Books in the Security Series

Computer Security Fundamentals
ISBN: 0-13-171129-6

Information Security: Principles and Practices
ISBN: 0-13-154729-1

Firewalls and VPNs: Principles and Practices
ISBN: 0-13-154731-3

Security Policies and Procedures: Principles and Practices
ISBN: 0-13-186691-5

Network Defense and Countermeasures: Principles and Practices
ISBN: 0-13-171126-1

Intrusion Detection: Principles and Practices
ISBN: 0-13-154730-5

Disaster Recovery: Principles and Practices
ISBN: 0-13-171127-X

Computer Forensics: Principles and Practices
ISBN: 0-13-154727-5

Network Defense and Countermeasures

Principles and Practices

CHUCK EASTTOM

Upper Saddle River, New Jersey 07458

Library of Congress Cataloging-in-Publication Data

Easttom, Chuck.
  Network defense and countermeasures : principles and practices / Chuck Easttom.
    p. cm. -- (Security series)
  Includes bibliographical references and index.
  ISBN 0-13-171126-1
  1. Computer networks--Security measures. I. Title. II. Security series (Upper Saddle River, N.J.)
  TK5105.59.E26 2005
  005.8--dc22
                              2005011756

Vice President and Publisher: Natalie E. Anderson
Executive Acquisitions Editor, Print: Stephanie Wall
Executive Acquisitions Editor, Media: Richard Keaveny
Editorial Project Manager: Emilie Herman
Editorial Assistants: Brian Hoehl, Bambi Dawn Marchigano, Alana Meyers, Sandra Bernales
Senior Media Project Managers: Cathi Profitko, Steve Gagliostro
Marketing Manager: Sarah Loomis
Marketing Assistant: Lisa Taylor
Managing Editor: Lynda Castillo
Production Project Manager: Vanessa Nuttry
Manufacturing Buyer: Natacha Moore
Design Manager: Maria Lange
Art Director/Interior Design/Cover Design: Blair Brown
Cover Illustration/Photo: Gettyimages/Photodisc Blue
Composition/Full-Service Project Management: Custom Editorial Productions Inc.
Cover Printer: Courier/Stoughton

Credits and acknowledgments borrowed from other sources and reproduced, with permission, in this textbook appear on appropriate page within text.

Microsoft® and Windows® are registered trademarks of the Microsoft Corporation in the U.S.A. and other countries. Screen shots and icons reprinted with permission from the Microsoft Corporation. This book is not sponsored or endorsed by or affiliated with the Microsoft Corporation.

Pearson Education LTD.
Pearson Education Singapore, Pte. Ltd
Pearson Education, Canada, Ltd
Pearson Education–Japan

Pearson Education Australia PTY, Limited
Pearson Education North Asia Ltd
Pearson Educación de Mexico, S.A. de C.V.
Pearson Education Malaysia, Pte. Ltd

10 9 8 7 6 5 4 3
ISBN 0-13-171126-1

Contents in Brief

Table of Contents

Security Series Walk-Through

The Prentice Hall Security Series prepares students for careers in IT security by providing practical advice and hands-on training from industry experts. All of the books in this series are filled with real-world examples to help readers apply what they learn to the workplace. This walk-through highlights the key elements in this book created to help students along the way.

Chapter Objectives. These short-term, attainable goals outline what will be covered in the chapter text.

Chapter Introduction. Each chapter begins with an explanation of why these topics are important and how the chapter fits into the overall organization of the book.

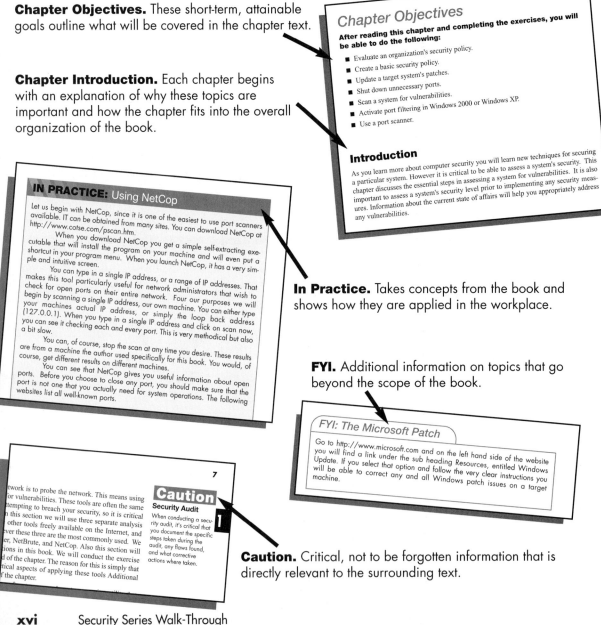

Chapter Objectives
After reading this chapter and completing the exercises, you will be able to do the following:

- Evaluate an organization's security policy.
- Create a basic security policy.
- Update a target system's patches.
- Shut down unnecessary ports.
- Scan a system for vulnerabilities.
- Activate port filtering in Windows 2000 or Windows XP.
- Use a port scanner.

Introduction
As you learn more about computer security you will learn new techniques for securing a particular system. However it is critical to be able to assess a system's security. It is also important to assess a system's security level prior to implementing any security measures. Information about the current state of affairs will help you appropriately address any vulnerabilities.

IN PRACTICE: Using NetCop
Let us begin with NetCop, since it is one of the easiest to use port scanners available. IT can be obtained from many sites. You can download NetCop at http://www.cotse.com/pscan.htm.

When you download NetCop you get a simple self-extracting executable that will install the program on your machine and will even put a shortcut in your program menu. When you launch NetCop, it has a very simple and intuitive screen.

You can type in a single IP address, or a range of IP addresses. That makes this tool particularly useful for network administrators that wish to check for open ports on their entire network. Four our purposes we will begin by scanning a single IP address, our own machine. You can either type your machines actual IP address, or simply the loop back address (127.0.0.1). When you type in a single IP address and click on scan now, you can see it checking each and every port. This is very methodical but also a bit slow.

You can, of course, stop the scan at any time you desire. These results are from a machine the author used specifically for this book. You would, of course, get different results on different machines.

You can see that NetCop gives you useful information about open ports. Before you choose to close any port, you should make sure that the port is not one that you actually need for system operations. The following websites list all well-known ports.

In Practice. Takes concepts from the book and shows how they are applied in the workplace.

FYI. Additional information on topics that go beyond the scope of the book.

FYI: The Microsoft Patch
Go to http://www.microsoft.com and on the left hand side of the website you will find a link under the sub heading Resources, entitled Windows Update. If you select that option and follow the very clear instructions you will be able to correct any and all Windows patch issues on a target machine.

7

...twork is to probe the network. This means using ...for vulnerabilities. These tools are often the same ...tempting to breach your security, so it is critical ...n this section we will use three separate analysis ...other tools freely available on the Internet, and ...ever these three are the most commonly used. We ...er, NetBrute, and NetCop. Also this section will ...ions in this book. We will conduct the exercise ...d of the chapter. The reason for this is simply that ...tical aspects of applying these tools Additional ...f the chapter.

Caution
Security Audit
When conducting a security audit, it's critical that you document the specific steps taken during the audit, any flaws found, and what corrective actions where taken.

Caution. Critical, not to be forgotten information that is directly relevant to the surrounding text.

Test Your Skills

Each chapter ends with exercises designed to reinforce the chapter objectives.
Four types of evaluation follow each chapter.

Multiple Choice Questions. Test the
reader's understanding of the text.

Exercises. Brief, guided projects
designed around individual concepts
found in the chapter.

Projects. Longer, guided projects that
combine lessons from the chapter.

Case Study. A real-world scenario to
resolve using lessons learned in the chapter.

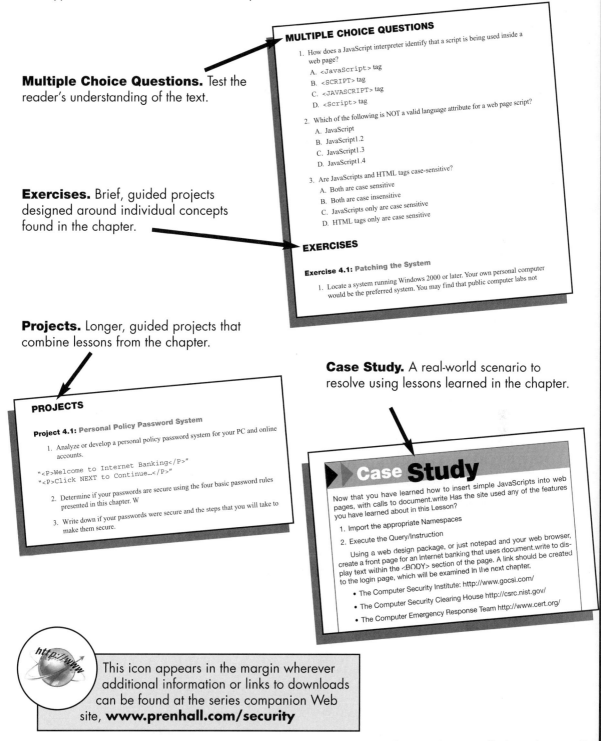

MULTIPLE CHOICE QUESTIONS

1. How does a JavaScript interpreter identify that a script is being used inside a web page?
   A. `<JavaScript>` tag
   B. `<SCRIPT>` tag
   C. `<JAVASCRIPT>` tag
   D. `<Script>` tag

2. Which of the following is NOT a valid language attribute for a web page script?
   A. JavaScript
   B. JavaScript1.2
   C. JavaScript1.3
   D. JavaScript1.4

3. Are JavaScripts and HTML tags case-sensitive?
   A. Both are case sensitive
   B. Both are case insensitive
   C. JavaScripts only are case sensitive
   D. HTML tags only are case sensitive

EXERCISES

Exercise 4.1: Patching the System

1. Locate a system running Windows 2000 or later. Your own personal computer would be the preferred system. You may find that public computer labs not

PROJECTS

Project 4.1: Personal Policy Password System

1. Analyze or develop a personal policy password system for your PC and online accounts.

   "`<P>`Welcome to Internet Banking`</P>`"
   "`<P>`Click NEXT to Continue...`</P>`"

2. Determine if your passwords are secure using the four basic password rules presented in this chapter. W

3. Write down if your passwords were secure and the steps that you will take to make them secure.

Case Study

Now that you have learned how to insert simple JavaScripts into web pages, with calls to document.write Has the site used any of the features you have learned about in this Lesson?

1. Import the appropriate Namespaces

2. Execute the Query/Instruction

   Using a web design package, or just notepad and your web browser, create a front page for an Internet banking that uses document.write to display text within the `<BODY>` section of the page. A link should be created to the login page, which will be examined in the next chapter,

   • The Computer Security Institute: http://www.gocsi.com/
   • The Computer Security Clearing House http://csrc.nist.gov/
   • The Computer Emergency Response Team http://www.cert.org/

This icon appears in the margin wherever
additional information or links to downloads
can be found at the series companion Web
site, **www.prenhall.com/security**

Preface

The hottest topic in the IT industry today is computer security. The news is replete with stories of hacking, viruses, and identity theft. The cornerstone of security is defending the organizational network. *Network Defense and Countermeasures: Principles and Practices* offers a comprehensive overview of network defense. It introduces students to network security threats and methods for defending the network. Three entire chapters are devoted to firewalls and intrusion-detection systems. There is also a chapter providing a basic introduction to encryption. Combining information on the threats to networks, the devices and technologies used to ensure security, as well as concepts like encryption provides students with a solid, broad-based approach to network defense.

This book provides a blend of theoretical foundations and practical applications. Each chapter ends with multiple choice questions, exercises, projects, and a case study. Students who successfully complete this textbook, including the end of chapter material, should have a solid understanding of network security. Throughout the book the student is directed to additional resources that can augment the material presented in the chapter.

Audience

This book is designed primarily as a textbook for students who have a basic understanding of how networks operate, including basic terminology, protocols, and devices. Students do not need to have an extensive math background or more than introductory computer courses.

Overview of the Book

This book will walk you through the intricacies of defending your network against attacks. It begins with a brief introduction to the field of network security in Chapter 1, Introduction to Network Security. Chapter 2, Types of Attacks, then explains the threats to a network—including denial of service attacks, buffer overflow attacks, and viruses.

Chapter 3, Fundamentals of Firewalls, Chapter 4, Firewall Practical Applications, Chapter 5, Intrusion-Detection Systems, and Chapter 7, Virtual Private Networks, give details on various security technologies including firewalls, intrusion-detection systems, and VPNs. These items are the core of any network's security, so a significant portion of this book is devoted to ensuring the reader fully understands both the concepts behind them and the practical applications. In every case, practical direction for selecting appropriate technology for a given network is included.

Chapter 6, Encryption, provides a solid introduction to encryption. This topic is critical because ultimately computer systems are simply devices for storing, transmitting, and manipulating data. No matter how secure the network is, if the data it transmits is not secure then there is a significant danger.

Chapter 8, Operating System Hardening, teaches operating system hardening. Chapter 9, Defending Against Virus Attacks, and Chapter 10, Defending Against Trojan Horses, Spyware, and Adware, give the reader specific defense strategies and techniques to guard against the most common network dangers. Chapter 11, Security Policies, gives readers an introduction to security policies.

Chapter 12, Assessing a System, teaches the reader how to do an assessment of a network's security. This includes guidelines for examining policies as well as an overview of network assessment tools. Chapter 13, Security Standards, gives an overview of common security standards such as the *Orange Book* and the Common Criteria. This chapter also discusses various security models such as Bell-Lapadula.

Chapter 14, Computer-Based Espionage and Terrorism, discusses computer-based espionage and terrorism, two topics of growing concern for the computer security community but often overlooked in textbooks.

Conventions Used in This Book

To help you get the most from the text, we've used a few conventions throughout the book.

IN PRACTICE: About In Practice

These show readers how to take concepts from the book and apply them in the workplace.

FYI: About FYIs

These boxes offer additional information on topics that go beyond the scope of the book.

Caution

About Cautions

Cautions appear in the margins of the text. They flag critical, not-to-be forgotten information that is directly relevant to the surrounding text.

Snippets and blocks of code are boxed and numbered, and can be downloaded from the companion Web site (**www.prenhall.com/security**).

New key terms appear in ***bold italics***.

 This icon appears in the margin wherever more information can be found at the series companion Web site, **www.prenhall.com/security**.

Instructor and Student Resources

Instructor's Resource Center on CD-ROM

The Instructor's Resource Center on CD-ROM (IRC on CD) is distributed to instructors only and is an interactive library of assets and links. It includes:

- Instructor's Manual. Provides instructional tips, an introduction to each chapter, teaching objectives, teaching suggestions, and answers to end-of-chapter questions and problems.

- PowerPoint Slide Presentations. Provides a chapter-by-chapter review of the book content for use in the classroom.

- Test Bank. This TestGen-compatible test bank file can be used with Prentice Hall's TestGen software (available as a free download at: **www.prenhall.com/testgen**). TestGen is a test generator that lets you view and easily edit test bank questions, transfer them to tests, and print in a variety of formats suitable to your teaching situation. The program also offers many options for organizing and displaying test banks and tests. A built-in random number and text generator makes it ideal for creating multiple versions of tests that involve calculations and provides more possible test items than test bank questions. Powerful search and sort functions let you easily locate questions and arrange them in the order you prefer.

Companion Web Site

The Companion Web site (**www.prenhall.com/security**) is a Pearson learning tool that provides students and instructors with online support. Here you will find:

- Interactive Study Guide, a Web-based interactive quiz designed to provide students with a convenient online mechanism for self-testing their comprehension of the book material.

- Additional Web projects and resources to put into practice the concepts taught in each chapter.

About the Author

Chuck Easttom spent many years in the IT industry, followed by three years teaching computer science at a technical college, including courses in computer security. He left academia to return to industry as the IT manager for a company in Dallas, TX. Among his other duties there, he is responsible for system security. He has authored seven other books on programming, Web development, and Linux. Chuck holds over 20 different industry certifications including CIW Security Analyst, MCSE, MCSA, MCDBA, MCAD, Server+, and more. He has served as a subject matter expert for the Computer Technology Industry Association (CompTIA) in the development or revision of four of their certification tests, including the initial creation of their Security+ certification. Chuck still works part-time as an adjunct teacher for a Dallas area college teaching a variety of courses, including computer security. He also does computer security consulting work from time to time.

Chuck is a frequent guest speaker for computer groups, discussing computer security. You can reach Chuck at his Web site (**www.chuckeasttom.com**) or by e-mail at chuckeasttom@yahoo.com.

Acknowledgments

While only one name goes on the cover of this book, it is hardly the work of just one person. I would like to take this opportunity to thank a few of the people involved. First of all, the editing staff at Prentice Hall worked extremely hard on this book. Without them this project would simply not be possible. I would also like to thank my wife, Misty, and my son, AJ, for their unwavering support. Anytime I am working on a project, their patience and understanding is key to the success of that project. Without that support neither this book, nor any of the others, would be possible.

Quality Assurance

We would like to extend our thanks to the Quality Assurance team for their attention to detail and their efforts to make sure that we got it right.

Technical Editors

Ken Dewey
Computer Information Technology
Rose State College

Lance Parks
Computer Information Science
Cosumnes River College

Reviewers

Jaime B. Sainz
Computer Science
Sierra College

Kathleen Murray
Computer Networking
Los Medanos Community College

Linda Woll
Computer Science
Montgomery County Community College

Chapter 1

Introduction to Network Security

Chapter Objectives

After reading this chapter and completing the exercises, you will be able to do the following:

- Identify the most common dangers to networks.
- Employ basic security terminology.
- Find the best approach to network security for your organization.
- Evaluate the legal issues that will affect your work as a network administrator.
- Use resources available for network security.

Introduction

News headlines for the first quarter of 2005 were filled with incidents of hackers getting sensitive data from systems with inadequate security. Even the most technically naïve person cannot go more than a few weeks without hearing of some new virus or some hacking incident, such as the dramatic attack in February 2003 when a hacker was able to get 5.6 million credit card numbers (CNN/Technology, 2003). Virus attacks like MyDoom became lead stories on national networks. On May 4, 2005, the United States Congress began discussing legislative ways to prevent identity theft (**www.wistv.com/Global/story.asp?S=3301014&nav=0RaPZSSe**). These events brought a great deal of attention to the field of computer security.

Despite this media attention, far too many computer professionals — including a surprising number of network administrators — do not have a clear understanding of the type of threats to which network systems are exposed, or which ones are most likely to actually occur. Mainstream media focuses attention on the most dramatic computer security breaches rather than giving an accurate picture of the most plausible threat scenarios.

This chapter looks at the threats posed to networks, defines basic security terminology, and lays the foundation for concepts covered in the chapters that follow. The steps required to ensure the integrity and security of your network are methodical and, for the most part, already outlined. By the time you complete this book, you will be able to identify the most common attacks, and explain how they are perpetrated in order to prevent them, and understand how to secure your data transmissions.

The Basics of a Network

Before we dive into how to protect your network, it would probably be a good idea to explore what networks are. For many readers this will be a review, but for some it might be new material.

A network is simply a way for computers to communicate. At the physical level, it consists of all the machines you want to connect and the devices you use to connect them. Individual machines are connected either with a physical connection (a category 5 cable going into a network interface card) or wirelessly. In order to connect multiple machines together, each machine will connect to a hub or switch, then those hubs/switches are connected together. In larger networks, each subnetwork is connected to the others by a router. We will look at many attacks in this book (including several in Chapter 2) that focus on the devices that connect machines together on a network (i.e., routers, hubs, and switches).

Basic Network Structure

There must be some connection point between your network and the outside world. A barrier is set up between that network and the Internet, usually in the form of a firewall. Many attacks discussed in this book work to overcome the firewall and get into the network.

The real essence of networks is communication — allowing one machine to communicate with another. However, every avenue of communication is also an avenue of attack. The first step in understanding how to defend a network is having a detailed understanding of how computers communicate over a network.

The previously mentioned network interface cards, switches, routers, hubs, and firewalls are the fundamental physical pieces of a network. The way they are connected and the format they use for communication is the network architecture.

Data Packets

Once you have established a connection (whether it is physical or wireless), you need to send data. The first part is to identify where you want to send it. All computers (as well as routers) have an IP address that is a series of four numbers between 0 and 255 and separated by periods, such as 192.0.0.5. The second part is to format the data for transmission. All data is ultimately in binary form (1s and 0s). This binary data is put into packets, all less than about 65,000 bytes. The first 20 bytes are the header. That header tells where the packet is going, where it came from, and how many more packets are coming as part of this transmission. There are attacks we will study (IP spoofing for example) that try to change the header of packets to give false information. There are other methods of attack that simply try to intercept packets and read the content (thus compromising the data).

What Does This Mean for Security?

This book covers security from numerous angles, but ultimately there are only two venues for attack, and thus two venues for security:

■ **The data itself:** Once data leaves your network, the packets are vulnerable for interception and even alteration. Later in this book when we discuss encryption and virtual private networks, you will learn how to secure this data.

■ **The network connection points:** Whether it is the routers or the firewall, any place where one computer connects to another is a place that can be attacked, and one that must be defended. When looking at a system's security, you should first look at the connectivity points.

As you proceed through this book, don't lose sight of the basic purpose, which is to secure networks and the data they store and transmit.

Assessing Likely Threats to the Network

Before we can explore the topic of computer security, we must first formulate a realistic assessment of the threats to those systems. The key word is *realistic*. Clearly one can imagine some very elaborate and highly technical potential dangers. But, as a network security professional, you will need to focus your attention — and resources — on the likely dangers. Before we delve into specific threats, let's get an idea of how likely attacks, of any type, are on your system.

In this regard, there seem to be two extreme attitudes toward computer security. The first is the assumption that there is no real threat to systems. This viewpoint holds that there is little real danger to computer systems and that much of the negative news is simply a reflection of unwarranted panic. People of this attitude often think that taking only minimal security precautions should ensure the safety of their systems. Unfortunately, some people in decision-making positions hold this point of view. The prevailing sentiment of these individuals is, "If our computer/organization has not been attacked so far, we must be secure."

This viewpoint often leads to a reactive approach to computer security, meaning that people will wait until *after* an incident to decide to address security issues. Waiting to address security until an attack occurs may be too late. In the best of circumstances, the incident may have only a minor impact on the organization and serve as a much needed wake-up call. In less fortunate cases, an organization may face serious, possibly catastrophic consequences. For example, there are organizations that did not have an effective network security system in place when the MyDoom virus attacked their systems. One of those companies estimated that lost productivity through downtime of the systems cost over $100,000. Avoiding this *laissez-faire* approach to security is imperative.

Any organization that embraces this extreme — and erroneous — philosophy is likely to invest little time or resources in computer security. They may have a basic firewall and antivirus software, but most likely expend little effort ensuring that they are properly configured or routinely updated.

IN PRACTICE: Reactive Security in the Real World

Whenever I am asked to perform some consulting or training task, I get to see a number of diverse network environments. From this experience, I have developed the opinion that a disturbingly large segment of the business world takes a very lax approach to computer security. Following are a few examples of behavior that indicate (to me) a lax view toward security:

- Companies that do not have any type of intrusion-detection system (covered in Chapter 5).
- Companies that do not use any type of spyware protection (covered in Chapter 10).
- Companies that leave their backup tapes on a table in an open area accessible to any number of people (discussed when we cover policies in Chapter 11).
- Companies with no plan for implementing patches (discussed in Chapter 8).

These are just a few indications of organizations that are not addressing network security in an appropriate manner.

At the other end of the spectrum, some executives overestimate security threats. They assume that very talented hackers exist in great numbers and that all of them are an imminent threat to their system. They may believe that virtually any teenager with a laptop can traverse highly secure systems at will. This viewpoint has, unfortunately, been fostered by a number of movies that depict computer hacking in a somewhat glamorous light. Such a worldview makes excellent movie plots, but is simply unrealistic. The reality is that many people who call themselves hackers are less knowledgeable than they think. Systems protected by even moderate security precautions have a low probability of being compromised by a hacker of this skill level.

This does not mean that skillful hackers do not exist. They most certainly do. However, people with the skill to compromise relatively secure systems must use rather time-consuming and tedious techniques to breach system security. These hackers must also weigh the costs and benefits of any hacking mission. Skilled hackers tend to target systems that have a high benefit, either financially or ideologically. If a system is not perceived as having sufficient benefit, a skilled hacker is less likely to expend the resources to compromise it. Burglars are one good analogy: There are certainly highly skilled burglars; however, they typically seek high-value targets. The thief who targets small businesses and homes usually has limited skills. The same is true of hackers.

FYI: Skilled vs. Unskilled Hackers

Skilled hackers usually target only highly attractive sites. Attractive sites offer valuable information or publicity. Military computers—even simple Web servers with no classified information—offer a great deal of publicity. Banks, on the other hand, generally have very valuable information. Novice hackers usually start with a low value and, consequently, often less secure system. Low value systems may not have any data of substantial value or offer much publicity. A college Web server would be a good example. While novice hackers' skills are not as well developed, their numbers are greater. Also, monetary gains are not the only factor that may make a system attractive to a skilled hacker. If a hacker objects to an organization's ideological stance (for example, if an organization sells large sport utility vehicles that the hacker feels is poor environmental policy), then she might target its system.

Both extremes of attitudes regarding the dangers to computer systems are inaccurate. It is certainly true that there are people who have both the comprehension of computer systems and the skills to compromise the security of many, if not most, systems. However, it is also true that many who call themselves hackers are not as skilled as they claim. They have ascertained a few buzzwords from the Internet and are convinced of their own digital supremacy, but they are not able to affect any real compromises to even a moderately secure system.

You may think that erring on the side of caution, or extreme diligence, would be the appropriate approach. In reality, you do not need to take either extreme view. You should take a *realistic* view of security and formulate practical strategies for defense. Every organization and IT department has finite resources: You only have so much time and money. If you squander part of those resources guarding against unrealistic threats you may not have adequate resources left for more practical projects. Therefore a realistic approach to network security is the only practical approach.

You may be wondering why some people overestimate dangers to their networks. The answer, in part at least, lies with the nature of the hacking community and with the media. Media outlets have a tendency to sensationalize. You don't get good ratings by downplaying danger; you get them by emphasizing, and perhaps outright exaggerating. Also the Internet is replete with people claiming significant skill as hackers. As with any field of human endeavor, the majority is merely average. The truly talented hacker is no more common than the truly talented concert pianist. Consider how many people take piano lessons at some point in their lives; then consider how many of those ever truly become virtuosos.

The same is true of computer hackers. Keep in mind that even those who do possess the requisite skill also need the motivation to expend the time and effort necessary to compromise your system. Keep this fact in mind when considering any claims of cyber prowess you may encounter.

The claim that many people who describe themselves as hackers lack real skill is not based on any study or survey. A reliable study on this topic would be impossible because hackers are unlikely to identify themselves and submit to skills tests. I came to this conclusion based on two considerations. The first is simply years of experience traversing hacker discussion groups, chat rooms, and bulletin boards. In more than a decade of work in this field, I have encountered talented and highly skilled hackers, yet I encounter far more who claim to be hackers but clearly demonstrate a lack of sufficient skill. The second consideration is that it is a fact of human nature that the vast majority of people in any field are, by definition, mediocre. Consider the millions of people who work out at a gym on a regular basis, and consider how few ever become competitive body builders. In any field, most participants will be mediocre.

This statement is also not meant to minimize the dangers of hacking. That is not my intent at all. Even an unskilled novice attempting to intrude on a system will get in, in the absence of appropriate security precautions. Even if the would-be hacker does not successfully breach security, he can still be quite a nuisance. Additionally, some forms of attack don't require much skill at all. We will be discussing these later in this book.

A more balanced view (and therefore, a better way to assess the threat level to any system) is to weigh the attractiveness of a system to potential intruders against the security measures in place. As we shall see, the greatest threat to any system is not actually hackers. Virus and other attacks are far more prevalent. As you will see, threat assessment is a complex task with multiple facets.

Classifications of Threats

Your network certainly faces real security threats, and these threats can manifest themselves in a variety forms. There are a variety of ways one might choose to classify the various threats to your system. You could choose to classify them by the damage caused, the level of skill required to execute the attack, or perhaps even by the motivation behind the attack. For our purposes we will categorize attacks by what they actually do. Based on that philosophy most attacks can be categorized as one of three broad classes:

- Intrusion
- Blocking
- Malware

The three categories are shown in Figure 1.1. The ***intrusion*** category includes attacks meant to breach security and gain unauthorized access to a system. This group of attacks includes any attempt to gain unauthorized access to a system. This is generally what hackers do. The second category of attack, ***blocking,*** includes attacks designed to prevent legitimate access to a system. Blocking attacks are often called ***Denial of Service*** attacks (or simply DoS). In these types of attacks the purpose is not to actually get into your system but simply to block legitimate users from gaining access.

Categories of Attack

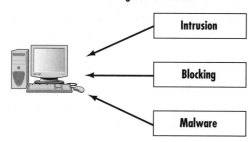

Intrusion

Blocking

Malware

FIGURE 1.1 Types of attacks.

> ### FYI: What About Other Attacks?
>
> In Chapter 2 you will learn about attacks such as **buffer overflows** that can be used for more than one category. For example, a buffer overflow can be used to shut down a machine, thus making it a blocking attack, or it can be used to breach system security, making it an intrusion attack. However, once implemented it will be in one category or the other.

The third category of threats is the installation of **malware** on a system. Malware is a generic term for software that has a malicious purpose. It includes virus attacks, Trojan horses, and spyware. Because this category of attack is perhaps the most prevalent danger to systems, we will examine it first.

Malware Malware is probably the most common threat to any system, including home users' systems, small networks, and large enterprise wide area networks. One reason is that malware is often designed to spread on its own, without the creator of the malware having to be directly involved. This makes this sort of attack much easier to spread across the Internet, and hence more widespread.

The most obvious example of malware is the computer **virus.** You probably have a general idea of what a virus is. If you consult different textbooks you will probably see the definition of a virus worded slightly differently. One definition for a virus is "a program that can 'infect' other programs by modifying them to include a possibly evolved copy of itself" (Landesman, 2004). That is a very good definition, one you will see throughout this book. A computer virus is analogous to a biological virus in that both replicate and spread. The most common method for spreading a virus is using the victim's e-mail account to spread the virus to everyone in his address book. Some viruses do not actually harm the system itself, but *all* of them cause network slowdowns or shutdowns due to the heavy network traffic caused by the virus replication.

> ### IN PRACTICE: Real Viruses
>
> The original MyDoom worm is discussed in detail in Chapters 2 and 9. MyDoom.BB virus is a variation on MyDoom that began to spread early in 2005. This particular worm appears on your hard drive as either *java.exe* or *services.exe*. This is an important thing to learn about viruses. Many try to appear as legitimate system files, thus preventing you from deleting them.

This particular worm sends itself out to everyone in your address book, thus spreading quite rapidly. This worm will attempt to download a backdoor program giving the attacker access to your system.

From a technological point of view, this worm was most interesting for how it extracts e-mail addresses. It should be noted that the worm uses a much improved algorithm for e-mail address recognition. Now it can catch such e-mail addresses as:

- chuck@nospam.domain.com
- chuck-at-domain-dot-com

These addresses are translated by the worm to the usable format. Many other e-mail extraction engines are foiled by these sorts of e-mail address permutations (which is why they are used).

Another type of malware, often closely related to the virus, is the ***Trojan horse.*** The term is borrowed from the ancient tale. In this tale, the city of Troy was besieged for a long period of time, but the attackers could not gain entrance. They constructed a huge wooden horse and left it one night in front of the gates to Troy one night. The next morning, the residents of Troy saw the horse and assumed it to be a gift, consequently rolling the wooden horse into the city. Unbeknownst to them, several soldiers were hidden inside the horse. That evening, the soldiers left the horse, opened the city gates, and let their fellow attackers into the city. An electronic Trojan horse works in the same manner, appearing to be benign software but secretly downloading a virus or some other type of malware onto your computer from within. In short you have an enticing gift that you install on your computer, and later find it has unleashed something quite different from what you expected. It is a fact that Trojan horses are more likely to be found in illicit software. There are many places on the Internet to get pirated copies of commercial software. It is not at all uncommon to find such software is actually part of a Trojan horse.

Trojan horses and viruses are the two most widely encountered forms of malware. A third category of malware is ***spyware,*** which is increasing in frequency at a dramatic pace. Spyware is software that literally spies on what you do on your computer. This can be as simple as a ***cookie*** — a text file that your browser creates and stores on your hard drive. Cookies are downloaded onto your machine by Web sites you visit. This text file is then used to recognize you when you return to the same site. That file can enable you to access pages more quickly and save you from having to enter your information multiple times on pages you visit frequently. However, in order to do this, that file must be read by the Web site; this means it can also be read by other Web sites. Any data that the file saves can be retrieved by any Web site, so your entire Internet browsing history can be tracked.

Another form of spyware, called a ***key logger,*** records all of your keystrokes. Some also take periodic screen shots of your computer. Data is then either stored for retrieval later by the party who installed the key logger or is sent immediately back via e-mail. In either case, every single thing you do on your computer is recorded for the interested party.

FYI: Key Loggers

While we defined a key logger as software, it is important to note that hardware-based key loggers do indeed exist. Hardware-based key loggers are much less common than software based key loggers. The reason for this is that software key loggers are easier to place on a targeted machine. Hardware key loggers require you to physically go to the machine and install hardware. If the key logger is being installed without the computer user's knowledge, then installing a physical device can be quite difficult. A software key logger can be installed via a Trojan horse with the perpetrator not even being in the same city as the target computer.

Compromising System Security One could make the argument that any sort of attack is aimed at compromising security. However in this instance we are talking about those attacks that are actually trying to intrude into the system. This is different from attacks that simply deny users access to the system, or attacks that are not focused at a particular target such as viruses and worms. Intrusion attacks are designed to gain access to a specific targeted system. Intrusion attacks are commonly referred to as hacking, although that is not the term hackers themselves use. Hackers call this type of attack ***cracking,*** which means intruding onto a system without permission, usually with malevolent intent. Any attack designed to breach security, either via some operating system flaw or any other means, can be classified as cracking. As you progress through this book you will encounter a few specific methods for intruding on a system. In many cases, if not most, the idea is to exploit some software flaw to gain access to the target system.

Using security flaws is not the only method for intruding into a system. In fact there are methods that can be technologically much easier to execute. For example one completely not technologically-based method for breaching a system's security is called ***social engineering,*** which, as the name implies, relies more on human nature than technology. This was the type of attack that the famous hacker Kevin Mitnick most often used. Social engineering uses standard con artist techniques to get users to offer up the information needed to gain access to a target system (Lemos, 2000). The way this method works is rather simple. The perpetrator obtains preliminary information about a target organization, such as the name of its system administrator, and leverages it to gain additional information from the system's users. For example, he might call someone in accounting and claim to be one of the company's technical support personnel. The intruder could use the system administrator's name to validate that claim. He could then ask various questions to learn additional details about the system's specifications. A savvy intruder might even get a person to provide a username and password. As you can see, this method is based on how well the intruder can manipulate people and actually has little to do with computer skills.

Social engineering and exploiting software flaws are not the only means of executing an intrusion attack. The growing popularity of wireless networks gives rise to new kinds of attacks. The most obvious and dangerous activity is **war-driving.** This type of attack is an offshoot of **war-dialing.** With war-dialing, a hacker sets up a computer to call phone numbers in sequence until another computer answers to try and gain entry to its system. War-driving, using much the same concept, is applied to locating vulnerable wireless networks. In this scenario, a hacker simply drives around trying to locate wireless networks (Poulsen, 2001). Many people forget that their wireless network signal often extends as much as 100 feet (thus, past walls). At DefCon 2003, the annual hackers' convention, contestants participated in a war-driving contest in which they drove around the city trying to locate as many vulnerable wireless networks as they could (DefCon II, 2003).

Denial of Service   The third category of attacks is blocking attacks. One type is called the Denial of Service attack (DoS). In this attack, the attacker does not actually access the system, but rather simply blocks access from legitimate users. In the words of the CERT (Computer Emergency Response Team) Coordination Center (the first computer security incident response team), "A 'Denial-of-Service' attack is characterized by an explicit attempt by attackers to prevent legitimate users of a service from using that service" (CERT, 2003). One common method is flooding the targeted system with so many false connection requests that it cannot respond to legitimate requests. DoS is an extremely common attack, second only to malware.

Likely Attacks

We have been examining various possible threats to a network. Clearly some threats are more likely than others. What are the realistic dangers facing individuals and organizations? What are the most likely attacks, and what are common vulnerabilities? Understanding the basics of existing threats and the likelihood that they will cause problems for users and organizations is important.

> ## FYI: Likelihood of Attacks
>
> The likelihood of a particular attack depends on the type of organization the network serves. The data presented here is applicable to most network systems. Clearly a number of factors (including how much publicity a system gets and the perceived value of the data on that system) influence the likelihood of an attack targeting a particular system. Always err on the side of caution when estimating the threats to your network.

The most likely threat to any computer or network is the computer virus. For example, in the first six weeks of 2005 the F-Secure Web site listed four new viruses (F-Secure, 2003). This number does not take into account the previously released viruses still circulating. Each month, several new virus outbreaks are typically documented. New viruses are constantly being created, and old ones are still out there.

It is also important to note that many people do not update their antivirus software as often as they should. This is evidenced by the fact that many of the viruses spreading around the Internet already have countermeasures released, but people are simply not applying them. As an example, in late 2004, all the major antivirus software vendors released protection for the SoBig virus. However, today alone I personally received 18 e-mail messages with that virus as an attachment. Therefore, even when a virus is known and there is protection against it, it can continue to thrive because many people do not update their protection or clean their systems regularly. If all computer systems and networks had regularly updated security patches and employed virus scanning software, a great many virus outbreaks would either be avoided altogether or their effects would at least be minimized.

Blocking has become the most common form of attack besides viruses. As you will learn later in this book, blocking attacks are easier to perpetrate than intrusions and are therefore more common. A resourceful hacker can find tools on the Internet to help her launch a blocking attack. You will learn more about blocking attacks, as well as malware, in Chapter 2.

Related to blocking attacks is internal misuse of systems. A recent survey by the Computer Security Institute of 223 computer professionals showed over $445 million in total losses due to computer security breaches. Seventy-five percent of respondents cited the Internet connection as a frequent point of attack, while 33% cited their internal systems. A rather astonishing 78% detected employee abuse of systems/Internet (Computer Security Institute, 2002). This means that one of the chief dangers in any organization might be its own employees.

IN PRACTICE: What Is "Misuse of Systems"?

Employers and employees often view misuse of a system differently. All systems at a workplace are the property of the employer. Computers, hard drives, even e-mail are all the property of the employer. United States law has consistently maintained that employers have a right to monitor employees' Web usage and even e-mail.

Most organizations have policies that strictly forbid use of computer equipment for any purpose other than work. The Internet connection is restricted to work-related use, not for reading the headlines on the Web. Some companies do not mind if an employee uses the Internet for personal purposes during lunch. From a security perspective, administrators must be concerned about the Web sites employees visit. Are they downloading Flash animations? Are they downloading their own screen savers? Anything that is downloaded is a potential threat to a system. Even without downloading, it is possible that Web sites are tracking information about users and their computers. From a security perspective, the less information about your network someone outside the organization has, the better. Any piece of information is potentially useful to a hacker.

As you will learn in Chapter 4, many firewall solutions allow administrators to block certain Web sites, a feature many use. At a minimum, companies should have a very clearly defined policy that describes exactly which activities are permissible and which are not. Any ambiguity in your policies can cause problems later. You will learn more about defining and implementing security policies in Chapter 11.

Threat Assessment

When attempting to assess the threat level for an organization, administrators must consider a number of factors. The first has already been mentioned: The attractiveness of the system to hackers. Some systems attract hackers due to the systems' monetary value. The systems of financial institutions provide tempting targets for hackers. Other systems attract hackers because of the public profile of the organizations they support. Hackers are attracted to government systems and computer security Web sites simply because of their high profiles. If a hacker successfully gets into one of those systems, he will achieve fame and prestige in the hacker community. Academic institutions also receive a high frequency of hacking attempts. High schools and colleges have a large population of younger, computer savvy students. The number of hackers and would-be hackers among such a group is likely to be higher than in the general populace. Additionally, academic institutions do not have a good reputation on information security.

The second risk factor is the nature of the information on the system. If the system has sensitive or critical information, then its security requirements are higher. Personal data such as Social Security numbers, credit card numbers, and medical records have a high security requirement. Systems with sensitive research data or classified information have even higher security needs.

A final consideration is traffic to the system. The more people who have some sort of remote access to the system, the more security dangers there are. For example, a number of people access e-commerce systems from outside the network. Each of these connections represents a danger. If, on the other hand, a system is self-contained with no external connections, its security vulnerabilities are reduced.

The attractiveness of the system to hackers, the nature of the information the system stores, and the number of remote connections to your system — consideration of these three items together allows administrators to provide a complete assessment of security needs.

The following numerical scale can provide a basic overview of a system's security requirements.

Three factors are considered (attractiveness, information content, and security devices present). Each of those factors is given a numeric designation between 1 and 10. The first two are added together, and then the third number is subtracted. The final score ranges from -8 (very low risk, high security) to 19 (very high risk, low security); the lower the number, the less vulnerable the system, the higher the number the greater the risk. The best rating is for a system that:

- Receives a 1 in attractiveness to hackers (i.e., a system that is virtually unknown, has no political or ideological significance, etc.).

- Receives a 1 in informational content (i.e., a system that contains no confidential or sensitive data).

- Receives a 10 in security (i.e., a system with an extensive layered, proactive security system complete with firewalls, ports blocked, antivirus software, IDS, anti-spyware, appropriate policies, all workstations and servers hardened, etc.).

Evaluating attractiveness is certainly quite subjective. However, evaluating the value of informational content or the level of security can be done with rather crude but simple metrics. This system will be reiterated and then further expanded in Chapter 12.

Obviously this is not an exact science and is contingent to some extent on a personal assessment of a system. This method will, however, provide a starting point for assessing a system's security. This metric is certainly not the final word in security metrics but rather a starting point.

Understanding Security Terminology

When studying the field of computer security, you must be cognizant of the fact that this discipline is an overlap of security professionals and amateur hackers. As such, the field combines terminology from both domains. The Glossary will be a useful reference tool throughout this course.

Hacking Terminology

We will begin by examining hacker terminology. It should be noted that this terminology is not precise, and that many definitions can be debated. There is no "official" hacker vocabulary. The terms evolve through their use by the hacker community. Clearly it would be prudent to begin this examination by defining *hacker,* a term used in movies and news broadcasts. Most people use it to describe any person who breaks into a computer system. However, security professionals and hackers themselves use this term differently. In the hacking community a hacker is an expert on a particular system or systems who wants to learn more about the system. Hackers feel that looking at a system's flaws is the best way to learn about it.

For example, someone well-versed in the Linux operating system who works to understand that system by learning its weaknesses and flaws would be a hacker. However, this does often mean seeing whether a flaw can be exploited to gain access to a system. This "exploiting" part of the process is where hackers differentiate themselves into three groups.

- *White hat hackers,* upon finding a vulnerability in a system, will report the vulnerability to the vendor of that system. For example, if they discovered some flaw in Red Hat Linux™, they would then e-mail the Red Hat company (probably anonymously) and explain what the flaw is and how it was exploited.

- *Black hat hackers* are the people normally depicted in the media. Once they gain access to a system, their goal is to cause some type of harm. They might steal data, erase files, or deface Web sites. Black hat hackers are sometimes referred to as crackers.

- *Gray hat hackers* are typically law-abiding citizens, but in some cases will venture into illegal activities. They may do so for a wide variety of reasons. Commonly, gray hat hackers conduct illegal activities for reasons they feel are ethical, such as hacking into a system belonging to a corporation that the hacker feels is engaged in unethical activities. Note that this term is not found in many textbooks, but is very common in the hacking community itself.

Regardless of how hackers view themselves, intruding on any system without permission is illegal. This means that, technically speaking, all hackers, regardless of the color of the metaphorical hat they may wear, are in violation of the law. However, many people feel that white hat hackers actually perform a service by finding flaws and informing vendors before those flaws are exploited by less ethically inclined individuals.

The various shades of hackers are only the beginning of hacker terminology. Recall that a hacker is an expert in a given system. If so, what is the term for someone who calls herself a hacker but lacks expertise? The most common term for an inexperienced hacker is **script kiddy** (*Glossary of Hacker Terminology,* 2004). The name derives from the fact that the Internet is full of utilities and scripts that one can download to perform some hacking tasks. Someone who downloads these tools without really understanding the target system would be considered a script kiddy. A significant number of the people who call themselves hackers are, in reality, merely script kiddies.

This brings us to some very specific types of hackers. A **cracker** is someone whose goal is to compromise a system's security for purposes other than to learn about the system (*Hacker Dictionary,* 2003). There is no difference between a black hat hacker and a cracker. Both terms refer to a person who breaks through a system's security and intrudes on that system without permission from the appropriate parties, with some malicious intent.

When and why would someone give permission to another party to hack/crack a system? The most common reason is to assess the system's vulnerabilities. This is yet another specialized type of hacker — the **ethical hacker** or **sneaker,** a person who legally hacks/cracks a system in order to assess security deficiencies. In 1992, Robert Redford, Dan Aykroyd, and Sydney Poitier starred in a movie about this very subject. There are consultants who perform work of this type, and you can even find firms that specialize in this very activity as more and more companies are soliciting these services to assess their vulnerabilities.

A word of caution for readers either considering becoming or hiring sneakers: Any person hired to assess the vulnerabilities of a system must be both technically proficient and morally sound. This means that a criminal background check should be done before engaging her services. You certainly would not hire a convicted burglar as your night watchman. Neither should you consider hiring someone with any criminal background, especially in computer crimes, as a sneaker. Some people might argue that a convicted hacker/cracker has the best qualifications to assess your system's vulnerabilities. This is simply not the case, for several reasons:

- There are legitimate security professionals who know and understand hacker skills but have never committed any crime. You can get the skills required to assess your system without using a consultant with a demonstrated lack of integrity.

- If you take the argument that hiring convicted hackers means hiring talented people to its logical conclusion, you could surmise that the person in question is not as good a hacker as he would like to think, since he was caught.

- Most importantly, giving a person with a criminal background access to your systems is comparable to hiring a person with multiple DWI convictions as your driver. In both cases you are inviting problems and, perhaps, assuming significant civil and criminal liabilities.

A thorough review of a sneaker's qualifications is also recommended. Just as there are people who falsely claim to be highly skilled hackers, there are those who will falsely claim to be skilled sneakers. An unqualified sneaker might pronounce your system sound when in fact it was a lack of skill that prevented him from successfully breaching your security. In Chapter 12, we discuss the basics of assessing a target system. In that chapter we also discuss the necessary qualifications of any consultant hired for this purpose.

Another specialized branch of hacking involves breaking into telephone systems. This sub-specialty of hacking is referred to as *phreaking.* The *New Hackers Dictionary* actually defines phreaking as "The action of using mischievous and mostly illegal ways in order to not pay for some sort of telecommunications bill, order, transfer, or other service" (Raymond, 2003). Phreaking requires a rather significant knowledge of telecommunications, and many phreakers have some professional experience working for a phone company or other telecommunications business. This type of activity is often dependent upon specific technology required to compromise phone systems more than simply knowing certain techniques. For example, there are certain devices used to compromise phone systems. Phone systems are often dependent on frequencies. (If you have a touchtone phone, you will notice that, as you press the keys, each has a different frequency.) Machines that record and duplicate certain frequencies are often essential to phone phreaking.

Security Terminology

Security professionals have specific terminology as well. Readers with any training or experience in network administration are probably already familiar with most of these terms. While most hacking terminology describes either the activity or the person performing it (phreaking, sneaker, etc.), much of the security terminology you will learn here deals with devices and policies. This is quite logical because hacking is an offensive activity centered on attackers and attack methodologies and security is a defensive activity concerned with defensive barriers and procedures.

The first and most basic security device is the *firewall.* A firewall is a barrier between a network and the outside world. Sometimes a firewall is a stand-alone server, sometimes a router, and sometimes software running on a machine. Whatever its physical form, the purpose is the same: to filter traffic entering and exiting a network. Firewalls are related to, and often used in conjunction with, a *proxy server.* A proxy server hides your internal network IP address and presents a single IP address (its own) to the outside world.

Firewalls and proxy servers are added to networks to provide basic perimeter security. They filter incoming and outgoing network traffic but do not affect traffic on the network. Sometimes these devices are augmented by an *Intrusion-Detection System,* or IDS. An IDS monitors traffic looking for suspicious activity that might indicate an attempted intrusion.

Access Control Authentication is another important computer security term that will be of particular interest to you in several of the later chapters. Access control is the aggregate of all measures taken to limit access to resources. This includes logon procedures, encryption, and any method that is designed to prevent unauthorized personnel from accessing a resource. Authentication is clearly a subset of access controls, perhaps the most basic security activity. Authentication is simply the process of determining whether the credentials given by a user or another system, such as a username and password, are authorized to access the network resource in question. When a user logs in with a username and password, the system attempts to authenticate that username and password. If they are authenticated, the user will be granted access.

Non-repudiation is another term you will encounter frequently in computer security. It is any technique that is used to ensure that someone performing an action on a computer cannot falsely deny that they performed that action. Non-repudiation provides reliable records of what user took a particular action at a specific time. In short it is methods to track what actions are taken by what user. Various system logs provide one method for non-repudiation. One of the most important security activities is *auditing.* Auditing is the process of reviewing logs, records, and procedures to determine whether they meet standards. This activity will be discussed throughout this book and is the focus of Chapter 12. Auditing is critical because checking that systems have appropriate security in place is the only way to ensure system security.

An entire book could be written on computer security terminology. These few terms you have been introduced to here are ubiquitous and it is important that you are familiar with them. Some of the exercises at the end of this chapter will help you expand your knowledge of computer security terminology. You might also find these links helpful:

- **www.microsoft.com/security/glossary.mspx** (Microsoft Security Glossary)

- **www.yourwindow.to/information%2Dsecurity/** (Information Security Glossary)

- **www.ietf.org/rfc/rfc2828.txt** (IETF Internet Security Glossary)

> ## FYI: Auditing and Sneakers
>
> The process a sneaker uses is really just an audit. You may wonder what the difference is between sneaking and auditing. The distinction between a normal audit and sneaking lies in the methodology. Many traditional security professionals rely on standardized processes and techniques to conduct an audit, whereas sneakers often simply try to crack the system in order to assess security. The traditional audit will consist of reviewing logs, checking system settings, and ensuring that the security meets some arbitrary standard. Sneakers will simply try to break into the system. If they can, then the system is deemed insecure.

Approaching Network Security

Organizations can choose from several approaches to network security. A particular approach, or paradigm, will influence all subsequent security decisions and set the tone for the entire organization's network security infrastructure. Network security paradigms can be classified by either the scope of security measures taken (perimeter, layered) or how proactive the system is.

Perimeter Security Approach

In a *perimeter security approach,* the bulk of security efforts are focused on the perimeter of the network. This focus might include firewalls, proxy servers, password policies, and any technology or procedure that makes unauthorized access of the network less likely. Little or no effort is made to secure the systems within the network. In this approach, the perimeter is secured, but the various systems within that perimeter are often vulnerable.

This perimeter approach is clearly flawed. So why do some companies use it? A small organization might use the perimeter approach if they have budget constraints or inexperienced network administrators. This method might be adequate for small organizations that do not store sensitive data, but it rarely works in a larger corporate setting.

Layered Security Approach

A *layered security approach* is one in which not only is the perimeter secured, but individual systems within the network are also secured. All servers, workstations, routers, and hubs within the network are secure. One way to accomplish this is to divide the network into segments and secure each segment as if it were a separate network so that, if perimeter security is compromised, not all internal systems are affected. Layered security is the preferred approach whenever possible.

You should also measure your security approach by how proactive and/or reactive it is. This is done by gauging how much the system's security infrastructure and policies are dedicated to preventive measures as opposed to how much are devoted to simply responding to an attack after it has occurred.

A *passive security approach* takes few or no steps to prevent an attack. Conversely a *dynamic security approach,* or proactive defense, is one in which steps are taken to prevent attacks before they occur. One example of a proactive defense is the use of an IDS, which works to detect attempts to circumvent security measures. These systems can tell a system administrator that an attempt to breach security has been made, even if that attempt is not successful. An IDS can also be used to detect various techniques intruders use to assess a target system, thus alerting a network administrator to the potential for an attempted breach before the attempt is even initiated.

Hybrid Approach

In the real world, network security is rarely completely in one paradigm or another. Networks generally fall along a continuum with elements of more than one security paradigm. The two categories also combine. One can have a network that is predominantly passive but layered, or one that is primarily perimeter, but proactive. It can be helpful to consider approaches to computer security along a Cartesian coordinate system, with the x axis representing the level of passive-active approaches and the y axis depicting the range from perimeter to layered defense. This is shown in Figure 1.2.

The most desirable hybrid approach is a layered paradigm that is dynamic. This means that, in Figure 1.2, the upper right-hand quadrant is the preferred approach to security.

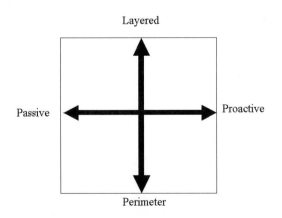

FIGURE 1.2 A security approach guide.

Network Security and the Law

An increasing number of legal issues affect how administrators approach network security. If your organization is a publicly traded company, a government agency, or does business with either, there may be legal constraints. Legal constraints include any laws that affect how information is stored or accessed. Sarbanes-Oxley (which will be discussed in more detail later in this chapter) is one example. Even if your network is not legally bound to these security guidelines, it is useful for administrators to review the various laws impacting computer security and perhaps to derive ideas that can apply to your own security standards.

One of the oldest pieces of legislation in the United States affecting computer security is the *Computer Security Act of 1987* (100th Congress, 1987). This act requires government agencies to identify sensitive systems, conduct computer security training, and develop computer security plans. This law is a vague mandate ordering federal agencies in the United States to establish security measures without specifying any standards.

This legislation established a legal mandate to enact specific standards, paving the way for future guidelines and regulations. It also helped define certain terms, such as what information is indeed "sensitive," according to the following quote found in the legislation itself:

> *Sensitive information* is any information, the loss, misuse, or unauthorized access to or modification of which could adversely affect the national interest or the conduct of Federal programs, or the privacy to which individuals are entitled under section 552a of title 5, United States Code (the Privacy Act), but which has not been specifically authorized under criteria established by an Executive order or an Act of Congress to be kept secret in the interest of national defense or foreign policy (100th Congress, 1987).

This definition should be kept in mind, for it is not just Social Security information or medical history that must be secured. When considering what information needs to be secure simply ask the question: Would the unauthorized access or modification of this information adversely affect my organization? If the answer is yes, then you must consider that information "sensitive" and in need of security precautions.

Another more specific federal law that applies to mandated security for government systems is *OMB Circular A-130* (specifically, Appendix III). This document requires that federal agencies establish security programs containing specified elements. This document describes requirements for developing standards for computer systems and for records held by government agencies.

Most states have specific laws regarding computer security, such as legislation like the *Computer Crimes Act of Florida,* the *Computer Crime*

Act of Alabama, and the *Computer Crimes Act of Oklahoma.* Any person responsible for network security might potentially be involved in a criminal investigation. This could be an investigation into a hacking incident or employee misuse of computer resources. Whatever the nature of the crime instigating the investigation, being aware of the computer crime laws in your state is invaluable. A list of computer crime laws by state is available at **www.alw.nih.gov/Security/FIRST/papers/legal/statelaw.txt**. This government list is from the Advanced Laboratory Workstation (ALW), National Institutes for Health (NIH), and Center for Information Technology.

It is also critical to keep in mind that any law that governs privacy (such as Health Insurance Portability and Accountability (HPPA), for medical records) also has a direct impact on computer security. If a system is compromised and data that is covered under any privacy statute is compromised, you may need to prove that you exercised due diligence to protect that data. A finding that you did not take proper precautions can result in civil liability.

A law that is probably even more pertinent to business network security is Sarbanes-Oxley, often called SOX (**www.sarbanes-oxley.com**). This law governs how publicly traded companies store and report on financial data, and keeping that data secure is a vital part of this. Obviously full coverage of this law is beyond the scope of this chapter, or even this book. It is mentioned to point out to you that in addition to network security being a technical discipline, there are business and legal ramifications.

Using Security Resources

As you read this book and when you move out into the professional world, you will have frequent need for additional security resources. Appendix A lists additional security resources, but this section highlights a few of the most important ones and those you may find useful now.

- **CERT** (**www.cert.org/**). CERT stands for Computer Emergency Response Team, a group sponsored by Carnegie-Mellon University. CERT was the first computer incident-response team and is still one of the most respected in the industry. Anyone interested in network security should visit the site routinely. On the Web site is a wealth of documentation including guidelines for security policies, cutting-edge security research, security alerts, and more.

- **Microsoft Security Advisor** (**www.microsoft.com/security/ default.mspx**). This site is particularly useful because so many computers run Microsoft operating systems. This site is a portal to all Microsoft security information, tools, and updates. Users of Microsoft software should visit this Web site regularly.

- **F-Secure Corporation** (**www.f-secure.com/**). This site is, among other things, a repository for detailed information on virus outbreaks.

Here you will find notifications and detailed information about specific viruses. This information includes how the virus spreads, ways to recognize the virus, and specific tools for cleaning an infected system of a particular virus.

■ **SANS Institute (www.sans.org/).** This site provides detailed documentation on virtually every aspect of computer security. The SANS Institute also sponsors a number of security research projects and publishes information about those projects on its Web site.

Summary

Threats to networks are growing. We are seeing an increase in the number of hacking attacks and viruses, as well as other forms of attack. Coupling this growing danger with increasing legal pressures (such as HIPAA and SOX), network administrators have an ever-increasing demand on network security. In order to meet this demand you must have a thorough understanding of the threats to your network, as well as the countermeasures you can employ. This begins with a realistic assessment of the dangers to your network.

This chapter has introduced you to the basic concepts of network security, the general classes of danger, and basic security terminology. Subsequent chapters will elaborate on this knowledge.

Test Your Skills

MULTIPLE CHOICE QUESTIONS

1. Which of the following is not one of the three major classes of threats?

    A. Denial of Service attacks

    B. a computer virus or worm

    C. actually intruding on a system

    D. online auction fraud

2. Which of the following is the most accurate definition of a virus?

    A. any program that spreads via e-mail

    B. any program that carries a malicious payload

    C. any program that self replicates

    D. any program that can damage your system

3. Are there any reasons not to take an extreme view of security, if that view errs on the side of caution?

   A. No, there is no reason not to take such an extreme view.

   B. Yes, that can lead to wasting resources on threats that are not likely.

   C. Yes, if you are going to err, assume there are few if any realistic threats.

   D. Yes, that can require that you increase your security skills in order to implement more rigorous defenses.

4. What is a computer virus?

   A. any program that is downloaded to your system without your permission

   B. any program that self replicates

   C. any program that causes harm to your system

   D. any program that can change your Windows registry

5. Which of the following gives the best definition of spyware?

   A. any software that logs keystrokes

   B. any software used to gather intelligence

   C. any software or hardware that monitors your system

   D. Any software that monitors which Web sites you visit

6. Which of the following is the best definition for the term *sneaker*?

   A. an amateur who hacks a system without being caught

   B. a person who hacks a system by faking a legitimate password

   C. a person who hacks a system to test its vulnerabilities

   D. an amateur hacker

7. What is the term for hacking a phone system?

   A. telco-hacking

   B. hacking

   C. cracking

   D. phreaking

8. Which of the following is the best definition of malware?

   A. software that has some malicious purpose

   B. software that self replicates

   C. software that damages your system

   D. any software that is not properly configured for your system

9. Which of the following is the best definition for war-driving?

    A. driving while hacking and seeking a computer job

    B. driving while using a wireless connection to hack

    C. driving looking for wireless networks to hack

    D. driving and seeking rival hackers

10. Which of the following is the most basic security activity?

    A. installing a firewall

    B. authenticating users

    C. controlling access to resources

    D. using a virus scanner

11. Blocking attacks seek to accomplish what?

    A. install a virus on the target machine

    B. shut down security measures

    C. prevent legitimate users from accessing a system

    D. break into a target system

12. What are the three approaches to security?

    A. perimeter, layered, and hybrid

    B. high security, medium security, and low security

    C. internal, external, and hybrid

    D. perimeter, complete, and none

13. An intrusion-detection system is an example of:

    A. proactive security

    B. perimeter security

    C. hybrid security

    D. good security practices

14. Which of the following would most likely be classified as misuses of systems?

    A. looking up information on a competitor using the Web

    B. getting an occasional personal e-mail

    C. using your business computer to conduct your own (non-company) business

    D. shopping on the Web during lunch

15. The most desirable approach to security is one which is:

    A. perimeter and dynamic

    B. layered and dynamic

    C. perimeter and static

    D. layered and static

16. When assessing threats to a system, what three factors should you consider?

    A. the system's attractiveness, the information contained on the system, and how much traffic the system gets

    B. the skill level of the security team, the system's attractiveness, and how much traffic the system gets

    C. how much traffic the system gets, the security budget, and the skill level of the security team

    D. the system's attractiveness, the information contained on the system, and the security budget

17. Which of the following is the best definition for non-repudiation?

    A. security that does not allow the potential intruder to deny his attack

    B. processes that verify which user performs what action

    C. It is another term for user authentication.

    D. access control

18. Which of the following types of privacy laws affect computer security?

    A. any state privacy law

    B. any privacy law applicable to your organization

    C. any privacy law

    D. any federal privacy law

19. The first computer incident response team is affiliated with what university?

    A. Princeton

    B. Carnegie-Mellon University

    C. Harvard University

    D. Yale

20. Which of the following is the best definition of "sensitive information"?

    A. military or defense related information

    B. any information that is worth more than $1,000

    C. any information that, if accessed by unauthorized personnel, could damage your organization in any way

    D. any information that has monetary value and is protected by any privacy laws

21. Which of the following best defines the primary difference between a sneaker and an auditor?

    A. There is no difference.

    B. The sneaker tends to be less skilled.

    C. The auditor tends to be less skilled.

    D. The sneaker tends to use more unconventional methods.

EXERCISES

Exercise 1.1: How Many Virus Attacks Have Occurred This Month?

1. Using various Web sites, determine the number of virus attacks reported this month. You may find that sites such as **www.f-secure.com** are helpful for finding this information.

2. Compare that figure to the number of virus outbreaks per month in the last three, nine, and twelve months.

3. Are virus attacks increasing or decreasing in frequency? Give examples to support your answer and state the estimated amount of change in virus attacks over the past year.

Exercise 1.2: Trojan Horse Attacks

1. Using the Internet, journals, books, or other resources, find one incident of a Trojan horse attack in the past nine months.

2. How was this Trojan horse delivered? What damage did it cause?

3. Describe the Trojan horse attack, including:

   ■ Any specific targets

   ■ Whether the perpetrators of the attack have been caught and/or prosecuted

   ■ What types of security warnings were issued about the attack as well as measures prescribed to defend against it.

Exercise 1.3: Recent Trends in Computer Crime

1. Using the Computer Security Institute Web site (**www.gocsi.com/awareness/fbi.jhtml**), find its most recent survey on computer crime.

2. Note which areas of computer crime have increased and decreased.

3. Describe the changes between this survey and the one published in 2002.

4. What do the two surveys tell you about trends in computer crime?

5. What area of computer crime appears to be increasing most rapidly?

Exercise 1.4: Hacking Terminology

Using the *New Hackers Dictionary* (**www.hack.gr/jargon/**), define the following terms. Then check the Internet (Web pages, chat rooms, or bulletin boards) to find an example of each term being used.

daemon

dead code

Dumpster diving

leapfrog attack

kludge

nuke

Exercise 1.5: Security Professional Terminology

Using the Microsoft Security Terminology Web site (**www.microsoft.com/ security/glossary.mspx**), define the following terms:

> access control list
>
> adware
>
> authentication
>
> backdoor
>
> buffer
>
> HotFix

PROJECTS

Project 1.1: Learning About a Virus

1. Using Web resources in Appendix A, find a virus that has been released in the last six months. You might find information on sites such as **www.f-secure.com**.

2. Describe how the virus you chose worked, including the method it used to spread.

3. Describe the amount of damage caused by the virus.

4. Were any specific targets identified?

5. Were the perpetrators of the virus attack caught and/or prosecuted?

6. What types of security warnings were issued about the virus attack?

7. What measures were prescribed to defend against it?

8. Would the virus most properly be described as a virus or a worm?

Project 1.2: Security Profession

Using various resources including the Web, find out qualifications required for computer security administrator jobs. You will need to find out specific technologies required, years of experience, educational level, and any certifications. This project should help you see what topics the industry considers most important for a security professional to understand. Web sites that might help you include:

www.computerjobs.com

www.monster.com

www.hotjobs.com

Project 1.3: Finding Web Resources

In this chapter we have utilized several very good Web resources for security information. You should now use the Internet to identify three Web sites you think provide reliable and valid information that would be beneficial to a security professional. Explain why you believe these to be valid sources of information.

Note: You will likely use these sources in later chapter exercises and projects, so make certain you can rely on the data they provide.

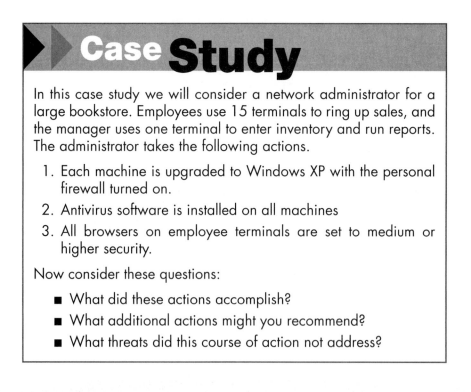

Case Study

In this case study we will consider a network administrator for a large bookstore. Employees use 15 terminals to ring up sales, and the manager uses one terminal to enter inventory and run reports. The administrator takes the following actions.

1. Each machine is upgraded to Windows XP with the personal firewall turned on.
2. Antivirus software is installed on all machines
3. All browsers on employee terminals are set to medium or higher security.

Now consider these questions:

- What did these actions accomplish?
- What additional actions might you recommend?
- What threats did this course of action not address?

Chapter | 2

Types of Attacks

Chapter Objectives

After reading this chapter and completing the exercises, you will be able to do the following:

- Describe the most common network attacks including session hacking, virus attacks, Trojan horses, Denial of Service, and buffer overflow.
- Explain how these attacks are executed.
- Identify basic defenses against those attacks.
- Configure a system to prevent Denial of Service attacks.
- Configure a system to defend against Trojan horse attacks.
- Configure a system to defend against buffer overflow attacks.

Introduction

Chapter 1 introduced some general dangers to computer systems and provided an overview of network security. In this chapter we will examine specific types of attacks much more closely. This chapter analyzes how systems are most commonly attacked. Particular attention will be paid to the Denial of Service (DoS) attack. This threat is one of the most common attacks on the Internet, so it is prudent for administrators to understand how it works and how to defend systems against them.

This chapter also describes virus attacks, Trojan horse attacks, and some less common methods of attack, such as session hacking and tunneling. In information security, the old adage "knowledge is power" is not only good advice but an axiom upon which to build an entire security outlook.

Defending Against Denial of Service Attacks

The first type of attack we will examine is the Denial of Service (DoS). Recall from Chapter 1 that a Denial of Service attack is any attack that aims to deprive legitimate users of the use of the target system. This class of attacks does not actually attempt to infiltrate a system or to obtain sensitive information. It simply aims to prevent legitimate users from accessing a given system. This type of attack is quite common; in fact it is one of the most common categories of attack. Many experts feel that it is so common because most forms of Denial of Service attacks are fairly easy to execute. The ease with which these attacks can be executed means that even attackers with minimal technical skills can often successfully perform a denial of service.

The concept underlying the denial of service attack is based on the fact that any device has operational limits. This fact applies to all devices, not just computer systems. For example, bridges are designed to hold weight up to a certain limit, aircraft have limits on how far they can travel without refueling, and automobiles can only accelerate to a certain point. All of these various devices share a common trait: They have set limitations to their capacity to perform work. Computers are no different than these, or any other machine; they, too, have limits. Any computer system, Web server, or network can only handle a finite load.

How a workload (and its limits) is defined varies from one machine to another. A workload for a computer system may be defined in a number of different ways, including by the number of simultaneous users, the size of files, the speed of data transmission, or the amount of data stored. Exceeding any of these limits will stop the system from responding. For example, if you can flood a Web server with more requests than it can process, it will be overloaded and will no longer be able to respond to further requests (*Webopedia, 2004*). This reality underlies the DoS attack. Simply overload the system with requests, and it will no longer be able to respond to legitimate users attempting to access the Web server.

DoS in Action

The concept of a Denial of Services is simple, however, most principles are easier to grasp if one can see a concrete example. In this case we need a safe way to simulate a DoS attack within a classroom or laboratory setting. One simple way to illustrate a DoS attack, especially in a classroom setting, involves the use of the ping command along with certain parameters. (Recall that typing in **ping /h** or **ping /?** will show you all the options for the ping command.) The first step is to start a Web server service running on a computer that will be used as the target for this attack. You can use any operating system and any Web server you like (such as Microsoft Internet Information Server or Apache.). Apache is a free download from **www.apache.org**.

Microsoft Windows 2000 professional comes with Internet Information Server, or you can download Personal Web Server for free from **www. studiodeluxe.net/pws/index.htm**, so you should have no trouble finding a Web server to install and run. For the purposes of this lab you would want to purposefully use a low capacity machine. An older machine, perhaps an older laptop, would be ideal. You want to pick a machine that will be easy to overload. In essence you are looking for the exact opposite of what you look for when setting up a real Web server.

Setting up a Web server is actually quite simple. Since Apache is available as a free download for both Linux and Windows (**www.apache. org**), let's examine it. Follow these steps to install and configure Apache on your system.

Installing for Windows

1. Download Apache for Windows from **www.apache.org**.
2. Look in *C:\Program Files\Apache Group\Apache2\conf* for the httpd.conf file and open it.
3. Set the ServerName = localhost.
4. Save the file.
5. From the command prompt type **httpd start**.
6. You should now be able to open a browser and see the default Apache Web site.

Installing for Linux

1. Download Apache for Linux (or if in many Linux distributions you can simply add the Apache Web server package) from **http://www. apache.org**.
2. You will need to look in */etc/httpd/conf* for the *httpd.conf* file. When you find it right-click and open with text editor.
3. Set the ServerName = localhost.
4. Save the file.
5. From a shell type **/etc/init.d/httpd start**. The server should start and you get an OK message.
6. Open your browser and go to **http://localhost/**.
7. You should see the Apache default Web site.
8. When you are ready to make your server live (reachable from other PCs):
9. In the */etc/httpd/conf/httpd.conf* file change the following settings:
   - Change servername to your registered URL or to your IP:port such as 10.10.10.117:80.

Caution

Changing the Configuration File

Any time you change the configuration file you must stop the Apache server and restart it. To stop Apache:
/etc/init.d/http stop

Caution

Conducting Labs Safely

This lab is potentially dangerous to the target server. In fact throughout this book, we will be examining labs that could cause significant disruption to live computer systems. You should conduct these labs only on computers that are disconnected from your main network and that do not contain any critical information. It is best to set up a lab specifically for security practice.

- Change listen to reflect the IP and port you wish (there is an example in the *config* file).
- Check the *documentroot* directory to make certain that is where you want your Web pages to be served up from. The default should be */var/www/html*.

From a shell type **/etc/init.d/httpd start**.

If you are using Windows 2000 or 2003 Server editions you can also choose to use Microsoft Internet Information Server as your Web server.

The next step is to verify that the Web server is actually running and that you can reach its default Web page. One person in the class can open his or her browser and type the target server machine's IP address in the address bar. They should then be viewing the default Web site for that Web server. Now you can do a rather primitive DoS attack on it.

The actual attack is done using the ping command. If you don't recall how to use the ping command, you should note that typing **ping /h** at the command prompt displays all of the options for the ping command. The options you will be using in this exercise are –**w** and –**t**. The –**w** option determines how many milliseconds the ping utility will wait for a response from the target. In this case, set that option to –0, so it does not wait at all. The –t instructs the ping utility to keep sending packets until explicitly told to stop. An additional option, the –l option, allows users to change the size of the packet you can send. Keep in mind that a TCP packet can only be of a finite size, so you are going to set these packets to be almost as large as you can send.

At the command prompt in Windows 2000/XP (that's the DOS prompt in Windows 98 and the Shell in Unix/Linux), type **ping <address of target machine goes here>–l 65000 –w 0 –t**. The machine's response should be similar to that shown in Figure 2.1. Note that in the figure I am pinging the

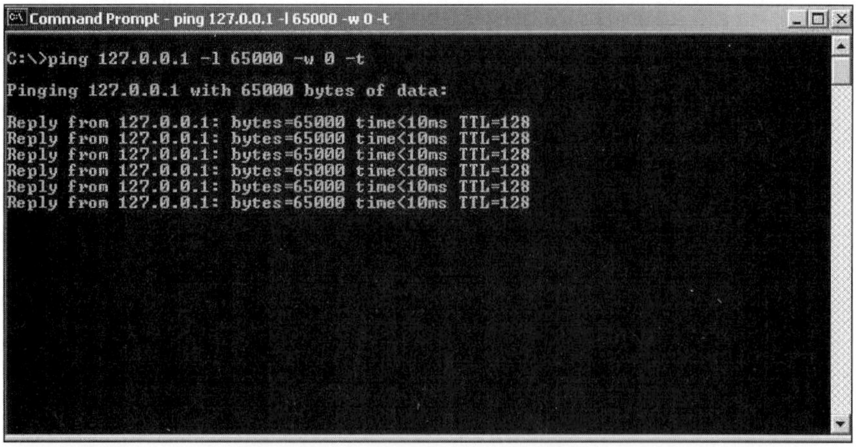

FIGURE 2.1 Ping from the command prompt.

loop back address for my own machine. You will want to substitute the address of the machine on which you are running the Web server.

What is happening as this series of pings is being executed is that this single machine is continually pinging away at the target machine. At this point in the exercise, having just one machine in a classroom or lab pinging on a Web server should not adversely affect the Web server. This is because that level of traffic is well within the capacity of the target Web server. However, after causing other machines to ping the server in the same way, you will begin to tax the target machine's capacity. If you get enough machines pinging the target, you will eventually reach a threshold at which the target machine will stop responding to requests, and you will no longer be able to access the Web page. The number of machines it will take to reach this threshold depends on the Web server you are using. This author has conducted this particular experiment in classrooms. In those situations Apache Web server was being run on a Pentium III laptop running Windows 98, with only 64 megabytes of RAM. In that scenario it only took about 15 machines simultaneously pinging to cause the Web server to stop responding to legitimate requests.

This experiment allows you to get a feel for how a Denial of Service is executed. It is meant to give you a better understanding of the principle behind the DoS. You should keep in mind that actual denial of service attacks use much more sophisticated methods. It should also be noted that no real Web server would be running on a simple laptop with Windows 98. However, this exercise demonstrates the basic principle behind the DoS attack: Simply flood the target machine with so many packets that it can no longer respond to legitimate requests. This basic concept is shown in Figure 2.2. What we have done, in this experiment, is simply to exceed the operational limits of the laboratory Web server.

Generally the methods used for DoS attacks are significantly more sophisticated than the illustration. While all DoS attacks seek to overload the

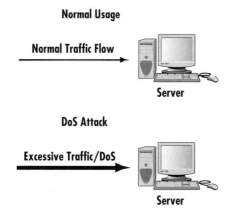

FIGURE 2.2 The DoS concept.

target machine, there are a variety of ways to do that, and a variety of ways to initiate the attack itself. For example, a hacker might develop a small virus whose sole purpose is to initiate a ping flood against a predetermined target. Once the virus has spread, the various machines that are infected with that virus begin their ping flood to the target system. This sort of DoS is easy to do, and can be hard to stop. A DoS attack that is launched from several different machines is called a *Distributed Denial of Service,* or *DDoS.*

The DDoS is becoming more common; in fact it is now the most common sort of DoS attack. Most of the real world examples we will examine later in this chapter are DDoS attacks. There are two reasons that this form of Denial of Service attack is becoming more common. The first is that it is easier to overload a target system if you have more than one machine attacking it. With newer servers capable of handling much higher workloads it becomes more difficult to execute a DoS attack from just one machine. Another reason the DDoS is becoming more common is because it allows the attacker to launch the attack from other people's machines, thus protecting his anonymity. Launching an attack from one's own machines can be risky because each packet has the potential to be traced back to its source. This would mean an almost certainty of being caught by the authorities.

The basic concept behind a DoS attack is simple. The real problem for the attacker is avoiding being caught. We will next examine some specific types of DoS attacks and review specific case studies.

SYN Flood

Simply sending a flood of pings is the most primitive method of performing a DoS. There are more sophisticated methods that use specific types of packets. One popular version of the DoS attack is the *SYN flood.* This particular attack depends on the hacker's knowledge of how connections are made to a server. When a session is initiated between the client and server in a network using the TCP protocol, a small buffer space in memory is set aside on the server to handle the "hand-shaking" exchange of messages that sets up the session. The session-establishing packets include a SYN field that identifies the sequence in the message exchange.

A SYN flood attempts to subvert this process. In this attack an attacker will send a number of connection requests very rapidly and then fail to respond to the reply that is sent back by the server. In other words, the attacker requests connections, then never follows through with the rest of the connection sequence. This has the effect of leaving connections on the server half open, and the buffer memory allocated for them is reserved and not available to other applications. Although the packet in the buffer is dropped after a certain period of time (usually about three minutes) without a reply, the effect of many of these false connection requests is to make it difficult for legitimate requests for a session to get established. This is shown in Figure 2.3.

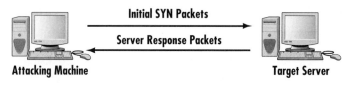

Initial SYN Packets

Server Response Packets

Attacking Machine

Target Server

FIGURE 2.3 The SYN flood.

There have been a number of well-known SYN flood attacks on Web servers. The reason for the popularity of this attack type is that any machine that engages in TCP communication is vulnerable to it — and all machines connected to the Internet engage in TCP communications. The TCP packet exchange is the entire basis for Web server communication. There are, however, several methods that protect against these attacks. Some of those methods require more technical sophistication than others. You can select the methods most appropriate for your network environment and your level of expertise.

Micro Blocks Micro blocks seek to avoid SYN floods by changing the way the server allocates memory for any given connection request. Instead of allocating a complete connection object, the server is altered so that it only allocates a micro-record. Newer implementations of this technique allocate as little as 16-bytes for the incoming SYN object. The specifics on how to setup micro blocks are specific to a given operating system.

SYN Cookies As the name *SYN cookies* suggests, this method uses cookies, not unlike the standard cookies used on many Web sites. With this method, the system does not immediately create a buffer space in memory for the hand-shaking process. Rather, it first sends a SYNACK (the acknowledgement signal that begins the hand-shaking process). The SYNACK contains a carefully constructed cookie, generated as a hash that contains the IP address, port number, and other information from the client machine requesting the connection. When the client responds with a normal ACK (acknowledgment), the information from that cookie will be included, which the server then verifies. Thus, the system does not fully allocate any memory until the third stage of the hand-shaking process. However, the cryptographic hashing used in SYN cookies is fairly intensive, so system administrators that expect a large number of incoming connections may choose not to use this defensive technique.

This defense mechanism also illustrates the fact that most defenses require some trade off between performance and security. The overhead resources required by the SYN cookie may degrade performance, especially when there is a large amount of traffic; however the SYN cookie is one of the more robust defenses against many forms of DoS. The optimal solution would be to have a very high performance server (or server farm) that can handle the overhead, and to implement SYN cookies.

RST Cookies Another cookie method that is easier to implement than SYN cookies is the *RST cookie.* In this method, the server sends a wrong SYNACK back to the client. The client should then generate an RST packet telling the server that something is wrong. Because the client sent back a packet notifying the server of the error, the server now knows the client request is legitimate and will now accept incoming connections from that client in the normal fashion. This method has two disadvantages. It might cause problems with Windows 95 machines and/or machines that are communicating from behind firewalls. Because Win95 machines often react poorly to error messages, the RST cookie might cause a problem on a legitimate client machine. Some firewalls might block the return SYNACK packet.

Obviously Windows 95 is not as common today as it once was. With each passing year there are fewer Windows 95 machines to be concerned about, so this particular defense mechanism becomes more viable. You can also configure your firewall to allow the returning SYNACK packet to pass.

Stack Tweaking The method of *stack tweaking* involves altering the TCP stack on the server so that it will take less time to timeout when a SYN connection is left incomplete. Unfortunately, this protective method will just make executing a SYN flood against that target more difficult; to a determined hacker, the attack is still possible. Stack tweaking is more complicated than the other methods and is discussed more fully in Chapter 8.

The specific implementation procedure of any of these methods depends on the operating system your Web server is using. Administrators should consult your operating system's documentation or appropriate Web sites in order to find explicit instructions. The most efficient way to defend against a DoS attack is a combination of these methods. The use of SYN cookies or RST cookies in conjunction with stack tweaking is a very good way to defend your Web server. By combining methods, each method can overcome the others' weaknesses. Combining these methods is rather like using both an alarm system and a security guard to protect a building. The guard can make decisions that the alarm system cannot, but the alarm system is never asleep, cannot be bribed, and is never distracted. The two methods together cover each other's weaknesses.

The Smurf Attack

The *Smurf attack* is a very popular type of DoS attack. It was named after the application first used to execute this attack. In the Smurf attack, an ICMP packet is sent out to the broadcast address of a network, but its return address has been altered to match one of the computers on that network, most likely

FYI: Stack Tweaking

The process of stack tweaking is often quite complicated, depending on the operating system. Some operating systems' documentation provides no help on this subject. Also, it only decreases the danger, but it does not prevent it. For this reason it is not used as frequently as other methods.

a key server. All the computers on the network will then respond by pinging the target computer (Huegen, 2004). ***ICMP packets*** use the Internet Control Message Protocol to send error messages on the Internet. Because the address the packets are sent to is a broadcast address, that address responds by echoing the packet out to all hosts on the network, who then send it to the spoofed source address. Continually sending such packets will cause the network itself to perform a DoS attack on one or more of its member servers. This attack is both clever and simple. The greatest difficulty is getting the packets started on the target network. This can be accomplished via some software such as a virus or Trojan horse that will begin sending the packets. This attack is shown in Figure 2.4

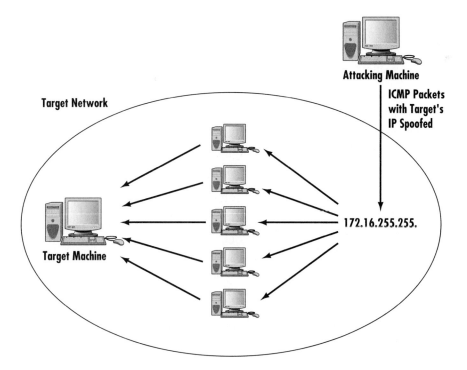

FIGURE 2.4 The Smurf attack.

The Smurf attack is an example of the creativity that some malicious parties can employ. It is sometimes viewed as the digital equivalent of the biological process in an autoimmune disorder. With such disorders, the immune system attacks the patient's own body. In a Smurf attack the network performs a DoS attack on one of its own systems. This method's cleverness illustrates why it is important that you attempt to work creatively and in a forward-thinking manner if you are responsible for system security in your network. The perpetrators of computer attacks are inventive, continually developing new techniques. If your defense is less creative and clever than the attackers' offense, then it is simply a matter of time before your system is compromised.

There are two ways to protect against the Smurf attack. The most direct method is to configure all of your routers so that they do not forward any directed broadcast packets. These packets are the cornerstone of the Smurf attack, and if routers do not forward them then the attack is contained within one subnetwork. The second approach is to guard against Trojan horses (covered in depth later in this chapter). Since the Smurf attack is launched from software delivered via a Trojan horse, preventing that initial delivery will prevent the attack. Policies that prohibit employees from downloading applications and guarding a system with adequate virus scanners can go a long way to protecting the system from a Trojan horse, and thus the Smurf attack.

Using a proxy server is also imperative. Proxy servers can hide the internal IP addresses of your machine, which makes your system a lot less vulnerable to a Smurf attack. Chapters 3 and 4 explore proxy servers and firewalls, another important tool, in detail.

The Ping of Death

The *Ping of Death* (PoD), perhaps the simplest and most primitive form of DoS attack, is based on overloading the target system. TCP packets are of limited size. In some cases simply sending a packet that is too large can shut down a target machine.

This attack is quite similar to the classroom example discussed earlier in this chapter. The aim in both cases is to overload the target system and cause it to quit responding. The PoD works to compromise systems that cannot deal with extremely large packet sizes. If successful, the server will actually shut completely down. It can, of course, be rebooted.

The only real safeguard against this type of attack is to ensure that all operating systems and software are routinely patched. This attack relies on vulnerabilities in the way a particular operating system or application handles abnormally large TCP packets. When such vulnerabilities are discovered, the vendor customarily releases a patch. The possibility of PoD is one reason, among many, why you must keep patches updated on all of your systems.

This attack is becoming less common as newer versions of operating systems are better able to handle the overly large packets that Ping of Death depends on. If the operating system is properly designed it will drop any oversized packets, thus negating any possible negative effects a PoD attack might have.

UDP Flood This attack is actually a variation on the experiment we described earlier in this chapter. UDP is a connectionless protocol and it does not require any connection setup procedure to transfer data. TCP packets connect and wait for the recipient to acknowledge receipt before sending the next packet. Each packet is confirmed. UDP packets simply send the packets without confirmation. This allows packets to be sent much faster, making it easier to perform a DoS attack.

A UDP Flood Attack occurs when an attacker sends a UDP packet to a random port on the victim system. When the victim system receives a UDP packet, it will determine what application is waiting on the destination port. When it realizes that there is no application that is waiting on the port, it will generate an ICMP packet of destination unreachable to the forged source address. If enough UDP packets are delivered to ports on the victim, the system will go down.

ICMP Flood The ICMP flood is a term you will frequently encounter in security literature. In reality it is simply another name for the ping flood we used in our previous experiment. ICMP packets are the type of packets used in the ping and tracert (this command is tracert in Windows, and traceroute in Linux) utilities.

Distributed Reflection Denial of Service

As we previously stated, Distributed Denial of Service attacks are becoming more common. Most such attacks rely on getting various machines (servers or workstations) to attack the target. The ***Distributed Reflection Denial of Service*** is a special type of DoS attack. As with all such attacks, it is accomplished by the hacker getting a number of machines to attack the selected target. However, this attack works a bit differently than other DoS attacks. Rather than getting computers to attack the target, this method tricks Internet routers into attacking a target.

Many of the routers on the Internet backbone communicate on port 179 (Gibson, 2003). This attack exploits that communication line and gets routers to attack a target system. What makes this attack particularly wicked is that it does not require the routers in question to be compromised in any way. The attacker does not need to get any sort of software on the router to get it to participate in the attack. Instead the hacker sends a stream of packets to the various routers requesting a connection. The packets have been altered so that they appear to come from the target system's IP address. The routers respond

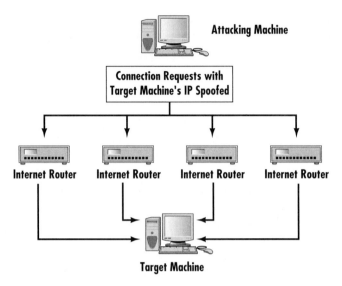

FIGURE 2.5 Distributed Reflection Denial of Service.

by initiating connections with the target system. What occurs is a flood of connections from multiple routers, all hitting the same target system. This has the effect of rendering the target system unreachable. This attack is illustrated in Figure 2.5.

DoS Tools

One reason that DoS attacks are becoming so common is that there are a number of tools available for executing DoS attacks. These tools are widely available on the Internet, and in most cases are free to download. This means that any prudent administrator should be aware of them. In addition to their obvious use as an attack tool, they can also be useful for testing your anti-DoS security measures.

IN PRACTICE: Attacking Your Own System

There is no better way to test your defense versus a particular sort of attack, than to simulate that attack. No matter what counter measures you implement, you won't really know if they are effective until you are attacked. It would be better to find out before a real attack occurs. The best way to do this is to use military style battle exercises.

This is not something you would try against a live machine. The preferred way to do this is to setup a machine for testing purposes. On that machine implement your various security measures. Then subject that machine to the types of attacks you hope to defend against. This will give you concrete evidence of the efficacy of your defenses.

When you conduct this sort of exercise, several guidelines should be followed:

- Always use a test system, not a live system.
- Carefully document the system's state prior to the attack (what operating system, patches, hardware configuration, CPU usage, memory usage, what software is installed, and how the system is configured).
- Carefully document exactly what security measures you implement.
- Very specifically document each type of attack you subject the machine to.
- Document how that machine responds.

When you have completed this battle drill, you should borrow one more idea from the military, and that is the after action review. Simply put, briefly write up how the system defenses performed and what this indicates about your system's security.

It is an unfortunate fact, however, that this particular security measure is one that is not frequently employed in industry. The primary reason for this is that it requires resources. You must dedicate a test machine, and more importantly, many hours to conducting the exercise. Most IT departments have a very heavy workload and simply cannot allocate the time necessary for this sort of drill. However this is something that security consultants should definitely engage in.

The Tribal Flood Network is perhaps the most widely known and used DoS tool. It is available in two versions — the original version, TFN, and a newer version, TFN2K. TFN2K supports both Windows NT and Unix platforms and has some features that make detection more difficult than its predecessor, including sending decoy information to avoid being traced. TFN or TFN2K work by configuring the software to attack a particular target, and then getting the target on a specific machine. Usually the attacker will seek to infect several machines with the TFN program in order to form a Tribal Flood Network.

Experts at using TFN2K can use the resources of a number of agents to coordinate an attack against one or more targets. TFN and TFN2K can perform various types of DoS attacks, such as UDP flood attacks, ICMP flood attacks, and TCP SYN flood attacks. You can get more details about TFN and TFN2K at these Web sites:

- Washington University: **http://staff.washington.edu/dittrich/misc/ tfn.analysis.txt**

- Packetstorm Security: **http://packetstormsecurity.com/distributed/ TFN2k_Analysis-1.3.txt**

- CERT: **www.cert.org/advisories/CA-1999-17.html**

Trin00 *Trin00* is another popular DoS tool. It was originally available only for Unix but now is available for Windows as well. It is actually a Distributed Denial of Service tool, much like TFN. The Trin00 package is delivered to multiple machines and will run as a ***daemon*** (a program that runs when the operating system starts, usually has no visual interface, and provides some background service; Web servers and FTP servers in Unix/ Linux operate as daemons) or service (Windows). How it is delivered to the target system varies depending on the attacker, however a common technique would be to use a Trojan horse to deliver the Trin00 packet.

The multiple infected machines essentially create a Trin00 network. In such a network the attacker connects to a central machine, referred to as the "master." When Trin00 is successfully installed on a machine it will notify the Trin00 master that it is installed and ready to work. These client installations of Trin00 are usually called daemon machines because the software runs as a daemon. One feature of Trin00 that makes it particularly insidious is that daemon machines are generally controlled by more than one master so that if a master is discovered it doesn't remove the entire network.

The daemon or client installations of Trin00 will usually carry one or several DoS routines that can be invoked remotely by one of the master machines. A master process can also control the targets and parameters for the attack. Some of the commands are password protected to prevent unauthorized activation or deactivation of the attacks.

A Trin00 network of at least 227 systems was used on August 17, 1999, to flood a single system at the University of Minnesota.

The following Web sites provide more information about Trin00:

- Security Team: **www.securiteam.com/securitynews/Trin00_DDoS_ tool_now_available_for_Windows.html**

- Washington University: **http://staff.washington.edu/dittrich/misc/ trinoo.analysis**

- University of Chicago: **http://security.uchicago.edu/seminars/ DDoS/trin00.shtml**

To stop a Trin00 attack you will first need to remove the application from infected machines on your network (assuming that your network is the

2

one that has been infected and is causing the Trin00 attack). Finding the Trin00 daemon program might be difficult, because the name of the executable can vary. The most common names are listed here:

1. ns
2. ttp
3. rpc.trinoo
4. rpc.listen
5. trinix
6. rpc.irix
7. irix

You can use any process viewer, including the Windows task manager, to see if one of these processes is running. If so, stop it from running and search your hard drive for that file. You will then need to delete that file.

If possible, you may want to trace the packets it is sending or receiving before you remove it. This can let you know where the master is located, as well as what the target machine for the DoS attack is. You should then contact the administrators of both systems letting them know what has occurred.

Real World Examples

You should now have a firm grasp of what a DoS attack is, and have a basic understanding of how it works. You should also have some basic ideas of how to defend your network from these attacks. It is now time to begin discussing specific, real-world examples of such attacks. The following analysis of several actual attacks illustrates the methods hackers use to launch them, their effects, their detection, and the steps administrators took to overcome them.

FYI: Virus or Worm?

You will see the terms *virus* and *worm* used in different books, sometimes interchangeably. However there is a difference between the two. A worm is a specific type of virus, one that can spread without any human interaction. Traditional virus attacks come as e-mail attachments, and a human operator must open the attachment to start the infection. A worm spreads without any activity on the part of the human user. Some books will use these terms rather strictly. The term *virus* accurately describes both situations.

Blaster This worm is a fascinating worm to study, for several reasons. First it had an interesting spread. It spread via e-mail, as all worms and viruses do, but it also would use a buffer overflow attack on Windows 2000 or XP machines, in order to load itself onto the target machine. This buffer overflow exploited a known flaw in Windows, called the DCOM RPC vulnerability. There were patches available for this vulnerability, but many machines were not patched.

Once the machine was infected, it would, on a pre-selected date, launch a Denial of Service attack against Microsoft's update Web site, the Web site Microsoft users visit to get their systems patched. The damage from this particular attack was minimal, simply because the attackers did not realize that the Web site they were hitting was actually simply a redirect Web site, not the actual server that handled patches. Microsoft simply changed the link from their main site.

However this entire incident illustrates several important items you should consider:

- If all machines were routinely patched, then Blaster would have been completely ineffectual. You will see this is the case with many viruses and worms.

- The perpetrators seemed to have been sending a message about patches. The worm did not cause any direct harm to the infected machines. Some experts believe that this was a misguided attempt to bring attention to the issue of patches, and perhaps to highlight some security flaws in the Microsoft operating systems.

MyDoom In early 2004 it would have been quite difficult to not hear about the MyDoom worm. This threat was a classically executed DDoS attack. The virus/worm would e-mail itself to everyone in your address book and then, at a preset time, all infected machines began a coordinated attack on **www.sco.com** (Delio, 2004). Estimates put the number of infected machines between 500,000 and 1 million. This attack successfully shut down the Santa Cruz Operations (SCO) Web site. It should be noted that well before the day that the DDoS attack was actually executed, network administrators and home users were well aware of what MyDoom would do. There were several tools available free of charge on the Internet for removing that specific virus/worm. However, it appears that many people did not take the steps necessary to clean their machines of this virus/worm.

This attack is interesting to study from several angles. First of all it is a classic example of a worm. It used multiple modes to spread. It could spread as an e-mail attachment, or it could copy itself over a network. It was also a fascinating attack because it ultimately was the vehicle for launching a Distributed Denial of Service attack on a very specific target. But what makes this attack most interesting is that it is clearly an example of domestic cyber terrorism (although it is certain that the creators of My-Doom would probably see it differently). For those readers who do not know the story, it will be examined here briefly. Santa Cruz Operations makes a version of the Unix operating system. Like most Unix versions, their version is copyright protected. Several months before this attack SCO began accusing certain Linux distributions of containing segments of SCO Unix code. SCO sent letters to many Linux users demanding license fees. Many people in the Linux community viewed this as an attempt to undermine the growing popularity of Linux, an open-source operating system. SCO went even further and filed suit against major companies distributing Linux (SCO/Linux, 2003). This claim seemed unfounded to many legal and technology analysts. It was also viewed with great suspicion since SCO had close ties to Microsoft, who had been trying desperately to stop the growing popularity of Linux.

Many analysts feel that the MyDoom virus/worm was created by some individual (or group of individuals) who felt that the Santa Cruz Operations tactics were unacceptable. This hacker (or group of hackers) launched the virus to cause economic harm to SCO and to damage the company's public image. This makes the MyDoom virus a clear case of domestic cyber terrorism: One group attacks the technological assets of another based on an ideological difference. There have been numerous incidents of Web site defacement and other small-scale attacks that arose from ideological conflicts. However, the MyDoom attack was the first to be so widespread and so successful. This incident began a new trend in information warfare. As technology becomes less expensive and the tactics more readily available, there will likely be an increase in this sort of attack in the coming years.

The exact monetary damage caused by such attacks is virtually impossible to calculate. It includes the loss of service to customers, lost sales, and the impact of the negative publicity. SCO offered a $250,000 reward to anyone providing information leading to the arrest of the individuals responsible, an indication that they felt that the impact of the attack exceeded that amount.

Of particular note is the fact that variations of the MyDoom virus have continued to arise long after the original intent was fulfilled. These variations use the basic MyDoom engine, and spread in similar fashion, but have differing effects. As late as February 2005, new variations of MyDoom were showing up.

W32.Storm Worm W32.Storm.Worm is a worm that seeks out systems running the Microsoft Internet Information Services Web server. There is a patch available that will prevent this, but this worm will infect any systems that have not applied that security patch. The payload of this worm performs a Denial of Service attack on **www.microsoft.com**.

If a system is infected with this worm, the worm will scan literally millions of IP addresses in an attempt to find a vulnerable system. A vulnerable system is any system running IIS that has not been patched. Once a machine is infected, the worm has two activities it accomplishes:

- A Denial of Service attack is initiated against **www.microsoft.com**.

- An e-mail bombing session is started that sends e-mail messages containing an obscene message to **gates@microsoft.com**.

Like the Blaster worm, this worm could easily have been prevented by proper patching. In this case the situation is even more egregious because the machines being infected are Web servers. This means they are presumably run by trained administrators. There is no excuse for these machines being unpatched. Clearly the perpetrators of this attack have some sort of disagreement with Microsoft, and used a worm to express that disagreement.

The Slammer Worm Another virus/worm responsible for DoS attacks in recent years was the *Slammer* virus. Some experts rate it as the fastest-spreading virus to ever hit the Internet (Moore, 2004). This worm achieved its DoS simply by spreading so quickly that it clogged up networks. It began spreading on January 25, 2003. It would scan a network for computers running the Microsoft SQL Server Desktop Engine. It then used a flaw in that application to infect the target machine. It would continually scan every computer connected to the infected machine, seeking one with Microsoft SQL Server Desktop Engine. At its peak it performed millions of scans per second, resulting in a tremendous number of packets going across infected networks. That flood of scanning packets brought many systems down.

This particular attack was interesting for two reasons. First, what defines this virus as also being a worm is its method of propagation. It was able to spread without anyone downloading it or opening an attachment on an e-mail. Instead, it would randomly scan IP addresses, looking for any machine it could infect. This method meant it spread much faster than many other virus/worm attacks had previously. The second interesting fact about this attack was that it was totally preventable. Microsoft had released a patch for this flaw weeks before the attack took place. This story should illustrate the critical need to frequently update your software.

How to Defend Against DoS Attacks

There is no guaranteed way to prevent all DoS attacks, just as there is no guaranteed way to prevent any hacking attack. However, there are steps to minimize the danger. In this section we will examine some steps administrators can take to make their systems less susceptible to a DoS attack in addition to the use of SYN and RST cookies discussed previously.

2

One of the first things to consider is how these attacks are perpetrated. They may be executed via ICMP packets that are used to send error messages on the Internet or are sent by the ping and traceroute utilities. Simply configuring your firewall to refuse ICMP packets from outside your network will be a major step in protecting your network from DoS attacks. Since DoS/DDoS attacks can be executed via a wide variety of protocols, you can also configure your firewall to disallow any incoming traffic at all, regardless of what protocol or port it occurs on. This may seem like a radical step, but it is certainly a secure one.

FYI: Blocking All Traffic

Most networks *must* allow some incoming traffic. This traffic might be to the network's Web server or to an e-mail server. For this reason you will not often see a firewall that blocks all incoming traffic. If you can't block all incoming traffic, be as selective as possible and only allow in the traffic that is absolutely necessary.

If your network is large enough to have internal routers, then you can configure those routers to disallow any traffic that does not originate with your network. In that way, should packets make it past your firewall, they will not be propagated throughout the network. Because all TCP packets have a source IP address, it is not difficult to determine whether a packet originated within the network or from outside the network. Another possibility is disabling directed IP broadcasts on all routers. This will prevent the router from sending broadcast packets to all machines on the network, thus stopping many DoS attacks.

Because many distributed DoS attacks depend on "unwitting" computers being used as launch points, one way to reduce such attacks is to protect your computer against virus/worm attacks and Trojan horses. Protecting against these attacks is discussed later in this chapter, but for now three points are important to remember:

- Always use virus-scanning software and keep it updated.

- Always keep operating system and software patches updated.

- Have an organizational policy stating that employees cannot download anything onto their machines unless the download has been cleared by the IT staff.

None of these steps will make your network totally secure from being the victim of a DoS attack or being the launch point for one, but they will help reduce the chances of either occurring. A good resource for this topic is the SANS institute Web site, **www.sans.org/dosstep/**. This site has many good tips on preventing DoS attacks.

Defending Against Buffer Overflow Attacks

Virus, DoS, and Trojan horse attacks are probably the most common ways to attack a system, but they are not the only methods of attack available. Another way of attacking a system is called a ***buffer overflow*** (or buffer overrun) attack. Some experts would argue that the buffer overflow is as common, if not more common, than the DoS attack, but this is less true now than it was a few years ago. A buffer overflow attack is designed to put more data in a buffer than the buffer was designed to hold (*Webopedia,* 2004). However recall that at least one worm used a buffer overflow to infect targeted machines. This means that while this threat may be less than it once was, it is still a very real threat.

Any program that communicates with the Internet or a private network must receive some data. This data is stored, at least temporarily, in a space in memory called a buffer. If the programmer who wrote the application was careful, the buffer will truncate or reject any information that exceeds the buffer limit. Given the number of applications that might be running on a target system and the number of buffers in each application, the chance of having at least one buffer that was not written properly is significant enough to cause any prudent system administrator some concern. A person moderately skilled in programming can write a program that purposefully writes more data into the buffer than it can hold. For example if the buffer can hold 1024 bytes of data and you try to fill it with 2048 bytes, the extra 1024 bytes is then simply loaded into memory. This concept is shown in Figure 2.6.

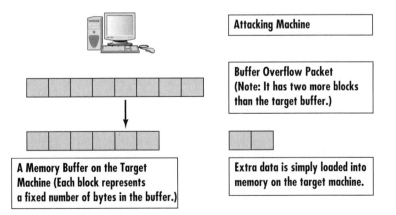

FIGURE 2.6 Buffer overflow attack.

If the extra data is actually a malicious program, then it has just been loaded into memory and is running on the target system. Or perhaps the perpetrator simply wants to flood the target machine's memory, thus over-writing other items that are currently in memory and causing them to crash. Either way, the buffer overflow is a very serious attack.

Fortunately, buffer overflow attacks are a bit harder to execute than the DoS or a simple MS Outlook script virus. To create a buffer overflow at-tack, a hacker must have a good working knowledge of some programming language (C or C++ is often chosen) and understand the target operating system/application well enough to know whether it has a buffer overflow weakness and how the weakness might be exploited.

FYI: What Is an Outlook Script Virus?

Microsoft Outlook is designed so that a programmer can write scripts using a subset of the Visual Basic programming language, called Visual Basic for Applications, or simply VBA. This scripting language is, in fact, built into all Microsoft Office products. Pro-grammers can also use the closely related VB Script language. Both languages are quite easy to learn. If such a script is attached to an e-mail and if the recipient is using Outlook, then the script can execute. That execution can do any number of things, includ-ing scanning the address book, looking for addresses, sending out e-mail, deleting e-mail, and more.

Susceptibility to a buffer overflow attack is entirely contingent on software flaws. A perfectly written program would not allow buffer over-flows. Since perfection is unlikely, the best defense against buffer overflow attacks is to routinely patch software so that flaws are corrected when the vendor discovers a vulnerability.

FYI: How Do Buffer Overflows Occur?

A buffer overflow attack can only occur if some flaw exists in the soft-ware, usually the operating system or Web server. This means that the only way to prevent this type of attack is to improve the quality of software. Unfortunately, many software vendors seem to place more emphasis on being quick to market rather than on extensive testing and review of their software. Security savvy administrators will pay attention to the testing methods used by their software vendors.

Defending Against IP Spoofing

IP spoofing is essentially a technique used by hackers to gain unauthorized access to computers. While this is the most common reason for IP spoofing, it is occasionally done simply to mask the origins of a DoS attack. In fact it is very common for DoS and DDoS attacks to mask the actual IP address from which the attack is originating.

With IP spoofing, the intruder sends messages to a computer system with an IP address indicating that the message is coming from a different IP address than it is actually coming from. If the intent is to gain unauthorized access, then the spoofed IP will be that of a system the target considers to be a trusted host. In order to successfully perpetrate an IP spoofing attack, the hacker must first find the IP address of a machine that the target system considers a trusted source. Hackers may employ a variety of techniques to find an IP address of a trusted host. Once they have that trusted IP address, they can then modify the packet headers of their transmissions so it appears that the packets are coming from that host

IP spoofing, unlike many other types of attacks, was actually known to security experts on a theoretical level before it was ever used in a real attack. The concept of IP spoofing was initially discussed in academic circles as early as the 1980s. While the concept behind this technique was known for sometime, it was primarily theoretical until Robert Morris discovered a security weakness in the TCP protocol known as sequence prediction. Stephen Bellovin (Tanase, 2003) discussed the problem in-depth in his famous paper *Security Problems in the TCP/IP Protocol Suite.*

IP spoofing attacks are becoming less frequent, primarily because the venues they use are becoming more secure and in some cases are simply no longer used. However, spoofing can still be used, and all security administrators should address it. There are a few different ways to address IP spoofing. The first is not to reveal any information regarding your internal IP addresses. This will help to prevent those addresses from being "spoofed." The second method is to monitor incoming IP packets for signs of IP spoofing using network monitoring software. One popular product is Netlog. Netlog and similar products seek incoming packets to the external interface that have both the source and destination IP addresses in your local domain. Essentially this means an incoming packet that claims to be from inside the network, when it is clearly coming from outside your network. Finding one means an attack is underway.

The danger from IP spoofing is that some firewalls do not examine packets that appear to come from an internal IP address. It is possible to route packets through filtering-router firewalls if they are not configured to filter incoming packets whose source address is in the local domain.

Examples of router configurations that are potentially vulnerable include

- Routers to external networks that support multiple internal interfaces
- Proxy firewalls where the proxy applications use the source IP address for authentication

- Routers with two interfaces that support subnetting on the internal network

- Routers that do not filter packets whose source address is in the local domain

The best method of preventing IP spoofing is to install a filtering router. Filtering routers filter incoming packets by not allowing a packet through if it has a source address from your internal network. In addition, you should filter outgoing packets that have a source address different from your internal network in order to prevent a source IP spoofing attack from originating at your site. Many of the most common commercial firewall vendors, such as Cisco, 3COM, and Bay Networks, offer this option.

If your vendor's router does not support filtering on the inbound side of the interface and you feel the need to immediately filter such packets, you may filter the spoofed IP packets by using a second router between your external interface and your outside connection. Configure this router to block, on the outgoing interface connected to your original router, all packets that have a source address in your internal network. For this purpose, you can use a filtering router or a Unix system with two interfaces that supports packet filtering.

Defending Against Session Hacking

Another form of attack is *session hacking.* TCP session hijacking is a process whereby a hacker takes over a TCP session between two machines. Because authentication frequently is done only at the start of a TCP session, this allows the hacker to break into the communication stream and take control of the session. Often a person might log on to a machine remotely. Once they have established a connection with the host, the hacker may use session hacking to take over that session and thereby gain access to the target machine.

One popular method for session hacking is using source-routed IP packets. This allows a hacker at point A on the network to participate in a conversation between B and C by encouraging the IP packets to pass through the hacker's machine.

The most common sort of session hacking is the "man-in-the-middle attack." In this scenario a hacker uses some sort of packet sniffing program to simply listen in on the transmissions between two computers, taking whatever information he or she wants but not actually disrupting the conversation. A common component of such an attack is to execute a DoS attack against one end point to stop it from responding. Since that end point is no longer responding, the hacker can now interject her own machine to stand in for that end point.

The point of hijacking a connection is to exploit trust and to gain access to a system to which one would not otherwise have access.

The only way to truly defend against session hacking is to use encrypted transmissions. Chapter 6 discusses various encryption methods. If the packets are not encrypted, then the communication is vulnerable to session hacking. Many network administrators do use encrypted transmissions when communicating outside their network, but fewer encrypt internal communications. For a truly high level of security, you should consider encrypting all transmissions.

Packet sniffers will be discussed in more detail in Chapter 14 (Computer-Based Espionage and Terrorism). Right now what you need to be aware of is that a packet sniffer is software that intercepts packets going across a network or the Internet and copies them. This gives the attacker a copy of every packet you send. These tools have legitimate uses in network traffic monitoring, but are also used by hackers to intercept communications and, in some cases, for session hacking.

Blocking Virus and Trojan Horse Attacks

In the preceding segments of this chapter we examined the Denial of Service attack, buffer overflow attack, and session hacking. However, virus attacks are the most common threat to any network. Therefore, protecting against virus attacks is essential for any security-conscious network administrator.

Viruses

By definition, a computer virus is a program that self replicates. Generally, a virus will also have some other unpleasant function, but the self-replication and rapid spread are its hallmarks. Often this growth, in and of itself, can be a problem for an infected network. Worms are viruses that can replicate without human interaction.

Earlier in this chapter, you learned about the Slammer virus and the effects of its rapid, high-volume scanning. Any rapidly spreading virus can reduce the functionality and responsiveness of a network. It can lead to too much network traffic and prevent the network from functioning properly. Simply by exceeding the traffic load a network was designed to carry, the network may be rendered temporarily nonfunctional.

How Does a Virus Spread? We have seen how viruses can impact infected systems, and we have looked at a few actual cases. Clearly the key to stopping a computer virus is to prevent it from spreading to other computers. In order to do this you need to have a good understanding of how viruses typically spread. A virus usually spreads in one of two ways. The first is by scanning a computer for connections to a network and then copying itself to other machines on the network to which that machine has access. This is the most efficient way for a virus to spread and is a typical spread method of worms. However, this method requires more programming skill than other methods. The more common method is reading the e-mail address book and sending itself to everyone in it. Programming this is a trivial task, which explains why it is so common.

The latter method is, by far, the most common method for virus propagation, and Microsoft Outlook may be the one e-mail program most often hit with such virus attacks. The reason is not so much a security flaw in Outlook as it is the ease of working with Outlook. All Microsoft Office products are made so that a legitimate programmer can access many of that application's internal objects and thereby easily create applications that integrate the applications within the Microsoft Office suite. For example, a programmer could write an application that would access a Word document, import an Excel spreadsheet, then use Outlook to automatically e-mail the resulting document to interested parties. Microsoft has done a good job of making this process very easy. It usually takes a minimum amount of programming to accomplish these tasks. In the case of Outlook it takes less than five lines of code to reference Outlook and to send out an e-mail. This means a program can literally cause Outlook itself to send e-mails, unbeknownst to the user. There are numerous code examples on the Internet that show exactly how to do this, free for the taking.

However a virus arrives, once it is on a system it will attempt to spread. In many cases the virus will also attempt to cause some harm to the system. Once a virus is on a system it can do anything a legitimate program can do. That means it could potentially delete files, change system settings, or cause other harm. The threat from virus attacks cannot be overstated. Let's take a moment to look at a few recent virus outbreaks, see how they operated, and describe the damage they caused.

The Sobig Virus The virus that received the most media attention and perhaps caused the most harm in 2003 was the Sobig virus. The first interesting thing about this virus was the multi-modal approach by which it spread. This means that it used more than one mechanism to spread and infect new machines. Sobig copied itself to any shared drives on the network *and* it e-mailed itself out to everyone in the address book. Because of this approach, Sobig can be classified as a worm rather than simply a virus. This multi-modal spread meant that this Sobig was particularly virulent — a term signifying that the virus spread rapidly and easily infected new targets.

This multi-modal spread is why it is so critical that each and every person in your organization be cautioned about proper security policies and procedures. If just one person on a network was unfortunate enough to open an e-mail containing the Sobig virus, it infected not only that machine but also every shared drive on the network that this person could access.

Like most e-mail distributed virus attacks, this one had tell-tale signs in the e-mail subject or title that could be used to identify the e-mail as one infected by a virus. The e-mail would have a title such as "here is the sample" or "the document" and encourage you to open the attached file. The virus then copied itself into the Windows system directory. One of the effects of some variants of Sobig was to download a file from the Internet that would then cause printing problems. Some network printers would just start printing junk. The Sobig.E variant even wrote to the Windows registry causing the virus to be included in the computer startup (F-Secure, 2003). These complex characteristics indicate that the creator of Sobig knew how to access the Windows registry, access shared drives, alter the Windows startup, and how to access Outlook.

A method I personally use and recommend to all security administrators is to routinely send out an e-mail to everyone in your organization telling them the telltale signs to be wary of in e-mails. Web sites like **www.f-secure.com** list current viruses and what to look for in an e-mail. I summarize this list and send it out once or twice a month to everyone in my organization. That way all members of the organization are aware of e-mails that they should definitely not open. If you couple this with instilling a healthy caution toward unexpected e-mails, you can drastically reduce the chance of becoming infected with a virus.

This particular virus spread so far and infected so many networks, that the multiple copying of the virus alone was enough to bring some networks to a standstill. This virus did not destroy files or damage the system, but it generated enough traffic to bog down the networks infected by it. The virus itself was of moderate sophistication. Once it was out, many variants began to spring up, further complicating the situation.

Virus Variations Sometimes, some intrepid programmer with malicious intent receives a copy of a virus (perhaps his or her own machine becomes infected) and decides to reverse engineer it. Many virus attacks are in the form of a script attached to an e-mail. This means that unlike traditional compiled programs, their source code is readily readable and alterable. The programmer in question then simply takes the original virus code, introduces some change, and then re-releases the variant. The people who are most frequently caught for creating viruses are the developers of variants who simply lack the skill of the original virus writer and are therefore easily caught.

The Mimail Virus The Mimail virus sprang up toward the end of 2003. While this virus did not get as much media attention as Sobig, it had its intriguing characteristics. This virus not only collected e-mail addresses from the address book, but also from other documents on the infected machine (Gudmundsson, 2003). Thus, if you had a Word document on the hard drive and an e-mail address was in that document, Mimail would find it. This enabled Mimail to spread farther than many other viruses. Mimail also had its own built-in e-mail engine so that it did not have to "piggyback" off of another computer's e-mail client. It could spread regardless of what e-mail software was installed.

These variations made Mimail interesting to people who study computer viruses. The fact that Mimail scanned a computer for any document that had an e-mail address is intriguing. There are a variety of programming techniques that enable programmers to open and process files on a computer; however, most virus attacks do not employ them. The scanning of the document for e-mail addresses in the Mimail virus indicates a certain level of skill and creativity by the virus writer. In this author's opinion, Mimail was not the work of an amateur but rather a person with professional-level programming skill.

FYI: The Economic Impact of Viruses

It is impossible to get an exact accounting of the damage caused by Mimail or any other virus. However, if one considers the number of hours IT professionals spend working on cleaning up a given virus, the worldwide cost of any virus is in the millions of dollars. If the amount of money spent trying to defend against such viruses through antivirus software, hiring consultants, and purchasing books like this one is included, the annual impact of all viruses can easily reach billions of dollars.

For this reason many security experts recommend that governments begin enacting stronger penalties for virus creators. It would also be helpful if federal law enforcement agencies took a more active role in investigating these crimes. Recently, private companies such as SCO and Microsoft have begun offering substantial bounties for information leading to the arrest of virus creators, a very positive step.

The Bagle Virus Another virus that spread rapidly in the fourth quarter of 2003 and well into 2004 was the Bagle virus. The e-mail it sent claimed to be from the system administrator, informing the user that his e-mail account had been infected by a virus and instructing the user to open an attached file in order to get instructions. One the attached file was opened, the system was infected. This virus was particularly interesting for several reasons. To begin with, it spread both through e-mail and copying itself to shared folders. Second, it also scanned files on the PC looking for e-mail addresses. Finally, it disabled processes used by antivirus scanners. In biological terms, this virus took out a computer's "immune system."

The method of delivering the payload was rather simplistic and relied more on end-user negligence than on the skill of the virus writer. Enticing users to go to Web sites or open files they should not is a common method for delivering a virus, and one that requires no programming skill. However, disabling virus scanners is a new twist that indicates at least moderate programming skills on the part of the virus creator.

You can read more about any virus, past or current, at the following Web sites:

- **www.f-secure.com/virus-info/virus-news/**

- **www.cert.org/nav/index_red.html**

- **http://securityresponse.symantec.com/**

- **http://vil.nai.com/vil/**

FYI: Why Write a Virus?

In the case of the MyDoom attack specifically targeting SCO, it was not hard to ascertain the virus writer's motivations. However, with other viruses such as Bagle and Mimail, it is difficult to understand why the virus was created in the first place. To the best of my knowledge, no formal psychological studies exist regarding the mentality of virus writers. However, having interacted with alleged virus writers in various forums, and having read interviews with convicted virus writers, I can provide you with some insight into their mentality.

In some cases the virus writer simply wished to prove that he could do it. For some people, simply knowing that they "outwitted" numerous security professionals gives them a feeling of satisfaction. For others, the ability to cause damage on a wide scale imbues them with a sense of power they probably do not otherwise feel. When virus writers are caught they usually turn out to be young, intelligent, and technically skilled; have strong antisocial leanings; and generally don't fit into any peer group. The writing of a virus gives them the same cathartic feeling that other people get from vandalism and graffiti.

The Virus Hoax Another new type of virus has been gaining popularity in the past few years: the "non-virus virus," or **virus hoax.** Rather than actually writing a virus, a hacker simply sends an e-mail to every address he has. The e-mail claims to be from some well known antivirus center and warns of a new virus that is circulating. The e-mail then instructs the user to delete a file from the computer in order to get rid of the virus. The file, however, is not really a virus but part of the computer's system. The *jdbg-mgr.exe* virus hoax used this scheme (*Vmyths.com,* 2002). It encouraged the reader to delete a file that was actually needed by the system. Surprisingly, a large number of people followed this advice and not only deleted the file but promptly e-mailed their friends and colleagues to warn them to delete the file from their machines.

A common theme with all virus attacks (except the hoax) is that they instruct the recipient to open some type of attachment. The most common way for a virus to spread is as an e-mail attachment. This realization leads to some simple rules that will drastically reduce the odds of a machine becoming infected with a virus:

- Always use a virus scanner. McAfee and Norton are the two most widely accepted and used virus scanners. Each costs about $30 a year to keep updated. Do it. Chapter 9 will discuss virus attacks and virus scanners in more detail.

- If you are unsure about an attachment, do not open it.

- You might even exchange a code word with friends and colleagues. Tell them that if they wish to send you an attachment, they should put the code word in the title of the message. Without seeing the code word, you will not open any attachment.

- Don't believe "security alerts" that are sent to you. Microsoft does not send out alerts in this manner. Check the Microsoft Web site regularly, as well as one of the antivirus Web sites previously mentioned. Microsoft's security Web site (**www.microsoft.com/security/default.mspx**) is the only reliable place to get Microsoft security updates. There are other security sites that might have accurate information (such as **www.sans.org**) but if you are using a particular vendor's software (such as Microsoft) then it is always best to go to their site to find alerts and to get patches.

These rules will not make systems 100% virus proof, but they will go a long way toward protecting them.

The Sasser Virus While this book was being written, several major new virus outbreaks took place, most notably, the Sasser virus. Sasser is a combination attack in that the virus (or worm) spreads by exploiting a buffer overrun. Sasser was first noticed at the end of April 2004.

The Sasser virus spreads by exploiting a known flaw in a Windows system program. Sasser copies itself to the Windows directory as *avserve.exe* and creates a registry key to load itself at startup. Once a machine is infected, the virus starts each time the machine is started. The virus then scans random IP addresses, listening on successive TCP ports starting at 1068 for exploitable systems—that is, systems that have not been patched to fix this flaw. When one is found, the worm exploits the vulnerable system by overflowing a buffer in *LSASS.EXE,* which is a file that is part of the Windows operating system. It creates a remote shell on TCP port 9996. Next, it creates an FTP script named *cmd.ftp* on the remote host and executes that script. This FTP script instructs the target victim to download and execute the worm (with the filename *#_up.exe*) from the infected host. It also acts as an FTP server on TCP port 5554, and creates a remote shell on TCP port 9996. Shutting down these ports on a router goes a long way towards nullifying some of the effects of this virus.

A computer infected with Sasser creates a file named *win.log* on the C: drive. This file contains the IP address of the localhost. Copies of the worm are created in the Windows System directory as *#_up.exe.* Examples are shown here:

- *c:\WINDOWS\system32\12553_up.exe*

- *c:\WINDOWS\system32\17923_up.exe*

- *c:\WINDOWS\system32\29679_up.exe*

A side effect of this virus is that it causes machines to reboot. A machine that repeatedly reboots without any known cause may well be infected with the Sasser virus.

This is another case in which infections can easily be prevented by several means. First, any system updated on a regular basis will not be vulnerable to this flaw. Second, networks routers or firewalls that block traffic on ports 9996 and 5554 will prevent most of Sasser's damage. In short, if you as the network administrator are aware of security issues and are taking prudent steps to protect the network, then the network will be safe. The fact that so many networks have been affected by this virus indicates that not enough administrators are properly trained in computer security.

Trojan Horses

You have seen this term used in this chapter, and you probably already have some idea of what it is. A Trojan horse is a term for a program that looks benign but actually has a malicious purpose. You might receive or download a program that appears to be a harmless business utility or game. More likely, the Trojan horse is just a script attached to a benign-looking e-mail. When you run the program or open the attachment, it does something else other than or in addition to what you thought it would. It might:

- Download harmful software from a Web site.

- Install a key logger or other spyware on your machine.

- Delete files.

- Open a backdoor for a hacker to use.

It is common to find combination virus plus Trojan horse attacks. In these scenarios the Trojan horse spreads like a virus. The MyDoom virus opened a port on machines that a later virus, Doomjuice, would exploit, thus making MyDoom a combination virus and Trojan horse.

FYI: Was MyDoom a Trojan Horse?

Some experts say that MyDoom was not actually a Trojan horse because it did not pretend to be benign software. However, one could argue that the e-mail attachment that delivered MyDoom did indeed claim to be a legitimate attachment and, thus, could be classified as a Trojan horse. Whether or not you agree that My-Doom is a Trojan horse, it is certainly a good illustration of how malicious software can take multiple avenues to cause harm.

A Trojan horse also could be crafted especially for an individual. If a hacker wished to spy on a certain individual, such as the company account-ant, she could design a program specifically to attract that person's atten-tion. For example, if she knew the accountant was an avid golfer, she could write a program that computed handicap and listed best golf courses. She would post that program on a free Web server. She would then e-mail a number of people, including the accountant, telling them about the free software. The software, once installed, could check the name of the cur-rently logged-on person. If the log-on name matched the accountant's name, the software could then go out, unknown to the user, and download a key logger or other monitoring application. If the software did not damage files or replicate itself then it would probably go undetected for quite a long time.

Such a program could be within the skill set of virtually any moder-ately competent programmer. This is one reason many organizations have rules against downloading *any* software onto company machines. I am un-aware of any actual incident of a Trojan horse being custom tailored in this fashion. However, it is important to remember that those creating virus at-tacks tend to be innovative people.

Another scenario to consider is one that would be quite devastating. Without divulging programming details, the basic premise will be outlined here to illustrate the grave dangers of Trojan horses. Imagine a small appli-cation that displays a series of unflattering pictures of Osama Bin Laden. This would probably be popular with many people in the United States, par-ticularly people in the military, the intelligence community, or defense-re-lated industries. Now assume that the application simply sits dormant on the machine for a period of time. It need not replicate like a virus because the computer user will probably send it to many of his or her associates. On a certain date and time, the software connects to any drive it can, including network drives, and begins deleting all files.

If such a Trojan horse were released "in the wild," within 30 days it would probably be shipped to thousands, perhaps millions, of people. Imagine the devastation when thousands of computers begin deleting files and folders.

This scenario is mentioned precisely to frighten you a little. Computer users, including professionals who should know better, routinely download all sorts of files from the Internet, including amusing Flash animations and cute games. Every time an employee downloads something of this nature, there is the chance of downloading a Trojan horse. One need not be a statistician to realize that if employees continue that practice long enough they will eventually download a Trojan horse onto a company machine. A user can only hope it is not one as vicious as the theoretical one just outlined here.

Summary

In this chapter we examined the most common threats to your systems: virus attacks, Denial of Service attacks, Trojan horses, and buffer over flow attacks. Other dangers such as identity theft and phishing (using fake e-mail and Web sites to solicit end user information that can be used in identity theft and fraud) are becoming more common, but don't pose as great a direct threat to an organizational network as they do to individuals. That is why this chapter focused on the four attacks it did — they are of the most concern to network security.

In each case the various defense mechanisms fell into one of two categories: technical or procedural. Technical defenses are those items you can install or configure to make your system safer. This includes things like micro blocks, RST cookies, stack tweaking, and antivirus software. Procedural defenses involve modifying the behavior of end users in order to increase security. Such measures include not downloading suspicious files and not opening unverified attachments. As you proceed through this text you will discover that network defense must be approached from both angles. In later chapters you will see detailed discussion of technical defenses (firewalls, virus scanners, and more) as well as entire chapters devoted to procedural defenses (policies and procedures). It is vital that you understand that both approaches are necessary in order to secure your network.

It should be obvious by this point that securing your system is absolutely critical. In the upcoming exercises, you will try out the antivirus programs by Norton and McAfee. There are so many ways for a hacker to attack a system that securing your system can be a rather complex task. Chapter 6 will deal with more specific methods whereby you can secure your system.

Test Your Skills

MULTIPLE CHOICE QUESTIONS

1. From the attacker's point of view, what is the primary weakness in a DoS attack?

   A. The attack must be sustained.

   B. The attack does not cause actual damage.

   C. The attack is easily thwarted.

   D. The attack is difficult to execute.

2. What DoS attack is based on leaving connections half open?

   A. Ping of Death

   B. Smurf attack

   C. Distributed Denial of Service

   D. SYN flood

3. What is the name for a DoS defense that is dependent on sending back a hash code to the client?

   A. Stack tweaking

   B. RST cookie

   C. SYN cookie

   D. Server reflection

4. Which of the following would be the best defense if your Web server had limited resources but you needed a strong defense against DoS?

   A. A firewall

   B. RST cookies

   C. SYN cookies

   D. Stack tweaking

5. What is a technical weakness of the Stack tweaking defense?

   A. It is complicated and requires very skilled technicians to implement.

   B. It only decreases time out but does not actually stop DoS attacks.

   C. It is resource intensive and can degrade server performance.

   D. It is ineffective against DoS attacks.

6. What is the name for a DoS attack that causes machines on a network to initiate a DoS against one of that network's servers?

   A. Smurf attack

   B. SYN flood

   C. Ping of Death

   D. Distributed Denial of Service

7. Which of the following virus attacks initiated a DoS attack?

   A. Faux

   B. Walachi

   C. Bagle

   D. MyDoom

8. Which of the following is a recommended configuration of your firewall to defend against DoS attacks?

   A. block ICMP packets that originate outside your network

   B. block all incoming packets

   C. block all ICMP packets

   D. block TCP packets that originate outside your network

9. Which of the following best describes a buffer overflow attack?

   A. an attack that overflows the target with too many TCP packets

   B. an attack that attempts to put too much data in a memory buffer

   C. an attack that attempts to send oversized TCP packets

   D. an attack that attempts to put misconfigured data into a memory buffer

10. What is the best way to defend against a buffer overflow?

    A. using a robust firewall

    B. blocking TCP packets at the router

    C. keeping all software patched and updated

    D. stopping all ICMP traffic

11. Which of the following is the best definition for IP spoofing?

    A. sending a packet that appears to come from a trusted IP

    B. rerouting packets to a different IP

    C. setting up a fake Web site that appears to be a different site

    D. sending packets that are misconfigured

12. What is the danger inherent in IP spoofing attacks?

    A. They are very damaging to target systems.

    B. Many of these attacks open the door for other attacks.

    C. They can be difficult to stop.

    D. Many firewalls don't examine packets that seem to come from within the network.

13. What is the best method of defending against IP spoofing?

    A. installing a router/firewall that blocks packets that appear to be originating within the network

    B. installing a router/firewall that blocks packets that appear to be originating from outside the network

    C. blocking all incoming TCP traffic

    D. blocking all incoming ICMP traffic

14. Which of the following best describes session hacking?

    A. taking over a target machine via a Trojan horse

    B. taking control of a target machine remotely

    C. taking control of the communication link between two machines

    D. taking control of the login session

15. Which of the following is the best definition of a virus?

    A. software that causes damage to system files

    B. software that self replicates

    C. software that causes damage to any files

    D. software that attaches to e-mail

16. What was the greatest danger from the Bagle virus?

    A. It shut down antivirus software.

    B. It deleted system files.

    C. It corrupted the Windows registry.

    D. It was difficult to detect.

17. What is a Trojan horse?

    A. software that self replicates

    B. software that appears to be benign but really has some malicious purpose

    C. software that deletes system files then infects other machines

    D. software that causes harm to your system

EXERCISES

Exercise 2.1: A Basic DoS Attack

1. Set up a machine with a Web server.

2. Use other machines in the lab to begin pinging the target machine.

3. Continue this until the target is no longer able to respond to legitimate requests.

4. Note the number of total packets per second required to successfully execute a DoS attack.

Exercise 2.2: Configuring a Firewall to Block DoS Attacks

(*Note:* This exercise is only for classes with access to a lab firewall.)

1. Using your firewall's documentation, find out how to block incoming ICMP packets.

2. Configure your firewall to block those packets.

3. Now try Exercise 2.1 through the firewall and see if it is successful.

Exercise 2.3: Installing Norton AntiVirus

1. Go to Norton's Web site and download the trial version of its antivirus program.

2. Configure it and scan your machine.

3. Go to McAfee's Web site and download the trial version of its antivirus program.

4. Configure it and scan your machine.

5. Note differences in usability, feel, and general performance between the two virus scanners. Which would you recommend and why?

Exercise 2.4: Configuring a Router

(*Note:* This exercise is only for classes with access to a lab router.)

1. Consult your router documentation to find out how to disallow traffic originating outside the network.

2. Configure your router to block traffic originating outside the network.

3. Ping the network's server to test whether the configuration you set has blocked outside traffic.

Exercise 2.5: Learning about Blaster

1. Use the Web or other resources to look up information about the Blaster virus.

2. Describe how that virus worked and how it spread.

3. Research and describe the type and amount of damage the virus caused.

4. Have the perpetrators of the attack been caught and/or prosecuted?

5. Make recommendations for defending against this specific virus.

Exercise 2.6: Learning about MyDoom

1. Use the Web or other resources to look up information about the My-Doom virus.

2. Describe how that virus worked and how it spread.

3. Research and describe the type and amount of damage the virus caused.

4. Have the perpetrators of the attack been caught and/or prosecuted?

5. Make recommendations for defending against this specific virus.

PROJECTS

Project 2.1: The Most Recent Virus Attacks

1. Use the Web or other resources to pick a new virus attack that has spread during the last 90 days.

2. Note how that virus is spreading, the damage it causes, and the recommended steps for guarding against it.

3. How does this virus compare to the Sasser virus and the MyDoom virus?

Project 2.2: Setting up Antivirus Policy

1. Use the Web to find an organization's antivirus policies. The preferred resources listed in Chapter 1 are good places to begin this search. Or, you can seek out the policies of some organization you have contact with, such as your school or your employer.

2. What changes would you recommend to that particular organization's antivirus policy?

3. Your recommendations should be specific and include detailed reasons that support them.

Project 2.3: Why Do Buffer Overflow Vulnerabilities Exist?

1. Considering how buffer overflow vulnerabilities arise, explain why you think they are present and provide recommendations to prevent or reduce the number of such flaws.

▶▶ Case Study

Juanita is a network administrator for a medium-sized company. She is charged with overseeing security for the network. The company is particularly concerned with virus attacks because it has had several virus infections in the past year. Juanita takes the following actions:

- She installs virus scanners on all machines.

- She establishes policies preventing any downloading from the Internet.

What other recommendations would you make to Juanita? Give the reasons for your recommendations.

Chapter 3

Fundamentals of Firewalls

Chapter Objectives

After reading this chapter and completing the exercises, you will be able to do the following:

- Explain how firewalls work.
- Evaluate firewall solutions.
- Differentiate between packet filtering and stateful packet filtering.
- Differentiate between application gateway and circuit gateway.
- Understand host-based firewalls and router-based firewalls.

Introduction

The first two chapters of this book discussed threats to network security and ways to defend against those threats. This and the following two chapters will address security devices. One of the most fundamental devices used to implement network security is the firewall. This is a key part of any security architecture. In fact, other systems such as the proxy server and intrusion detection systems work in conjunction with the firewall and are to some extent dependent upon the firewall.

This chapter will explore the basics of how firewalls work to provide a basis for evaluating which firewall is most appropriate in a given situation.

What Is a Firewall?

A firewall is a barrier between your network and the outside world. A particular firewall implementation might use one or more of the methods listed here to provide that barrier.

- Packet filtering

- Stateful packet filtering

- User authentication

- Client application authentication

At a minimum a firewall will filter incoming packets based on parameters such as packet size, source IP address, protocol, and destination port. Figure 3.1 shows the essentials of the firewall concept.

As you may already know, both Linux and Windows XP ship with a simple firewall built into the operating system. Norton and McAfee both offer personal firewall solutions for individual PCs. These firewalls are meant for individual machines. There are more advanced solutions available for networks. In an organizational setting, you will want a dedicated firewall between your network and the outside world. This might be a router that also has built-in firewall capabilities. (Cisco Systems is one company that is well-known for high quality routers and firewalls.) Or, it might be a server that is dedicated solely to running firewall software. There are a number of firewall solutions that you can examine, and Appendix B has

---

FYI: High-Speed Home or Small Office Connections

With the growing popularity of cable and DSL connections for homes and small offices, more emphasis is being placed on securing computer systems in these locations. Very inexpensive router-based firewalls for your high-speed Internet connection are available. Consumers can also purchase a router that is separate from the DSL or cable router or one that includes the functions of the cable or DSL router with the firewall. The following Web sites provide more information about these:

- Linksys: **www.linksys.com/products/ product.asp?prid=20&grid=5**
- Home PC Firewall Guide: **www.firewallguide.com**
- Broadband Guide: **www.firewallguide.com/ broadband.htm**

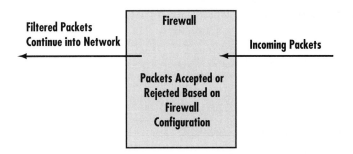

FIGURE 3.1 Basic firewall operations.

some links to get you started. Selecting a firewall is an important decision. This chapter will give you the essential skills necessary for you to be able to select the appropriate firewall for your network.

Types of Firewalls

Packet filtering firewalls are the simplest and often the least expensive type of firewalls. Several other types of firewalls offer their own distinct advantages and disadvantages. The basic types of firewalls are

■ Packet filter

■ Application gateway

■ Circuit level gateway

■ Stateful packet inspection

Packet Filter Firewall

The *packet filter firewall* is the most basic type of firewall. In a packet-filtering firewall, each incoming packet is examined. Only those packets that match the criteria you set are allowed through. Many operating systems, such as Windows XP and many Linux distributions, include basic packet-filtering software with the operating system. Packet filter firewalls are also referred to as screening firewalls. They can filter packets based on packet size, protocol used, source IP address, and many other parameters. Many routers offer this type of firewall protection in addition to their normal routing functions.

Packet filtering firewalls work by examining a packet's source address, destination address, source port, destination port, and protocol type. Based on these factors and the rules that the firewall has been configured to use, they either allow or deny passage to the packet. These firewalls are very easy to configure and inexpensive. Some operating systems, such as Windows XP and Linux, include built-in packet filtering capabilities. Chapter 4 discusses specific firewall products in detail. Here is a brief summary of some commonly used packet filtering products:

- **Firestarter:** This is a free packet filtering application for Linux available at **www.fs-security.com**. This software is installed on a Linux machine designed to be used as your network firewall.

- **Norton Personal Firewall:** This product is inexpensive and is available for multiple operating systems. A free trial download is available from **www.symantec.com**.

- **McAfee Personal Firewall:** This product is similar in price and basic function to Norton Personal Firewall. You can find out more about this product at **us.mcafee.com**.

- **Outpost Firewall:** This product is designed for the home or small office user. It has both a free version and an enhanced commercial version. You can find out more about this product at **www.agnitum. com/products/outpost/**.

There are a few disadvantages to the screening/packet-filtering firewall solution. One disadvantage is that they do not actually examine the packet or compare it to previous packets; therefore, they are quite susceptible to either a ping flood or SYN flood. They also do not offer any user authentication. Because this type of firewall looks only at the packet header for information, it has no information about the packet contents. It also does not track packets, so it has no information about the preceding packets. Therefore, if thousands of packets came from the same IP address in a short period of time, a screened host would not notice that this pattern is unusual. Such a pattern often indicates that the IP address in question is attempting to perform a DoS attack on the network.

To configure a packet filtering firewall, simply establish appropriate filtering rules. A set of rules for a given firewall would need to cover the following:

- What types of protocols to allow (FTP, SMTP, POP3, etc.)

- What source ports to allow

- What destination ports to allow

- What source IP addresses to allow (you can block certain IP addresses if you wish)

These rules will allow the firewall to determine what traffic to allow in and what traffic to block. Because this sort of firewall uses only very limited system resources, is relatively easy to configure, and can be obtained inexpensively or even for free, it is frequently used. Although it is not the most secure type of firewall, you are likely to encounter it frequently.

IN PRACTICE: Packet Filtering Rules

Unfortunately in many real world networks there are so many different applications sending different types of packets that setting up proper rules for packet filtering can be more difficult than you might think. On a simple network with only a few servers running a small number of services (perhaps a Web server, an FTP server, and an e-mail server), configuring packet filtering rules can, indeed, be rather simple. In other situations it can become quite complicated.

Consider the wide area network connecting multiple sites in geographically diverse regions. When you set up a packet filtering firewall in this scenario, you need to be aware of any application or service that uses network communications of any type, on any machine, in any of the sites your WAN connects to. Failure to take these complexities into account can result in your firewall blocking some legitimate network service.

Application Gateway

An *application gateway* (also known as *application proxy* or *application-level proxy*) is a program that runs on a firewall. This type of firewall derives its name from the fact that it works by negotiating with various types of applications to allow their traffic to pass the firewall. In networking terminology negotiation is a term used to refer to the process of authentication and verification. In other words, rather than looking at the protocol and port the packet is using, it will examine the client application and the server side application to which it is trying to connect. It will then determine if that particular client application's traffic is permitted through the firewall. This is significantly different from a packet filtering firewall, which examines the packets and has no knowledge of what sort of application sent them. Application gateways enable the administrator to allow access only to certain specified types of applications, such as Web browsers or ftp clients.

When a client program, such as a Web browser, establishes a connection to a destination service, such as a Web server, it connects to an application gateway, or proxy. The client then negotiates with the proxy server in order to gain access to the destination service. In effect, the proxy establishes the connection with the destination behind the firewall and acts on behalf of the client, hiding and protecting individual computers on the network behind the firewall. This process actually creates two connections. There is one connection between the client and the proxy server and another connection between the proxy server and the destination.

Once a connection is established, the application gateway makes all decisions about which packets to forward. Since all communication is conducted through the proxy server, computers behind the firewall are protected.

With an application gateway, each supported client program requires a unique program to accept client application data. This sort of firewall allows for individual user authentication, which makes them quite effective at blocking unwanted traffic. However, a disadvantage is that these firewalls use a lot of system resources. The process of authenticating client applications uses more memory and CPU time than simple packet filtering.

FYI: Unique Logons

Be aware that having a unique logon for each user is probably not the ideal solution for sites with a great deal of public traffic, such as an e-commerce site. On sites such as this, you want to attract a high volume of traffic, mainly from new customers. New visitors to your site will not have a logon ID or password. Making them go through the process of setting up an account just to visit your Web site will likely turn off many potential customers. However, this can be an ideal solution for a corporate network.

Application gateways are also susceptible to various flooding attacks (SYN flood, ping flood, etc.) for two reasons. The first potential cause of a flooding attack may be the additional time it takes for an application to negotiate authenticating a request. Remember that both the client application and the user may need to be authenticated. This takes more time than simply filtering packets based on certain parameters. For this reason, a flood of connection requests can overwhelm the firewall, preventing it from responding to legitimate requests. Application gateways may also be more susceptible to flooding attacks because once a connection is made, packets are not checked. If a connection is established, then that connection can be used to send a flooding attack to the server it has connected to, such as a Web server or e-mail server. This vulnerability is mitigated somewhat by authenticating users. Provided the user logon method is secure (appropriate passwords, encrypted transmission, etc.), the likelihood that someone can use a legitimate connection through an application gateway for a flooding attack is reduced.

Chapter 4 discusses specific firewall implementations; however, a brief summary of a few application gateway products is provided here:

- The company Teros offers an application gateway specifically tailored for Web servers. This solution is relatively inexpensive and can be ideal for companies whose primary function is to provide Web sites or Web services. Information is available at **www.teros.com/ products/appliances/gateway/index.shtml**.

■ The Firebox, from Watchguard Technologies (**www.watchguard. com/products/fireboxx.asp**), is an application gateway firewall that is router-based. It is relatively easy to set up and configure and is appropriate for medium-sized networks.

Circuit Level Gateway

Circuit level gateway firewalls are similar to application gateways but are more secure and generally implemented on high-end equipment. These types of firewalls also employ user authentication, but they do so earlier in the process. With an application gateway, first the client application is checked to see if access should be granted, and then the user is authenticated. With circuit level gateways, authenticating the user is the first step. The user's logon ID and password are checked, and the user is granted access before the connection to the router is established. This means that each individual, either by username or IP address, must be verified before any further communication can take place.

Once this verification takes place and the connection between the source and destination is established, the firewall simply passes bytes between the systems. A virtual "circuit" exists between the internal client and the proxy server. Internet requests go through this circuit to the proxy server, and the proxy server delivers those requests to the Internet after changing the IP address. External users only see the IP address of the proxy server. Responses are then received by the proxy server and sent back through the circuit to the client. It is this virtual circuit that makes the circuit level gateway secure. The private secure connection between the client application and the firewall is a more secure solution than some other options, such as the simple packet filtering firewall and the application gateway.

While traffic is allowed through, external systems never see the internal systems. The differences between the application gateway and the circuit level gateway are shown in Figure 3.2.

While highly secure, this approach may not be appropriate for some communication with the general public, such as e-commerce sites. This type of firewall is also difficult to configure because each client must be set up to have a circuit connection with the firewall. One very interesting circuit level gateway is offered by Amrita labs.

Amrita Labs (**http://aitf.amrita.edu/gw.htm**) provides an open source software circuit level gateway. The source code for this firewall can be downloaded, compiled, and run in a network host-based configuration. The fact that this is open source and can be modified by the organization

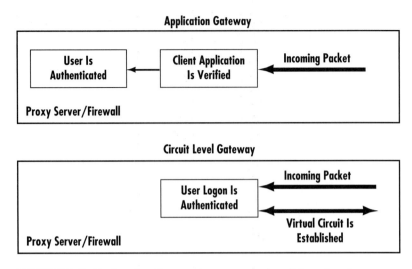

FIGURE 3.2 Application gateway vs. circuit level gateway.

using it makes it an attractive choice for organizations that have sufficiently experienced staff programmers.

Stateful Packet Inspection

The *stateful packet inspection (SPI)* firewall will examine each packet, denying or permitting access based not only on the examination of the current packet, but also on data derived from previous packets in the conversation. This means that the firewall is aware of the context in which a specific packet was sent. This makes these firewalls far less susceptible to ping floods and SYN floods, as well as being less susceptible to spoofing. SPI firewalls are less susceptible to these attacks for the following reasons:

- They can tell whether the packet is part of an abnormally large stream of packets from a particular IP address, thus indicating a possible DoS attack in progress.

- They can tell whether the packet has a source IP that appears to come from inside the firewall, thus indicating IP spoofing is in progress.

- They can also look at the actual contents of the packet, allowing for some very advanced filtering capabilities.

SPI firewalls are an improved version of the packet filtering firewall. Most high-end firewalls use the stateful packet inspection method; when possible, this is the recommended type of firewall for most systems. The name *stateful packet inspection* derives from the fact that in addition to examining the packet, the firewall is examining the packet's state in relationship to the entire IP conversation. This means the firewall can refer to the preceding packets as well as those packets' contents, source, and destination. As you might suspect, SPI firewalls are becoming quite common. We will examine several of them in Chapter 4. The following is a list of some well-known products:

■   SonicWALL (**www.sonicwall.com/**) makes a number of different SPI firewall products for various sized networks, in different price ranges. It is a well-known vendor of firewall products.

■   Linksys (**www.linksys.com/**) makes a number of small office/ home office firewall router products that use SPI technologies. These are very inexpensive and easy to configure.

■   Cisco (**www.cisco.com**) is a very well-known and highly respected vendor for many different types of network products, including router based firewalls that use SPI technology.

3

FYI: Stateless Packet Filtering

Stateful packet inspection is clearly the preferred method. The natural follow-up question is: What about stateless packet filtering? This term is not generally used by security professionals; it merely denotes the standard packet filtering method.

Hybrid Firewalls

As you will see later in this chapter and Chapter 4, there are a growing number of manufacturers creating hybrid firewalls. These are firewalls that use a mix of approaches, rather than a single approach. This sort of mixed approach is often even more effective than any of the pure approaches.

One very powerful firewall approach is a design that uses both a circuit level gateway and stateful packet filtering. Such a configuration has the best firewall methods combined into a single unit. In Chapter 4, we will examine some real world examples of hybrid solutions.

Implementing Firewalls

Administrators must be able to evaluate implementation issues to achieve a successful security solution for their systems. Understanding the type of firewall means knowing how the firewall will evaluate traffic and deciding what to allow and what not to allow. Understanding the firewall's implementation means understanding how that firewall is set up in relation to the network it is protecting. The most widely used configurations include:

- Network host-based
- Dual-homed host
- Router-based firewall
- Screened host

Network Host-Based

In the *network host-based* scenario the firewall is a software solution installed on an existing machine with an existing operating system. The most significant concern in this scenario is that, no matter how good the firewall solution is, it is contingent upon the underlying operating system. In such a scenario, it is absolutely critical that the machine hosting the firewall have a hardened operating system. Hardening the operating system refers to taking several security precautions including:

- Ensuring all patches are updated
- Uninstalling unneeded applications or utilities
- Closing unused ports
- Turning off all unused services

Operating system hardening is covered in greater depth in Chapter 8.

In the network host-based implementation, you install the firewall software onto an existing server. Sometimes, the server's operating system may come with such software. It is not at all uncommon for administrators to use a machine running Linux, configure its built-in firewall, and use that server as a firewall. The primary advantage to this option is cost. It is much cheaper to simply install firewall software onto an existing machine, and use that machine as your firewall.

IN PRACTICE: DMZ

More and more organizations are opting to use DMZs. A **DMZ** is a demilitarized zone. A DMZ is created using two separate firewalls. One firewall faces the outside world, or the Internet, and the other faces the inside, or corporate network. It allows for an additional layer of protection between Internet-facing services and back-end corporate resources.

Typically Web servers, e-mail servers, and FTP servers are located inside the DMZ. Domain controllers, database servers, and file servers are located inside the corporate network. This means that if a hacker should breach the security of the first firewall she would only be able to affect the Web server or e-mail server. She would not be able to get directly at the corporate data. Getting at that data would require the hacker to break through the security of yet another firewall.

This sort of arrangement is the preferred method, regardless of what type of firewall you use. Often administrators choose to use a weaker and cheaper firewall, such as a simple packet filtering firewall, on the outer side of the DMZ. They then use a much more rigorous firewall such as a sateful packet filter on the inner side of the DMZ. If an intrusion-detection system (these are discussed in detail in Chapter 5) is used on the outer firewall, then any breach of that firewall is likely to be detected long before the hacker can successfully breach the inner firewall. This is also one reason why media stories abound about hackers defacing Web sites, but stories of hackers actually getting at sensitive data are much less common.

Some vendors now offer a single box that implements a DMZ. It does this by creating two virtual firewalls in one device, so you can buy a single appliance (usually a router) that implements the entire DMZ. Figure 3.3 shows a DMZ.

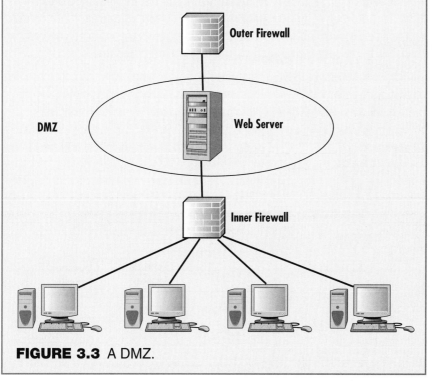

FIGURE 3.3 A DMZ.

Dual-Homed Hosts

A *dual-homed host* is a firewall running on a server with at least two network interfaces. The server acts as a router between the network and the interfaces to which it is attached. To make this work, the automatic routing function is disabled, meaning that an IP packet from the Internet is not routed directly to the network. The administrator can choose what packets to route and how to route them. Systems inside and outside the firewall can communicate with the dual-homed host, but cannot communicate directly with each other. Figure 3.4 shows a dual-homed host.

The dual-homed host configuration is simply an expanded version of the network host firewall implementation. That means it is also contingent on the security of the underlying operating system. Any time a firewall is running on a server of any kind, the security of that server's operating system becomes even more critical than normal.

This option has the advantage of being relatively simple and inexpensive. The primary disadvantage is its dependency on the underlying operating system.

Router-Based Firewall

Administrators can implement firewall protection on a router. In larger networks with multiple layers of protection, this is often the first layer of protection. Although various types of firewalls can be implemented on a router, the most common type uses packet filtering. Users of a broadband connection in a home or small office can get a packet-filtering firewall router to replace the basic router provided by the broadband company.

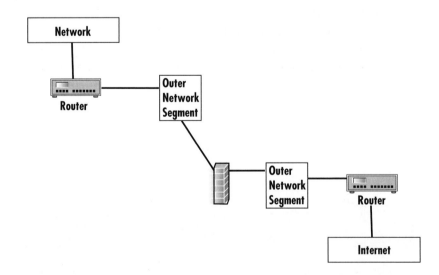

FIGURE 3.4 The dual-homed host.

In many cases this solution is also ideal for the firewall novice. A number of vendors supply router-based firewalls that can be preconfigured by the vendor based on the customer's needs. The customer can then install it between her network and external Internet connection. Also, most of the more widely known brands (Cisco, 3Com, etc.) offer vendor-specific training and certifications in their hardware, making it relatively easy to find qualified administrators or to train current staff.

Another valuable way to implement router-based firewalls is between sub-sections of a network. If a network is divided into segments, each segment needs to use a router to connect to the other segments. Using a router that also includes a firewall significantly increases security. If the security of one segment of the network is compromised, the rest of the network is not necessarily breached.

Perhaps the best advantage to router-based firewalls is the ease of setup. In many cases the vendor will even configure the firewall for you, and you simply plug it in.

Screened Hosts

A *screened host* is really a combination of firewalls. In this configuration, a combination of a bastion host and a screening router is used. The combination creates a dual firewall solution that is effective at filtering traffic. The two firewalls can be different types. The bastion host might be an application gateway and the router packet screening (or visa versa). This approach (shown in Figure 3.5) gives the advantages of both types of firewalls and is similar in concept to the dual-homed host.

The screened host has some distinct advantages over the dual-homed firewall. Unlike the dual-homed firewall, the screened needs only one network interface and does not require a separate subnet between the application gateway and the router. This makes the firewall more flexible but perhaps less secure because its reliance on only one network interface card means that it

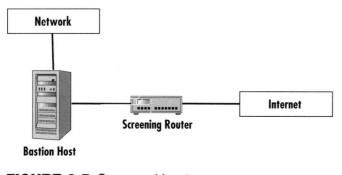

FIGURE 3.5 Screened host.

might be configured to pass certain trusted services to the application gateway portion of the firewall and directly to servers within the network.

The most significant concern when using the screened host is that it essentially combines two firewalls into one. Therefore any security flaw or misconfiguration affects both firewalls. When you use a DMZ there are physically two separate firewalls, and the likelihood of any security flaw being propagated to both is low.

FYI: Bastion Hosts

A **bastion host** is a single point of contact between the Internet and a private network. It usually will only run a limited number of services (those that are absolutely essential to the private network) and no others. The bastion host is often the packet-filtering firewall that is between the network and the outside world.

In addition to these firewall configurations, there are also different methods for how the firewall examines packets. Packet filters work at the network layer of the OSI model and simply block certain packets based on criteria such as protocol, port number, source address, and destination address. For example, a packet filter might deny all traffic on ports 1024 and up, or it might block all incoming traffic using the TFTP protocol. Incoming and outgoing filters can dictate what information passes into or out of the local network.

The screening router adds security by allowing you to deny or permit certain traffic from the bastion host. It is the first stop for traffic, which can continue only if the screening router lets it through.

IN PRACTICE: Utmost Security

Organizations that want the utmost level of security often use multiple firewalls. The perimeter of the network may actually have two firewalls, perhaps a stateful packet inspecting firewall and an application gateway, one following the other (the order will determine how they are configured). This enables the organization to get the benefit of both types of firewalls. This type of configuration is not as common as it should be, but it is used by some organizations.

One common multiple firewall scenario is the use of screened firewall routers separating each network segment. The network will still have a perimeter firewall blocking incoming traffic, but it will also have packet filtering separating each network segment. This means that if an attack breaches the perimeter, not all network segments will be affected.

For the highest possible level of firewall protection, the ideal scenario is to have the dual perimeter firewall, to use packet screening on all routers, and then to have individual packet filtering firewalls (such as those built into some operating systems) on every server and perhaps even on individual workstations. Such a configuration can be expensive to set up and difficult to maintain, but it would provide an extremely robust level of firewall protection. Figure 3.6 shows a possible configuration with multiple firewalls. In this image each workstation has its own operating system firewall configured and running.

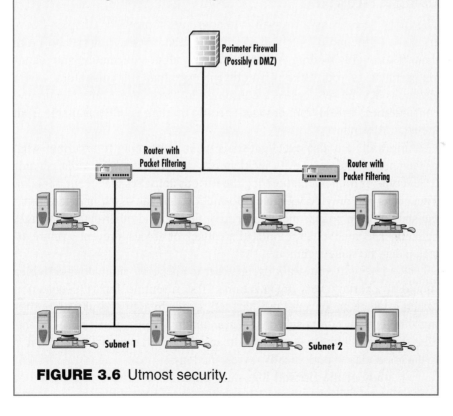

FIGURE 3.6 Utmost security.

Selecting and Using a Firewall

There is a variety of commercial firewall products from which you can choose. Many software vendors offer a basic packet-filtering solution. Major antivirus software vendors (including those previously mentioned in this chapter) often offer the firewall software as a bundled option with their antivirus software. Other companies, such as Zone Labs, sell firewall and intrusion-detection software. The major manufacturers of routers and hubs such as Cisco also offer firewall products.

The amount of security necessary for a particular system is always difficult to pinpoint. A bare minimum recommendation is to have a packet-filtering firewall/proxy server between your network and the Internet—but that is a bare minimum. As a rule of thumb, administrators should buy the most robust firewall that the budget allows. Chapter 4 examines some of the more widely used firewall solutions in detail.

Using a Firewall

The first rule in using a firewall is to configure it properly. Chapter 4 covers some of the more widely used firewall solutions and how to configure them. Thoroughly reading and understanding all documentation and manuals pertinent to your firewall solution is essential. Administrators should also consider the services of a consultant to assist in the initial setup and configuration. In addition, product-specific training is often available from the firewall vendor.

Firewalls are also excellent tools when attempting to ascertain what has happened after a security incident occurs. Almost all firewalls, regardless of type or implementation, log the various activities that occur on them. These logs can provide valuable information that can assist in determining the source of an attack, methods used to attack, and other data that might help either locate the perpetrator of an attack or at least prevent a future attack using the same techniques.

Reviewing the firewall logs in order to check for anomalous activities should be a part of every organization's IT staff routine. Intrusion detection systems, which are covered in Chapter 5, can help a great deal with notifying the network administrator when anomalies occur, particularly anomalies that might indicate a potential attack. However, even with an IDS, it is still a good idea to periodically review the logs.

A study of the firewall logs during normal activity over a period of time will establish a baseline. That baseline should show average number of incoming and outgoing packets per hour, minute, and day. It should also identify the types of packets (for example, 73% of incoming packets are HTTP packets destined for your Web server). Defining normal activity on a firewall helps administrators notice abnormal activity, should it occur.

Using Proxy Servers

A proxy server is often used with a firewall to hide the internal network's IP (Internet Protocol) address and present a single IP address (its own) to the outside world. A proxy server is a server that sits between a client application, such as a Web browser, and a real server. Proxy servers prevent hackers from seeing the IP addresses of internal machines, knowing how many machines are behind the proxy server, or learning anything about the network configuration. Proxy servers also provide a valuable control mechanism because most proxy servers log all outgoing traffic. This enables network administrators to see where employees go on the Internet. A proxy server normally runs as software on the same machine as your firewall.

The proxy server is configured to redirect certain traffic. For example, incoming traffic using the HTTP protocol is usually allowed through the proxy server but is redirected to the Web server. That means that all outgoing and incoming HTTP traffic first goes through the proxy server. A proxy server can be configured to redirect any traffic you want. If an e-mail server or ftp server is on the network, all incoming and outgoing traffic for that network will run through the proxy server.

Using a proxy server means that when a machine inside the network visits a Web site, the Web site will only detect that the proxy server visited it. In fact, if dozens of different machines on the network visit a site that logs the IP addresses of incoming connections, they will all be logged with the same IP address—that of the proxy server.

This hiding of the network is a very valuable service because knowledge of internal IP addresses can be used to execute certain forms of attack. For example, IP spoofing is contingent upon knowing the IP address of some internal server. Hiding those IP addresses is an important step in network security. It can also be very useful to know where employees go on the Internet. Proxy servers track such information, and many network administrators use this to restrict employees from using the company Internet connection for illicit purposes. This can also be a useful tool for stopping attacks. An employee that visits hacker Web sites might be a potential security risk. They may elect to try some of the techniques they read about on the network. Administrators can also detect potential industrial espionage. An employee who spends a lot of time on a competitor's Web site might be considering a job change and might consider taking valuable data with him.

The WinGate Proxy Server

There are a number of proxy server solutions available. Some are commercial products, while others are open source. In order to help you understand proxy servers better we will examine one such product. WinGate is an inexpensive commercial product that also offers a free trial download (available at **www.wingate.com**). This product has all of the standard features of a proxy server including:

■　Internet connection sharing

■　Hiding internal IP addresses

■　Allowing virus scanning

■　Filtering of sites

The free download option makes it ideal for students. You can use the 30-day trial version to learn how the proxy server works, without incurring any expense. The installation routine is simple, and the product has an easy-to-use graphical user interface.

Of course there are other proxy server solutions you can find, and many of them are quite good. This one is being shown because it is:

■　Easy to use

■　Inexpensive

■　Available as a free download

WinGate is also a good solution outside the classroom. The ability to filter certain Web sites is quite attractive to many companies. One way companies reduce abuse of system resources is by blocking sites they don't want employees to use. The ability to also scan for viruses is valuable in any setting.

NAT

For many organizations, proxy servers have been superseded by a newer technology known as ***network address translation*** (NAT). First and foremost, NAT translates internal addresses and external addresses to allow communication between network computers and outside computers. The outside sees only the address of the machine running NAT (often the firewall). From this perspective it is functioning exactly like a proxy server.

NAT also provides significant security because, by default, it allows only connections that are originated on the inside network. This means that a computer inside the network can connect to an outside Web server, but an outside computer cannot connect to a Web server inside the network. You can make some internal servers available to the outside world via inbound mapping, which maps certain well-known TCP ports (80 for HTTP, 21 for FTP, etc.) to specific internal addresses, thus making services such as FTP or Web sites available to the outside world. However, this inbound mapping must be done explicitly; it is not present by default.

As you will see in subsequent chapters, NAT is frequently offered as a part of another product, such as a firewall. Unlike proxy servers, it is less likely to be found as a standalone product. However, Chapter 4 shows several firewall solutions that include a network address translation functionality feature.

Summary

It is absolutely critical that any network have a firewall and proxy server between the network and the outside world. There are a number of firewall types and implementations to consider. Some are easy to implement and inexpensive. Others may be more resource intensive, difficult to configure, or more expensive. Organizations should use the most secure firewall that their circumstances allow. For some firewalls, vendor-specific training may be essential for proper configuration of the firewall. A poorly configured firewall can be as much of a security hazard as having no firewall at all.

We have examined the various types of firewalls (packet screening, application gateway, circuit level gateway, and stateful packet inspection) as well as the implementations (network host-based, router-based, dual-homed, and screened). Understanding how a firewall works is essential for selecting an appropriate solution for a network's security needs.

Test Your Skills

MULTIPLE CHOICE QUESTIONS

1. Which of the following are four basic types of firewalls?

   A. screening, bastion, dual-homed, circuit level

   B. application gateway, bastion, dual-homed, screening

   C. packet filtering, application gateway, circuit level, stateful packet inspection

   D. stateful packet inspection, gateway, bastion, screening

2. Which type of firewall creates a private virtual connection with the client?

   A. bastion

   B. dual-homed

   C. application gateway

   D. circuit level gateway

3. Which type of firewall is considered the most secure?

   A. dual-homed

   B. stateful packet inspection

   C. circuit-level gateway

   D. packet screening

4. What four rules must be set for packet filtering firewalls?

   A. protocol type, source port, destination port, source IP

   B. protocol version, destination IP, source port, username

   C. username, password, protocol type, destination IP

   D. source IP, destination IP, username, password

5. What type of firewall requires individual client applications to be authorized to connect?

   A. screened gateway

   B. stateful packet inspection

   C. dual-homed

   D. application gateway

6. Why might a proxy gateway be susceptible to a flood attack?

   A. It does not properly filter packets.

   B. It does not require user authentication.

   C. It allows multiple simultaneous connections.

   D. Its authentication method takes more time and resources.

7. Why might a circuit level gateway be inappropriate for some situations?

   A. It has no user authentication.

   B. It blocks Web traffic.

   C. It requires client side configuration.

   D. It is simply too expensive.

8. Why is an SPI firewall less susceptible to spoofing attacks?

   A. It examines the source IP of all packets.

   B. It automatically blocks spoofed packets.

   C. It requires user authentication.

   D. It requires client application authentication.

9. Why is an SPI firewall more resistant to flooding attacks?

   A. It automatically blocks large traffic from a single IP.

   B. It requires user authentication.

   C. It examines each packet in the context of previous packets.

   D. It examines the destination IP of all packets.

10. What is the greatest danger in a network host-based configuration?

    A. SYN flood attacks

    B. ping flood attacks

    C. IP spoofing

    D. operating system security flaws

11. Which of the following is an advantage of the network host-based configuration?

    A. It is resistant to IP spoofing.

    B. It is inexpensive or free.

    C. It is more secure.

    D. It has user authentication.

12. Which of the following can be shipped preconfigured?

    A. stateful packet inspection firewalls

    B. network host-based firewalls

    C. router-based firewalls

    D. dual-homed firewalls

13. Which of the following solutions is actually a combination of firewalls?

    A. screened firewalls

    B. router-based firewalls

    C. dual-homed firewalls

    D. bastion host firewalls

14. It should be routine for someone in the IT security staff to

    A. test the firewall by attempting a ping flood

    B. review firewall logs

    C. reboot the firewall

    D. physically inspect the firewall

15. A device that hides internal IP addresses is called

    A. screened host

    B. bastion firewall

    C. proxy server

    D. dual-homed host

16. What is the most important security advantage to NAT?

    A. It blocks incoming ICMP packets.

    B. It hides internal network addresses.

    C. By default it blocks all ICMP packets.

    D. By default it only allows outbound connections.

EXERCISES

Caution

Don't Use Live Systems for Labs

With all exercises you should use only lab computers specifically set up for the purpose of experimentation. Never perform these Lab exercises on live systems.

Exercise 3.1: Turning on Windows 2000 Packet Filtering

Note: This exercise requires access to a machine with Windows 2000.

1. Go to *Start*, choose *Settings,* and click *Control Panel*.

2. Double-click *Network* and *Dial-up connections*.

3. Right-click *Local Area Connection* and choose *Properties*.

4. Highlight *Internet Protocol (TCP/IP)* and then click *Properties*.

5. Click the button labeled *Advanced*.

6. Choose the tab labeled *Options*, highlight *Filtering*, and click the *Properties* button. You can now filter out any protocols you wish.

Exercise 3.2: Turning on the Windows XP Firewall

Note: This exercise requires access to a machine with Windows XP.

1. Start your computer and log on with an account that has full administrative privileges.

2. Click the *Start* button.

3. Click the *Control Panel*.

4. Double-click the *Network Connections* icon.

5. In the Network Connections window, right-click the connection that you want to protect with ICF (Internet Connection Firewall) and choose *Properties*.

6. In the Properties window, click the *Advanced* tab, and then check the *Internet Connection Firewall* box.

7. Click *OK* to make the change effective.

If you experience adverse effects or otherwise want to turn ICF off, follow the same steps above, but uncheck the box and click *OK* to make the change effective.

If your computer is not being used as a server, you can choose to block virtually all incoming packets. Blocking HTTP will not keep you from going to Web pages, it will just keep people from accessing your machine as a Web server.

Exercise 3.3: Linux Firewall

Note: This exercise requires access to a Linux machine. Given the various Linux distributions, it is not possible to list step-by-step instructions for all of them here.

1. Use the Web to find the firewall documentation for your particular Linux distribution.

   The following sites might help you:

   www.linux-firewall-tools.com/linux/
   www.linux.com/
   www.linuxsecurity.com/resources/firewalls-1.html

2. Use those instructions to turn on and configure your Linux firewall.

Exercise 3.4: Free Firewalls

There are many commercial firewall solutions, but free solutions are also available. In this exercise you should:

1. Find one of them on the Web. The following Web sites might be useful to you:

    www.free-firewall.org/

    http://smb.sygate.com/products/spf_standard.htm

2. Download and install it.

3. Configure it.

Exercise 3.5: Free Proxy Servers

There are a number of proxy servers that are available for free (or at least offer a free trial version) on the Web. The following Web sites should help you locate one:

Analog Proxy: **www.analogx.com/contents/download/network/proxy.htm**

Proxy+: **www.proxyplus.cz/**

Free Downloads Center: **www.freedownloadscenter.com/Network_and_Internet/Proxy_Server_Tools/**

1. Download your chosen proxy server.

2. Install it.

3. Configure it according to vendor specifications.

PROJECTS

Project 3.1: The Cisco Firewall

Using Web resources or documentation to which you have access, look up the detailed specifications of the Cisco PIX 500 series firewall. Determine what type of firewall it is and what implementation it is. Also note any specific advantages or disadvantages. The following Web sites will probably be useful to you:

www.cisco.com/warp/public/cc/pd/fw/sqfw500/

www.cisco.com/en/US/products/hw/vpndevc/ps2030/

Project 3.2: Zone Labs Firewalls

Using Web resources or documentation to which you have access, look up the detailed specifications of the Zone Labs Check Point Integrity firewall. Determine what type of firewall it is and what implementation it is. Also note any specific advantages or disadvantages. The following Web sites will probably be useful to you:

> **www.zonelabs.com/store/content/company/corpsales/ intOverview.jsp?lid=enthmintps**
>
> **www.checkpoint.com/products/integrity/**

Project 3.3: Windows XP Firewall

Using Web resources or documentation to which you have access, look up the detailed specifications of the Windows XP service pack 2 firewall. Determine what type of firewall it is and what implementation it is. Also note any specific advantages or disadvantages. The following Web sites will probably be useful to you:

> **www.microsoft.com/windowsxp/using/security/Internet/ sp2_wfintro.mspx**
>
> **www.microsoft.com/windowsxp/using/networking/learnmore/ icf.mspx**

Basil is the administrator for a Web-hosting company. The company has several small business clients who host their business sites on his company's server. Basil is deeply concerned about Denial of Service attacks bringing down the entire server and all of the sites hosted on it. However, he has no experience in setting up firewalls. He decides to implement an application gateway firewall that is router-based. He orders it from a vendor that ships it preconfigured for him.

1. What mistakes did Basil make?

2. What correct choices did he make?

3. What would you recommend?

Chapter

Firewall Practical Applications

Chapter Objectives

After reading this chapter and completing the exercises, you will be able to:

- Explain the requirements of single machine, small office, network, and enterprise firewalls.
- Evaluate the needs and constraints of an individual or company to determine what type of firewall solution is appropriate.
- Compare popular firewall solutions.
- Recommend an appropriate firewall solution for a given situation.

Introduction

Chapter 3 discussed the conceptual basis for the firewall. It described the various approaches to packet filtering used by different sorts of firewalls. This chapter examines the practical aspects of firewall selection. Firewalls can be classified based on a number of different criteria. In Chapter 3 these were classified based on configuration and type. This chapter classifies firewalls based on the practical situation in which they will be used.

Each section of this chapter examines the practical requirements of each category. We will look at the security needs, as well as budget limitations. Then we will examine one or more actual products designed for that environment. However, in no case am I specifically endorsing any product. I chose firewalls based on how widely they are used because the most widely used firewall solutions are the ones you are most likely to encounter in your career, regardless of their technical merits.

Using Single Machine Firewalls

A *single machine firewall* is a firewall solution running on an individual PC. Home users often protect their computers with single machine firewalls. In many cases, security-conscious organizations set up individual firewalls on all workstations on their network in addition to the firewall solution used for the network itself. I recommend that strategy over simply having a perimeter firewall. Regardless of which scenario you are working in, single machine firewalls have many things in common:

■ Most are packet filtering/screening firewalls.

■ All are software based.

■ Most are easy to configure and set up.

Most single machine firewalls were designed with the home user in mind. The idea is not to keep out a concerted breach attempt by a skilled hacker or to fend off a DoS attack but rather to give a higher level of security to a home user. This accounts for the fact that these firewalls are typically simple packet filtering solutions that are quite easy to configure. Nonetheless, they can be quite helpful in bolstering network security.

For example, more than one virus has spread by scanning nearby machines on a network, looking for open ports and connecting to that port. One version of the infamous MyDoom virus used port 1034 to facilitate its spread. A network that had all individual machines with their own firewalls blocking port 1034, would be immune to this avenue of attack (Canavan and Andres, 2004), even if one of the machines on the network was infected. In short, having individual firewalls on all workstations means that even if one machine is breached, the breach will not necessarily affect all machines on the network. We will examine the Windows XP firewall, a Linux firewall, and a couple of commercial firewalls (i.e., ones that don't come with the operating system but must be purchased separately).

When you select a single machine firewall solution, keep in mind that most were designed with several assumptions. Since the home user is the primary target customer for these products, ease of use is generally a high priority. Secondly, most of these products are very low cost and in some cases free. Finally, you should keep in mind that they are not meant for highly secure situations but merely to provide essential security for a home user.

Windows XP

Windows XP ships with Internet Connection Firewall (ICF). Prior to Service Pack 2 it was disabled by default. Now it is enabled by default. This

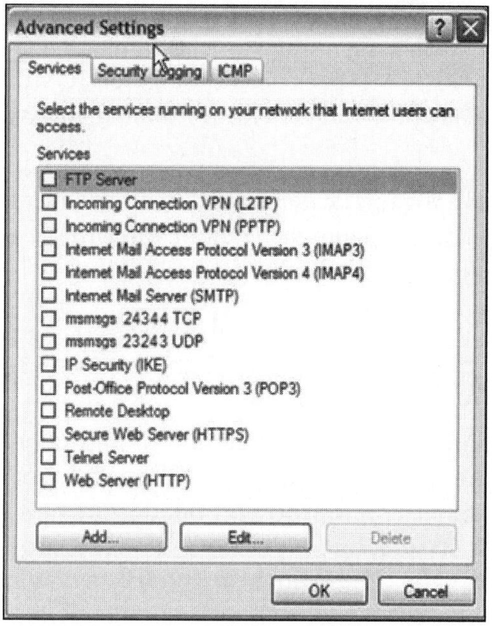

FIGURE 4.1 ICF.

firewall is designed to block incoming packets. Like most single machine firewalls, it is a packet filtering firewall. It is important to realize that ICF blocks only inbound traffic, not outbound traffic. Some home users avoid blocking port 80 for fear it will prevent them from using the Web. In fact blocking that port is a concern only for machines being used as a Web server. Remember that when you visit a Web site it is outbound packets going to the Web site. Most firewalls (including ICF) do not block return packets you requested, so blocking port 80 will not prevent that PC from being able to access Web pages.

The main advantage to ICF is that it is simple to set up and use. This makes it ideal for the home user who may not have a great deal of computer expertise. Configuring ICF is as simple as selecting boxes for items you wish to allow or disallow. An example of an ICF configuration screen is shown in Figure 4.1.

Administrators should always follow these rules with all packet-filtering firewalls:

- If you do not explicitly need a port, then block it. For example if you are not running a Web server on that machine, then block all in-bound port 80 traffic. With home machines you can usually block all ports. With individual workstations on a network you may need to keep some ports open in order to allow for various network utilities to access the machine.

- Unless you have a compelling reason not to, always block ICMP traffic because many utilities such as ping, tracert, and many port scanners use ICMP packets. If you block ICMP traffic, you will prevent many port scanners from scanning your system for vulnerabilities.

ICF also has a logging feature, but it is disabled by default. Turn this feature on (when you configure the firewall you will see a place to turn on logging). Check this log periodically.

FYI: Log Files

If you are using ICF on a workstation within a network that already has a perimeter firewall and ICF on all workstations, you may not want to turn on the logging because reviewing the log for your perimeter firewall and all the workstations' firewall logs is impractical. The sheer cumbersome nature of reviewing all of those logs makes it likely that they will never be reviewed.

Typically, you will review logs on your perimeter firewall and on all server firewalls, but not on workstation firewalls. Of course, if your security needs dictate that you log all system firewalls and you have the resources to routinely review those logs, it is certainly a good idea to do so.

As with any technology, ICF has advantages and disadvantages, as listed below.

Advantages

- ICF comes with the operating system and costs nothing extra.
- ICF is very easy to set up. Even a novice can do it.
- With Windows XP Service Pack 2, ICF is automatically turned on.
- ICF has logging features and can block inbound ICMP packets.

Disadvantages

- ICF does not block any outbound traffic at all. That means a Trojan horse on a machine with ICF can broadcast outbound traffic.
- ICF uses only packet filtering, the least robust firewall type.

ICF is a low-end, basic firewall. However, it is easy to configure and the fact that it ships with the operating system makes it inexpensive. If you are using Windows XP on your workstations (or on a home computer) there is no reason why you should not be using ICF in addition to your perimeter firewall.

Symantec Norton Firewall

The makers of Norton AntiVirus also sell a personal, single machine firewall. It can be purchased in a bundle along with Norton antivirus software. Like ICF, the Norton firewall is a basic packet filtering firewall. But Norton has an advantage over ICF: It enables you to also block outbound traffic. Blocking outbound traffic is a very significant feature in any firewall (and included in most network firewalls, but not in all personal firewalls) for the following reasons:

- If an individual machine is infected with a virus that tries to spread via a particular port that will be blocked.

- Many Trojan horses try to communicate via a certain port.

The Norton firewall also includes some additional features such as popup ad blocking and privacy protection. It accomplishes the latter task by preventing information about you from being transmitted via the browser without your knowledge. This firewall gives you a relatively easy-to-use interface, similar to Window's Explorer, that also enables you to set browser security. It also has a feature that enables you to connect to Norton's Web site and have that site scan your system for vulnerabilities. This feature is shown in Figure 4.2.

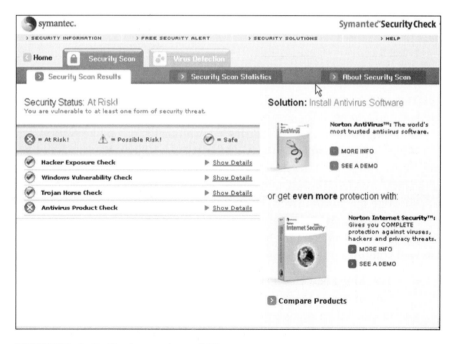

FIGURE 4.2 Norton vulnerability scan.

It should be noted that all of these tasks can be done without Norton. You can set your browser security settings, and you can scan your machine for vulnerabilities (even using free tools downloaded from the Internet, some of which will be discussed in Chapter 12). You can also use the built-in ICF to block incoming traffic. However, with Norton you can accomplish all of this via a simpler interface. This is particularly appealing to novice users. It should also be stressed that, unlike ICF, Norton's firewall can block outgoing traffic as well.

The advantages and disadvantages of Norton Firewall are summarized below.

Advantages:

- Norton firewall can be purchased as a bundle with Norton Anti-Virus software.

- Norton firewall is easy to use and set up.

- Norton firewall has several extra features, such as the ability to scan your system for vulnerabilities.

- Norton firewall also enables you to block outbound traffic.

Disadvantages

- Norton firewall costs almost $50 per copy.

- Many of Norton firewall's features can be done with separate, free tools.

McAfee Personal Firewall

McAfee and Norton are the most widely used antivirus software vendors. Both manufacturers offer personal firewalls for individual PCs. McAfee Personal Firewall offers a packet filtering firewall that is much like Norton and ICF. Like Norton's firewall, the McAfee Personal Firewall can also block outbound traffic. It is also quite easy to use. Figure 4.3 shows the initial screen for McAfee firewall, and Figure 4.4 shows filtering with McAfee.

Unlike the Norton firewall, the McAfee firewall does not offer a feature that enables you to scan your system for vulnerabilities. However, it does offer a few interesting features that are not found in most personal firewall solutions:

- **Tracking:** McAfee Personal Firewall has a utility that will show you on a map the path from which an attack is coming. It does this in much the same way as the traceroute command, but instead performing trace route commands on the incoming packets and then displaying those routes on a map.

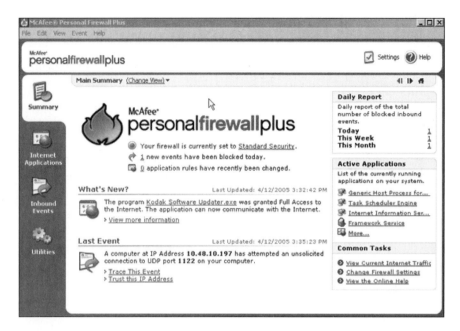

FIGURE 4.3 The initial McAfee firewall screen.

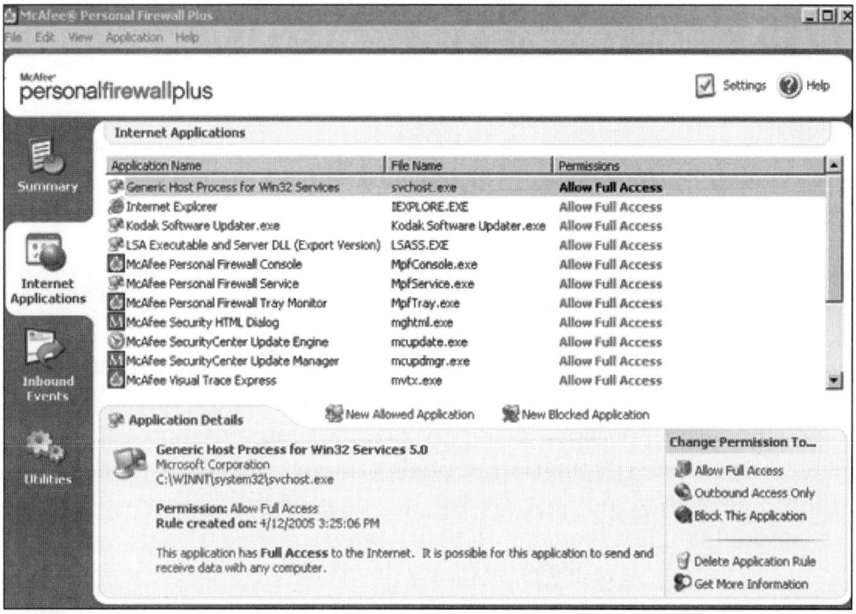

FIGURE 4.4 Filtering with McAfee.

4

> ## FYI: Traceroute
>
> Traceroute is a command available from the command prompt in Windows or the shell in Unix/Linux that is used to trace where a packet is coming from.

- **Connected to HackerWatch.org:** McAfee Personal Firewall is connected to **HackerWatch.org**, an anti-hacking Web site that enables you to get tips and news on the latest threats.

Like Norton and ICF, Personal firewall has advantages and disadvantages, listed below:

Advantages:

- McAfee Personal Firewall blocks outbound and inbound traffic.

- McAfee Personal Firewall is easy to use and setup.

- McAfee Personal Firewall links to anti-hacking news and tips.

Disadvantages

- McAfee Personal Firewall costs from $30 to $50 depending on the version.

- Some extra features in McAfee Personal Firewall (like the link to anti-hacking news) can be obtained without this product.

IN PRACTICE: Extra Firewall Features

You may have noted that many of the firewall solutions come with a variety of extra features not directly related to packet filtering/blocking. You have probably also noticed that many of these features can be obtained from other sources for free. So, the question arises: Why not just use ICF or some other free firewall, and then get the other features on your own?

The answer is really ease of use. In addition to functionality, any technology product has to be evaluated based on usability. For example, you can do traceroute commands, scan your machine for vulnerabilities, and monitor various Web sites to keep current with attacks, but given that most administrators are quite busy, isn't it more convenient to have these features all in one place?

Home users certainly do not have access to a dedicated network administrator and certainly do not have a dedicated network security professional. Many small- to medium-sized organizations are in the same boat. They may or may not have a basic general technical support person on site. In this case the person handling security is likely to have limited skills and will benefit from tools that do much of the work for him.

From a practical point of view, some of these features might be superfluous to a security-savvy network administrator or a dedicated network security professional. However, for the home or small office user, they can be absolutely critical. You will be asked to recommend security solutions on the job as well as in your private life. You must keep in mind not only the technical strengths of each product, but how easy the product will be for the person who uses it.

4

There are other personal firewall solutions. Most Linux distributions have one or more built-in firewalls. A Google or Yahoo search on "free firewall" will provide several options. In most cases, personal firewalls will simply be packet-filtering firewalls. Most free solutions have rather limited features, whereas many commercial products will add in additional features.

FYI: McAfee and Norton

McAfee and Norton firewall solutions are quite similar as far as core functionality goes. However they are the two most commonly used personal or small business firewall solutions, so it is imperative that as a security professional you are familiar with both.

Wolverine

Wolverine is a robust commercial firewall solution for Linux available from **www.coyotelinux.com/**. Wolverine provides Stateful Packet Inspection, built-in VPN capabilities (VPNs are discussed in detail in Chapter 7), several encryption methods (AES, DES, and more), and offers a Web-based administration utility. This is an excellent solution for any network using Linux.

The advantages and disadvantages of the Wolverine firewall are summarized below.

Advantages

- Wolverine is a very low cost solution. The most expensive version of this product is under $200.

- Wolverine includes built-in VPN capabilities.

- Wolverine offers built-in encryption.

- Wolverine provides Web-based administration.

Disadvantages Frankly, when compared to any other firewall in its price range, Wolverine only has two disadvantages.

- Wolverine is Linux-based, and many organizations are standardized on Microsoft.

- Wolverine is network host-based, which means that it is dependent upon the security of the underlying operating system.

Using Small Office/Home Office Firewalls

The small office/home office system (often referred to as SOHO) will frequently have needs similar to the individual PC firewall. The personnel maintaining the firewall will likely have limited network administration and security training. Both Norton and McAfee offer solutions designed to be perimeter firewalls for a small network. These products are quite similar to their individual PC firewalls, but with added features and a slightly higher cost. However, there are other solutions for the SOHO which we will examine here. Keep in mind that one critical consideration with any firewall for this environment is ease of installation and use.

SonicWALL

SonicWALL is a vendor of several firewall solutions. Their T170 series is made specifically for small networks with 10 to 25 users. It costs between $350 and $700, depending on the version and retailer. T170 is a router-based firewall, as shown in Figure 4.5.

Most importantly, this product uses Stateful Packet Inspection, which is significantly more secure than basic packet filtering.

One additional feature that SonicWALL products offer is built-in encryption so that all transmissions are encrypted. Currently their products offer AES and 3DES encryption. While not strictly a firewall feature, this is an important part of network security. When packets are being sent around a network and outside the network, it is not difficult to intercept those packets with a packet sniffer and get the data if the packets are not encrypted.

Management of the SonicWALL firewall should be easy to master for those familiar with Windows 2000 and later versions of Windows because the management is based on objects, such as users, groups, and even IP address ranges (SonicWALL Data Sheet, 2004). Once a group is defined, you can apply filtering/blocking properties to that group.

FIGURE 4.5 The SonicWALL Firewall.

4

FYI: AES and 3DES Encryption

Chapter 6 describes encryption in detail, including how various encryption methods work. At this point it is important to understand that both AES and 3DES are considered highly secure encryption methods and should be appropriate for almost any network security situation.

SonicWALL, as well as many other modern firewalls, offers built-in NAT. This technology is designed to replace proxy servers. It accomplishes the same goal of hiding internal network IP addresses from the external world.

The advantages and disadvantages of SonicWALL are briefly listed here.

Advantages:

- SonicWALL firewalls provide stateful packet inspection.
- SonicWALL firewalls provide built-in encryption.
- SonicWALL firewalls provide management and configuration that is easy for Windows administrators.
- SonicWALL firewalls provide built-in NAT.

Disadvantages:

- The price of SonicWALL firewalls may be prohibitive for small offices on a tight budget.
- SonicWALL firewalls require some skill to configure and are not intended for the complete novice.

D-Link DFL–300 Office Firewall

D-Link makes a number of products for home users and for small offices. Its Office firewall product is a router-based firewall that uses Stateful Packet Inspection to filter network traffic. It allows for remote users to connect to it using DES encryption, which is a widely used, very secure encryption method. It logs all Web traffic, and it also enables administrators to filter certain Web addresses. The DFL-300 is specifically designed to detect many common DoS attacks and to block that traffic. The DFL-300 is shown in Figure 4.6.

This firewall is fairly easy to configure and has a Web-based interface, similar to the type used by many home wireless router manufacturers. By using any computer connected directly to the router, you can enter the router's IP address and you will be presented with a Web page that enables you to configure the router. Of course, one of the first things you should do is change the password to prevent other parties from reconfiguring your router-based firewall. This firewall solution can cost anywhere from $350 to $500. Unlike many firewall solutions, the vendor does not require any additional licenses for additional users, so if your company goes from 20 to 50 users, it need not purchase additional licenses (D-Link Data Sheet, 2004).

Here are the advantages and disadvantages of the DFL-300:

Advantages

- The DFL-300 includes built-in reliable encryption.
- The DFL-300 is inexpensive compared to other SOHO firewalls.
- The DFL-300 has a liberal licensing policy.
- The DFL-300 is easy to configure.
- The DFL-300 uses Stateful Packet Inspection.

FIGURE 4.6 The DFL-300.

Disadvantages

- The DFL-300 lacks some security features that more advanced systems might offer.

- DFL-300 combines multiple firewall types.

- DFL-300 includes built-in NAT.

- DFL-300 includes built-in VPN.

Using Medium-Sized Network Firewalls

Medium-sized networks can be defined as having as few as 25 users up to several hundred users all on a single LAN at a single location. Administrators of medium-sized networks face configuration and security issues beyond what an administrator in a home or small offices might encounter. To begin with, medium-sized networks are likely to have a more diverse group of users and applications running. Each of these presents different access needs and security requirements. On the other hand, medium-sized networks typically benefit from the support of dedicated network administration personnel. This means there is someone on site who has at least a basic understanding of computer security.

Check Point Firewall-1

Check Point is a well known manufacturer of security equipment, and its Firewall-1 product is designed explicitly for use on medium- to large-sized networks. Firewall-1 features host-based configuration. Recall from Chapter 3 that this means the firewall must be installed on an existing server that will serve as the firewall. Firewall-1 is available for Windows 2000 (Server and Advanced Server editions), Sun Solaris (8 and 9), as well as Red Hat Linux.

In addition to filtering packets, Firewall-1 provides filtering based on application. It also requires that a computer connecting to the network from outside the firewall must be authenticated. This makes it a sort of hybrid between packet filtering and application gateway, but its packet filtering uses Stateful Packet Inspection, not simple packet screening. Perhaps most importantly, Firewall-1 automatically blocks and then logs any oversized packets or packets that appear to be part of a SYN flood. As you learned in Chapter 2, oversized packets and SYN floods are two common DoS techniques.

Check Point offers a number of other security products, including intrusion-detection systems (IDS will be discussed in detail in Chapter 5). Check Point sells many package solutions that include a firewall as well as some of these additional security products, though such packages can cost anywhere from $3000 to more than $50,000 (Checkpoint Firewall-1 Data

Sheet, 2004).

The advantages and disadvantages of Firewall-1 are as follows:

Advantages:

- Firewall-1 works with multiple operating systems.

- Firewall-1 combines Stateful Packet Inspection with an application gateway.

- Firewall-1 protects against common DoS techniques.

Disadvantages

- All host-based firewalls such as Firewall-1 are dependent on the security of the underlying operating system.

- Firewall-1 requires at least moderate skill to administer and configure.

- The cost of Firewall-1 can be prohibitive to some organizations.

Cisco PIX 515E

Cisco is a very well known manufacturer of networking equipment, especially routers, so it should come as no surprise that it also makes firewalls. It should also be stressed that their PIX series has multiple models, some for SOHO solutions and others for large-scale enterprise solutions. The 515E is designed for small- to medium-sized networks. The 515E is shown in Figure 4.7.

The PIX 515E firewall solution utilizes Stateful Packet Inspection to filter traffic. It also has built-in intrusion-detection software and NAT. All of the PIX series firewalls offer AES, DES, or 3DES encryption built in. The 515E model also has security features that monitor voice over IP and multimedia transmissions for potential threats.

Most importantly, the PIX 515E has a range of capabilities for identifying potentially malicious packets. It looks for oversized packets, malformed packets, packets from fake IP sources, and other telltale signs that a packet might be part of an attack. If it detects a probable attack, it blocks the traffic and logs the event. The PIX 515E sells for between $1800 and $2600, depending on whether you purchase a refurbished or new unit as well as the retail vendor.

FIGURE 4.7 The Cisco PIX 515E.

One of the strengths of Cisco products is the extensive training available for their systems. Cisco sponsors a number of certifications for their products. Their highest certification, the Cisco Certified Internetworking Engineer (CCIE) is one of the most widely respected and most rigorous certifications in networking. This certification process enables you to easily identify qualified people to work with your Cisco equipment. It also enables you to identify appropriate training plans for your existing staff.

The advantages and disadvantages of the PIX 515E are listed below.

Advantages:

- The PIX 515E uses SPI filtering.

- The PIX 515E features built-in robust encryption.

- Cisco product-specific training is available for the PIX 515E.

- The PIX 515E includes NAT.

- The PIX 515E includes voice over IP and multimedia security options.

Disadvantages:

- The PIX 515E may be cost prohibitive for some organizations.

- The PIX 515E requires at least moderate skill to configure and administer.

Using Enterprise Firewalls

An enterprise network is a large network that is often made up of several local networks connected over a wide area network, or WAN. Large corporations and government agencies frequently use this type of environment. The enterprise environment presents a number of challenges not found in smaller networks. First, each small local network that is connected to the enterprise must be secured. You should also recognize that most enterprise networks include many different types of users, applications, and even operating systems. You may have Unix, Linux, Windows, and Macintosh running a combination of hard wired and wireless network connections. In addition, your end users will probably be quite diverse, including everything from clerical workers to skilled IT professionals. This presents a very complex security challenge, but all enterprise networks are supported by multiple network administrators. Many enterprise networks are supported by a dedicated network security professional. This provides the skill set necessary to deal with such complex situations.

Fortigate 3600

The Fortigate 3600 received SearchNetworking.com's Gold Award for 2003. It is a hardware (router-based) solution that provides total network protection. It provides virus scanning at the firewall before packets ever reach individual machines. This also means that non-e-mail packets such as FTP and TCP messages are scanned for virus infections before being allowed into your network. The Fortigate 3600 is shown in Figure 4.8.

The entire Fortigate series also has built-in intrusion-detection. And like many firewall solutions, it also enables administrators to configure content filtering to block certain Web sites and e-mail messages. Fortigate's content filtering also enables them to set cookie handling, ActiveX handling, and script handling at the firewall. This can be very useful, as it prevents worries about the browser settings on each and every machine in an organization.

This firewall solution provides NAT and your choice of encryption using AES, DES, or 3DES. One very interesting feature is that Fortigate's maintenance package includes a 24-hour-a-day service that constantly monitors new threats (new viruses, worms, etc.). This service pushes new patches to your firewall within hours of a new threat appearing on the Internet. The firewall implements user authentication as well as Stateful Packet Inspection, but the system is quite expensive and requires at least moderate knowledge to be able to configure and administer.

The advantages and disadvantages of the Fortigate firewall include the following:

Advantages:

- The Fortigate firewall offers SPI and user authentication.

- The Fortigate firewall has built-in IDS and virus scanning.

- The Fortigate firewall features 24-hour update service.

- The Fortigate firewall has built-in robust encryption.

- The Fortigate firewall provides very extensive content filtering.

FIGURE 4.8 The Fortigate 3600.

Disadvantages

- The Fortigate firewall requires trained personnel to administer it.

- The Fortigate firewall itself can cost more than $20,000 depending on the model, and the service contracts cost several thousand dollars per year.

Summary

4

The type of firewall that is most appropriate for a network depends, at least in part, on the size of the network. Within each size category there are a number of options for a firewall solution, each with its own advantages and disadvantages.

It is important to consider both the technical merits of a firewall solution and the ease of use. A firewall solution's degree of user-friendliness is largely contingent upon the skill set of the support staff that will implement it. Administrators also must balance cost verses benefit. Clearly, the more expensive firewalls have some impressive features, but they may not be necessary for an organization and may negatively impact its overall IT budget.

Test Your Skills

MULTIPLE CHOICE QUESTIONS

1. Which of the following is a common problem when seeking information on firewalls?

    A. It is difficult to find information on the Web.

    B. Unbiased information may be hard to find.

    C. Documentation is often incomplete.

    D. Information often emphasizes price rather than features.

2. Which of the following is not a common feature of most single PC firewalls?

    A. software-based

    B. packet filtering

    C. ease of use

    D. built-in NAT

3. What is ICF?

   A. Windows XP Internet Connection Firewall

   B. Windows XP Internet Control Firewall

   C. Windows 2000 Internet Connection Firewall

   D. Windows 2000 Internet Control Firewall

4. Should a home user with ICF block port 80, and why or why not?

   A. She should not because it would prevent her from using Web pages.

   B. She should because port 80 is a common attack point for hackers.

   C. She should not because that will prevent her from getting updates and patches.

   D. She should unless she is running a Web server on her machine.

5. Should a home user block ICMP traffic, and why or why not?

   A. It should be blocked because such traffic is often used to transmit a virus.

   B. It should be blocked because such traffic is often used to do port scans and flood attacks.

   C. It should not be blocked because it is necessary for network operations.

   D. It should not be blocked because it is necessary for using the Web.

6. Which of the following is found in Norton's personal firewall but not in ICF?

   A. NAT

   B. a visual tool to trace attacks

   C. vulnerability scanning

   D. strong encryption

7. What tool does McAfee Personal Firewall offer?

   A. a visual tool to trace attacks

   B. NAT

   C. strong encryption

   D. vulnerability scanning

8. What type of firewall is SonicWALL T170?

   A. packet screening

   B. application gateway

   C. circuit-level gateway

   D. Stateful Packet Inspection

9. Which type of encryption is included with the T170?

   A. AES and DES

   B. WEP and DES

   C. PGP and AES

   D. WEP and PGP

10. NAT is a replacement for what technology?

    A. firewall

    B. proxy server

    C. antivirus software

    D. IDS

11. Which of the following is an important feature of D-Link DFL 300?

    A. built-in IDS

    B. WEP encryption

    C. vulnerability scanning

    D. liberal licensing policy

12. Medium-sized networks have what problem?

    A. lack of skilled technical personnel

    B. diverse user group

    C. need to connect multiple LANs into a single WAN

    D. low budgets

13. What type of firewall is Check Point Firewall-1?

    A. application gateway

    B. packet filtering/application gateway hybrid

    C. SPI/application gateway hybrid

    D. circuit level gateway

14. What implementation is Check Point Firewall-1?

    A. router based

    B. network based

    C. switch based

    D. host based

15. Which of the following is a benefit of Cisco firewalls?

    A. extensive training available on the product

    B. very low cost

    C. built-in IDS on all products

    D. built-in virus scanning on all products

16. What is an advantage of an enterprise environment?

    A. multiple operating systems to deal with

    B. skilled technical personnel available

    C. lower security needs

    D. IDS systems not needed

17. What is one complexity found in enterprise environments that is unlikely in small networks or SOHO environments?

    A. multiple operating systems

    B. diverse user groups

    C. users running different applications

    D. Web vulnerabilities

18. Which of the following is not an advantage of the Fortigate firewall?

    A. built-in virus scanning

    B. content filtering

    C. built-in encryption

    D. low cost

EXERCISES

Note: Some of the exercises here use commercial tools. All of these exercises can also be completed using free software from the following sites:

- **www.free-firewall.org/**
- **www.homenethelp.com/Web/howto/free-firewall.asp**
- **www.firewallguide.com/freeware.htm**

Exercise 4.1: The McAfee Firewall

1. Download the McAfee personal firewall. You may wish to download one copy to one machine for the entire class to take turns using, or contact McAfee and request an academic discount or free copy. **us.mcafee.com/root/package.asp?pkgid=101&WWW_URL=ww w.mcafee.com/myapps/firewall/ov_firewall.asp**

2. Install and configure the McAfee firewall on your machine.

3. Examine the firewall's configuration utilities.

4. Examine extra features such as its attack tracing utility.

5. Attempt to send packets to blocked ports on that firewall.

Exercise 4.2: The Norton Firewall

1. Download the Norton personal firewall from **www.symantec.com/ sabu/nis/npf/** for $49.95.

2. Install and configure the firewall on your machine.

3. Examine the firewall's configuration utilities.

4. Pay particular attention to extra features such as its vulnerability scanning.

5. Attempt to send packets to blocked ports on that firewall.

Exercise 4.3: Router-based Firewall

Note: For cost reasons a specific router is not mentioned here. Many companies and vendors will donate old routers they no longer use to academic labs. You can go to a used computer equipment outlet and find an older router-based firewall for use in the lab.

1. Using the firewall's documentation, set up this firewall. It should be connected to at least one machine.

2. Attempt to send packets to blocked ports on that firewall.

Exercise 4.4: Zone Alarm Firewall

This product was not covered in this chapter, but you can work with it quite easily. Simply follow these steps:

1. Download the free version from **zonelabs.com/store/content/ company/ zap_za_grid.jsp.**

2. Install and configure this firewall.

3. Observe how it works and compare it to Norton and McAfee.

PROJECTS

Project 4.1: Finding Firewall Solutions in Your Organization

Contact an organization you are associated with (an employer, your school, a local company, etc.). Explain to the organization that you are doing a school project and arrange to discuss its firewall solution with the network administrator. Determine why the organization selected its particular solution. Was cost a major factor? Was ease of use a major factor? What features were most important to them? Explain your findings and discuss whether you agree or disagree with that organization's choice.

Project 4.2: Finding a Different SOHO Solution

Using the Web or other resources, find a SOHO firewall not mentioned in this chapter. Briefly compare and contrast it to the solutions that were mentioned in the chapter. Evaluate whether the firewall you found is a better choice than the ones mentioned in the chapter and discuss why or why not.

Project 4.3: Selecting the Proper Firewall

Analyze the environment of your academic institution. Is it a medium-sized network or enterprise? What types of users utilize the network? Are there multiple operating systems? Is there sensitive data that requires additional security? Based on the factors you analyze, write a brief essay describing the environment and recommending a firewall solution. Explain your recommendation.

▶▶ Case Study

Hans is the network administrator for a stock brokerage firm. This firm has a total of 75 users. Fifty of them are brokers who routinely use the Web for data collection and marketing efforts. All employees work at a single office location. The firm has allocated a generous amount for security, but Hans has limited knowledge of firewalls. He makes the following choices:

1. He purchases the D-Link DFL 300.

2. He turns on ICF on all machines.

Did Hans make the best choices given his resources and company's needs? Explain your answer.

Chapter | 5

Intrusion-Detection Systems

Chapter Objectives

After reading this chapter and completing the exercises, you will be able to do the following:

■ Explain how intrusion-detection systems work.

■ Implement strategies for preventing intrusion.

■ Identify and describe several popular intrusion-detection systems.

■ Define the term *honey pot.*

■ Identify and describe at least one honey pot implementation.

Introduction

Chapter 4 discussed several firewall solutions that have built-in Intrusion-Detection Systems (IDS). An IDS is designed to detect signs that someone is attempting to breach a system and to alert the system administrator that suspicious activity is taking place. This chapter analyzes how an IDS works and how to implement some specific IDS solutions.

IDS has become much more widely used in the last few years. An IDS inspects all inbound and outbound port activity on a machine/firewall/system and looks for patterns that might indicate an attempted break-in. For example, if the IDS finds that a series of ICMP packets were sent to each port in sequence from the same source IP address, this probably indicates that a system is being scanned by network-scanning software such as Cerberus (scanners are discussed at length in Chapter 12). Since this is often a prelude to an attempt to breach a system's security, it can be very important to know that someone is performing preparatory steps to infiltrate a system. The IDS may also detect an abnormally large flow of packets from the same

IP address, all in a brief period of time. This may indicate a DoS attack. In either case, these are situations the network administrator should be aware of and should take steps to prevent.

Understanding IDS Concepts

A full discussion of intrusion-detection systems, the subject of entire books, is beyond the scope of this section. However, this section provides an overview of IDS to explain how these systems work. There are six basic approaches to intrusion-detection and prevention. Some of these methods are implemented in various software packages, and others are simply strategies that an organization can employ to decrease the likelihood of a successful intrusion. The following paragraphs describe and examine each.

Preemptive Blocking

Preemptive blocking, sometimes called *banishment vigilance,* seeks to prevent intrusions before they occur. This is done by noting any danger signs of impending threats and then blocking the user or IP address from which these signs originate. Examples of this technique include attempting to detect the early foot printing stages of an impending intrusion, then blocking the IP or user that is the source of the foot printing activity. If you find that a particular IP address is the source of frequent port scans and other scans of your system, then you would block that IP address at the firewall.

This sort of intrusion-detection and avoidance can be quite complicated, and there is the potential of blocking a legitimate user by mistake. The complexity arises from distinguishing legitimate traffic from that indicative of an impending attack. This can lead to the problem of *false positives,* in which the system mistakenly identifies legitimate traffic as some form of attack. Usually, a software system will simply alert the administrator that suspicious activity has taken place. A human administrator will then make the decision whether or not to block the person. If the software automatically blocks any addresses it deems suspicious, you run the risk of blocking out legitimate users. It should also be noted that nothing prevents the offending user from moving to a different machine to continue his or her attack. This sort of approach should only be one part of an overall intrusion-detection strategy and not the entire strategy.

Infiltration

Infiltration refers to proactive efforts on the part of the administrator or security specialist to acquire information from various illicit sources about potential threats. This is usually done to supplement vendor bug reports and security warnings. In other words, it is not a software or hardware implementation, but rather a process of infiltrating hacker/cracker online groups in order to keep tabs on what sort of vulnerabilities are currently being exploited by these groups and what systems are considered attractive targets.

This form of intrusion-detection has two main drawbacks. The first is that it is quite time-consuming, and most network administrators have a very full schedule. The second is that most IT professionals are not trained in gathering intelligence or doing detective work, so there is the very real possibility that the information gathered could be inaccurate or incomplete. This strategy should only be used in cases in which an extraordinary level of security is required. Furthermore, this cannot be the only method of intrusion-detection; it must be coupled with other methods.

IN PRACTICE: Dangers Inherent in Using Infiltration

The process of infiltrating illicit groups (such as black hat hacker groups or those who trade in copyright protected software) can be very difficult. Such people are, first and foremost, naturally quite suspicious. They do not trust new contacts easily. Additionally, at least some of them are technically very proficient and respect only those who are equally technically proficient. Both of these facts place rather serious practical limitations on an administrator's ability to infiltrate any such group. It would take a great deal of time and care to have any hope of successfully accomplishing this task.

There are also other reasons one may wish to avoid this practice. The first is that if such a group detects the infiltration, the odds of multiple retaliatory attacks, including Denial of Service, virus attacks, and other threats to your computer security, are quite high. Additionally, the practice of spying on other people can be a tricky proposition from a legal standpoint. Consulting an attorney before attempting any such project is advisable.

Only those organizations with very high security needs, the resources of full-time computer security staff, and a likelihood of being targeted specifically by particular groups will feel compelled to implement the infiltration method. The following are guidelines for doing so:

- Research the target group or groups thoroughly before making an attempt to intrude. You must know the players, their ideology, and their history.

- Create a complete and plausible identity. Simply setting up an e-mail address front will not work. This identity must have a personality, a history, quirks, and so on.

▶▶ CONTINUED ON NEXT PAGE

▸▸ **CONTINUED**

- Be prepared to be on the fringe of the group or groups in question for many months as trust builds.

- Be prepared for the very serious adverse affects that might occur if the intrusion is detected.

Infiltration is a drastic step that most organizations avoid. However, a company in the business of providing computer security can use the infiltration strategy to keep an eye on the "dark side" of the Internet.

Intrusion Deflection

Intrusion deflection is becoming increasingly popular among security-conscious administrators. The essence of it is quite simple. An attempt is made to attract the intruder to a sub-system set up for the purpose of observing him. This is done by tricking the intruder into believing that he has succeeded in accessing system resources when, in fact, he has been directed to a specially designed environment. Being able to observe the intruder while he practices his art will yield valuable clues and can lead to his arrest.

This is often done by using what is commonly referred to as a *honey pot.* Essentially, you set up a fake system, possibly a server that appears to be an entire subnet. The administrator makes that system look attractive to hackers, perhaps making it appear to have sensitive data, such as personnel files, or valuable data, such as account numbers or research. The actual data stored in this system is fake. The real purpose of the system is to carefully monitor the activities of any person who accesses the system. Since no legitimate user ever accesses this system, it is a given that anyone accessing it is an intruder.

This sort of system can be difficult to set up and maintain. It also presupposes that someone is able to successfully compromise security. Intrusion deflection systems are typically only employed at sites requiring very high security. They should only be a part of the overall IDS strategy—not the entire strategy.

Intrusion Deterrence

Intrusion deterrence involves simply trying to make the system seem like a less palatable target. In short, an attempt is made to make any potential reward from a successful intrusion attempt appear more difficult than it is worth. This approach includes tactics such as attempting to reduce the apparent value of the current system's worth through camouflage. This essentially means working to hide the most valuable aspects of the system. The other tactic in this methodology involves raising the perceived risk of a potential intruder being caught. This can be done in a variety of ways, including conspicuously displaying warnings and warning of active monitoring. The perception of the security of a system can be drastically improved, even when the actual system security has not been improved.

Because this approach costs almost nothing to implement and is relatively easy to set up, it is a good option for any system when used in conjunction with other strategies.

To implement this strategy, warn the user at every step in the process of connecting that her activities are being closely monitored, whether they are or are not. In addition, avoid advertising that the system or machine contains sensitive data by giving it an innocuous name. For example a database server that contains research material might be named "print_server 1" rather than "research_server" to make it less attractive. When using this approach, it is important to maintain a master list and develop a naming scheme. For example, all real print servers might end with X and all false print server names end in Y so that staff know that "print_server1x" is a real print server and "print_server1y" is actually a sensitive server being hidden from intruders. There must be some way of keeping track of the real purpose of the servers.

The purpose of the multiple warnings is to scare off less skilled hackers. While such people might not have a great deal of technical prowess, their attempts to invade a system are a nuisance and can cause problems. Many of these attackers are new to hacking and appropriate warnings can scare off a significant percentage of them.

Anomaly Detection

Anomaly detection involves actual software that works to detect intrusion attempts and notify the administrator. This is what many people think of when they talk about intrusion-detection systems. The general process is simple: the system looks for any anomalous behavior. Any activity that does not match the pattern of normal user access is noted and logged. The software compares observed activity against expected normal usage profiles. Profiles are usually developed for specific users, groups of users, or applications. Any activity that does not match the definition of normal behavior is considered an anomaly and is logged. The specific ways in which an anomaly is detected include:

- threshold monitoring
- resource profiling
- user/group work profiling
- executable profiling

Threshold Monitoring *Threshold monitoring* presets acceptable behavior levels and observes whether these levels are exceeded. This could include something as simple as a finite number of failed login attempts or something as complex as monitoring the time a user is connected and the amount of data that user downloads. Thresholds provide a definition of acceptable behavior. Unfortunately, characterizing intrusive behavior solely by the threshold limits can be somewhat challenging. It is often quite difficult to establish proper threshold values or the proper time frames at which to check those threshold values. This can result in a high rate of false positives in which the system misidentifies normal usage as a probable attack.

Resource Profiling *Resource profiling* measures system-wide use of resources and develops a historic usage profile. Looking at how a user normally utilizes system resources enables the system to identify usage levels that are outside normal parameters. Such abnormal readings can be indicative of illicit activity underway. However, it may be difficult to interpret the meaning of changes in overall system usage. An increase in usage might simply indicate something benign like increased workflow rather than an attempt to breach security.

User/Group Work Profiling In *user/group work profiling*, the IDS maintains individual work profiles about users and groups. These users and groups are expected to adhere to these profiles. As the user changes his activities, his expected work profile is updated to reflect those changes. Some systems attempt to monitor the interaction of short-term versus long-term profiles. The short-term profiles capture recent changing work patterns, whereas the long term profiles provide a view of usage over an extended period of time. However it can be difficult to profile an irregular or dynamic user base. Profiles that are defined too broadly enable any activity to pass review, whereas profiles that are defined too narrowly may inhibit user work.

Executable Profiling *Executable profiling* seeks to measure and monitor how programs use system resources with particular attention to those whose activity cannot always be traced to a specific originating user. For example, system services usually cannot be traced to a specific user launching them. Viruses, Trojan horses, worms, trapdoors, and other such software attacks are addressed by profiling how system objects such as files and printers are normally used not only by users, but also by other system subjects on the part of users. In most conventional systems, for example, any program, including a virus, inherits all of the privileges of the user executing the software. The software is not limited by the principle of least privilege to only those privileges needed to properly execute. This openness in the architecture permits viruses to surreptitiously change and infect totally unrelated parts of the system.

Executable profiling enables the IDS to identify activity that might indicate an attack. Once a potential danger is identified, the method of notifying the administrator, such as by network message or e-mail, is specific to the individual IDS.

Understanding and Implementing IDS Systems

Many vendors supply IDS systems, and each of these systems has its own strengths and weaknesses. Deciding which system is best for a particular environment depends on many factors including the network environment, security level required, budget constraints, and the skill level of the person who will be working directly with the IDS. This section discusses the most common IDS systems.

Snort

Snort is perhaps the most well known *open-source* IDS available. It is a software implementation installed on a server to monitor incoming traffic. It typically works with a host-based firewall in a system in which both the firewall software and Snort run on the same machine. Snort is available for Unix, Linux, Free BSD, and Windows. The software is free to download, and documentation is available at the Web site: **www.snort.org/.**

FYI: What Is Open Source?

Open source is a way of licensing software. It means that the software is freely distributable and contains the source code. This means that users can make copies, give them to friends, and even get a copy of the source code. Users can even modify the source code and then release their own version (though that release must also be open source).

The idea behind open source is to encourage users to examine the source code for a product and, if possible, to improve it. The belief is that through review and improvements by so many people, a product will reach a higher level of quality faster than commercial ones. There are a number of products available via open source licenses besides Snort, including products such as Open Office (**www.openoffice.org**), Linux (**www.linux.org**), and Gimp (**www.gimp.org**).

More details about open source software are available at **www.opensource.org/docs/definition.php.**

Snort works in one of three modes: sniffer, packet logger, and network intrusion-detection.

Sniffer In packet *sniffer mode,* the console (shell or command prompt) displays a continuous stream of the contents of all packets coming across that machine. This can be a very useful tool for a network administrator. Finding out what traffic is traversing a network can be the best way to determine where potential problems lie. It is also a good way to check whether transmissions are encrypted.

Packet Logger *Packet logger mode* is similar to sniffer mode. The difference is that the packet contents are written to a text file log rather than displayed in the console. This can be more useful for administrators who are scanning a large number of packets for specific items. Once the data is in a text file, users can scan for specific information using a word processor's search capability.

Network Intrusion-Detection In *network intrusion-detection* mode, Snort uses a heuristic approach to detecting anomalous traffic. This means it is rules-based and it learns from experience. A set of rules initially governs a process. Over time Snort combines what it finds with the settings to optimize performance. It then logs that traffic and can alert the network administrator. This mode requires the most configuration because the user can determine the rules she wishes to implement for the scanning of packets.

Snort works primarily from the command line (Shell in Unix/Linux, command prompt in Windows). Configuring Snort is mostly a matter of knowing the correct commands to enter and understanding their output. Anyone with even moderate experience with either Linux shell commands or DOS commands can quickly master the Snort configuration commands. Perhaps Snort's greatest advantage is its price: It is a free download. For any organization to not be using some IDS is inexcusable when a free product is available. Snort is a good tool when used in conjunction with host-based firewalls or as an IDS on each server to provide additional security.

Cisco Intrusion-Detection

The Cisco brand is widely recognized and well respected in the networking profession. As with their firewalls and their routers, Cisco has several models of intrusion-detection, each with a different focus/purpose. We will focus our attention on two of those products, the Cisco IDS 4200 Series Sensors and Cisco Catalyst 6500 Series Intrusion-Detection System (IDSM-2) Services Module. Information about all Cisco IDS solutions is available at: **www.cisco.com/warp/public/cc/pd/sqsw/sqidsz/index.shtml**.

Cisco IDS 4200 Series Sensors These devices are a bit different from what many people think of as IDS. Rather than being deployed at the perimeter in conjunction with a main firewall, the product is deployed anywhere in the network. That means that it can be used with the perimeter firewall or between any two subnets on a network. It utilizes heuristic methods and anomaly detection to detect potential attacks.

The purpose of these sensors is to provide protection within the network. Most IDS are designed with the perimeter of the network in mind. Having IDS inside the network provides a much more robust defense. Recall from Chapter 1 that a layered defense is always preferred over a perimeter defense. However, many organizations simply cannot afford to place sensors on every subnetwork, and this level of protection is beyond the needs of most organizations. Figure 5.1 shows an example of the deployment of such sensors.

It must be stressed that the configuration shown in Figure 5.1 is only one possible deployment. The sensors can be placed anywhere on a network.

These sensors also protect the communication between the administration software and the sensor itself. All communication with the sensor is secured either with SSH (Secure Shell, a protocol for securely logging into a remote Unix or Linux machine) or IPSec (Internet Protocol Security, a protocol used with Virtual Private Networks). Both technologies are discussed at some length in Chapter 6.

Perhaps the most interesting feature of the IDS 4200 is that when a sensor is set to monitor the firewall, it monitors for any change in the firewall policy or access control list (ACL). This is particularly important because a more talented hacker may attempt to compromise the firewall, thus making further incursions into the network much easier.

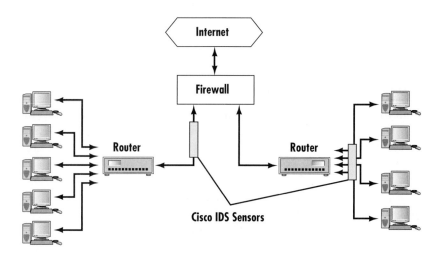

FIGURE 5.1 Cisco sensor deployment.

FYI: ACL

An Access Control List defines which users can access a device as well as which ports can be used for communication. Firewalls and routers use ACLs to determine who has what rights on that device. They also define what ports should be open for communication and which ones are blocked. If skilled hackers gain initial entry into a system, they will attempt to modify the ACL to allow them to re-enter with less difficulty in the future.

You can monitor the sensors through a relatively user-friendly Web interface. You can also configure them to send alerts about potential threats via many different methods, such as through an e-mail or pop up alert.

Cisco Catalyst 6500 Series Intrusion-Detection System (IDSM-2) Services Module This product is a rack-mounted hardware module that plugs into the network and monitors packets. Figure 5.2 shows this model.

The hardware uses Red Hat Linux as its operating system. This IDS solution monitors packets and logs anomalous activity. It also can be configured to alert the system administrator that some anomaly has occurred. This device is a traditional IDS designed to be used as part of a complete Cisco security solution, but it can certainly be used in conjunction with non-Cisco products.

One of the chief benefits of using Cisco security products is their widespread use across the industry and the availability of good training. The fact that so many organizations use Cisco indicates a high level of successful field testing, which generally indicates a reliable product. Cisco also sponsors a range of certifications on its products, making it easier to determine whether someone is qualified on a particular Cisco product.

Understanding and Implementing Honey Pots

A honey pot is a single machine set up to simulate a valuable server or even an entire subnetwork. The idea is to make the honey pot so attractive that if a hacker breaches the network's security, she will be attracted to the honey

FIGURE 5.2 The Cisco Catalyst 6500 IDS.

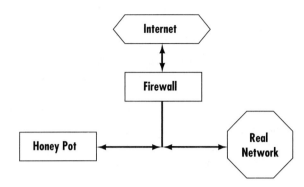

FIGURE 5.3 Honey pots.

pot rather than to the real system. Software can closely monitor everything that happens on that system, enabling tracking and perhaps identification of the intruder.

The underlying premise of the honey pot is that any traffic to the honey pot machine is considered suspicious. Because the honey pot is not a real machine, no legitimate users should have a reason to connect to it. Therefore, anyone attempting to connect to that machine can be considered a possible intruder. The honey pot system can entice him to stay connected long enough to trace where he is connecting from. Figure 5.3 illustrates the honey pot concept.

Specter

Specter is a software honey pot solution. Complete product information is available at **www.specter.com**. The Specter honey pot is comprised of a dedicated PC with the Specter software running on it. The Specter software can emulate the major Internet protocols/services such as HTTP, FTP, POP3, SMTP, and others, thus appearing to be a fully functioning server. The software runs on Windows 2000 or XP, but can simulate AIX, Solaris, Unix, Linux, Mac, and Mac OS X. Figure 5.4 shows the primary configuration window for Specter.

Specter works by appearing to run a number of services common to network servers. In fact in addition to simulating multiple operating systems, it can also simulate the following services:

- SMTP

- FTP

- TELNET

- FINGER

- POP3

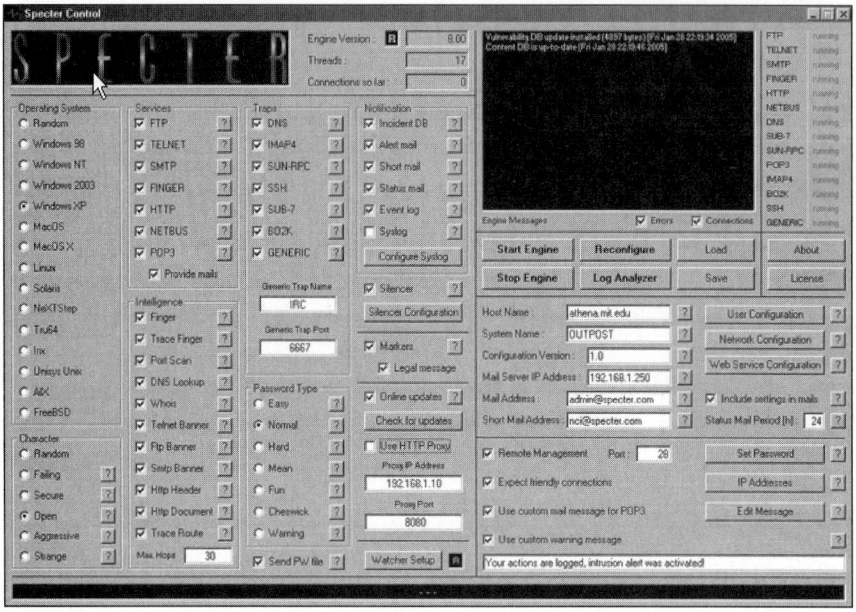

FIGURE 5.4 The Specter configuration window.

- IMAP4

- HTTP

- SSH

- DNS

- SUN-RPC

- NETBUS

- SUB-7

- BO2K

- GENERIC TRAP

Even though Specter appears to be running these servers, it is actually just monitoring all incoming traffic. Because it is not a real server for your network, no legitimate user should be connecting to it. Specter logs all traffic to the server for analysis. Users can set it up in one of five modes:

- **Open** – In this mode the system behaves like a badly configured server in terms of security. The downside of this mode is that you are most likely to attract and catch the least skillful hackers.

- **Secure** – This mode has the system behaving like a secure server.

- **Failing** – This mode is interesting in that it causes the system to behave like a server with various hardware and software problems. This might attract some hackers because such a system is likely to be vulnerable.

- **Strange** – In this mode the system behaves in unpredictable ways. This sort of behavior is likely to attract the attention of a more talented hacker and perhaps cause her to stay online longer trying to figure out what is going on. The longer the hacker stays connected, the better the chance of tracing her.

- **Aggressive** – This mode causes the system to actively try and trace back the intruder and derive his identity. This mode is most useful for catching the intruder.

In all modes, Specter logs the activity, including all information it can derive from the incoming packets. It also attempts to leave traces on the attacker's machine, which can provide clear evidence should civil or criminal action later be required.

Users can also configure a fake password file in all modes. These are particularly useful because most hackers attempt to access a password file to crack the passwords. If they are successful they can then log on as a legitimate user. The holy grail of hacking is getting the administrator's password. There are multiple ways to configure this fake password file:

- **Easy** – In this mode the passwords are easy to crack, leading a would-be intruder to believe that she has actually found legitimate passwords and usernames. Often a hacker with a legitimate logon will be less careful covering her tracks. If you know that logon is fake and the system is set up to monitor it, you can track it back to the hacker.

- **Normal** – This mode has slightly more difficult passwords than the easy mode.

- **Hard** – This mode has even harder passwords to crack. There is even a tougher version of this mode called *mean,* in which the passwords are very difficult to break so that the hacker can be traced while he is taking time to crack the passwords.

- **Fun** – This mode uses famous names as usernames. In my opinion this one, and the related one named *Cheswick,* have dubious security value.

- **Warning** – In this mode the hacker gets a warning telling him he has been detected if he is able to crack the password file. The theory behind this mode is that most hackers are simply trying to see if they can crack a system and do not have a specific objective. Letting this sort of hacker know he has been detected is often enough to scare him off.

The cost of this software system is about $900, and it requires a PC to install it on. The purpose of honey pots like Specter is not preventing intrusion. Instead, they minimize the damage once someone is in. They serve to direct the hacker's attention away from critical systems. They also can be very helpful in tracking down hackers.

Symantec Decoy Server

Because Symantec is such a prominent vendor for both antivirus software and firewall solutions, it should come as no surprise that it also has a honey pot solution. The Symantec product, Decoy Server, simulates being a real server by simulating many server functions, such as incoming and outgoing e-mail traffic. Full details about this product are available at **http://enterprisesecurity. symantec.com/content/displaypdf.cfm?pdfid=292**.

As the Decoy Server works as a honey pot, it also works as an IDS monitoring the network for signs of intrusion. If an attack is detected all traffic related to that attack is recorded for use later in whatever investigative, criminal, or civil procedures that may arise.

Decoy Server is designed to be part of a suite of enterprise security solutions that work together, including enterprise versions of Symantec's antivirus software, firewall software, and antispyware. The product is usually purchased as part of a volume licensing agreement for a complete security package.

Summary

A variety of IDS are available. Some are designed to run on the perimeter with the perimeter firewall, often in a host-based configuration. Others are designed to be sensors throughout your network or are a router-type appliance. Honey pots entice hackers to explore phantom servers with the goal of keeping them long enough to identify them.

A complete IDS solution should have a perimeter IDS working in conjunction with a perimeter firewall. The most complete IDS solution includes multiple sensors for each subnet. Ideally, an administrator places some IDS on each major server and implements a honey pot solution.

Clearly, such a level of expenditure and complexity is not possible in all circumstances. This level certainly provides the greatest security, but many organizations do not require, nor can they afford, this level of security. At a minimum, an organization should have an IDS running with the perimeter firewall. Because free IDS solutions are available, there is no reason not to have one.

Test Your Skills

MULTIPLE CHOICE QUESTIONS

1. IDS is an acronym for:
    A. intrusion-detection system
    B. intrusion deterrence system
    C. intrusion deterrence service
    D. intrusion-detection service

2. A series of ICMP packets sent to your ports in sequence might indicate what?
    A. a DoS attack
    B. a ping flood
    C. a packet sniffer
    D. a port scan

3. What is another term for preemptive blocking?
    A. intrusion deflection
    B. banishment vigilance
    C. user deflection
    D. intruder blocking

4. Which of the following is not a reason to avoid choosing infiltration as part of an IDS strategy?
    A. It can be time consuming.
    B. It requires knowledge of the target group.
    C. The group may retaliate.
    D. It can be expensive.

5. Attempting to attract intruders to a system set up to monitor them is called what?
    A. intrusion deterrence
    B. intrusion deflection
    C. intrusion banishment
    D. intrusion routing

6. A system that is set up for attracting and monitoring intruders is called what?

   A. fly paper

   B. trap door

   C. honey pot

   D. hacker cage

7. Attempting to make your system appear less appealing is referred to as what?

   A. intrusion deterrence

   B. intrusion deflection

   C. system camouflage

   D. system deterrence

8. Which of the following is not a profiling strategy used in anomaly detection?

   A. threshold monitoring

   B. resource profiling

   C. executable profiling

   D. system monitoring

9. Setting up parameters for acceptable use, such as the number of login attempts, and watching to see if those levels are exceeded is referred to as what?

   A. threshold monitoring

   B. resource profiling

   C. system monitoring

   D. executable profiling

10. Which of the following is a problem with the approach described in Question 8?

    A. It is difficult to configure.

    B. It misses many attacks.

    C. It yields many false positives.

    D. It is resource intensive.

11. A profiling technique that monitors how applications use resources is called what?

    A. system monitoring

    B. resource profiling

    C. application monitoring

    D. executable profiling

12. Snort is which type of IDS?

    A. router-based

    B. OS-based

    C. host-based

    D. client-based

13. Which of the following is not one of Snort's modes?

    A. sniffer

    B. packet logger

    C. network intrusion-detection

    D. packet filtering

14. Which type of IDS is the Cisco Sensor?

    A. anomaly detection

    B. intrusion deflection

    C. intrusion deterrence

    D. anomaly deterrence

15. Why might you run Specter in strange mode?

    A. It may confuse hackers and deter them from your systems.

    B. It will be difficult to determine the system is a honey pot.

    C. It may fascinate hackers and keep them online long enough to catch them.

    D. It will deter novice hackers.

16. What is the purpose of the *warning* configuration for Specter's e-mail file?

    A. to track hackers back to their source IPs

    B. to scare off at least novice hackers

    C. to keep your normal users honest

    D. to deter highly skilled hackers

EXERCISES

Exercise 5.1: Using Snort

Note: This is a longer exercise appropriate for groups. Refer to the chapter text for an explanation of the Snort product and features.

1. Go to the Snort.org Web site (**www.snort.org**).

2. Download Snort.

3. Using the vendor documentation or other resources, configure Snort as a packet sniffer. Use that resource to observe traffic on your network.

4. Compile statistics about your network's normal traffic. These statistics include mean packets per minute, top five destination IP addresses, top 10 source IP addresses, and so on.

Exercise 5.2: Using Snort as an IDS

1. Using the Snort installation from Exercise 5.1, configure Snort to do network intrusion-detection.

2. Set up rules for alerts by Snort.

Exercise 5.3: Open Source Honey Pots

Note: This exercise requires you to use an open source honey pot. One such free solution can be found at **www.projecthoneypot.org**, but feel free to use any solution you like. In fact, if possible, it is best to test out multiple solutions in order to compare results.

1. Install the honey pot on a lab machine.

2. Configure it according to the vendor documentation.

3. Have one student pose as a hacker attacking the honey pot.

4. The other student(s) should use the honey pot to detect that intrusion

Exercise 5.4: Infiltration

Note: In this exercise students should conduct only the preliminary steps and not the actual infiltration.

1. Identify an online group that would be a valuable target for infiltration.

2. Identify information that would assist in successfully intruding.

3. Create a fake identity that could be used for such an infiltration.

Exercise 5.5: Recommend an IDS

1. Assume you are working for a small organization that has a moderate security budget.

2. Select a particular IDS solution you would recommend for that organization.

3. Write your recommendations, including your reasons, in a memo format as if submitting them to a CIO or other decision maker.

PROJECTS

Project 5.1: IDS Strategy

Using Web sites and vendor documentation create a document that outlines a complete IDS plan for a network. Plan your entire IDS strategy assuming a budget of $2,000.

Project 5.2: Firewall-Based IDS

Using Web resources, books, or other resources as well as your own opinions, determine whether you think a firewall-based IDS or a separate IDS is a better solution. Write a memo (as if you were submitting it to a CIO or other decision maker) explaining your position, including your reasons for coming to this conclusion.

Project 5.3: How to Improve Honey Pots

By now you should have a good understanding of how honey pots work, and you should have actually used at least one honey pot. But like all security technology, honey pots are evolving. Describe, in detail, at least two improvements you would like to see in honey pot technology. This could include features not currently available, improved detection, or more aggressive responses. The following sites describe current honey pot technology and might be of use to you.

- **www.projecthoneypot.org/**
- **www.giac.org/practical/gsec/Michael_Sink_GSEC.pdf**
- **www.tracking-hackers.com/papers/honeypots.html**

Case Study

Tom is the security administrator for a defense contractor with highly sensitive data. The company has had threats from various antiwar groups threatening cyber attacks. Tom has been tasked with detecting intrusions and preventing them, and he has been given an extensive budget. He takes the following steps:

1. He implements Snort on the perimeter firewall.

2. He installs the Specter honey pot.

Are these steps adequate? If not, what other steps would you recommend?

Chapter | 6

Encryption

Chapter Objectives

After reading this chapter and completing the exercises, you will be able to do the following:

- Explain encryption concepts.
- Describe the history of encryption and modern encryption methods.
- Describe virtual private networks (VPNs).
- Use some simple decryption techniques.

Introduction

Encryption is a vital part of any network security strategy. As Chapter 4 explained, many firewall solutions have built-in encryption. No matter how secure the network is, if the data is not encrypted during transmission, then that data is vulnerable. Even most basic wireless routers for home users now offer encryption.

This chapter offers a basic overview of encryption and an explanation of how it works in order to help you make good decisions for your organization. A complete examination is beyond the scope of this book, but this chapter provides a "manager's understanding" of cryptography to help you ask the right questions about your organization's encryption needs.

The History of Encryption

Encrypting communications is a very old idea. People have found the need to send private communications for most of the history of civilization. The need for privacy originally arose from military and political needs, but has expanded beyond that. Businesses need to keep data private in order to maintain a competitive edge. People wish to keep certain information, such as their medical records and financial records, private.

For much of human history private communications meant encrypting written communiqués. Over the past century that has expanded to radio transmission, telephone communications, and computer/Internet communications. In the past several decades the encryption of computerized transmissions has actually become common. In fact it is more common to find computer/Internet communications encrypted than phone or radio. The digital environment makes implementing a particular type of encryption much easier.

Whatever the nature of the data you are encrypting, or the mode of transmitting the data, the basic concept is actually quite simple. Messages must be changed in such a way that they cannot be read easily by any party that intercepts them but can be decoded easily by the intended recipient. In this section you will examine a few historical methods of encryption. It should be noted that these are very old methods, and they cannot be used for secure communication today. An amateur could easily crack the methods discussed in this section. However, they are wonderful for conveying the concept of encryption without having to incorporate a great deal of math, which is required of the more complex encryption methods.

FYI: False Claims About Encryption

As you will see in this chapter, the basic concepts of encryption are very simple. Anyone with even rudimentary programming skills can write a program that implements one of the simple encryption methods examined here. However these methods are *not* secure and are included to illustrate fundamental encryption concepts only.

From time to time someone new to encryption discovers these basic methods, and in his enthusiasm attempts to create his own encryption method by making some minor modifications. While this can be a very stimulating intellectual exercise, it is only that. Users without training in advanced math or cryptography are extremely unlikely to stumble across a new encryption method that is effective for secure communications.

Amateurs frequently post claims that they have discovered the latest, unbreakable encryption algorithm on the Usenet newsgroup sci.crypt (if you are not familiar with Usenet, those groups are now accessible via the Groups link on **www.google.com**). Their algorithms are usually quickly broken. Unfortunately some people implement such a method into a software product and market it as secure.

Some distributors of insecure encryption methods and software do so out of simple greed and are intentionally defrauding an unsuspecting public. Others do so out of simple ignorance, honestly believing that their method is superior. Methods for evaluating encryption claims are discussed later in this chapter.

The Caesar Cipher

One of the oldest recorded encryption methods is the Caesar cipher. This name is based on a claim that this method was used by ancient Roman emperors. This method is very simple to implement, requiring no technological assistance. You choose some number by which to shift each letter of a text. For example if the text is

```
A cat
```

And you choose to shift by two letters, then the message becomes

```
C ecv
```

Or, if you choose to shift by three letters, it becomes

```
D fdw
```

In this example, you can choose any shifting pattern you wish. You can shift either to the right or left by any number of spaces you like. Because this is a very simple method to understand, it makes a good place to start our study of encryption. It is, however, extremely easy to crack. You see, any language has a certain letter and word frequency, meaning that some letters are used more frequently than others (Letter Frequency Distributions in the English Alphabet, 1998). In the English language, the most common single-letter word is *a*. The most common three-letter word is *the*. Those two rules alone could help you decrypt a Caesar cipher. For example, if you saw a string of seemingly nonsense letters and noticed that a three-letter word was frequently repeated in the message, you might easily surmise that this word was *the*—and the odds are highly in favor of this being correct.

Furthermore, if you frequently noticed a single-letter word in the text, it is most likely the letter *a*. You now have found the substitution scheme for *a*, *t*, *h*, and *e*. You can now either translate all of those letters in the message and attempt to surmise the rest or simply analyze the substitute letters used for *a*, *t*, *h*, and *e* and derive the substitution cipher that was used for this message. Decrypting a message of this type does not even require a computer. It could be done in less than ten minutes using pen and paper by someone with no background in cryptography.

Caesar ciphers belong to a class of encryption algorithms known as substitution ciphers. The name derives from the fact that each character in the unencrypted message is substituted by one character in the encrypted text. The particular substitution scheme used (e.g., $+2$ or $+1$) in a Caesar cipher is called a substitution alphabet (i.e., *b* substitutes for *a*, *u* substitutes for *t*, and so on). Because one letter always substitutes for one other letter, the Caesar cipher is sometimes called a ***mono-alphabet substitution*** method, meaning that it uses a single substitution for the encryption.

The Caesar cipher, however, is not useless. Since most programming languages have some function to convert a character or number to its ASCII code, a programmer can write a simple function that loops through text converting each character to its ASCII code, then either adding or subtracting the appropriate number. Again, it must be stressed that this is not a secure method of encrypting messages, but an interesting exercise to begin introducing you to the basic concepts of encryption.

Readers with a programming background are probably aware that most programming languages have some function to convert a character or number to its *ASCII code*. You can then write a simple function that loops through text converting each character to its ASCII code and then either adding or subtracting the appropriate number. Because ASCII codes exist for every key on a computer's keyboard, a cryptographer can use this to encrypt all the characters—not just the letters. Furthermore, the limitation against shifting more than 26 characters does not apply to ASCII codes. With ASCII codes, the maximum effective shift is 255. Although this method is not secure, it makes for an excellent learning exercise.

FYI: ASCII Codes

ASCII is a numeric code corresponding to every letter (both upper and lower cases), number, and key on a keyboard. All key strokes can be converted to a numeric ASCII code. For example, capital A is ASCII code 65, and the Return key is ASCII code 13. Table 6.1 shows the full ASCII conversion chart.

TABLE 6.1 ASCII chart.

Decimal	Value	Decimal	Value
000	NUL (Null char.)	008	BS (Backspace)
001	SOH (Start of Header)	009	HT (Horizontal Tab)
002	STX (Start of Text)	010	LF (Line Feed)
003	ETX (End of Text)	011	VT (Vertical Tab)
004	EOT (End of Transmission)	012	FF (Form Feed)
		013	CR (Carriage Return)
005	ENQ (Enquiry)	014	SO (Shift Out)
006	ACK (Acknowledgment)	015	SI (Shift In)
007	BEL (Bell)	016	DLE (Data Link Escape)

Decimal	Value	Decimal	Value
017	DC1 (XON) (Device Control 1)	047	/ (forward slash)
018	DC2 (Device Control 2)	048	0
019	DC3 (XOFF) (Device Control 3)	049	1
		050	2
020	DC4 (Device Control 4)	051	3
021	NAK (Negative Acknowledgment)	052	4
		053	5
022	SYN (Synchronous Idle)	054	6
023	ETB (End of Trans. Block)	055	7
024	CAN (Cancel)	056	8
025	EM (End of Medium)	057	9
026	SUB (Substitute)	058	: (colon)
027	ESC (Escape)	059	; (semi-colon)
028	FS (File Separator)	060	< (less than)
029	GS (Group Separator)	061	= (equal sign)
030	RS (Request to Send)(Record Separator)	062	> (greater than)
		063	? (question mark)
031	US (Unit Separator)	064	@ (AT symbol)
032	SP (Space)	065	A
033	! (exclamation mark)	066	B
034	" (double quote)	067	C
035	# (number sign)	068	D
036	$ (dollar sign)	069	E
037	% (percent)	070	F
038	& (ampersand)	071	G
039	' (single quote)	072	H
040	((left/opening parenthesis)	073	I
		074	J
041	) (right/closing parenthesis)	075	K
		076	L
042	* (asterisk)	077	M
043	+ (plus)	078	N
044	, (comma)	079	O
045	- (minus or dash)	080	P
046	. (dot)	081	Q

6

▶▶ CONTINUED ON NEXT PAGE

▶▶ CONTINUED

Decimal	Value	Decimal	Value
082	R	105	i
083	S	106	j
084	T	107	k
085	U	108	l
086	V	109	m
087	W	110	n
088	X	111	o
089	Y	112	p
090	Z	113	q
091	[(left/opening bracket)	114	r
092	\ (back slash)	115	s
093	] (right/closing bracket)	116	t
094	^ (caret/circumflex)	117	u
095	_ (underscore)	118	v
096	`	119	w
097	a	120	x
098	b	121	y
099	c	122	z
100	d	123	{ (left/opening brace)
101	e	124		(vertical bar)
102	f	125	} (right/closing brace)
103	g	126	~ (tilde)
104	h	127	DEL (delete)

Multi-Alphabet Substitution

Eventually, a slight improvement on the Caesar cipher was developed, called *multi-alphabet substitution.* In this scheme, you select multiple numbers by which to shift letters (i.e., multiple substitution alphabets). For example, if you select three substitution alphabets ($+2, -2, +3$), then

A CAT

becomes

C ADV

Notice that the fourth letter starts over with another $+2$, and you can see that the first A was transformed to C and the second A was transformed to *D*. This makes it more difficult to decipher the underlying text. While this is harder to decrypt than a Caesar cipher, it is not overly difficult. It can be done with simple pen and paper and a bit of effort. It can be cracked very quickly with a computer. In fact, no one would use such a method today to send any truly secure message, for this type of encryption is considered very weak.

Binary Operations

Shifting letters by a certain amount using mono-alphabet or multi-alphabet ciphers is only one approach to encryption; various operations on **binary numbers** (numbers made of only zeroes and ones) are well known to programmers and programming students. But for those readers not familiar with them, a brief explanation follows. When working with binary numbers, there are three operations not found in normal math: AND, OR, and XOR operations. Each is illustrated below.

AND To perform the AND operation, you take two binary numbers and compare them one place at a time. If both numbers have a one in both places, then the resultant number is a one. If not, then the resultant number is a zero, as you see here:

```
1  1  0  1
1  0  0  1
-------
1  0  0  1
```

OR The OR operation checks to see whether there is a one in either or both numbers in a given place. If so, then the resultant number is one. If not, the resultant number is zero, as you see here:

```
1  1  0  1
1  0  0  1
-------
1  1  0  1
```

XOR The XOR operation impacts your study of encryption the most. It checks to see whether there is a one in a number in a given place, but not in both numbers at that place. If it is in one number but not the other, then the resultant number is one. If not, the resultant number is zero, as you see here:

```
1  1  0  1
1  0  0  1
-------
0  1  0  0
```

XORing has a very interesting property in that it is reversible. If you XOR the resultant number with the second number, you get back the first number. And, if you XOR the resultant number with the first number, you get the second number.

```
0  1  0  0
1  0  0  1
-------
1  1  0  1
```

Binary encryption using the XOR operation opens the door for some rather simple encryption. Take any message and convert it to binary numbers and then XOR that with some key. Converting a message to a binary number is really a simple two-step process. First, convert a message to its ASCII code, then convert those codes to binary numbers. Each letter/number will generate an eight-bit binary number. Then you can use a random string of binary numbers of any given length as the key. Simply XOR your message with the key to get the encrypted text, then XOR it with the key again to retrieve the original message.

This method is easy to use and great for computer science students; however, it does not work well for truly secure communications because the underlying letter and word frequency remains. This exposes valuable clues that even an amateur cryptographer can use to decrypt the message. Yet, it does provide a valuable introduction to the concept of single-key encryption, which will be discussed in more detail in the next section. While simply XORing the text is not the method typically employed, single-key encryption methods are widely used today. For example, you could simply include a multi-alphabet substitution that was then XORed with some random bit stream—variations of which do exist in a few actual encryption methods currently used.

Modern cryptography methods, as well as computers, make decryption a rather advanced science. Therefore, encryption must be equally sophisticated in order to have a chance of success.

What you have seen so far regarding encryption is simply for educational purposes. As has been noted several times, you would not have a truly secure system if you implemented any of the previously mentioned encryption schemes. You may feel that this has been overstated in this text. However, it is critical that you have an accurate view of what encryption methods do and do not work. It is now time to discuss a few methods that are actually in use today.

The following Web sites offer more information about cryptography:

- Trinity College Computer Science Department History of Cryptography: **http://starbase.cs.trincoll.edu/~crypto/**

- The Stanford University History of Cryptography: **www-cs-education. stanford.edu/classes/sophomore-college/projects-97/cryptography/history.html**

- Cybercrimes.net: **www.cybercrimes.net/Cryptography/Articles/Hebert.html**

- Cypher Research Laboratories: **www.cypher.com.au/crypto_history.htm**

Understanding the simple methods described here and other methods listed on the aforementioned Web sites should give you a sense of how cryptography works as well as what is involved in encrypting a message. Regardless of whether you go on to study modern, sophisticated encryption methods, it is important for you to have some basic idea of how encryption works at a conceptual level. Having a basic grasp of how encryption works, in principle, will make you better able to understand the concepts of any encryption method you encounter in the real world.

FYI: Careers in Cryptography

Some readers might be interested in a career in cryptography. Basic knowledge of cryptography is enough to be a security administrator, but not enough to be a cryptographer. A strong mathematics background is essential for in-depth exploration of cryptography, particularly when pursuing a career in this field. An adequate background includes a minimum of the complete calculus sequence (through differential equations), statistics through basic probability theory, and number theory. A double major in computer science and mathematics is ideal. A minimum of a minor in mathematics is required, and familiarity with existing encryption methods is critical.

Learning About Modern Methods

Not surprisingly, modern methods of encryption are more secure than the historical methods just discussed. All of the methods discussed in this section are in use today and are considered reasonably secure.

In some cases the algorithm behind these methods requires a sophisticated understanding of mathematics. Number theory often forms the basis for encryption algorithms. Fortunately for our purposes it is not important that you have the exact details of these encryption algorithms; this means that you don't require a strong mathematics background to follow this material. More important is a general understanding of how a particular encryption method works and how secure it is.

PGP

PGP, a public key system, stands for ***Pretty Good Privacy.*** It is a widely used system that is considered very secure by most experts (International

Caution

Encryption Strength

Federal law prohibits the exportation of encryption beyond a certain strength. This means that if you are in the United States, you cannot market any product outside the United States if that product has any encryption technology that exceeds the federal limits. The exact limit is currently being contested in various court cases. It is recommended that you consult current federal guidelines before implementing encryption in your organization.

PGP Web site, 2004). There are several software implementations available as freeware for most desktop operating systems. There are PGP plug-ins for Netscape Messenger, MSN Messenger, and many other popular communications software packages (McCune, 2004). A simple Yahoo or Google search for *PGP* will help you find many of these software products.

The following Web pages are also good sources of information for finding implementations of PGP:

- The International PGP page: **www.no.pgpi.org/**

- The MIT PGP page: **http://web.mit.edu/network/pgp.html**

- Freeware PGP versions: **www.pgpi.org/products/pgp/versions/freeware/**

- Where to get PGP: **http://cryptography.org/getpgp.htm**

PGP was invented by Phil Zimmerman (Zimmerman, 2004). Before creating PGP, Mr. Zimmerman had been a software engineer for 20 years and had experience with existing forms of cryptography. A great deal of controversy surrounded the birth of PGP because it was created without an easy means for government intrusion and its encryption was considered too strong for export. This caused Zimmerman to be the target of a three-year government investigation. However those legal matters are now resolved, and PGP is now one of the most widely used encryption methods available.

PGP is a ***public key system***. That means one key encrypts the message, and a separate one decrypts it. The important things to know about PGP are that it is:

- A public key encryption.

- Considered quite secure.

- Available free of charge.

These facts make it well worth your time to investigate PGP as a possible solution for your organization's encryption needs.

Public Key Encryption

In our discussion of PGP we mentioned the term public key encryption. This of course leads us to the question of what is public key encryption? Public key encryption is essentially the opposite of single-key encryption. With any public key encryption algorithm, one key is used to encrypt a message (called the public key) and another is used to decrypt the message. You can freely distribute your public key so that anyone can encrypt a message to send to you, but only you have the private key and only you can decrypt the message. The actual mathematics behind the creation and applications of the keys is a bit complex and beyond the scope of this book. Many public key algorithms are dependent, to some extent, on large prime numbers, factoring, and number theory.

Many commonly used algorithms, such as PGP, use public key encryption. It is very easy to implement since the public key can be freely distributed to anyone, and sometimes put on a Web site for download.

Data Encryption Standard

Data Encryption Standard, or *DES* as it is often called, was developed by IBM in the early 1970s. DES uses a *symmetric key system.* Recall from our earlier discussion that this means the same key is used to encrypt and to decrypt the message. The DES uses short keys and relies on complex procedures to protect its information. The actual DES algorithm is quite complex. The basic concept, however, is as follows (Federal Information Processing Standards, 1993):

1. The data is divided into 64-bit blocks, and those blocks are then transposed.
2. Transposed data is then manipulated by 16 separate steps of encryption, involving substitutions, bit-shifting, and logical operations using a 56-bit key.
3. The data is then further scrambled using a swapping algorithm.
4. Finally, the data is transposed one last time.

More information about DES is available at the Federal Information Processing Standards Web site at **www.itl.nist.gov/fipspubs/fip46-2.htm**.

One advantage that DES offers is efficiency. Some implementations of DES offer data throughput rates on the order of hundreds of megabytes per second. In plain English, what this means is that it can encrypt a great deal of data very quickly. You might assume that 16 steps would cause encryption to be quite slow; however, that is not the case using modern computer equipment. The problem with DES is the same problem that all symmetric key algorithms have: How do you transmit the key without it becoming compromised? This issue led to the development of public key encryption.

Another advantage of DES is the complexity with which it scrambles the text. DES uses 18 distinct steps to scramble the text. This yields a very scrambled text that is very difficult to break.

It should also be noted that while DES is still used widely today, a more recent version of DES known as DES3 is available. This algorithm is also commonly referred to as Triple DES. Triple DES is just the next step in the evolution of DES operation, hence its operation is quite simple. Its single key is actually divided into three 64-bit keys, for an overall key length of 192 bits. The entire 192-bit key is entered, and then Triple DES DLL breaks that key into three sub-keys. The procedure for encryption is exactly the same as regular DES, but it is repeated three times (hence the name Triple DES). You can find more information on Triple DES at these Web sites:

- Triple DES Encryption (an Overview): **www.tropsoft.com/ strongenc/des3.htm**

- What is Triple DES: **www.tropsoft.com/strongenc/ des3.htm**

- Wikipedia Triple DES: **http://en.wikipedia.org/wiki/Triple_DES**

RSA

The *RSA* method is a very widely used encryption algorithm. You cannot discuss cryptography without at least some discussion of RSA. This is a public key method developed in 1977 by three mathematicians, Ron Rivest, Adi Shamir, and Len Adleman. The name RSA is derived from the first letter of each mathematician's last name (Burnett and Paine, 2001).

One significant advantage of RSA is that it is a public key encryption

---

FYI: Basic Math Behind RSA

The following is a brief primer on the basic math underlying RSA.

Two large prime numbers are selected and then multiplied together: $n=p*q$.

We then let $f(n) = (p-1)(q-1)$, and $e>1$ such that *greatest common denominator* $(e, f(n))=1$. Here e will have a large probability of being co-prime to $f(n)$, if n is large enough and e will be part of the encryption key.

If we solve the equation for d, the pair of integers (e, n) are the public key and (d, n) form the private key. (The actual equation is based on linear algebra and is not really critical for this discussion. You can reference details in the RSA Security's Official Guide to Cryptography, or you can do a Web search and find the details on the Web sites below). Encryption of M can be accomplished by an equation using these integers for the keys.

---

method. That means there are no concerns with distributing the keys for the encryption. However RSA is much slower than DES.

RSA has become a very popular encryption method. It is considered quite secure and is often used in situations where a high level of security is needed. More details are available at these Web sites:

- The math behind RSA: **http://world.std.com/~franl/crypto/ rsa-guts.html**

- RSA from MathWorld: **http://mathworld.wolfram.com/ RSAEncryption.html**

- How RSA works: **www.muppetlabs.com/~breadbox/txt/rsa.html**

Blowfish

Blowfish is a symmetric block cipher. This means that it uses a single key to both encrypt and decrypt the message and works on "blocks" of the message at a time. It uses a variable-length key ranging from 32 to 448 bits (MyCrypto.net, 2004). This flexibility in key size allows you to use it in various situations. Blowfish was designed in 1993 by Bruce Schneier. It has been analyzed extensively by the cryptography community and has gained wide acceptance. It is also a non-commercial (i.e., free of charge) product, thus making it attractive to budget-conscious organizations.

In short, this is an alternative to DES. One advantage it has over DES is its broader range of key lengths. One disadvantage is that it has not been around as long as DES and, therefore, has not been as thoroughly tested yet. Additionally, some studies have shown Blowfish to be even faster than DES (which is faster than RSA). The speed of the algorithm is an important consideration when a large amount of data must be encrypted.

6

FYI: Block Ciphers and Stream Ciphers

A block cipher operates on blocks of fixed length, often 64 or 128 bits. In a block cipher, a cryptographic key and algorithm are applied to a block of data (for example, 64 contiguous bits) at once as a group rather than to one bit at a time. Stream ciphers simply take the text as an ongoing stream, encrypting each bit as it encounters it. Stream ciphers tend to be faster than block ciphers. A stream cipher generates what is called a *keystream* (a sequence of bits used as a key). Encryption is accomplished by combining the keystream with the plaintext, usually with the bitwise XOR operation.

AES

AES stands for *Advanced Encryption Standard.* This standard uses the *Rijndael algorithm.* The developers of this algorithm have suggested multiple alternative pronunciations for the name, including "reign dahl," "rain doll," and "rhine dahl." This algorithm was developed by two Belgian researchers, Joan Daemen of Proton World International and Vincent Rijmen, a postdoctoral researcher in the Electrical Engineering Department of Katholieke Universiteit Leuven.

The AES specifies three key sizes: 128, 192, and 256 bits. By comparison, DES keys are 56 bits long, and Blowfish allows varying lengths up to 448 bits. AES uses a block cipher. Interested readers can find detailed specifications for this algorithm, including a detailed discussion of the mathematics, at: **http://csrc.nist.gov/CryptoToolkit/aes/rijndael/Rijndael-ammended.pdf.**

This algorithm is widely used (as shown in the discussion of firewalls in Chapter 4), considered very secure, and therefore a good choice for many encryption scenarios.

IDEA Encryption

IDEA is another block cipher. The acronym IDEA stands for ***International Data Encryption Algorithm.*** This particular algorithm works with 64 bit blocks of data, 2 at a time and uses a 128-bit key. The procedure is fairly complicated and uses sub-keys generated from the key to carry out a series of modular arithmetic and XOR operations on segments of the 64-bit plaintext block. The encryption scheme uses a total of 52 16-bit sub-keys. These are generated from the 128-bit sub-key with the following procedure:

- The 128-bit key is split into eight 16-bit keys, which are the first 8 sub-keys.

- The digits of the 128-bit key are shifted 25 bits to the left to make a new key, which is then split into the next eight 16-bit sub-keys.

- The second step is repeated until the 52 sub-keys have been generated. The encryption consists of eight rounds of encrypting.

You can find out more about this algorithm from the following Web sites:

- The IDEA Encryption Algorithm: **www.finecrypt.net/ idea.html**

- IDEA Implementation: **www.haenni.info/thesis/tutorials/ idea_ia64/**

- IDEA: **www.cs.nps.navy.mil/curricula/tracks/security/notes/ chap04_43.html**

Selecting a Block Cipher

If you have decided on a block cipher, which one do you choose? We have examined three here, all with different strengths and weaknesses. There is no single answer that is right for everyone. Several factors are involved in the selection of an encryption algorithm. Here are a few things to keep in mind:

- If you encrypt large amounts of data, then speed of the encryption might be almost as important as security.

- If you have standard business data, then almost any of the well known, accepted encryption methods will probably be secure enough, and you can focus on things like key length and speed in your decision-making process. However if you are sending highly sensitive data, such as research or military data, you should be more concerned about security, even at the expense of speed.

- Variable length keys are important only if you need them. If you have some encryption products used inside the United States and some outside, then at least two lengths are needed. If you have some data you wish more strongly encrypted even if it means slower speed, and other data that needs to be fast but not as secure, then a variable length key is also important.

Identifying Good Encryption

Dozens of other encryption methods are released to the public for free or patented and sold for profit every year. However, this particular area of the computer industry is replete with frauds and charlatans. One need only search any search engine for "encryption" to find a plethora of ads for the latest greatest "unbreakable" encryption. If you are not knowledgeable about encryption, how do you separate legitimate encryption methods from frauds?

While there is never any guaranteed way to detect fraud, the following guidelines should help you avoid most fraudulent encryption claims:

- **"Unbreakable":** Anyone with any experience in cryptography knows that there is no such thing as an unbreakable code. There are codes that have not yet been broken. There are codes that are very hard to break. However, when someone claims that his method is completely unbreakable, you should be suspicious.

- **"Certified":** There is no recognized certification process for encryption methods, so any "certification" the company has is totally worthless.

- **Inexperienced vendors:** Find out about the experience of any company marketing a new encryption method. What is the experience of the people working with it? Do they have a background in math, encryption, or algorithms? If not, have they submitted their method to experts in peer reviewed journals? Are they at least willing to disclose how their method works so that it can be fairly judged?

Some experts claim you should only use widely known methods like Blowfish and PGP. I disagree. It is certainly possible to have a very secure system using less well-known or even new encryption methods. All of the widely used methods of today were once new and untested. However, it is necessary to take extra precautions to ensure that you are not being mislead when using a less well known method.

A Web site designed by Matt Curtin and titled "Snake Oil Warning Signs" gives its own list of warning signs to avoid (**www.interhack.net/ people/cmcurtin/snake-oil-faq.html**). It also explains some of the basics of cryptography.

Understanding Digital Signatures and Certificates

There has been much discussion of *digital signatures* in technical magazines in the past few years. However a digital signature is not a signature in the traditional sense, as in a signature on a document. A digital signature is an extra piece of data sent along with a message, often with an e-mail attachment, that is used to verify that the message actually comes from the person who claims to have sent it.

Digital signatures are based on public/private key encryption. They also use digital certificates. Certificates are issued by a *certificate authority (CA).* Getting such a certificate requires one to submit a great deal of personal information, as well as a fee. That fee can vary depending on the particular certificate authority. It can range from a small nominal fee to several hundred dollars. You also supply the CA with your public key. The CA uses all this information to generate a certificate encrypted with its private key and sends it back to you. The standard for digital certificates is *X.509*. It contains information about your identity, your public key, and the length of times for which it is valid. Choose a well-known and widely trusted CA.

Certificates are also sometimes used with software, especially software that is deployed on the Internet. When used with downloadable software, a certificate verifies that the software is from a reputable source and is not a Trojan horse or other malware. Whether used with software or documents, the purpose of the digital signature or certificate is to verify the original sender's identity. Various laws have held that digital signatures are as valid as traditional signatures. The following Web sites offer more details on the legal aspects of digital signatures:

- Ladas & Perry Intellectual Property Law: **www.ladas.com/ BULLETINS/2002/0202Bulletin/USElectronicSignature.html**

- AdLaw: **www.adlawbyrequest.com/legislation/digsigpass.shtml**

- BBC: **http://news.bbc.co.uk/1/hi/business/1446426.stm**

For reputable certificate authorities consider these Web sites:

- Verisign: **www.verisign.com/**

- Thwate: **www.thawte.com/**

- GCFN: **www.gcfn.net/ca.html**

Understanding and Using Decryption

Obviously if one can encrypt a message, one can decrypt it as well. The preferred method is, of course, to have the key and the algorithm, and hopefully the software used to encrypt and then easily decrypt the message. However people attempting to breach your security will not have the algorithm and key and will want to break your encrypted transmissions or data.

Decryption is a science much like encryption. It employs various mathematical methods to crack encryption. You can find a number of utilities on the Web that will actually crack encryption for you. As discussed earlier, there really is no such thing as unbreakable encryption. However the more secure an encryption technique is, the longer it will take to crack. If it takes months or years of dedicated effort to crack, then your data is secure. By the time someone cracks it, the information will likely no longer be relevant or useful to them.

Security professionals and security-savvy network administrators frequently use the same tools to inspect their systems. Using the tools of hackers to try to crack an encryption method is a practical and straightforward way of testing the security of data.

Though not exactly the same as breaking encrypted transmissions, cracking passwords is similar. If someone is able to successfully crack a password, particularly the administrator password, then other security measures are rendered irrelevant.

SolarWinds

The SolarWinds Web site, **www.solarwinds.net/Tools/Professional+/index.htm**, lists commercial tools for decrypting passwords. Most notable is their router password decryption that attempts to crack router passwords. This tool, designed specifically for Cisco routers, can be very helpful for checking the password security of routers—a vital part of a security audit.

SolarWinds has a wide range of other security utilities. Most are very inexpensive and available in free evaluation versions. Their products have very user-friendly interfaces. This is important because many of the commonly used hacking tools are command-line based and not intuitive to use.

Brutus

Brutus is a well-known and widely used password cracker, popular in the hacking community. It is available for multiple Windows versions and can be downloaded for free from **www.hoobie.net/brutus/**. It uses a text file as the basis for attempting to "guess" passwords. Using this tool you can take information about a target and come up with a lengthy list of possible passwords to try. The main screen of Brutus is shown in Figure 6.1.

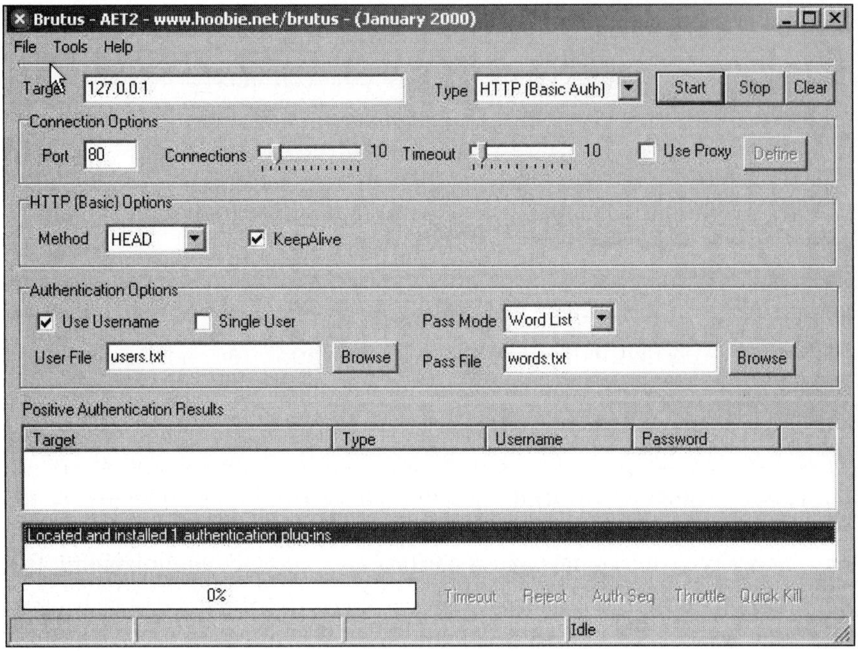

FIGURE 6.1 Brutus.

Select an IP address, which uses the loop back address by default. Then choose a mode. A segment in the middle of the screen labeled *Authentication Options* contains most of the things you will use to set up your password cracking scan. This segment is displayed in Figure 6.2. Note that you can choose one text file for it to use to guess usernames and one for passwords.

Brutus includes a text file of commonly used passwords. If you were trying to guess a person's password, you would simply add to that text file probable words. For example, you might add jones, cowboys, aikman, and so on to the list if trying to crack the password of a Dallas Cowboys fan. This example also illustrates the importance of not choosing passwords related to your life or interest, which can be guessed.

Also, note that you can select a Pass Mode. The mode determines whether Brutus will use your list or simply brute force. When Brutus uses brute force, it simply tries every possible combination within the parame-

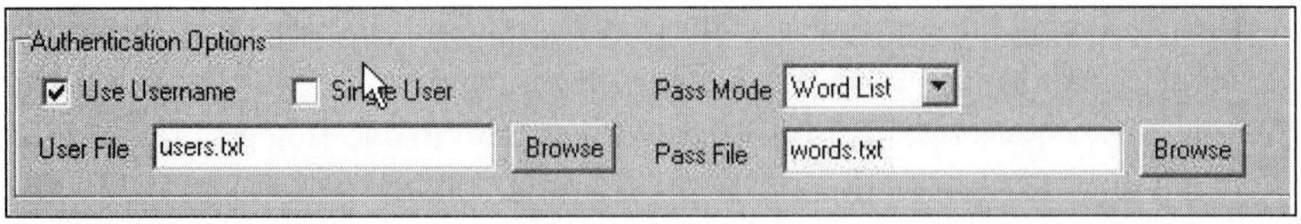

FIGURE 6.2 Authentication options.

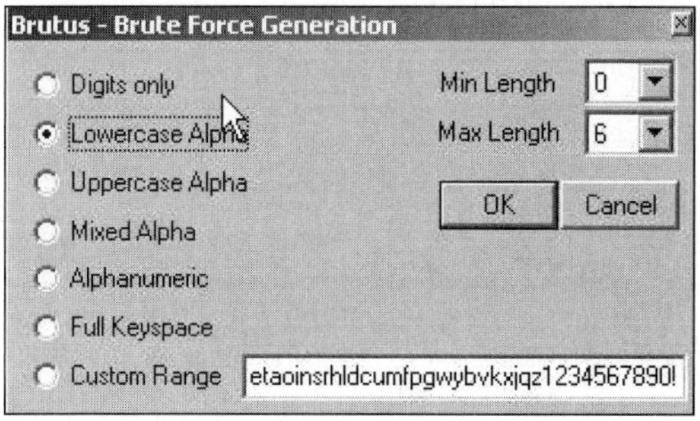

FIGURE 6.3 Brute force options.

ters you set. When you select brute force you will see a button with the caption *range*. Clicking that button brings up a screen such as the one shown in Figure 6.3. It allows you to determine the parameters for the brute force attack.

You can choose to use digits only, alphabet characters, some mix, and even to use a custom list of characters. You can also choose minimum and maximum lengths. If you know the target machine has a policy of passwords that must contain numbers and letters and must be 6 to 10 characters long, then select that range to do your scan.

An examination of Brutus and other password crackers ought to accomplish two things. First it provides you with a tool for checking the security of your own passwords. Second, it should make clear the critical nature of good password policies. Longer passwords are tougher to crack, and limiting the number of failed log in attempts prevents a product such as Brutus from simply hammering away until it succeeds.

John the Ripper

John the Ripper is another password cracker very popular with both network administrators and hackers. It can be downloaded for free from **www.openwall.com/john/**.

This product is completely command-line based and has no Windows interface. It enables the user to select text files for word lists to attempt cracking a password. While John the Ripper is less convenient to use because of its command-line interface, it has been around for a long time and is well regarded by both the security and hacking communities. Interestingly, there is a tool available at **www.openwall.com/passwdqc/** that ensures your passwords cannot easily be cracked by John the Ripper.

John the Ripper works with password files rather than attempting to crack live passwords on a given system. Passwords are usually encrypted and in a file on the operating system. Hackers frequently try to get that file off of a machine and download it to their own system so they can crack it at will. They might also look for discarded media in your dumpster in order to find old backup tapes that might contain password files. Each operating system stores that file in a different place:

- In Linux, it is */etc/passwd*.
- In Windows 95, it is in a *.pwl* file.
- In Windows 2000, it is in a hidden *.sam* file.

After you have downloaded John the Ripper, you can run it by typing in (at a command line) the word *john* followed by the file you wish it to try and crack:

```
john passwd
```

To make it use a wordlist with rules only, type:

```
john -wordfile:/usr/dict/words -rules passwd
```

Cracked passwords will be printed to the terminal and saved in a file called *john.pot,* found in the directory into which you installed John the Ripper.

Other Password Crackers

There are many other password crackers, many of which can be found on the Internet and downloaded for free. The following list of Web sites may be useful in that search:

- Russian password crackers: **www.password-crackers.com/ crack.html**
- Password recovery: **www.elcomsoft.com/prs.html**
- Crak Software: **www.crak.com/**
- LastBit password recovery: **http://lastbit.com/mso/Default.asp**

Password crackers should be used only by administrators to test their own systems' defenses. Attempting to crack another person's password and infiltrate her system has both ethical and legal ramifications.

Exploring the Future of Encryption

With improved mathematical methods for decryption and increased computing power, it is only a matter of time before the widely used encryption methods of today are cracked. That is simply the way technology works: Today's hottest new technology will be tomorrow's outdated, obsolete history lesson. The question remains: Where is encryption headed in the future? One direction is to simply create longer and more complex keys. New encryption algorithms also pop up from time to time. However the most promising method on the horizon seems to be quantum encryption.

Quantum encryption is based on basic quantum physics. Quantum physics is a theory of physics used to describe subatomic particles. This theory has shown that at the subatomic level everything is structured in discrete levels. For example the energy that an electron or any other subatomic particle can have is discrete. It can be at one level or at another level but not in between (this is why there are electron shells where electrons are found and certain discrete energy levels). Quantum physicists have also found that the subatomic world behaves much differently than the reality we experience in our day-to-day world.

One of the ways in which subatomic particles behave differently is *quantum entanglement*. In this rather bizarre phenomenon, two particles become "entangled" so that their states (properties such as polarization and spin) are linked. Changing the state of one particle immediately changes the state of the other particle. This effect is not limited by distance. The two particles might be 10 meters or 10,000 kilometers apart. How this occurs is simply unknown. There does not appear to be any transmission between the two particles. This has lead to experiments with "quantum teleportation," or the instantaneous transfer of information. For more information on quantum physics (for the layman) consider these sources:

- What is Quantum Physics: **www.jracademy.com/~jtucek/science/what.html**

- Wikipedia Quantum Mechanics: **http://en.wikipedia.org/wiki/Quantum_physics**

- *In Search of Schrodinger's Cat* by John Gribbon

One might enlist the aid of quantum physics in order to improve encryption in a number of ways. One way that quantum physics might aid in encryption is via the use of computers based on quantum mechanics. Such computers, though purely theoretical at this point, would be orders of magnitude faster than the fastest current computers, allowing for better methods of both encryption and decryption.

Another way in which quantum physics could aid in encryption is by assisting in the transfer of keys. If keys are transferred using the states of subatomic particles, any interference with those particles (such as trying to read them) would actually change the state, thus destroying the key. More information on quantum encryption is available at the following sources:

- Wikipedia Quantum Encryption: **http://en.wikipedia.org/wiki/Quantum_cryptography**

- The Oxford Center for Quantum Computation: **www.qubit.org/**

- The Dartmouth Quantum Cryptography Tutorial: **www.cs.dartmouth.edu/~jford/crypto.html**

- *PC Magazine*, Quantum Cryptography: **www.pcmag.com/article2/0%2C4149%2C1132786%2C00.asp**

Summary

Encryption is a basic element of computer security. You should never send sensitive data that has not been encrypted. Encrypting your system's hard drives is also a very good idea, so that if they are stolen, the valuable data on the drives is less likely to be compromised. Reading this chapter won't qualify you as a cryptographer, but it does offer a basic outline of how cryptography works. In the following exercises, you will practice using different cipher methods and learn more about a number of encryption methods.

Test Your Skills

MULTIPLE CHOICE QUESTIONS

1. Why is encryption an important part of security?
   A. No matter how secure your network is, the data being transmitted is still vulnerable without encryption.
   B. Encrypted transmissions will help stop Denial of Service Attacks.
   C. A packet that is encrypted will travel faster across networks.
   D. Encrypted transmissions are only necessary with VPNs.

2. Which of the following is the oldest known encryption method?
   A. PGP
   B. multi-alphabet
   C. Caesar cipher
   D. cryptic cipher

3. Which of the following is the primary weakness in the Caesar cipher?
   A. It does not disrupt letter frequency.
   B. It does not use complex mathematics.
   C. It does not use a public key system.
   D. There is no significant weakness; the Caesar cipher is adequate for most encryption uses.

4. An improvement on the Caesar cipher that uses more than one shift is called a what?

   A. DES encryption

   B. multi-alphabet substitution

   C. IDEA

   D. Triple DES

5. Which binary mathematical operation can be used for a simple encryption method?

   A. bit shift

   B. OR

   C. XOR

   D. bit swap

6. Why is the method described in Question 5 not secure?

   A. It does not change letter or word frequency.

   B. The mathematics are flawed.

   C. It does not use a symmetric key system.

   D. The key length is too short.

7. Which encryption method is most widely available as an add-in for various applications, including e-mail clients?

   A. DES

   B. RSA

   C. Caesar cipher

   D. PGP

8. Which of the following is a symmetric key system using blocks?

   A. RSA

   B. DES

   C. PGP

   D. Blowfish

9. What is the primary advantage of the encryption algorithm described in Question 8?

   A. It is complex.

   B. It is unbreakable.

   C. It uses asymmetric keys.

   D. It is relatively fast.

10. What size key does this system use?

    A. 255 bit

    B. 128 bit

    C. 56 bit

    D. 64 bit

11. What type of encryption uses a different key to encrypt the message than it uses to decrypt the message?

    A. private key

    B. public key

    C. symmetric

    D. secure

12. Which of the following is an encryption method developed by three mathematicians in the 1970s?

    A. PGP

    B. DES

    C. DSA

    D. RSA

13. Which encryption algorithm uses a variable length symmetric key?

    A. RSA

    B. ADEA

    C. DES

    D. PGP

14. Which of the following encryption algorithms uses three key ciphers in a block system, and uses the Rijndael algorithm?

    A. DES

    B. RSA

    C. AES

    D. NSA

15. If you are using a block cipher to encrypt large amounts of data, which of the following would be the most important consideration when deciding which cipher to use (assuming all of your possible choices are well known and secure):

    A. size of the keys used

    B. speed of the algorithm

    C. whether or not it has been used by any military group

    D. number of keys used

16. Which of the following uses a total of 52 16-bit sub-keys?

    A. AES

    B. DES

    C. Triple DES

    D. IDEA

17. Which of the following is the most common legitimate use for a password cracker?

    A. There is no legitimate use for a password cracker.

    B. military intelligence agents using it to break enemy communications

    C. testing the encryption of your own network

    D. trying to break the communications of criminal organizations in order to gather evidence

18. What is a digital signature?

    A. a piece of encrypted data added to other data to verify the sender

    B. a scanned-in version of your signature, often in .jpg format

    C. a signature that is entered via a digital pad or other device

    D. a method for verifying the recipient of a document

19. What is the purpose of a certificate?

    A. to verify that software is virus free

    B. to guarantee that a signature is valid

    C. to validate the sender of a digital signature or software

    D. to validate the recipient of a document

20. Who issues certificates?

    A. the UN encryption authority

    B. the United States Department of Defense

    C. a private certificate authority

    D. the Association for Computing Machinery

6

EXERCISES

Exercise 6.1: Using the Caesar Cipher

Note: This exercise is well suited for group or classroom exercises.

1. Write a sentence in normal text.

2. Use a Caesar cipher of your own design to encrypt it.

3. Pass it to another person in your group or class.

4. Time how long it takes that person to break the encryption.

5. (optional) Compute the mean time for the class to break Caesar ciphers.

Exercise 6.2: Using Binary Block Ciphers

1. Write a single sentence in normal text.

2. Convert the text to ASCII. There are several Web sites with ASCII code tables, such as **http://www.asciitable.com**.

3. Then convert each character to binary.

4. Now create a random 16 bit key. You can literally simply write down a random string of 1s and 0s.

5. XOR that key with your text.

6. Pass it to another student in class and give them a chance to decipher it.

7. When you have given all students adequate opportunity to break their fellow students' encryption, have them give each other the appropriate key.

Exercise 6.3: Using PGP

1. Download a PGP attachment for your favorite e-mail client. A Web search for PGP and your e-mail client (e.g., "PGP and Outlook" or "PGP and Eudora") should locate both modules and instructions.

2. Install and configure the PGP module.

3. Send encrypted messages to and from a classmate.

Exercise 6.4: Certificate Authorities

1. Search the Web for certificate authorities.

2. Compare two certificate authorities. Which of the two would you recommend?

3. What reasons would you give a client for recommending the certificate authority you chose?

Exercise 6.5: Password Cracking

1. Download a password cracker of your choice.

2. Attempt to crack the password on your own PC.

3. Describe the results of your experiment. Were you able to crack the password?

4. How long did it take? How does changing your password to make it more difficult affect the time it takes to crack the password?

PROJECTS

Project 6.1: RSA Encryption

Using the Web or other resources, write a brief paper about quantum encryption. Of particular interest should be the current state of research in that field (as opposed to simple background/history). You should also address what significant impediments there are to implementing quantum encryption.

Project 6.2: Programming Caesar Cipher

Note: This project is for those students with some programming background.

Write a simple program, in any language you prefer or in the language your instructor recommends, that can perform a Caesar cipher. This chapter explains how this cipher works and offers some ideas for how to use ASCII codes for encryption in any standard programming language.

Project 6.3: Historical Encryption

Find an encryption method that has been used historically but is no longer used (such as the Enigma cipher of the Germans in World War II). Describe how that encryption method works, paying particular attention to how it contrasts with more modern methods.

Project 6.4: Password Cracking

Follow the steps in Exercise 6.5 with at least 2 other password cracking utilities. Then write a report comparing and contrasting the password crackers. Note which one you think is most efficient. Also explain how using such a utility can be beneficial to a network administrator.

Case Study

Bob is the network administrator for an insurance company. The data they send and receive via e-mail is not classified, but for legal reasons should remain confidential. Bob chooses a commercial encryption package using a brand new encryption algorithm. The vendor assures him that their method is unbreakable and is military grade encryption.

Was this choice the best one for Bob? If not, what would you have chosen?

Chapter | 7

Virtual Private Networks

Chapter Objectives

After reading this chapter and completing the exercises, you will be able to do the following:

- Use a virtual private network (VPN).
- Use point-to-point tunneling protocol (PPTP) as an encryption tool for VPNs.
- Use layer 2 tunneling protocol (L2TP) as an encryption tool for VPNs.
- Add security and privacy to a communication using IPSec.
- Understand and evaluate VPN solutions.

Introduction

Earlier chapters have focused primarily on security within a network. However, what happens when remote users wish to log on to a network, as distinct from a remote user simply accessing a Web server or ftp server on the network? This process involves a remote user, perhaps an entire remote office, connecting to the network and accessing resources just as if he were on your local network. This clearly presents significant security issues.

Virtual private networks, or VPNs, are becoming a common way to connect remotely to a network in a secure fashion. A VPN creates a private network connection over the Internet to connect remote sites or users together. Instead of using a dedicated connection such as leased lines, a VPN uses virtual connections routed through the Internet from the remote site or user to the private network. Security is accomplished by encrypting all of the transmissions.

The concept behind a VPN is to allow a remote user network access just as if she were local to the private network. This means not only connecting her to the network as if she were local but also making the connection secure. Because most organizations have many employees traveling and working from home, remote network access has become a very important security concern. Users want access, and administrators want security. The VPN is the current standard for providing both.

Basic VPN Technology

In order to accomplish its purpose, the VPN must emulate a direct network connection. This means it must provide both the same level of access and the same level of security. In order to emulate a dedicated point-to-point link, data is **encapsulated,** or wrapped, with a header that provides routing information allowing it to transmit across the Internet to reach its destination. This creates a virtual network connection between the two points. The data being sent is also encrypted, thus making that virtual network private.

Internet Week (Salamone, 1998) gives an excellent definition of a VPN: "a combination of tunneling, encryption, authentication, and access control technologies and services used to carry traffic over the Internet, a managed IP network, or a provider's backbone."

A VPN does not require separate technology, leased lines, or direct cabling. It is a *virtual* private network. This means it can use existing connections to provide a secure connection. In most cases it is used over normal Internet connections. Basically the VPN is a way to "piggy back" over the Internet to create secure connections. Figure 7.1 illustrates a VPN.

A variety of methods are available for connecting one computer to another. With dial-up Internet connections, for example, the user's modem dials the Internet service provider's number, where it connects to one modem in a group of modems called a modem bank. This connection is not secure and is not even designed to mirror direct network connections. If the user is using a high-speed access (such as cable or DSL), the difference is one of speed only — the fundamental fact that the connection is neither dedicated nor secure has not changed.

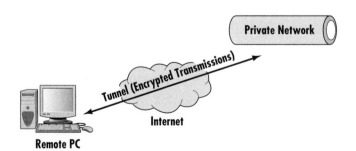

FIGURE 7.1 VPN technology.

This sort of arrangement is generally acceptable for an ISP. The customers connecting merely want a conduit to the Internet and do not need to connect directly or securely to a specific network. However, this is inadequate for remote users attempting to connect to an organization's network. In such cases the private and secure connection a VPN provides is critical.

Individual remote users are not the only users of VPN technology. Many larger organizations have offices in various locations. Achieving reliable and secure site-to-site connectivity for such organizations is an important issue. The various branch offices must be connected to the central corporate network through tunnels that transport traffic over the Internet.

Using VPN technology for site-to-site connectivity enables a branch office with multiple links to move away from an expensive, dedicated data line and to simply utilizing existing Internet connections.

Using VPN Protocols for VPN Encryption

There are multiple ways to achieve the encryption needs of a VPN. Certain network protocols are frequently used for VPNs. The two most commonly used protocols for this purpose are *point-to-point tunneling protocol (PPTP) and layer 2 tunneling protocol (L2TP).* The part of the connection in which the data is encapsulated is referred to as the *tunnel.* L2TP is often combined with IPSec in order to achieve a very high level of security. IPSec is discussed in more detail later in this chapter.

7

PPTP

PPTP is a tunneling protocol that enables an older connection protocol, *PPP (point-to-point protocol),* to have its packets encapsulated within *Internet Protocol (IP)* packets and forwarded over any IP network, including the Internet itself. PPTP is often used to create VPNs. PPTP is an older protocol than L2TP or IPSec. Some experts consider PPTP to be less secure than L2TP or IPSec, but it consumes fewer resources and is supported by almost every VPN implementation. It is basically a secure extension to the point-to-point protocol (PPP). This is shown in Figure 7.2.

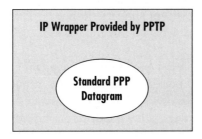

FIGURE 7.2 PPTP wrapping PPP.

FYI: PPP

Because PPTP is based on PPP, it may interest you to know a little bit about PPP. PPP was designed for moving datagrams across serial point-to-point links. It sends packets over a physical link, a serial cable set up between two computers. It is used to establish and configure the communications link and the network layer protocols, and also to encapsulate datagrams. PPP has several components and is actually made up of several protocols:

- MP, PPP multilink protocol.
- MP+, PPP Ascend's multilink protocol plus
- MPLS multiprotocol label switching
- SDTP, PPP serial data transport protocol

Each of these handles a different part of the process. PPP was originally developed as an encapsulation protocol for transporting IP traffic over point-to-point links. PPP also established a standard for a variety of related tasks including:

- assignment and management of IP addresses
- asynchronous and bit-oriented synchronous encapsulation
- network protocol multiplexing
- link configuration
- link quality testing
- error detection

PPP supports these functions by providing an extensible Link Control Protocol (LCP) and a family of Network Control Protocols (NCPs) to negotiate optional configuration parameters and facilities. In addition to IP, PPP supports other protocols, including Novell's Internetwork Packet Exchange (IPX).

PPTP was originally proposed as a standard in 1996 by the PPTP Forum — a group of companies that included Ascend Communications, ECI Telematics, Microsoft, 3Com and U.S. Robotics. This group's purpose was to design a protocol that would allow remote users to communicate securely over the Internet.

Although newer VPN protocols are available, PPTP is still widely used in part because almost all VPN equipment vendors support PPTP. Another important benefit of PPTP is that it operates at layer 2 of the OSI model (the data link layer), allowing different networking protocols to run over a PPTP tunnel. For example, PPTP can be used to transport IPX, Net-BEUI, and other data.

FYI: The OSI Model

The OSI model, short for Open Systems Interconnect model, is a standard description of how networks communicate. It describes the various protocols and activities, and delineates how they relate to each other. This model is divided into seven layers, as shown in Table 7.1.

TABLE 7.1 The OSI model.

Layer	Function	Protocols
Application	Interfaces directly to the application and performs common application services for the application processes	None
Presentation	Relieves the application layer of concern regarding syntactical differences in data representation within the end-user systems	POP, SMTP, DNS, FTP, Telnet, ARP
Session	Provides the mechanism for managing the dialogue between end-user application processes	NetBIOS
Transport	Provides end-to-end communication control	TCP
Network	Routes the information in the network	IP, ICMP
Data Link	Encodes and decodes data packets into bits at this layer	SLIP, PPP
Physical	Represents the actual physical devices at this layer, such as the network interface card	None

The following sources provide more information:

- Webopedia: **www.Webopedia.com/quick_ref/ OSI_Layers.asp**
- About.com: **http://compnetworking.about.com/ cs/designosimodel/g/bldef_osi.htm**
- HowStuffWorks.com: **http://computer.howstuff- works.com/osi.htm**

PPTP supports two generic types of tunneling, voluntary and compulsory. In the case of *voluntary tunneling,* a remote user dials into a service provider's network and a standard PPP session is established that enables the user to log on to the provider's network. The user then launches the VPN software to establish a PPTP session back to the PPTP remote-access server in the central network. This process is called voluntary tunneling because the user initiates the process and has the choice of whether to establish the VPN session. While not advisable, the user could simply use a standard PPP connection without the benefits of a VPN.

In a *compulsory tunneling* setup the only connection available to the host network is via a VPN. A simple PPP connection is not available, only the full PPTP connection, forcing users to use a secure connection. From a security standpoint this is the preferred option.

PPTP Authentication

When connecting to a remote system, encrypting the data transmissions is not the only facet of security. You must also authenticate the user. PPTP supports two separate technologies for accomplishing this: *Extensible Authentication Protocol (EAP) and Challenge Handshake Authentication Protocol (CHAP).*

EAP EAP was designed specifically with PPTP and is meant to work as part PPP. EAP works from within PPP's authentication protocol. It provides a framework for several different authentication methods. EAP is meant to supplant proprietary authentication systems and a variety of authentication methods to be used including passwords, challenge-response tokens, and public key infrastructure certificates.

CHAP CHAP is actually a three-part *handshaking* (a term used to denote authentication processes) procedure. After the link is established, the server sends a challenge message to the client machine originating the link. The originator responds by sending back a value calculated using a one-way hash function. The server checks the response against its own calculation of the expected hash value. If the values match, the authentication is acknowledged; otherwise the connection is usually terminated. This means that there are three stages in the authorization of a client connection. This process is illustrated in Figure 7.3.

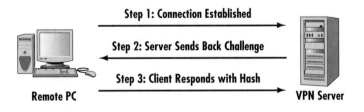

FIGURE 7.3 CHAP authentication.

What makes CHAP particularly interesting is that it periodically repeats the process. This means that even after a client connection is authenticated, CHAP repeatedly seeks to re-authenticate that client, providing a robust level of security.

FYI: What Is a Hash Function?

The term *hash function* comes up quite a bit in discussions of encryption and authentication. It is therefore important that you have a solid understanding of what it is. A hash function (H) is a transformation. This transformation takes a variable-sized input (m) and returns a fixed-length string. The fixed-length string that is returned is called the hash value (h). Expressed as a mathematical equation, this is $h = H(m)$. More details about hash functions are available at the following Web sites:

- RSA Security: **www.rsasecurity.com/rsalabs/node. asp?id=2176**
- MathWorld: **http://mathworld.wolfram.com/ HashFunction.html**

7

L2TP

Layer 2 tunneling protocol is an extension or enhancement of the point-to-point tunneling protocol that is often used to operate virtual private networks over the Internet. Essentially it is a new and improved version of PPTP. As its name suggests it operates at the data link layer of the OSI model (like PPTP). Both PPTP and L2TP are considered by many experts to be less secure than IPSec. However it is not uncommon to see IPSec used together with L2TP to create a secure VPN connection.

L2TP Authentication

Like PPTP, L2TP supports EAP and CHAP. However, it also offers support for other authentication methods, for a total of five:

- EAP
- CHAP
- MS-CHAP
- PAP
- SPAP

EAP and CHAP were discussed in the previous section. The following section discusses the remaining three.

MS-CHAP As the name suggests, *MS-CHAP* is a Microsoft-specific extension to CHAP. Microsoft created MS-CHAP to authenticate remote Windows workstations. The goal is to provide the functionality available on the LAN to remote users while integrating the encryption and hashing algorithms used on Windows networks.

Wherever possible, MS-CHAP is consistent with standard CHAP. However, there are some basic differences between MS-CHAP and standard CHAP:

- The MS-CHAP response packet is in a format designed for compatibility with Microsoft's Windows products networking products.

- The MS-CHAP format does not require the authenticator to store a clear-text or reversibly encrypted password.

- MS-CHAP provides authenticator-controlled authentication retry and password changing mechanisms. These retry and password changing mechanisms are compatible with the mechanisms used in Windows networks.

- MS-CHAP defines a set of reason-for-failure codes that are returned in the failure packet's message field if the authentication fails. These are codes that Windows software is able to read and interpret, thus providing the user with the reason for the failed authentication.

PAP *PAP,* an acronym for *password authentication protocol,* is the most basic form of authentication. With PAP, a user's name and password are transmitted over a network and compared to a table of name-password pairs. Typically, the passwords stored in the table are encrypted. However, the transmissions of the passwords are in clear text, unencrypted, the main weakness with PAP. The basic authentication feature built into the HTTP protocol uses PAP. This authentication is shown in Figure 7.4.

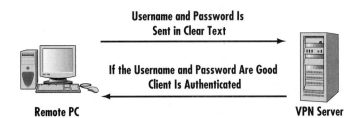

Username and Password Is
Sent in Clear Text

If the Username and Password Are Good
Client Is Authenticated

Remote PC

VPN Server

FIGURE 7.4 PAP.

FIGURE 7.5 SPAP.

SPAP *SPAP,* an acronym for *Shiva Password Authentication Protocol,* is a proprietary version of PAP. Most experts consider SPAP somewhat more secure than PAP because the username and password are both encrypted when they are sent, unlike with PAP. This protocol is illustrated in Figure 7.5.

Because SPAP encrypts passwords, someone capturing authentication packets will not be able to read the SPAP password. However, SPAP is still susceptible to *playback attacks* (i.e., a person records the exchange and plays the message back to gain fraudulent access). Playback attacks are possible because SPAP always uses the same reversible encryption method to send the passwords over the wire.

L2TP Compared to PPTP

L2TP is actually the convergence of the layer 2 forwarding protocol (developed by Cisco) and PPTP (discussed in the previous section). The development of L2TP was spurred on by perceived shortcomings in PPTP. One of those shortcomings was that PPTP only supports public IP addresses. Many dial-up networking services support only registered IP addresses, which limits the types of applications that are implemented over VPNs. In other words, only the public IP addresses registered with interNIC are acceptable. Given that many VPNs ultimately connect with an internal server that might use a private IP address, this presents some limitations. L2TP supports multiple protocols and unregistered and privately administered IP addresses over the Internet.

Another important improvement in L2TP over PPTP is that it uses IPSec for encryption, whereas PPTP only uses *Microsoft Point-to-Point Encryption (MPPE).* MPPE is actually a version of DES (discussed in Chapter 6) and as such is secure enough for most situations. However, most experts consider IPSec to be more secure. Table 7.2 provides a comparison of PPTP to L2TP.

Windows NT only supports PPTP, but Windows 2000 and later versions also support L2TP, making it a very attractive option for Windows network administrators because it supports more network connection and authentication options and is more secure.

TABLE 7.2 L2TP versus PPTP.

Non IP networks	Yes, L2TP can work over X.25 networks and ATM networks	No, IP only
Encryption	Yes, using IPSec	Yes, using MPPE
Authentication	Yes, using EAP or MS-CHAP	Yes, EAP, MS-CHAP, CHAP, SPAP, and PAP

These sources provide more data on L2TP:

- Wikipedia: **en.wikipedia.org/wiki/L2TP**
- The Cisco L2TP Web page: **www.cisco.com/univercd/cc/td/doc/ product/software/ios120/120newft/120t/120t1/l2tpt.htm**

IPSec

IPSec, short for *Internet Protocol Security,* is a technology used to create virtual private networks. IPSec is a security used in addition to the IP protocol that adds security and privacy to TCP/IP communication. IPSec is incorporated with Microsoft Operating Systems as well as many other operating systems. For example, the security settings in the Internet Connection Firewall that ships with Windows XP enables users to turn on IPSec for transmissions. IPSec is a set of protocols developed by the IETF (Internet Engineering Task Force, **www.ietf.org**) to support secure exchange of packets. IPSec has been deployed widely to implement VPNs.

IPSec has two encryption modes: transport and tunnel. The *transport mode* works by encrypting the data in each packet but leaves the header unencrypted. This means that the source and destination address, as well as other header information, are not encrypted. The *tunnel mode* encrypts both the header and the data. This is more secure than transport mode but can work more slowly. At the receiving end, an IPSec-compliant device decrypts each packet. For IPSec to work, the sending and receiving devices must share a key, an indication that IPSec is a single-key encryption technology. IPSec also offers two other protocols beyond the two modes already described. Those protocols are *AH (Authentication Header)* and *ESP (Encapsulated Security Payload).*

AH and ESP use the same algorithms to encrypt the data. AH also provides optional anti-replay protection, which protects against unauthorized retransmission of packets, a process to which SPAP is vulnerable. Anti-replay protection prevents packets from being rerouted to a destination other than the intended one, a very valuable security feature for a VPN. The authentication header is inserted into the packet between the IP header and packet contents.

AH, by itself, protects only the packet's origin, destination, and contents from tampering. It does not hide the sender or protect the data. If data is intercepted and only AH is used, the message contents can be read. In essence the AH is part of the tunneling portion of the VPN helping to establish the dedicated virtual connection. ESP is used to protect the actual data.

In addition to ESP and AH, IPSec also uses IPComp and IKE. *IPComp,* or *IP payload compression,* provides a way to compress packets before encryption by ESP. *IKE,* or *Internet Key Exchange,* manages the exchange of encryption keys. For communication between distant locations, VPNs must provide ways to negotiate keys in secrecy. IKE makes this possible.

As you can see IPSec is actually comprised of four protocols:

- AH
- ESP
- IPComp
- IKE

More details about IPSec are available at:

- The IPSec FAQ: **www.zyxel.com/support/supportnote/zywall10/ faq/vpn_faq.htm#4.%20What%20is%20PPTP?**
- The Internet Engineering Task Force IPSec Web site: **www.ietf.org/ html.charters/ipsec-charter.html**
- The High Performance Computing Group: **www.fys.ruu.nl/~wwwfi/ ipv6/ahesp**
- IPSec for Free BSD: **www.netbsd.org/Documentation/ network/ ipsec/#getting_started**

Implementing VPN Solutions

Regardless of which protocols you use for your VPN, you will need to implement your choice in some software/hardware configuration. Many operating systems have built-in VPN server and client connections. These are generally fine for small office or home situations. However, they may not be adequate for larger scale operations in which multiple users connect via VPN. For those situations, a dedicated VPN solution may be necessary. In this section we will discuss some of those solutions.

Cisco Solutions

Cisco offers VPN solutions, including a module (**www.cisco.com/en/US/ products/hw/modules/ps2706/ps4221/index.html**) that can be added to many of their switches and routers to implement VPN services. It also offers client side hardware (**www.cisco.com/en/US/products/sw/secursw/ps5299/index.html**) that is designed to provide an easy-to-implement yet secure client side for the VPN.

The main advantage of this solution is that it incorporates seamlessly with other Cisco products. Administrators using a Cisco firewall or Cisco routers might find this solution to be preferable. However, this solution might not be right for those not using other Cisco products and those who don't have knowledge of Cisco systems. However, there are many attractive specifications for this product:

- It uses 3DES encryption (an improved version of DES).

- It can handle packets larger than 500 bytes.

- It can create up to 60 new virtual tunnels per second, a good feature if a lot of users might be logging on or off.

Service Solutions

In some cases, especially with large WAN VPN situations, you may not wish to invest the time, energy, and cost to establish, secure, and monitor VPN connections. You can contract this entire process, the setup and the administration, to VPN vendors. ATT (**www.business.att.com/service_portfolio.jsp?repoid=ProductCategory&repoitem=vpn&serv_port=vpn&CMP=KNL-AR9974192875**) provides this service for many companies. In the United Kingdom companies such as VPlus (**www.vplusnetworks.com/index2.html**) provide similar services.

Service solutions have the advantage of not requiring any particular VPN skill on the part of the internal IT department. A department that lacks these specific skill areas but wants to implement a VPN might find that using an outside service is the right solution.

Free S/WAN

This product (**www.freeswan.org/**) is an open source VPN solution available for Linux operating systems. As an open source product, one of its biggest advantages is that it is free. Free S/WAN uses IPSec, making it a highly secure VPN solution.

Free S/WAN supports either remote users logging on via VPN, or site-to-site connections. It also supports wireless connections. However, it does not support NAT (the new alternative to proxy servers).

Other Solutions

Clearly there are many possible VPN solutions. A simple Google or Yahoo! search for "VPN Solutions" generates many responses. The following VPN solutions are encountered most frequently. Your organization's specific data usage requirements must be examined to determine the most appropriate VPN solution.

IN PRACTICE: Setting up a VPN Server
with Windows 2000

It is relatively easy to set up a virtual private network with Windows 2000 Server (this will not work with the professional edition). Simply follow these basic steps, and you will have a VPN server that any client can connect to:

1. The server you intend to use as your VPN server should use a static IP address (as opposed to a dynamically assigned one).

2. Go to Start > Programs > Settings > Administrative Tools > Routing and Remote Access, and then click on the icon next to your server's name.

3. Click Action | Configure and enable Routing and Remote Service. This will start a simple wizard that will walk you through the process of configuring your VPN server.

Once you are through the wizard you can check your configuration or change it by right-clicking on your server icon and choosing Properties. Check to make sure the following settings are in place:

1. You have on-demand dialing and LAN connection, as shown in Figure 7.6.

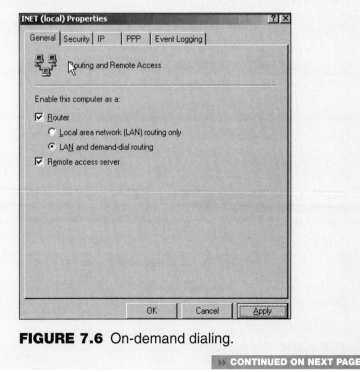

FIGURE 7.6 On-demand dialing.

▶▶ CONTINUED ON NEXT PAGE

▶▶ **CONTINUED**

2. It is set for IP routing and IP remote access, as shown in Figure 7.7.

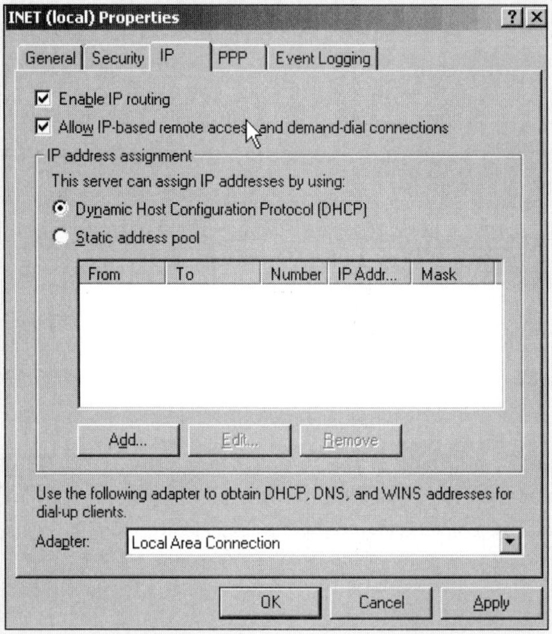

FIGURE 7.7 IP routing and remote access.

3. Set up the port to use either L2TP or PPTP, as shown in Figure 7.8.

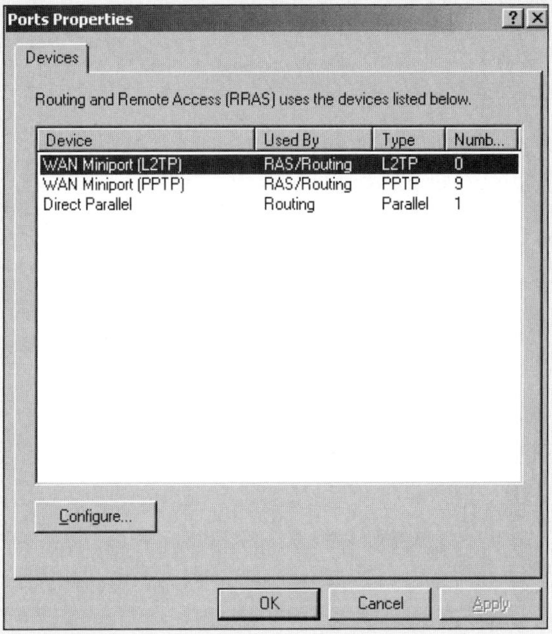

FIGURE 7.8 Protocols to use.

Depending on your network environment, you will need to configure your firewall to allow the VPN traffic through.

Summary

Virtual private networks are secure connections over the Internet that enable remote users and sites to connect to a central network. You can use PPTP, L2TP, or IPSec to create a VPN. IPSec is considered the most secure of the three. Administrators creating a VPN protocol should consider how the packets are encrypted, what sort of authentication is used, and whether the current hardware and software supports that technology.

Test Your Skills

MULTIPLE CHOICE QUESTIONS

1. PPTP is an acronym for which of the following?
   A. point-to-point transmission protocol
   B. point-to-point tunneling protocol
   C. point-to-point transmission procedure
   D. point-to-point tunneling procedure

2. What does L2TP stand for?
   A. level 2 transfer protocol
   B. layer 2 transfer protocol
   C. level 2 tunneling protocol
   D. level 2 transfer protocol

3. PPTP is based on what earlier protocol?
   A. SLIP
   B. L2TP
   C. IPSec
   D. PPP

4. At what layer of the OSI does PPTP operate?
   A. physical
   B. network
   C. data link
   D. transport

5. What is the difference between voluntary and compulsory tunneling in PPTP?
   A. Only voluntary tunneling allows the user to choose which network to connect to.
   B. Only compulsory tunneling forces the user to send his password.
   C. Only voluntary tunneling allows standard PPP/non VPN connection.
   D. Only compulsory tunneling forces 3DES encryption.

6. Which authentication protocols are available under PPTP?

    A. MS-CHAP, PAP, SPAP

    B. EAP, CHAP

    C. PAP, EAP, MS-CHAP

    D. SPAP, MS-CHAP

7. Which of the following is an important security feature in CHAP?

    A. It periodically re-authenticates.

    B. It uses 3DES encryption.

    C. It is immune to IP spoofing.

    D. It uses AES encryption.

8. Which authentication protocols are available with L2TP that are not available with PPTP?

    A. MS-CHAP, PAP, SPAP

    B. EAP, CHAP

    C. PAP, EAP, MS-CHAP

    D. SPAP, MS-CHAP

9. Which of the following is generally considered the least secure?

    A. PAP

    B. SPAP

    C. MS-CHAP

    D. X-PAP

10. What is the primary vulnerability in SPAP?

    A. weak encryption

    B. playback attacks

    C. clear text passwords

    D. no hash code

11. What encryption does PPTP use?

    A. MPPE

    B. IPSec

    C. 3DES

    D. AES

12. Which of the following is a weakness in PPTP?

    A clear text passwords

    B. no encryption

    C. used only with IP networks

    D. not supported on most platforms

13. What protocols make up IPSec?

    A. AH, IKE, ESP, IPComp

    B. AH, PAP, CHAP, IPComp

    C. IPComp, MS-CHAP, PAP, AH

    D. AH, SPAP, CHAP, IPComp

14. What is the difference between transport mode and tunnel mode in IPSec?

    A. Only transport mode is unencrypted.

    B. Only tunneling mode is unencrypted.

    C. Only tunneling mode does not encrypt the header.

    D. Only transport mode does not encrypt the header.

15. What advantage does AH have over SPAP?

    A. AH uses stronger encryption.

    B. AH protects the data as well as the header.

    C. AH is not susceptible to replay attacks.

    D. None; SPAP is more secure.

16. What protects the actual packet data in IPSec?

    A. AH

    B. ESP

    C. SPAP

    D. CHAP

17. What is the purpose of IKE?

    A. key exchange

    B. packet encryption

    C. header protection

    D. authentication

EXERCISES

Exercise 7.1: Setting up a Windows XP VPN Server

Windows XP has an easy-to-use VPN Wizard that allows you to set up your XP machine as a VPN server.

1. Click *Start,* and then select *Control Panel.*

2. In the Control Panel, select *Network Connections.*

3. In the Network Connections window, choose *Create a New Connection,* which launches the Welcome To The New Connection Wizard.

4. Click *Next* on the first screen of the wizard.

5. On the Network Connection Type screen, choose the *Set Up An Advanced Connection* option.

6. On the Advanced Connection Options screen, select the *Accept Incoming Connection* and click *Next.*

7. On the *Devices For Incoming Connections* screen, select the optional devices on which you want to accept incoming connections.

8. On the Incoming virtual private network (VPN) Connection screen, select the *Allow Virtual Private Connections* option and click *Next.*

9. On the User Permissions screen, select the users that are allowed to make incoming VPN connections. Click *Next.*

10. On the Networking Software screen, click on the *Internet Protocol (TCP/IP)* entry and click the *Properties* button.

11. In the Incoming TCP/IP Properties dialog box, place a check mark in the *Allow Callers To Access My Local Area Network* check box to allow VPN callers to connect to other computers on the LAN. If this check box isn't selected, VPN callers will be able to connect only to resources on the Windows XP VPN server itself. Click *OK* to return to the Networking Software screen and then click *Next.*

12. Click *Finish* to create the connection on the Completing The New Connection Wizard screen.

13. After the Incoming Connection is complete, right-click on the *Connection* you made in the Network Connections window and select the *Properties.*

14. You now have a VPN server.

7

Exercise 7.2: Setting up a Windows XP VPN Client

1. Click *Start,* and then select *Control Panel.*

2. In the Control Panel, select *Network Connections.*

3. Open the New Connection Wizard. Click *Connect to the network at my workplace,* and click *Next.*

4. Click *virtual private network connection,* and click *Next.*

5. Enter a name for this connection, and then click *Next.*

6. Choose whether Windows will automatically dial the initial connection to the Internet you created previously or let you do that manually. If you use multiple connections to the Internet, you should use manual, but if you always use the same connection you might consider the automatic method.

7. Click *Next,* and then type in the host name or IP address of your RRAS server. If you don't know this, check with your IT department. Click *Next* again, and select *My use only* for this connection. Click *Next* again and then *Finish* to create the VPN connection

8. You can test this by connecting to the server you created in Exercise 7.1.

Exercise 7.3: Setting up a Linux VPN

Linux can vary from distribution to distribution, so consult your particular distribution's documentation. However, several sources are given for you here in the order I recommend. The first is the easiest to follow:

■ **home.houston.rr.com/move2lin/vpn.htm**

■ **vpnlabs.org/linux-vpn.php**

■ **brneurosci.org/linuxsetup46.html**

■ **www.wown.com/articles_tutorials/Client_Based_VPN_via_ PPTP.html**

Exercise 7.4: Intercepting Packets

Chapter 5 discussed the open source IDS Snort. One of its modes is to simply intercept and read packets. You will use that in this exercise.

1. Run Snort in packet sniffing mode on your VPN Server.

2. Intercept the incoming packets.

3. Determine whether they are encrypted.

Exercise 7.5: Installing and Configuring Free S/WAN

1. Go to the Web site mentioned in the chapter for Free S/WAN.

2. Download the product to your Linux server.

3. Install and configure according to the product documentation.

Exercise 7.6: OS Independence

This exercise demonstrates that different operating systems can communicate easily over a VPN connection.

1. Using a Linux machine, connect to the Windows VPN server you created in Exercise 7.1.

2. Using a Windows machine, connect to the Linux VPN Server you created in Exercise 7.3 or 7.5.

PROJECTS

Project 7.1: Comparing Authentication Protocols

1. Using the Web or other resources look up each of the authentication protocols mentioned in this chapter.

2. Compare the protocols by pointing out the strengths and weaknesses of each.

3. Which one would you recommend for your school, company, or organization?

4. State the reasons behind your recommendation.

Project 7.2: Internet Key Exchange

1. Using the Web and other resources, look up information on how IKE works.

2. Describe the methods used in keeping the key exchange secure.

3. What are possible weaknesses in the IKE method?

4. Do you consider this a secure method for key exchange?

Project 7.3: Cost Efficiency

Unfortunately, technical strength is not the only criterion by which any solution is judged. Cost must be taken into account. For this project you will do cost estimates. This will require you to research product Web sites and perhaps even call sales representatives.

1. Assume a local area network that is small (under 100 users, 5 servers).

2. Assume 20 remote users, not all connected at the same time.

3. Assume an average of five to eight connections at any given time.

4. Research three solutions that can support this scenario, and report on the cost of each.

Case Study

Nancy is the network administrator for a defense research company. Many of its researchers do some work from home, particularly work on mathematics, algorithms, and so on. The data they send must be absolutely secure. These remote users wish to use VPN connections to the company network. Nancy takes the following actions:

1. She implements a PPTP VPN using Windows XP as the VPN server.

2. All remote users are set up for compulsory tunneling.

3. All remote users are given very strong passwords that change every 30 days.

Are the steps Nancy took adequate and appropriate? What other steps, if any, should she have taken?

Chapter 8

Operating System Hardening

Chapter Objectives

After reading this chapter and completing the exercises, you will be able to do the following:

- Properly configure a Windows system for secure operations.
- Properly configure a Linux system for secure operations.
- Apply appropriate operating system patches to Windows.
- Apply application patches.
- Securely configure a Web browser.

Introduction

Protecting the system's perimeters and subnets via firewalls, proxy servers (or NAT enabled machines), and intrusion detection systems is only one part of securing a network. Even installing antivirus software and anti-spyware does not complete a network's security. To achieve a completely secure network, you must perform ***operating system hardening.*** This is the process of properly configuring each machine, and especially servers, for the optimum security settings. The word *optimum* rather than *maximum* is used for a reason. Maximum security is also the least usable. Optimum security strikes a balance between ease of use and security.

In this chapter you will learn how to properly configure Windows 2000, Windows XP, Linux, and various Web browsers. Securely configuring the operating system and its software is a critical step in system security that is frequently ignored. Even relatively naïve security administrators often think of installing a firewall or antivirus software, but many fail to harden the individual machines against attacks.

Configuring Windows Properly

Properly configuring Windows (we will focus on Windows 2000 and Windows XP) consists of many facets. You must disable unnecessary services, properly configure the registry, enable the Internet Connection Firewall (for XP), properly configure the browser, and more. Chapter 4 discussed the Internet connection firewall, and a later section of this chapter discusses browser security. For now we will deal with the other important factors in Windows security configuration.

FYI: What about Windows 2003?

Throughout this chapter we will use Windows 2000 and Windows XP as our examples. You may wonder if these issues apply to Windows 2003. First and foremost, Windows XP is the desktop operating system currently supported by Microsoft; Windows 2003 is a server-only product at this point. We include Windows 2000 because many businesses are still using it.

The second reason for not discussing Windows 2003 is that from an operating system hardening perspective, it is virtually identical to Windows XP. It uses the same Internet Connection Firewall that Windows XP introduced. However there are a few options in Windows 2003 that are not present in Windows 2000 or Windows XP, and we will discuss those few differences as necessary.

Accounts, Users, Groups, and Passwords

Any Windows system (Windows 2000, XP, or 2003) comes with certain default user accounts and groups. These can frequently be a starting point for intruders who wish to crack passwords for those accounts and thereby gain entrance onto a server or network. Simply renaming or disabling some of these default accounts can improve your security.

In Windows 2000 or Windows XP you find user accounts by going to *Start > Settings > Control Panel > Users and Groups.* Figure 8.1 shows a screen similar to the one you will see.

Next select the *Advanced* tab, which takes you to the screen shown in Figure 8.2. Then select the *Advanced* button, which brings you to the screen shown in Figure 8.3.

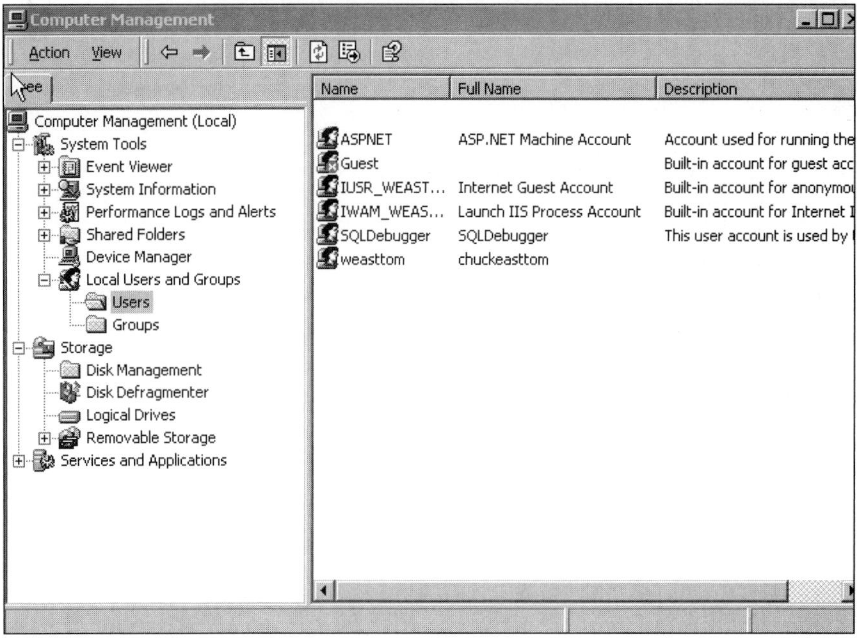

FIGURE 8.1 Users and Groups.

FIGURE 8.2 Manage users and passwords from this dialog box.

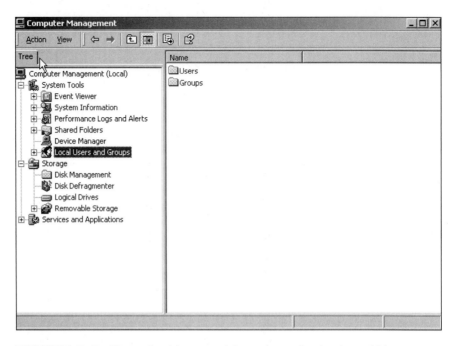

FIGURE 8.3 Alter, disable, or add accounts in the Local Users and Groups dialog box.

From here you can alter, disable, or add accounts. The following paragraphs demonstrate how to use this utility to adjust various default accounts.

Administrator Accounts The default administrator account has administrative privileges, and hackers frequently seek to obtain the log-on information for an administrator account. Guessing a log on is a two-fold process of first identifying the username, then the password. Default accounts allow the hacker to bypass the first half of this process.

Administrators should disable this account. If you double-click on any account (recall the users and groups utility previously shown in Figure 8.3) you will see a screen much like that shown in Figure 8.4. From here you can disable the default administrator account.

Obviously having an account with administrative privileges is necessary for maintaining your server. The next step is adding a new account, one with an innocuous name (e.g., *temp_clerk, receptionist,* etc.), and giving that account administrative privileges. Doing so makes a hacker's task more difficult, as he must first ascertain what account actually has administrative privileges before he can even attempt to compromise that account.

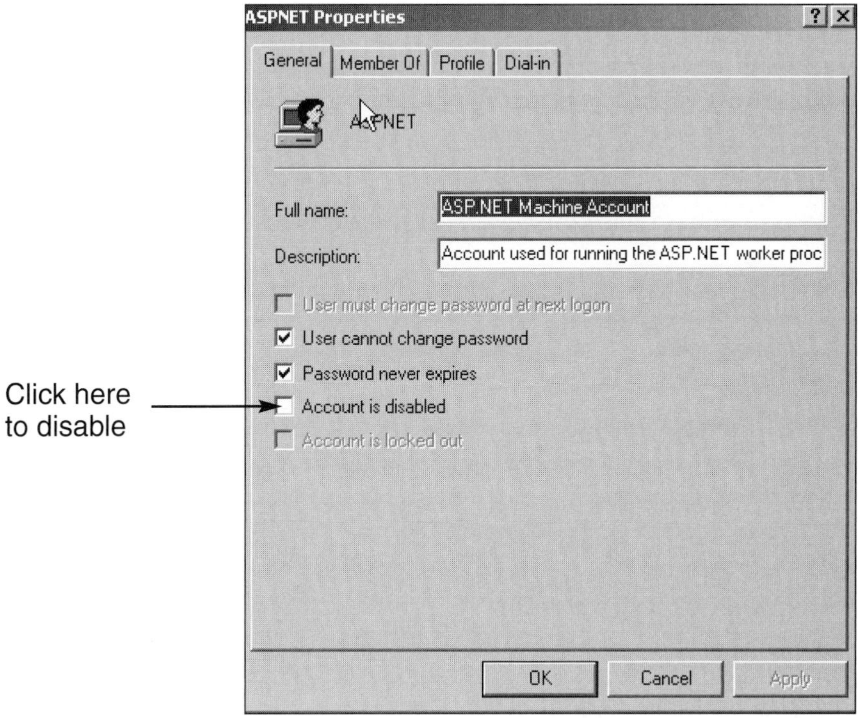

Click here
to disable

FIGURE 8.4 Disabling the default administrator account.

Some experts suggest simply renaming the administrator account, or using an administrator account that has a username that indicates its purpose. That is not the recommendation of this book for the following reasons:

- The entire idea is that a hacker should not be able to readily tell which username has administrative privileges.

- Simply renaming the administrator account to a different name, but one that still indicates its administrative rights, will not help this situation.

Other Accounts We have concentrated on the administrator account because it is the one most often targeted by hackers, but Windows also includes other default user accounts. It is a good idea to apply an equally rigorous treatment to all default accounts. Any default account can be a gateway for a hacker to compromise a system. A few accounts that you should pay particular attention to include:

- **IUSR_Machine name:** When you are running IIS, a default user account is created for IIS. Its name is *IUSR_* and the name of your machine. This is a common account for a hacker to attempt to compromise. Altering this one in the manner suggested for the administrator account is advisable.

- **ASP.NET:** If your machine is running ASP.NET, a default account is created for Web applications. A hacker that is familiar with .Net could target this account.

- **Database accounts:** Many relational database management systems, such as SQL Server, create default user accounts. An intruder, particularly one who wants to get at your data, could target these accounts.

FYI: Alternatives to Disabling the Administrative Account

Another secure option is to leave the default administrator account enabled, but to change it from being a member of the administrator's group to being a very restricted user account. Then make sure that none of your administrators use this account. At this point you can simply monitor server logs for attempts to log on to this account. Repeated attempts in a short period of time could mean someone is attempting to breach your system's security.

Leaving the administrator account enabled with significantly reduced access and monitoring any attempts to use that account provides you with a virtual trap for hackers.

Of course you must have accounts for all of these, and other services. The suggestion here is to ensure that the names of these accounts are not obvious and that default accounts are not used.

When adding any new account, always give the new account's user or group the least number and type of privileges needed to perform their job, even accounts for IT staff members. Here are a few examples of places to restrict user access/privileges that you might not think of:

- A PC technician does not need administrative rights on the database server. Even though she is in the IT department, she does not need access to everything in that department.

- Managers may use applications that reside on a Web server, but they certainly should not have rights on that server.

- Just because a programmer develops applications that run on a server does not mean that he should have full rights on that server.

These are just a few examples of things to consider when setting up user rights. Remember: Always give the least access necessary for that person to do her job.

Setting Security Policies

Setting appropriate security policies is the next step in hardening a Windows server. This does not refer to written policies an organization might have regarding security standards and procedures. In this case security policies refers to the individual machines' policies. When you select *Start > Settings > Control Panel > Administrative Tools,* you will also note local security policy. Selecting this takes you to the screen shown in Figure 8.5. The various subfolders in the dialog box shown in Figure 8.5 are expanded. Normally when you open this utility they will not be.

The first matter of concern is setting secure password policies. The default settings for Windows passwords are not secure. Table 8.1 shows the default ***password policies.*** Maximum password age refers to how long a password is effective before the user is forced to change that password. Password history refers to how many previous passwords the system remembers, thus preventing the user from reusing passwords. Password length defines the maximum number of characters allowed in a password. Password complexity means that the user must use a password that combines numbers, letters, and other characters. These are the default security settings for all Windows versions from Windows NT 4.0 forward.

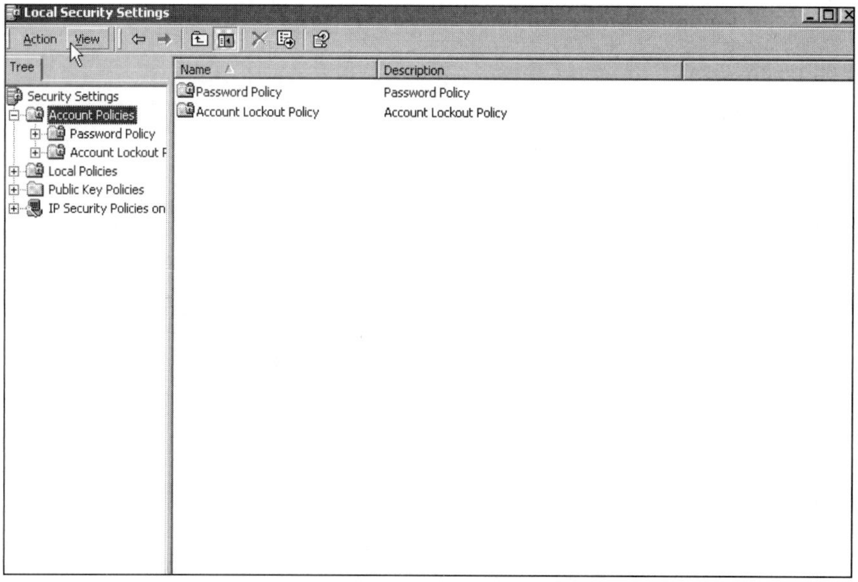

FIGURE 8.5 Local security policies.

TABLE 8.1 Default Windows password policies.

Enforce password history	1 password remembered
Maximum password age	42 days
Minimum password age	0 days
Minimum password length	0 characters
Passwords must meet complexity requirements	Disabled
Store password using reversible encryption for all users in the domain	Disabled

The default password policies are not secure enough, but what policies should you use instead? Different experts answer that question differently. Table 8.2 shows the recommendations of Microsoft, the National Security Agency, and the author's personal recommendations (along with an explanation when they differ significantly from the Microsoft or NSA recommendations).

TABLE 8.2 Password setting recommendations.

Policy	Microsoft	NSA	Author
Password history	3	5	3
Maximum password age	42	42	60 days. I recommend this because 42 is a rather odd number. Also, changing passwords too frequently causes end users to forget passwords.
Minimum password age	2	2	2
Minimum password length	8	12	I recommend 8 for most organizations, but for situations requiring more enhanced security the NSA guideline should be used.
Passwords must meet complexity requirements	No recommendation (left to user discretion)	Yes	Yes
Store password using reversible encryption for all users in the domain	No recommendation (left to user discretion)	No recommendation	No recommendation (left to user discretion)

Developing appropriate password policies depends largely on the requirements of your network environment. If your network stores and processes highly sensitive data and is an attractive target to hackers, you must always skew your policies and settings towards greater security. However, bear in mind that if security measures are too complex, your users will find it difficult to comply. For example, very long, complex passwords (such as *$%Tbx38T@_FgR$$*) make your network quite secure, but such passwords are virtually impossible for users to remember. Many users will simply write the password on a note and keep it in a handy but insecure location, such as the top drawer of their desks, a major security problem.

Account Lockout Policies When you open the Local Security Settings dialog, your options are not limited to setting password policies. You can also set *account lockout policies.* These policies determine how many times a user can attempt to log in before being locked out, and for how long to lock them out. The default Windows settings are shown in Table 8.3.

These default policies are not secure. Essentially they allow for an infinite number of log-in attempts, making using password crackers very easy and virtually guaranteeing that someone will eventually crack one or more passwords and gain access to your system. Recommendations from Microsoft, National Security Agency, and the author are given in Table 8.4.

8

TABLE 8.3 Windows default account lockout policy settings.

Account lockout duration	Not defined
Account lockout threshold	0 invalid log on attempts
Reset account lockout counter after	Not defined

TABLE 8.4 Recommended account lockout policies.

Policy	Microsoft	NSA	Author
Account lockout duration	0, indefinite	15 hours	48 hours. If someone is attempting to crack passwords on weekends/ holidays, you want the account locked until an administrator is aware of the attempt.
Account lockout threshold	5	3	3
Reset account after	15	30	30

FYI: More Guidelines

Guidelines for Windows 2000 Security are available on the following Web sites. These guidelines also apply to Windows XP and Windows 2003:

- National Security Agency: **svcaacs.conxion.com/win2k/**
- All NSA configuration guides: **www.nsa.gov/snac/**
- InfoSec guidelines: **www.infosec.uga.edu/windows.html**
- Microsoft Windows XP security guides: **www.microsoft.com/downloads/details.aspx?FamilyID=2d3e25bc-f434-4cc6-a5a7-09a8a229f118&DisplayLang=en**
- Microsoft Windows 2003 server security guide: **www.microsoft.com/technet/security/prodtech/Win2003/W2003HG/SGCH00.mspx**

Some of the links in this chapter are rather long. That is because they take you directly to the item in question. You can always go to the root domain (such as **www.microsoft.com**) and search for the item in question.

All of these sites provide other perspectives on securing a Windows 2000, Windows XP, or Windows 2003 server.

Other Issues Some account and password issues cannot be handled with computer settings. These involve setting organizational policies regarding user and administrator behavior. Chapter 11 discusses such organizational policies in greater depth. For now simply consider this basic list of the most important organizational security policies:

- Users must never write down passwords.

- Users must never share passwords.

- Administrators must use the least required access rule. That means most users should not have administrative privileges even on their own desktops.

Registry Settings

Secure registry settings are critical to securing a network. Unfortunately my experience has been that this area is often overlooked by otherwise security

FYI: An Addition in 2003

A few additions to Windows 2003 are pertinent to operating system hardening. One interesting new item is the ability to set application policies. This means that you can set how, when, and from where an application can execute. For example, you can set up a policy that allows an application to run only from a specific location.

This is useful because some viruses, Trojan horses, and other malware use files that contain the same name as some system file. For example, *explorer.exe* runs your Windows desktop; however, there are viruses that are named *explorer.exe*. The malware will almost always run from a different directory than the legitimate application. If you set up applications so they can run only from certain directories, then you protect your system from many types of malware. More information about this Windows 2003 feature is available at Microsoft's Windows 2003 page: **www.microsoft.com/windowsserver2003/evaluation/ overview/technologies/default.mspx**.

8

conscious administrators. The Windows Registry is a database used to store settings and options for Microsoft Windows operating systems. This database contains critical information and settings for all the hardware, software, users, and preferences on a particular computer. Whenever users are added, software is installed, or any other change is made to the system (including security policies), that information is stored in the registry.

Registry Basics The physical files that make up the registry are stored differently depending on which version of Windows you are using. Older versions of Windows (i.e., Windows 95 and 98) kept the registry in two hidden files in your Windows directory, called *USER.DAT* and *SYSTEM.DAT*. Later versions of Windows (such as Windows 2000 and XP) keep the registry in a separate directory: *%SystemRoot%\System32\Config* directory. Windows XP has named the file *ntuser.dat*. Regardless of the version of Windows you are using, you cannot edit the registry directly by opening and editing these files. Instead you must use a tool, *regedit.exe*, to make any changes. You can also use *regedit32.exe* to edit the registry for Windows 2000, Windows XP, and Windows 2003. However many users find that the older *regedit* has a more user friendly "find" option for searching the registry. Either one will work.

Although the registry is referred to as a "database," it does not actually have a relational database structure (like a table in MS SQL Server or

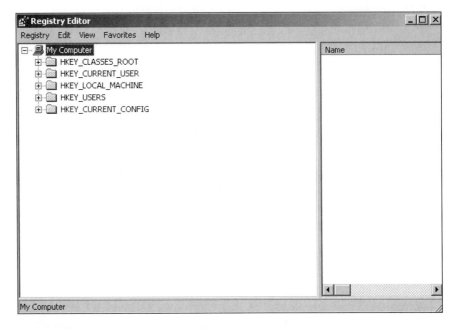

FIGURE 8.6 The Windows Registry.

Oracle). The registry has a hierarchical structure similar to the directory structure on the hard disk. In fact when you use *regedit*, you will note it is organized like Windows Explorer. To view the registry, go to *Start > Run* and type **regedit**. You should see the Registry Editor dialog box, shown in Figure 8.6. Some of the folders in your dialog box may be expanded. If so, simply collapse them so that your registry looks like the one shown in Figure 8.6.

Your Registry Editor dialog box will likely have the same five main folders as the one shown in Figure 8.6. Each of these main branches of the registry is briefly described below. These five main folders are the core registry folders. A system may have additions, but these are the primary folders containing information necessary for your system to run.

- *HKEY_CLASSES_ROOT* — This branch contains all of your file association types, OLE information, and shortcut data.

- *HKEY_CURRENT_USER* — This branch links to the section of HKEY_USERS appropriate for the user currently logged on to the PC.

- *HKEY_LOCAL_MACHINE* — This branch contains computer-specific information about the type of hardware, software, and other preferences on a given PC.

- *HKEY_USERS* — This branch contains individual preferences for each user of the computer.

- *HKEY_CURRENT_CONFIG* — This branch links to the section of *HKEY_LOCAL_MACHINE* appropriate for the current hardware configuration.

If you expand a branch by double-clicking on it, you will see its subfolders. Many of these have, in turn, more subfolders, possibly as many as four or more before you get to a specific entry. A specific entry in the Windows Registry is referred to as a key. A key is an entry that contains settings for some particular aspect of your system. If you alter the registry, you are actually changing the settings of particular keys.

This is just a brief overview of the registry. If you intend to do more extensive work with the registry than setting the proper security, you can use the following sources:

- Windows Registry Guide: **www.winguides.com/registry/**

- Windows Registry Tips: **www.activewin.com/tips/reg/index.shtml**

- Microsoft's Windows Registry support page: **http://support. microsoft.com/default.aspx?scid=kb%3BEN-US%3B256986**

Secure Registry Settings Remember that the Windows Registry controls everything about Windows. Therefore, to truly secure Windows, you must configure the register securely. Unfortunately, the registry's default settings are not secure. This section describes how to apply secure registry settings on your machines. Chapter 12 provides more information about secure registry settings in the section on assessing a system. There you will learn about software products available online that notify you of any insecure registry settings on your machine. These tools are sold by third-party vendors and are not part of Windows.

To find and check your registry settings for any of these keys, simply expand the appropriate node and work your way down to the specific key. For example, the first one on our list is *HKLM\SYSTEM\ CurrentControlSet\Services\LanmanServer*. You could first expand the *LOCAL_MACHINE* node, then the *SYSTEM* node, then the *CurrentControlSet* node, then the *Services* node. You should then be able to find the specific registry key you are looking for; in this example, we found *LanmanServer*. The same process can be applied to find any key; the *LanmanServer* key was randomly chosen for this example.

Restrict Null Session Access *Null sessions* are a significant weakness that can be exploited through the various shares that are on the computer. A null session is Windows' way of designating anonymous connections. Any time you allow anonymous connections to any server, you are inviting significant security risks. Modify null session access to shares on the computer by adding RestrictNullSessAccess, a registry value that toggles null session shares on or off to determine whether the Server service restricts access to clients logged on to the system account without username and password authentication. Setting the value to 1 restricts null session access for unauthenticated users to all server pipes and shares except those listed in the NullSessionPipes and NullSessionShares entries.

> Key Path: *HKLM\SYSTEM\CurrentControlSet\Services*
> *LanmanServer*
> Action: Ensure that it is set to: Value = 1

Restrict Null Session Access Over Named Pipes   This registry setting should be changed for much the same reason as the first null session registry setting. Restricting such access helps prevents unauthorized access over the network. To restrict null session access over named pipes and shared directories, edit the registry and delete the values, as shown in Table 8.5.

> Key Path: *HKLM\SYSTEM\CurrentControlSet\Services*
> *LanmanServer*
> Action: Delete all values

Restrict Anonymous Access   This registry setting allows anonymous users to list domain user names and enumerate share names. It should be shut off. The possible settings for this key are:

- 0 - Allow anonymous users

- 1 - Restrict anonymous users

- 2 - Allow users with explicit anonymous permissions

> Key Path: *HKLM\System\CurrentControSet\Control\Lsa*
> Action: Set Value = 2

TCP/IP Stack Settings   A number of registry settings affect how the TCP/IP stack handles incoming packets. Setting these properly can help reduce your vulnerability to DoS attacks. This process, stack tweaking, is described in Chapter 2. Because these settings are all related and are found in the same key path, they are shown together in Table 8.5.

As Table 8.5 shows, most of these settings prevent the redirection of packets, change the timeout on connections, and generally alter how Windows handles TCP/IP connections. You can find more details about Microsoft's recommendations for setting the TCP/IP stack registry settings at its Web site: **http://support.microsoft.com/default.aspx?scid=kb;en-us; Q315669&sd=tech.**

TABLE 8.5 TCP/IP Stack Registry settings.

Key path	Recommended value
DisableIPSourceRouting	2
EnableDeadGWDetect	0
EnableICMPRedirect	0
EnablePMTUDiscovery	0
EnableSecurityFilters	1
KeepAliveTime	300,000
NoNameReleaseOnDemand	1
PerformRouterDiscovery	0
SynAttackProtect	2
TcpMaxConnectResponseRetransmissions	2
TcpMaxConnectRetransmissions	3
TCPMaxPortsExhausted	5

Note: All keys are found in this path: HKLM\SYSTEM\CurrentControlSet\
Services\Tcpip

Default Shares The Windows operating system opens default shared folders on each installation for use by the system account. Since they are default shares, they are identical for all Windows machines, with identical permissions. These default shares can be used by a skilled hacker as a starting point for intruding upon your machine. You can disable the default Administrative shares two ways:

1. Stop or disable the Server service, which removes the ability to share folders on your computer. (However, you can still access shared folders on other computers.)

2. Edit the registry.

To change the default share folders setting in the registry, go to *HKey_Local_Machine\SYSTEM\CurrentControlSet\Services\LanManServer\Parameters*. For servers, edit *AutoShareServer* with a value of 0. For workstations, edit the key *AutoShareWks*. For more information on default shares or to view security advisories about them, consult the following Web sites:

- **www.cert.org/advisories/CA-2003-08.html**

- **www.sans.org/top20/**

Remote Access to the Registry Remote access to the registry is another potential opening for hackers. The Windows 2000 registry editing tools support remote access by default, but only administrators should have remote access to the registry. In fact some experts advise that there should be no remote access to the registry for any person. This point is certainly debatable. If your administrators frequently need to remotely alter registry settings, then completely blocking remote access to them will cause a reduction in productivity of those administrators. However, completely blocking remote access to the registry is certainly more secure. To restrict network access to the registry:

1. Add the following key to the registry: *HKEY_LOCAL_MACHINE* *\SYSTEM \CurrentControlSet\Control\SecurePipeServers\winreg*.

2. Select *winreg*, click the Security menu, and then click *Permissions*.

3. Set the Administrator's permission to *Full Control*, make sure no other users or groups are listed, and then click *OK*.

Recommended Value = 0

Other Registry Settings Adjusting the previously discussed registry settings will help you avoid some of the most common security flaws in the default Windows Registry settings and will certainly increase the security of any server. However, for maximum security an administrator must take the time to carefully study the Windows Registry for any additional areas that can be made more secure. A few of the additional settings you might want to look into include:

■ Restricting anonymous access to the registry

■ NTLMv2 Security (affects security of passwords being sent to the server)

■ KeepAlive (affects how long to keep a connection active)

■ SynAttackProtect (protects against a very specific type of SYN attack)

Several Web sites can help you understand secure registry settings, including the following:

■ Stanford University: **http://windows.stanford.edu/docs/ security2000.html#regsec**

■ Tech Republic: **http://techrepublic.com.com/ 5100-6329-1051224.html**

■ Error Nuker: **www.error-nuker.com/errornuker/article989.html**

Services

A *service* is a program that runs without direct intervention by the computer user. In Unix/Linux environments, these are referred to as ***daemons.*** Many items on your computer are run as services. Internet Information Service,

FTP Service, and many system services are good examples. Any running service is a potential starting point for a hacker. Obviously, you must have some services running for your computer to perform its required functions. However, there are services your machine does not use. If you are not using a service, it should be shut down.

Shutting Down a Service in Windows Shutting down a service in Windows is relatively easy. In our example we will shut down the FTP service on a machine that does not require FTP.

Go to *Start*, select *Settings* (in Windows 2000 only), and choose *Control Panel*. Then double-click *Administrative Tools*.

Double-click *Services*. You should see the Services dialog box, which looks similar to the one shown in Figure 8.7.

The Services dialog box shows all services installed on your machine, whether they are running or not. Notice that the dialog box also displays information about whether a service is running, whether it starts up automatically, and so forth. In Windows XP, more information can be seen by selecting an individual service. When you double-click on an individual service, you

Caution

Don't Know—Don't Touch

Caution should be taken when shutting down services so that you do not inadvertently shut down a service that you need. Always check with your operating system documentation. The rule of thumb is that if you are not sure, do not touch it.

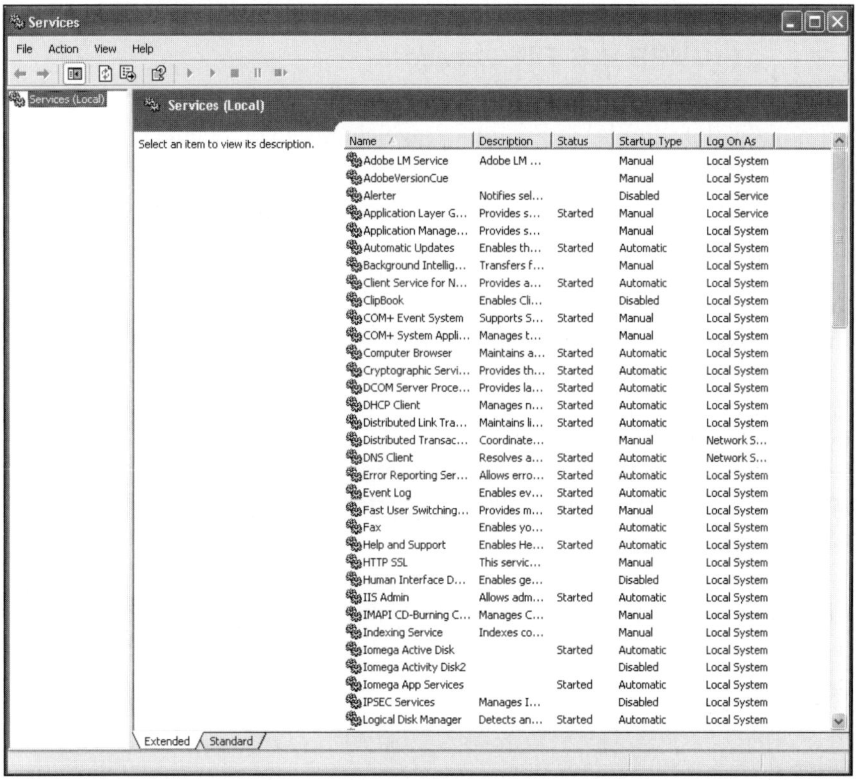

FIGURE 8.7 Services.

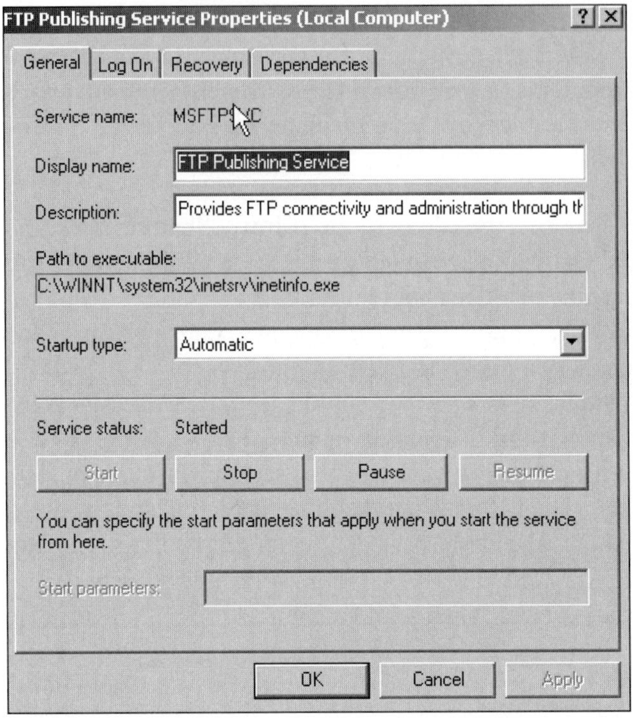

FIGURE 8.8 FTP services.

Caution

Dependencies

We are going to turn off the FTP service; but before you ever turn off any service, click on the "Dependencies" tab to see if other services depend on the one you are about to shut off. If other services depend on that service, you will then be causing them to malfunction by shutting it down.

see a dialog box similar to Figure 8.8, which gives you detailed information about the service and enables you to change the service's settings. In Figure 8.8, we are examining the FTP service on a machine that does not require it.

In this particular case there are no other dependencies, so you can go to the *General* tab and do two things. First, change the *Startup type* option to *Disabled.* Then click the *Stop* button. When you're done, the screen will show the status as disabled. The service is now shut down.

Shutting down unneeded services is an essential and very basic part of hardening an operating system. Every running service is a possible avenue for a hacker or a virus to get to your machine, so the rule for services is: If you don't need it, shut it down. Chapter 12 discusses utilities that scan systems for vulnerabilities. Many of these utilities will point out running services and open ports.

It is also possible to start and stop services from the command prompt. Many administrators prefer command prompts because it is often faster than going through several layers of the Windows graphical user interface. The syntax is quite simple:

```
net start servicename
```

-or-

```
net stop servicename
```

For example:

```
net stop messenger
net start messenger
```

FYI: Erroneous Information on Net Stop

When writing this book I actually found more than one Web site that stated that you could not start or stop a service from the command prompt. This is inaccurate, but has somehow become somewhat of an urban legend among some Windows users. The following documentation from Microsoft's own Web site confirms that you can indeed start and stop a service from the command prompt.

www.microsoft.com/resources/documentation/ windows/xp/all/proddocs/en-us/net_stop.mspx

Port Filtering and Firewalls in Windows Chapters 4 and 5 discuss the Windows XP Firewall and Windows 2000's basic port filtering capabilities. Turning on the Windows port filters is a basic part of operating system hardening. The instructions for doing this have been previously given in Chapters 4 and 5 and will be re-explored in exercises at the end of this chapter.

Encrypting File System

Beginning with Windows 2000, the Windows operating system has offered the *Encrypting File System (EFS),* which is based on public key encryption and takes advantage of the CryptoAPI architecture in Windows 2000. With this system, each file is encrypted using a randomly generated file encryption key, which is independent of a user's public/private key pair; this method makes the encryption resistant to many forms of cryptoanalysis-based attacks. For our purposes the exact details of how EFS encryption works are not as important as the practical aspects of using it.

User Interaction The default configuration of EFS enables users to start encrypting files with no administrator effort. EFS automatically generates a public key pair and file encryption certificate for file encryption the first time a user encrypts a file.

File encryption and decryption is supported per file or for an entire folder. Folder encryption is transparently enforced. All files and folders created in a folder marked for encryption are automatically encrypted. Each file has a unique file encryption key, making it safe to rename. If you rename a file from an encrypted folder to an unencrypted folder on the same volume, the file remains encrypted. However, if you copy an unencrypted file into

---

FYI: What If a User Leaves?

A user might encrypt a file and then be unavailable to decrypt it. They may become unavailable due to leaving the company, illness, or other reasons. Fortunately, EFS does give administrators a method by which they can recover the encryption key used to encrypt files, and thereby decrypt them. EFS allows recovery agents to configure public keys that are used to recover encrypted data if a user leaves the company. Only the file encryption key is available using the recovery key, not a user's private key. This ensures that no other private information is revealed to the recovery agent.

---

an encrypted folder, the file state will change. The file becomes encrypted. Command-line tools and administrative interfaces are provided for advanced users and recovery agents.

The best thing about EFS is that it is virtually transparent to the user. You don't have to decrypt a file to open it and use it. EFS automatically detects an encrypted file and locates a user's file encryption key from the system's key store. However, if the file is moved from the originating computer to another computer, a user trying to open it will find it is encrypted. The following steps will allow you to encrypt any file you wish:

1. Locate the file or folder you wish to encrypt (using either Windows Explorer or My Computer). Then right-click on that file and select *Properties*. You will see the Properties dialog box, similar to the one shown in Figure 8.9.
2. Click on the *Advanced* tab to bring up an option that you can check to encrypt the file, as shown in Figure 8.10.
3. Click *Encrypt contents* to secure data.

Once you have done this, your file or folder is now encrypted. As long as the same user on the same machine opens the file, it will be decrypted automatically. A hacker who transfers the file to his or her own system (or an employee attempting industrial espionage, who takes the file home on a disk) will find it is encrypted. Because EFS is built into Windows, costs nothing extra, and is so easy to use, it is difficult to find any reason not to use it. If you want more details, the following Web sites should be helpful to you:

- Microsoft's step-by-step guide to EFS: **www.microsoft.com/ windows2000/techinfo/planning/security/efssteps.asp**

- ServerWatch review of EFS: **www.serverwatch.com/tutorials/ article.php/2106831**

- A utility for retrieving EFS encryption keys: **www.lostpassword. com/efs.htm**

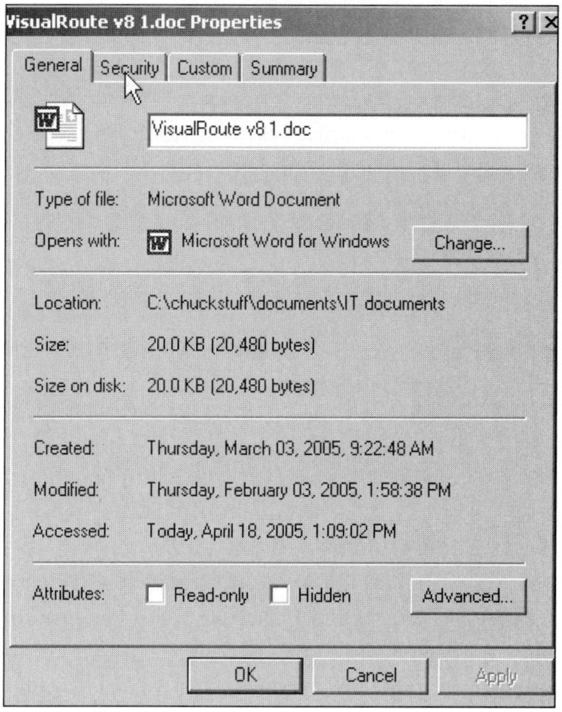

FIGURE 8.9 File properties.

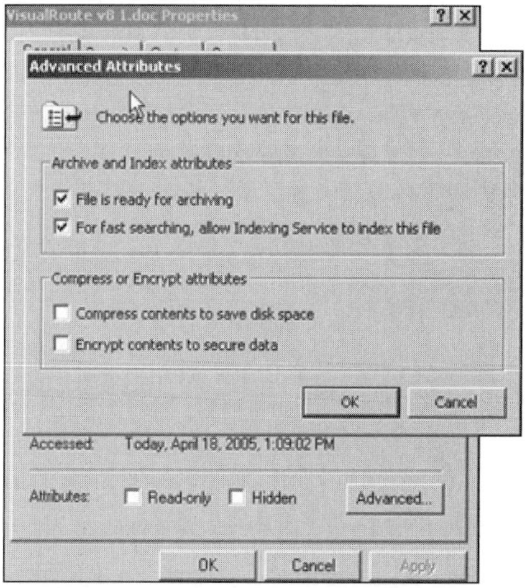

FIGURE 8.10 Encrypting a file.

> ## FYI: EFS in Windows 2003
>
> Encrypting File System was introduced in Windows 2000. However it was continued in Windows XP and Windows 2003. You can read about EFS in XP and Windows 2003 here:
>
> **www.microsoft.com/technet/prodtechnol/winxppro/deploy/cryptfs.mspx**

Security Templates

We have been discussing a number of ways for making a Windows system more secure, but exploring services, password settings, registry keys, and other tools can be a daunting task for the administrator who is new to security. Applying such settings to a host of machines can be a very tedious task for even the most experienced administrator. The best way to simplify this aspect of operating system hardening is to use *security templates.* A security template contains hundreds of possible settings that can control a single or multiple computers. Security templates can control areas such as user rights, permissions, and password policies, and they enable administrators to deploy these settings centrally by means of *Group Policy Objects (GPOs).*

Security templates can be customized to include almost any security setting on a target computer. A number of security templates are built into Windows. These templates are categorized for domain controllers, servers, and workstations. These security templates have default settings designed by Microsoft. All of these templates are located in the *C:\Windows\Security\ Templates* folder. The following is a partial list of the security templates that you will find in this folder:

- *DC security.inf* — This template is used to configure security of the Registry and File system of a computer that was upgraded from Windows NT to Windows 2000/2003.

- *Hisecdc.inf* — This template is designed to increase the security and communications with domain controllers.

- *Hisecws.inf* — This template is designed to increase security and communications for client computers and member servers.

- *Securedc.inf* — This template is designed to increase the security and communications with domain controllers, but not to the level of the High Security DC security template.

- *Securews.inf* — This template is designed to increase security and communications for client computers and member servers.

- *Setup security.inf* — This template is designed to reapply the default security settings of a freshly installed computer. It can also be used to return a system that has been misconfigured to the default configuration.

Installing security templates simplifies network security for the administrator. You will have the opportunity to walk through the process of installing a security template in one of the end-of-chapter exercises.

Configuring Linux Properly

An in-depth review of Linux security would be a lengthy task indeed. One reason is the diversity of Linux setups. Users could be using Debian, Red Hat, Mandrake, or other Linux distributions. Some might be working from the shell, while others work from some graphical user interfaces such as KDE or GNOME (for Windows users not familiar with Linux you may wish to consult my book *Moving from Windows to Linux*). However, it is fortunate that many of the same security concepts that apply to Windows can be applied to Linux. The only differences lie in the implementation, as explained in the following list:

- User and account policies should be set up the same in Linux as they are in Windows, with only a few minor differences. These differences are more a matter of using different names in Linux than in Windows. For example Linux does not have an administrator account; it has a root account.

- All services (called daemons in Linux) not in use should be shut down.

- The browser must be configured securely.

- Routinely patch the operating system.

In addition to these tactics that are common to Windows and Linux, there are a few approaches that are different for the two operating systems:

- No application should run as the root user unless absolutely necessary. Remember that the root user is equivalent to the administrator account in Windows. Also remember that all applications in Linux run as if started by a particular user, and therefore having an application run as root user would give it all administrative privileges.

- The root password must be complex and must be changed frequently. This is the same as with Windows administrator passwords.

- Disable all console-equivalent access for regular users. This means blocking access to programs like shutdown, reboot, and halt for regular users on your server. To do this, run the following command: *[root@kapil /]# rm -f /etc/security/console.apps/<service-name>,* where *<servicename>* is the name of the program to which you wish to disable console-equivalent access.

■ Hide your system information. When you log in to a Linux box, it displays by default the Linux distribution name, version, kernel version, and the name of the server. This information can be a starting point for intruders. You should just prompt users with a "Login:" prompt.

To do this, Edit the */etc/rc.d/rc.local* file and place # in front of the following lines, as shown:

```
# This will overwrite /etc/issue at every boot.
So, make any changes you
# want to make to /etc/issue here or you will lose
them when you reboot.
#echo "" > /etc/issue
#echo "$R" >> /etc/issue
#echo "Kernel $(uname -r) on $a $(uname -m)" >>
/etc/issue
#
#cp -f /etc/issue /etc/issue.net
#echo >> /etc/issue
Remove the following files: "issue.net" and
"issue" under "/etc" directory:
[root@kapil /]# rm -f /etc/issue
[root@kapil /]# rm -f /etc/issue.net
```

In general security concepts apply regardless of operating system. However, truly hardening any operating system requires a certain level of expertise with that particular operating system.

The following Web sites provide information useful for helping you secure your Linux Server:

■ Linux Security Administrators Guide:
www.linuxsecurity.com/docs/SecurityAdminGuide/ SecurityAdminGuide.html

■ National Security Administration's Secure Linux:
www.nsa.gov/selinux/

■ Linux security tips: **www.linuxgazette.com/issue58/ sharma.html**

■ Linux.com: **www.linux.com/**

Patching the Operating System

From time to time, security flaws are found in operating systems. As software vendors become aware of flaws, they usually write corrections to their code, known as patches or updates. Whatever operating system you use, you must apply these patches as a matter of routine. Windows patches are probably the most well known, but patches can be released for any operating system. You should patch your system any time a critical patch is released. You might consider scheduling a specific time simply to update patches. Some organizations find once per quarter or even once per month is necessary.

For Windows you can go to **www.microsoft.com**. On the left-hand side you should notice a link that says "Update Windows." If you click on this, you can scan your machine for missing patches and download them from the Web site. Red Hat offers a similar service for Red Hat Linux users. On the Web site **www.redhat.com/security/**, users can scan for updates.

> **Caution**
>
> **Patch Conflicts**
>
> A patch could possibly conflict with some software or settings on your system. To avoid these conflicts, you should first apply patches to a test machine to ensure there are no conflicts before you apply it to production machines.

Configuring Browsers

Most computers, including corporate workstations, are used to access the Internet. This means that proper browser configuration is absolutely essential for hardening a system. The Internet is probably the single greatest threat to an individual system or a corporate network. Safe use of the Internet is critical. This section describes how to set both Internet Explorer and Netscape Navigator for safe Internet use.

Securing Browser Settings for Microsoft Internet Explorer

Some experts claim that Internet Explorer simply is not a secure browser. We won't spend time engaging in the Internet Explorer vs. Netscape vs. Mozilla debate. Because many people use Internet Explorer, you must understand how to make it as secure as possible.

1. Open Microsoft Internet Explorer.
2. Select *Tools* on the menu bar, and then select *Internet Options*. You will see a screen like the one shown in Figure 8.11.

The Options window includes a Privacy tab and a Security tab. We will discuss both of these tabs and the settings you should select.

Privacy Settings With spyware a growing problem, privacy settings are as important to operating system hardening as security settings. Clicking on the Advanced button allows you to alter how your browser handles

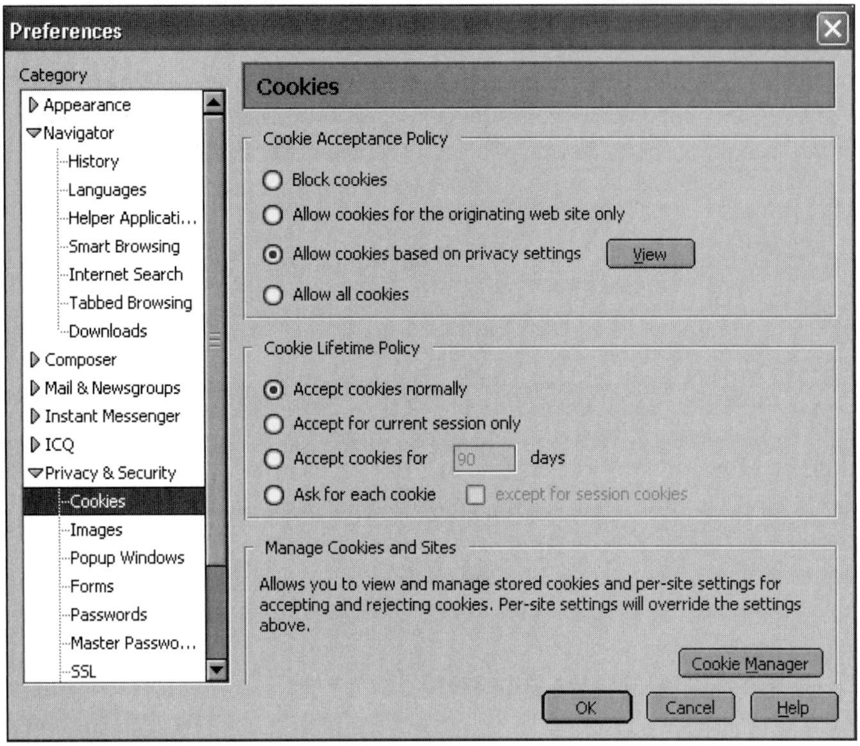

FIGURE 8.11 Internet Explorer options.

cookies. Unfortunately it is difficult to surf the Web without accepting some cookies. The following settings are recommended:

- Block third-party cookies
- Prompt for first-party cookies
- Always allow session cookies

These settings will help you avoid some of the problems associated with cookies. You may also want to click the *Edit* button and set up the browser to allow cookies from certain sites and to never allow cookies from others.

Security Settings Security settings are more complex than privacy settings, and there are many more security options to select. You can simply choose the default levels of low, medium, high in your browser, but most security conscious administrators use the *Custom* button to set up security specific to their organization. When you select *Custom,* you will see a dialog box like the one shown in Figure 8.12. We will not discuss every single setting, but we will explain many of the more important ones.

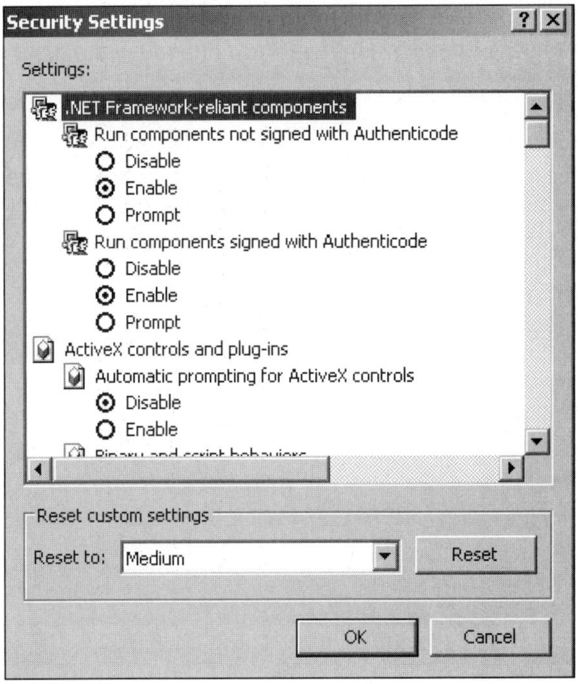

FIGURE 8.12 Internet Explorer custom security settings.

As you can see, there are many different settings for you to work with. Table 8.6 summarizes the most important ones and the recommended settings for each.

Because the Web is often the weakest part in an organization's security, having secure browser settings is critical to operating system security and to network security in general.

Secure Browser Settings for Netscape Navigator

Microsoft Internet Explorer is probably the most widely used browser for Windows systems. However Linux systems are becoming more popular every year, and some Windows users will choose to use Netscape instead. Anyone in the security business should be familiar with alternative software rather than simply specializing in one vendor for a given type of product. Netscape Navigator can be downloaded for free at **channels.netscape.com/ns/browsers/ default.jsp**. Once installed, you access Netscape Navigator privacy and security settings by the following method:

1. Open Netscape Navigator.
2. Select *Edit* on the menu bar and then select *Preferences*. You will see the screen shown in Figure 8.13.

TABLE 8.6 Internet Explorer custom security settings.

Setting	Purpose	Recommendation
Run components not signed with Authenticode	Allows unsigned software components to execute on your system.	At a minimum set this to prompt you, but consider disabling it altogether.
Run components signed with Authenticode	Allows signed software components to execute on your system.	Prompt.
Download Signed ActiveX	Allows ActiveX components that are signed to be downloaded automatically to your system.	Prompt.
Download Unsigned ActiveX	Allows ActiveX components that are not signed to be automatically downloaded to your system.	Prompt. You might think disable, but many Flash animations are not signed, and if you simply disable you will not be able to see those.
Initialize and script ActiveX controls not marked as safe	Allows ActiveX components to run scripts.	Disable is recommended, but at least prompt.
Script ActiveX controls marked safe	Allows those ActiveX components to run scripts.	Prompt.
Downloads (font, file, etc.)	Downloads files, fonts, and so on that a Web page needs.	Prompt.
Java permissions	This setting simply allows you to determine what a Java applet can or cannot do on your system. Java applets can be a vehicle for malicious code, but all applets need to perform some actions on your system.	High safety.
All others	This is the catch all for miscellaneous non-critical items that don't fit in elsewhere. These various settings are not as critical to safety as the ones previously discussed.	You can always have prompts if you do not wish to outright disable something. In most cases simply disabling all settings will render some Web sites unviewable, so for practical purposes the "prompt before..." setting is preferred.

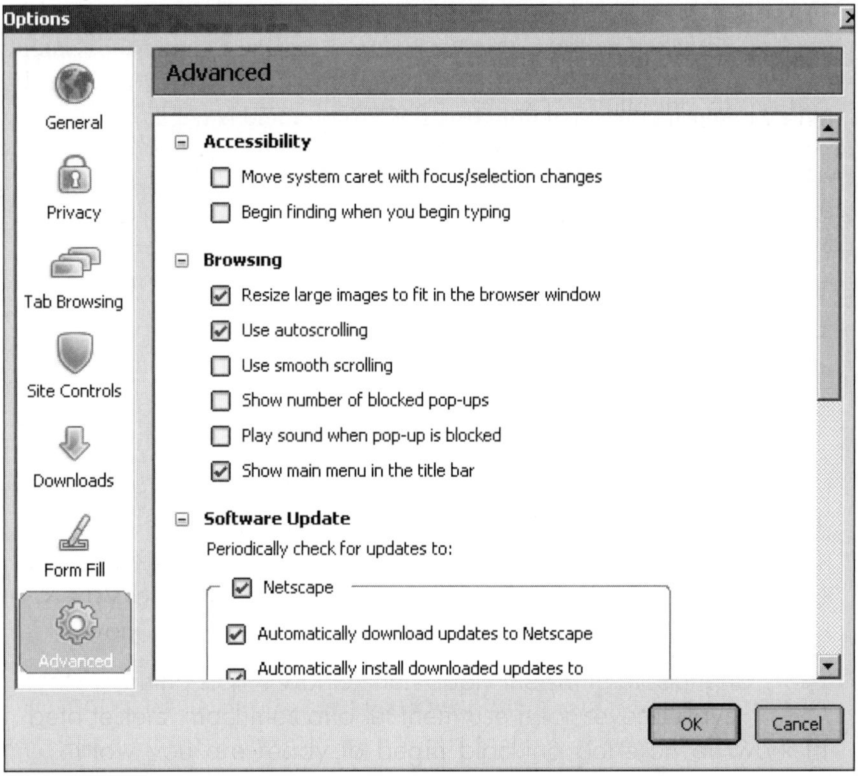

FIGURE 8.13 Netscape preferences.

3. Double-click the *Privacy and Security* option near the bottom of the Category panel. It will expand, giving you several options.

Netscape offers more details regarding privacy settings than Internet Explorer. In addition to enabling cookies for the originating site or third-party sites, you can set how long any cookie stays. This duration should be short, perhaps 3 days or less, so that if your machine gets cookies you do not want, they will not be there long.

Of particular interest is the third option under Privacy and Security, Popup Windows, which you can use to block popup windows. Some readers may think such windows are merely a nuisance to users, but they can often be used to deposit adware on a system. If the popup window is never loaded, then it cannot download the adware.

The fifth option defines how to handle passwords. Many users prefer to have passwords remembered, but this option is not particularly secure. For security reasons you should have this unchecked. You should also check the box that encrypts sensitive data. Examine the various settings with a mindset that you wish to close any potential avenue for an intruder or malware to get into your system.

Other Browsers In addition to Internet Explorer and Netscape Navigator, other browsers are available, including Mozilla, Opera, and Galeon (Linux only). Each of these have different methods for setting up security, but the same principles that hold true for Explorer and Navigator also apply to these browsers: Limit cookies, do not allow ActiveX components to run without your knowledge, and do not allow any scripts to execute without your knowledge. If you apply the same principles to other browsers, you should be able to achieve similar security to what you can have with Navigator or Internet Explorer.

FYI: What About Firefox?

The Firefox browser has received a great deal of attention lately. It is actually simply the latest version of Mozilla. That means its underlying security will be similar. Mozilla and Netscape Navigator have similar settings and are based on the same underlying architecture. Many reviewers have commented that Firefox is the most customizable browser they have ever used. This can be a boon to security, if you use that customization to tighten security. It can also be a security flaw if end users use the customization to loosen security.

Summary

Operating system hardening is a critical part of network security, and it has many facets. It involves securing the operating system, applying patches, using appropriate security settings, and securing your browser. All of these factors must be addressed in order to secure a machine.

Careful configuration of the operating system can make many hacking techniques more difficult. It can also make a system more resistant to DoS attacks. Setting up appropriate policies for users and accounts can make hacking into those accounts much more difficult. Policies should cover issues such as appropriate password length, password type, and password age/history.

With Windows you can also use the Encrypted File System to protect your data should it be moved off of your system. EFS was first introduced in Windows 2000 and has continued through Windows 2003. It is a valuable tool that can and should be used to protect any sensitive data.

With any version of Microsoft Windows, proper registry settings are key to security. The registry is the heart and soul of the Microsoft Windows operating system, and failure to address proper registry settings will leave gaping holes in security.

Proper configuration of the browser makes a system less susceptible to malware. Limiting cookies can help ensure that privacy is protected. Blocking browsers from executing scripts or any active code without your knowledge is a critical step for protecting a system from malware.

Test Your Skills

MULTIPLE CHOICE QUESTIONS

1. What do disabling the default administrator account and setting up an alternative account accomplish?

    A. makes it more difficult for someone to guess the log on information

    B. keeps administrators conscious of security

    C. allows closer management of administrator access

    D. makes the password stronger

2. What level of privileges should all users have?

    A. administrator

    B. guest

    C. most privileges possible

    D. least possible

3. What minimum password length does the NSA recommend?

    A. 6

    B. 8

    C. 10

    D. 12

4. What maximum password age does Microsoft recommend?

    A. 20 days

    B. 3 months

    C. 1 year

    D. 42 days

8

5. What account lockout threshold does the NSA recommend?

    A. 5 tries

    B. 3 tries

    C. 4 tries

    D. 2 tries

6. Which of the following most accurately describes the registry?

    A. a relational database containing system settings

    B. a database containing system settings

    C. a database where software is registered

    D. a relational database where software is registered

7. What is changing the TCP/Settings in the registry called?

    A. stack tweaking

    B. stack altering

    C. stack compression

    D. stack building

8. What type of encryption does EFS utilize?

    A. single key

    B. multi-alphabet

    C. public key encryption

    D. a secret algorithm proprietary to Microsoft

9. What happens if you copy an unencrypted file into an encrypted folder?

    A. It remains unencrypted.

    B. The folder becomes unencrypted.

    C. Nothing happens.

    D. The file becomes encrypted.

10. Which of the following templates is used to provide the most security for the domain controllers?

    A. Hisecdc.inf

    B. Securedc.inf

    C. Hisecws.inf

    D. Sectopdc.inf

11. Which of the following is a security recommendation for Linux not common to Windows?

   A. Shut down all services that you are not using (called daemons in Linux).

   B. Configure the browser securely.

   C. Routinely patch the operating system.

   D. Disable all console-equivalent access for regular users.

12. What is the rule for unused services on any computer?

   A. Turn them off only if they are critical.

   B. Turn them off.

   C. Monitor them carefully.

   D. Configure them for minimal privileges.

13. What operating systems require periodic patches?

   A. Windows

   B. Linux

   C. all

   D. Macintosh

14. What is the minimum secure setting in Internet Explorer for *Run components not signed with Authenticode*?

   A. disable

   B. enable

   C. forbid

   D. prompt

15. What is the recommended secure setting in Internet Explorer for *Initialize and script ActiveX controls not marked as safe*?

   A. disable

   B. enable

   C. forbid

   D. prompt

8

EXERCISES

Exercise 8.1: User Accounts and Password Policies

Note: This exercise is best done with a lab computer, not a machine actually in use. Following the guidelines given in this chapter, accomplish the following tasks:

1. Create a new account with administrative privileges.

2. Disable all default accounts, or if they cannot be disabled, change them to the lowest possible permissions.

3. Implement the NSA recommendations for password policies and account lockout policies.

Exercise 8.2: Secure Registry Settings

Note: This exercise should be done on a laboratory Windows machine, not on one in normal use. Using the guidelines given in the chapter, check your machine's settings to see that the following recommendations are implemented:

- Restrict null session access.

- Restrict anonymous access.

- Default shares.

- Restrict null session access over named pipes.

Exercise 8.3: Stack Tweaking

Note: This exercise should be done on a laboratory machine, not one in normal use.

Following the guidelines given in the chapter, change the registry settings to make DoS attacks more difficult.

Exercise 8.4: Installing Security Templates

This exercise should be done on a laboratory Windows machine, not on one in normal use. By following the steps given here you should be able to apply a security template to a Windows 2000 or XP machine. You may use one of the default templates mentioned in the chapter or one you download from a Web site of your choice.

1. From the *Command* prompt, or from *Start > Run,* type **MMC**. You will see a screen like the one shown in Figure 8.14:

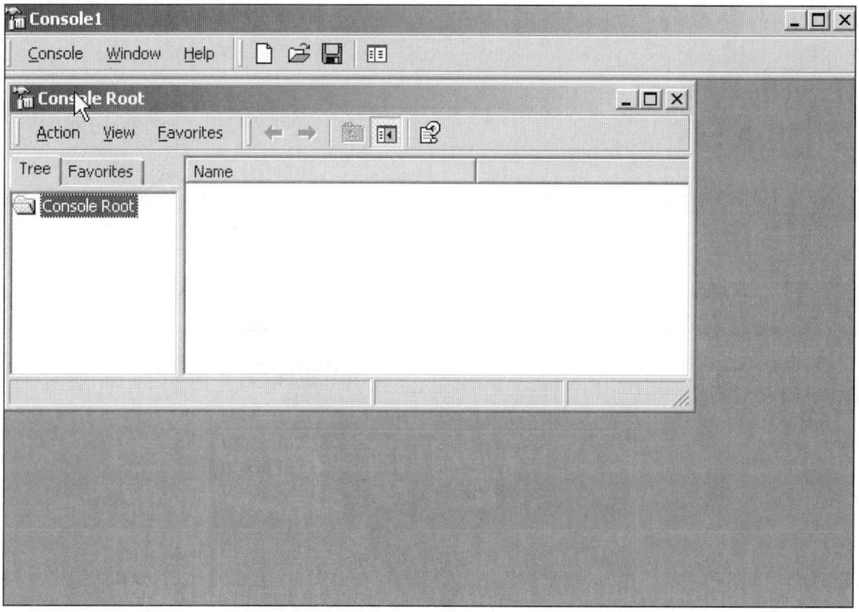

FIGURE 8.14 The MMC console.

2. Go to the drop down menu *Console* and choose *Add/remove* console.

3. When you click the *Add* button, you will see a screen like the one shown here. Find and select *Security Configuration and Analysis*.

4. Once you have added this to the console, you can right-click on it and choose *Open database.* Then give the database any name you like. When you click *Enter,* your dialog will change to display a list of all templates. Select the one you want.

Exercise 8.5: Securing Linux

Using a laboratory Linux machine (any distribution will work) and the data presented in this chapter, accomplish the following:

1. Ensure that user accounts are set up securely.

2. Shut down unused and unneeded daemons.

3. Apply the Linux-specific settings given in this chapter.

Exercise 8.6:

Using a laboratory computer, secure Microsoft Internet Explorer by following the steps given here:

1. Block all unsigned ActiveX components.

2. Limit cookies to only first-party and session cookies.

3. Block all scripting.

Exercise 8.7: Patching Windows

Using a laboratory computer, preferably one that has not been patched in quite some time:

1. Go to **www.microsoft.com**.

2. Scan for patches.

3. Update all patches, and document the patches you update.

PROJECTS

Project 8.1: Account and Password Settings

This chapter provides recommendations on accounts and passwords from the NSA, Microsoft, and the author. Using the Web (including but not limited to resources identified in this chapter), find recommendations from some other reliable source (CERT, SANS, any of the security certification vendors, etc.). Write a brief paper discussing those recommendations, paying particular attention to areas in which they differ from the recommendations given in this chapter.

Project 8.2: Registry Settings

Note: This project is appropriate either for students with a strong understanding of the registry or perhaps as a group project.

Write about at least three additional registry settings you think should be modified to create a more secure Windows operating system. Explain your reasons fully.

Project 8.3: Encrypted File System

Using the Web or other resources find out specifics about the Encrypted File System that is part of Windows. Describe this file system, and any strengths and any weaknesses you find.

▶▶ Case Study

Leah is a network administrator for an insurance company. The company has 6 servers and 40 workstations. The claims department, in particular, keeps sensitive documents on its workstations. Also most employees frequently use the Internet for work-related purposes. She takes the following actions to harden the operating systems of all servers and workstations:

1. She applies all patches and schedules to check patches every two months.
2. She disables default accounts on all machines.
3. She sets Internet Explorer to high security.

Are these steps adequate? Is there anything she missed?

8

Chapter

Defending Against Virus Attacks

Chapter Objectives

After reading this chapter and completing the exercises, you will be able to do the following:

- Explain how virus attacks work.
- Explain how viruses spread.
- Distinguish between different types of virus attacks.
- Employ virus scanners to detect viruses.
- Formulate an appropriate strategy to defend against virus attacks.

Introduction

Chapter 2 introduced virus attacks. In this chapter you will learn more about how virus attacks work and learn how to defend against a virus attack.

One thing already pointed out in Chapter 2 is that the most prevalent danger on the Internet is the computer virus or worm. This is due to the fact that once a virus is released it spreads rapidly and unpredictably. Other attacks, such as DoS, session hacking, and buffer overflow, are generally targeted at a specific system or network. The virus simply spreads to any computer it can get to. It is a fact that any system will eventually encounter a virus. How significantly your network is affected by this encounter is entirely up to you, and the security measures you implement.

Since the virus poses such a significant threat, defending against such attacks is of paramount importance to any network administrator. Unfortunately some administrators feel that simply because they have a virus scanner installed they are safe. This assumption is inaccurate. In this chapter you will learn how virus attacks work and explore some real world examples of virus attacks. Then you will learn more about how antivirus software works and look at a few commercial solutions. You will also learn about appropriate policies your organization can implement to reduce the chance of your systems being infected by a virus. Finally, you will learn about configuration options on other devices (firewalls, routers, etc.) that can help reduce the threat of a virus infection.

Understanding Virus Attacks

Understanding what a virus is, how it spreads, and the different variations are essential for combating virus threats. You will also need to have a firm understanding of how a virus scanner works in order to make intelligent decisions about purchasing a virus scanner for your organization. In this section we will explore these topics in sufficient detail to equip you with the skills needed to establish a solid defense against virus attacks.

What Is a Virus?

Most people are familiar with computer viruses, but may not have a clear definition of what one is. A computer virus is a program that self-replicates. Generally, a virus will also have some other negative function such as deleting files or changing system settings. However, it is the self-replication and rapid spread that define a virus. Often this growth, in and of itself, can be a problem for an infected network. It can lead to excessive network traffic and prevent the network from functioning properly. Recall in Chapter 2 that we discussed the fact that all technology has a finite capacity to perform work. The more a virus floods a network with traffic, the less capacity is left for real work to be performed.

What Is a Worm?

A worm is a special type of virus. Some texts go to great lengths to differentiate worms and viruses, while others treat the worm as simply a subset of a virus. A worm is a virus that can spread without human intervention. In other words, a virus requires some human action in order to infect a machine (downloading a file, opening an attachment), but a worm can spread without such interaction. In recent years, worm outbreaks have become more common than the standard, nonworm virus.

How a Virus Spreads

The best way to combat viruses is to limit their spread, so it's critical that you understand *how* they spread. A virus will usually spread in one of two ways. The most common, and the simplest, method is to read your e-mail address book and e-mail itself to everyone in your address book. Programming this is a trivial task, which explains why it is so common. The second method is to simply scan your computer for connections to a network, and then copy itself to other machines on the network to which your computer has access. This is actually the most efficient way for a virus to spread, but it requires more programming skill than the other method.

The first method is, by far, the most common method for virus propagation. Microsoft Outlook may be the one e-mail program most often hit with such virus attacks. The reason is not so much a security flaw in Outlook as it is the ease of working with Outlook.

FYI: Ease of Use vs. Security

There will always be a conflict between ease of use and security. The easier it is to use a system, the less secure it is. The opposite is true as well: The more secure you make a system, the more difficult it is to work with. Some security professionals focus merely on the security side without giving enough thought to usability issues. This leads some security experts to completely avoid Microsoft products, as Microsoft's focus has always been usability, not security.

To become an effective network administrator, you must have a balanced view of these considerations. The most secure computer in the world is one that is unplugged from any network, never has any software installed on it, and has all portable media drives (CD-ROM, floppy, USB) removed. Such a computer would also be completely useless.

9

There are a number of theories about why Microsoft Outlook is so frequently struck with virus attacks. One explanation is its prevalence in the marketplace. Virus writers wish to cause havoc. The best way to do that is to target the most commonly used systems.

Another reason that Outlook is so often targeted is that writing viruses for it is relatively easy. We previously mentioned the fact that many e-mail applications allow programmers to create extensions to the application. All Microsoft Office products are made so that a legitimate programmer who is writing software for a business can access many of the application's internal objects and thereby easily create applications that integrate the applications within the Microsoft Office suite. For example, a programmer could write an application that would access a Word document, import an Excel spreadsheet, and then use Outlook to automatically e-mail the resulting document to interested parties. Microsoft has done a good job of making this process very easy, for it usually takes a minimum amount of programming to accomplish these tasks. Using Outlook, it takes less than five lines of code to reference Outlook and send out an e-mail. This means a program can literally cause Outlook itself to send e-mail, unbeknownst to the user. There are numerous code examples on the Internet that show exactly how to do this, free for the taking. For this reason, it does not take a very skilled programmer to be able to access your Outlook address book and automatically send e-mail. Essentially, the ease of programming Outlook is why there are so many virus attacks that target Outlook.

While the overwhelming majority of virus attacks spread by attaching themselves to the victim's existing e-mail software, some recent virus outbreaks have used other methods for propagation. One method that is becoming more common is for viruses to have their own internal e-mail engine. A virus that has its own e-mail engine does not need to "piggy-back" off of the machine's e-mail software. This means that, regardless of what e-mail software you use, this virus can still propagate from your machine. Another virus propagation method is to simply copy itself across a network. Virus outbreaks that spread via multiple routes are becoming more common.

Another way a virus can spread is by examining the affected system looking for any connected computers and copying itself to them. This sort of self-propagation does not require user interaction, so the program that uses this method to infect a system is classified as a worm.

Regardless of the way a virus arrives at your doorstep, once it is on your system, it will attempt to spread and, in many cases, will also attempt to cause some harm to your system. Once a virus is on your system, it can do anything that any legitimate program can do. That means it could potentially delete files, change system settings, or cause other harm. The threat from virus attacks cannot be overstated. Some recent virus outbreaks even went so far as to disable existing security software, such as antivirus scanners and firewalls. Let's take a moment to examine a few virus attacks that are common as of this writing. Examining real-world virus outbreaks provides a firm understanding of how these work. For our purposes we will look at examples of both virus and worm attacks in this section.

The Zafi Worm The first version of this worm was released only in the Hungarian language, so its spread was somewhat limited. However, by version Zafi.d it was spreading in English. This version of the virus, which purported to be a holiday greeting card, spread widely just before Christmas 2004. The use of the holiday greeting as a subject line for the e-mail significantly increased its chances of being read. Its strategic timing probably lead to its infecting more systems than it otherwise would have. The virus has its own SMTP e-mail engine and sends itself out to as many addresses as it can find. This worm grabs e-mail addresses from a number of different file types it might find on a computer, including HTML, ASP, text files, and others.

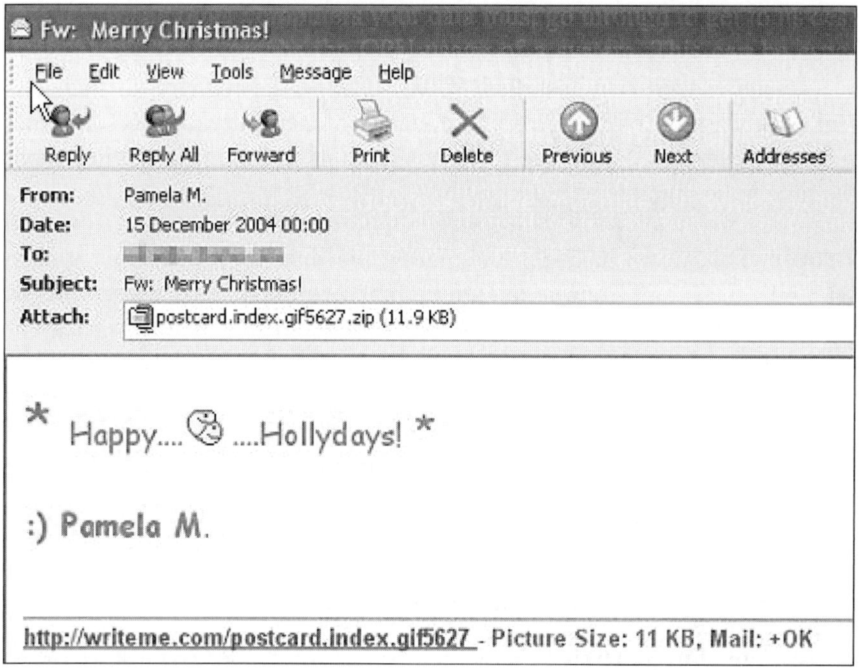

FIGURE 9.1 The Zafi worm.

Once a system is infected, in addition to e-mailing itself out to e-mail addresses, it attempts to detect antivirus program files on the computer and overwrite them with a copy of itself. This disabling of antivirus software made Zafi.d particularly dangerous. Some versions of Zafi (Kaspersky Labs, 2004) also attempt a DoS attack on the following sites:

- **www.2f.hu**
- **www.parlament.hu**
- **www.virusbuster.hu**
- **www.virushirado.hu**

A typical Zafi worm e-mail is shown in Figure 9.1.

Mabutu This virus also has its own built-in e-mail engine and harvests e-mail addresses from text files, HTML files, and other files on the victims' computers (F-Secure, 2004). You should note how common it is becoming for a virus to:

- Have its own built-in e-mail engine, freeing it from dependence upon the victims' e-mail software.

- Derive e-mail addresses from sources other than the victims' address books.

- Disable the virus scanner of the infected machine, thus allowing even more viruses to infect that machine, a particularly disturbing trend.

Once the virus is installed, it will change the registry so that it is loaded at startup. It will also try to connect to one of several IRC (Internet relay chat) servers. It will use these connections to send information about the infected computer.

Bropia This worm has been circulating the Internet for several months, with new variations coming as late as February 2005. This worm spreads via MSN Messenger. It may also be able to spread using Windows Messenger. It drops a variant of the Rbot worm family, *Win32.Rbot.BPR*. Many variations of the Rbot worm actually open a backdoor on the target system allowing intruders access. It then attempts to send this file using MSN Messenger to all active MSN contacts. The recipient has to accept and open the file to get infected by the worm.

Three factors make this worm interesting. First, it spreads through instant messaging. As instant messaging and chat rooms become more widely used, you can expect to see more viruses and worms that affect them. Second, it drops two worms on the affected machine: its own, and a second worm that it has in its payload. This two-pronged attack makes it more difficult to defend against. That second worm is *C:\osm.exe* (a variant of *W32.Spybot.Worm*). The third interesting aspect of this virus is the number of variations — over a dozen so far. This is important for two reasons:

- They indicate that more virus writers are producing versions of this virus.

- The different variations make it more difficult to detect and avoid the virus.

Santy The Santy worm exploits a vulnerability in bulletin boards and online forums that are written with the very popular phpBB software, using the Google search engine to find vulnerable servers. It does *not* infect end user computers.

The worm is written in the Perl scripting language. As previously mentioned, the worm uses the Google search engine to look for hosts that have phpBB software in use. It accomplishes this by searching for URLs that contain the string *viewtopic.php*. In order to get varied results with different searches, the worm uses a random string in the search as well.

If a suitable URL is found, the worm then attempts to exploit a vulnerability in phpBB software. This vulnerability, known as the *Highlight Vulnerability,* can be used to execute arbitrary code on the server running a vulnerable version of phpBB. If it successfully infects the target server, all

FYI: The Future of Virus Infections

In recent years many computer security professionals have lamented the security holes in Microsoft operating systems and applications. One of the claims (but not by any means the only claim) made is that the prevalence of Outlook-specific virus attacks is indicative of a fundamental security flaw in Microsoft products. With the increasing number of virus attacks that are not specific to any e-mail system, it is likely that we will see more virus attacks that infect non-Microsoft products.

affected Web pages will be replaced with a simple message stating, "This Site is Defaced."

The Virus Hoax

In recent years a new virus phenomenon has become more common — the virus hoax. Rather than actually writing a virus, a person sends an e-mail to every address he has. The e-mail claims to be from some well known antivirus center, and warns of a new virus that is circulating that might damage the user's computer. Often the e-mail instructs people to delete some file from their computer to get rid of the virus. The file, however, is not really a virus but part of a computer's system. The *jdbgmgr.exe* virus hoax used this scheme. It encouraged the reader to delete a file that was actually needed by the system. Surprisingly, a number of people followed this advice and not only deleted the file, but promptly e-mailed their friends and colleagues to warn them to delete the file from their machines.

Jdbgmgr Hoax This particular virus hoax is perhaps the most well known and well examined. You will see some mention of it in almost any comprehensive discussion of viruses. The jdbgmgr.exe virus hoax (Vmyths.com, 2004) encouraged the reader to delete a file that was actually needed by the system. The typical message looked like this:

I found the little bear in my machine because of that I am sending this message in order for you to find it in your machine. The procedure is very simple:

The objective of this e-mail is to warn all Hotmail users about a new virus that is spreading by MSN Messenger. The name of this virus is jdbgmgr.exe and it is sent automatically by the Messenger and by the address book too. The virus is not detected by McAfee or Norton and it stays quiet for 14 days before damaging the system.

9

The virus can be cleaned before it deletes the files from your system. In order to eliminate it, it is just necessary to do the following steps:

1. *Go to* Start, *click* Search.
2. *In the* Files or Folders *option write the name* jdbgmgr.exe.
3. *Once you have found that file, delete it.*

Jdbgmgr.exe is actually the Microsoft Debugger Registrar for Java. Deleting it may cause Java-based programs and Web applets not to function properly.

Tax Return Hoax This hoax first surfaced in 2003. The essential point of the e-mail was to make the recipient think that submitting federal taxes in the United States via the Internet was not safe (McAfee Virus Hoax Listings, 2003). The fact was that such online submissions were perfectly safe and usually resulted in much faster refunds for the taxpayer. The e-mail body looked something like this:

WARNING

Nobody still knows if it's true, but it's worthwhile to protect yourself.

Don't send your tax return by the Internet (for the time being).

A new virus has been unleashed through the Internet to capture your tax return. The author created this virus to intercept all files using the extensions generated by the Federal Revenue program. If there is a rebate, the virus changes the current account indicated by the victim, changing it to the author's account. After that the changed file goes to the Federal Revenue Database. The victim receives the usual return-receipt, because the tax return doesn't fail to be delivered. There is a small increase in time of shipping, necessary because of the changed account information, which is not apparent to the person waiting for the tax return, therefore the recipient of the rebate assumes that it is due to a high volume of traffic or problems with the telephone line, etc. ...all problems that we are accustomed to, being on the Internet. The new virus still informs its author about the rebates that he managed to capture, including the values that he'll pocket.

Send this e-mail to all your friends.

Fortunately this particular hoax did not cause any actual damage to the infected machine. However, it did dissuade victims from using a valuable and efficient service, online tax return processing, thus causing a great deal of inconvenience for the victim. You should remember this incident when we discuss information warfare in Chapter 14. This e-mail hoax was clearly designed to erode confidence in a government service.

The W32.Torch Hoax This hoax, like most others, causes no direct harm but can become a huge annoyance — the Internet equivalent of a prank phone call. Unlike the *jdbmgre.exe* hoax, it does not encourage you to delete files from your system. However it does induce a fair amount of concern in recipients. In this hoax a message is sent stating the following:

NEW VIRUS DESTROYS HARDWARE

A new virus found recently is capable of burning the CPU of some computers and even causing damage to the motherboard. Yes, it's true, this virus damages the hardware of your computer. The virus, called w32.torch, *uses the* winbond w83781d *chip, present in most modern motherboards, which is responsible for controlling the speed of the CPU and system fans. The infection takes place using the well-known Microsoft DCOM net-trap Vulnerability, and when installed, the virus spreads to other computers in the local network using this method. Reverse-engineering the virus code, we find no evidence of code other than that responsible for the CPU burnout. The virus turns off the high temperature detection in the BIOS (already disabled by default) and then slowly decreases the speed of the fans, leading the system to a deadly increase of the internal temperature. If you feel that your computer is becoming "quiet," it's better to check it out because it may be stopping, and you may have only a few minutes left to disconnect it. The virus contains the text "Moscow Dominates - out/27/03" which is shown in the tray of some machines based on their IP address, perhaps indicating Soviet origin. There is no payload set to activate on this date, but it may be an indication that something is supposed to happen on this day. Some antiviruses already detect it, check if yours is up to date.*

To date, there have not been any viruses that directly damage hardware.

Virus Scanners

The most obvious defense against viruses is the virus scanner. A virus scanner is essentially software that tries to prevent a virus from infecting your system. Usually it scans incoming e-mail and other incoming traffic. Most virus scanners also have the ability to scan portable media devices such as floppy drives. Most people are aware, in a general way, of how virus scanners work. In this section you will learn in more detail how scanners operate.

In general, virus scanners work in two ways. The first method is that they contain a list of all known virus files. Generally, one of the services that vendors of virus scanners provide is a periodic update of this file. This list is typically in a small file, often called a *.dat* file (short for data). When you update your virus definitions, what actually occurs is that your current file is replaced by the more recent one on the vendor's Web site.

Every virus scanner I have ever personally examined also allows you to configure it to periodically download the latest such updates. It is critical that, no matter which virus scanner you choose, you configure it to automatically update itself.

The antivirus program then scans your PC, network, and incoming e-mail for known virus files. Any file on your PC or attached to an e-mail is compared to the virus definition file to see whether there are any matches. With e-mail, this can be done by looking for specific subject lines and content. Known virus files often have specific phrases in the subject line and the body of the messages they are attached to. Yet viruses and worms can have a multitude of headers, some of which are very common, such as *re:hello* or *re:thanks.* Scanning against a list of known viruses alone would result in many false positives. Therefore, the virus scanner also looks at attachments to see whether they are of a certain size and creation date that matches a known virus or whether it contains known viral code. The file size, creation date, and location are the telltale signs of a virus. Depending on the settings of your virus scanner, you may be prompted to take some action, the file may be moved to a quarantine folder, or the file may simply be deleted outright. This type of virus scanning works only if the *.dat* file for the virus scanner is updated, and only for known viruses.

Another way a virus scanner can work is to monitor your system for certain types of behavior that are typical of a virus. This might include programs that attempt to write to a hard drive's boot sector, change system files, alter the system registry, automate e-mail software, or self-multiply. Another technique virus scanners often use is searching for files that stay in memory after they execute. This is called a Terminate and Stay Resident (TSR) program. Some legitimate programs do this, but it is often a sign of a virus.

Many virus scanners have begun employing additional methods to detect viruses. Such methods include scanning system files and then monitoring any program that attempts to modify those files. This means the virus scanner must first identify specific files that are critical to the system. With a Windows system, these include the registry, the *boot.ini*, and possibly other files. Then, if any program attempts to alter these files, the user is warned and must first authorize the alteration before it can proceed.

It is also important to differentiate between on-demand virus scanning and ongoing scanners. An ongoing virus scanner runs in the background and is constantly checking a PC for any sign of a virus. On-demand scanners run only when you launch them. Most modern antivirus scanners offer both options.

Virus Scanning Techniques

Now that you have learned the general strategies virus scanners use, let's take a more detailed look at specific virus scanning techniques employed by various virus scanners.

E-mail and Attachment Scanning Since the primary propagation method for a virus is e-mail, e-mail and attachment scanning is the most important function of any virus scanner. Some virus scanners actually examine your e-mail on the e-mail server before downloading it to your machine. Other virus scanners work by scanning your e-mail and attachments on your computer before passing it to your e-mail program. In either case, the e-mail and its attachments should be scanned prior to your having any chance to open it and release the virus on your system. This is a critical difference. If the virus is first brought to your machine, and then scanned, there is a chance, however small, that the virus will still be able to infect your machine. Most commercial network virus scanners will scan the e-mail on the server before sending it on to the workstations.

Download Scanning Anytime you download anything from the Internet, either via a Web link or through some FTP program, there is a chance you might download an infected file. Download scanning works much like e-mail and attachment scanning, but does so on files you select for downloading.

File Scanning Download and e-mail scanning will only protect your system against viruses that you might get downloading from a site, or that come to you in e-mail. Those methods will not help with viruses that are copied over a network, deposited on a shared drive, or that are already on your machine before you install the virus scanner.

This is the type of scanning in which files on your system are checked to see whether they match any known virus. This sort of scanning is generally done on an on-demand basis instead of an ongoing basis. It is a good idea to schedule your virus scanner to do a complete scan of the system periodically. I personally recommend a weekly scan, preferably at a time when no one is likely to be using the computer.

It does take time and resources to scan all the files on a computer's hard drive for infections. This type of scanning uses a method similar to e-mail and download scanning. It looks for known virus signatures. Therefore this method is limited to finding viruses that are already known and will not find new viruses.

Heuristic Scanning This is perhaps the most advanced form of virus scanning. This sort of scanning uses rules to determine whether a file or program is behaving like a virus, and is one of the best ways to find a virus that is not a known virus. A new virus will not be on any virus definition list, so you must examine its behavior to determine whether it is a virus. However, this process is not foolproof. Some actual virus infections will be missed, and some non-virus files might be suspected of being a virus.

The unfortunate side effect of heuristic scanning is that it can easily lead to false positives. This means that it might identify a file as a virus, when in fact it is not. Most virus scanners do not simply delete viruses. They put them in a quarantined area, where you can manually examine them to determine whether you should delete the file or restore it to its original location. Examining the quarantined files rather than simply deleting them all is important because some can be false positives. In this author's personal experience, false positives are relatively rare with most modern virus scanners.

As the methods for heuristic scanning become more accurate, it is likely that more virus scanners will employ this method, and will rely on it more heavily. Right now it offers the most promise for the greatest protection for your system. However the various algorithms used in heuristic scanning are relatively new, and time and research is required to realize their full potential.

Active Code Scanning Modern Web sites frequently embed active codes, such as Java applets and ActiveX. These technologies can provide some stunning visual effects to any Web site. However, they can also be vehicles for malicious code. Scanning such objects before they are downloaded to your computer is an essential feature in any quality virus scanner. Also recall from Chapter 8 we discussed altering your browser to prompt you before executing any such active code on a Web site. Combining that browser configuration with an antivirus software package that scans for active code can significantly reduce the chances of your being infected with this sort of virus.

Instant Messaging Scanning Instant message scanning is a relatively new feature of virus scanners. Virus scanners using this technique scan instant messaging communications looking for signatures of known virus or Trojan horse files. In recent years the use of instant messaging has increased dramatically. It is now frequently used for both business and recreational purposes. This growing popularity makes virus scanning for instant messaging a vital part of effective virus scanning. If your antivirus scanner does not scan instant messaging, then you should either avoid instant messaging or select a different antivirus package.

Most commercial virus scanners use a multi-modal approach to scanning. They employ a combination of most, if not all, of the methods we have discussed here. Any scanner that does not employ most of these methods will have very little value as a security barrier for your system.

Commercial Antivirus Software

There are a number of antivirus packages available for individual computers and for network-wide virus scanning. We will examine some of the more commonly encountered antivirus software here. It is important that you consider the following factors when purchasing a virus scanning solution for your own organization or recommending a solution to a client:

- Budget: Price should not be the only, or even the most important, consideration, but it certainly must be considered.

- Vulnerability: An organization with diverse users who frequently get e-mail from outside the organization or download from the Internet will need more antivirus protection than a small homogeneous group that uses the Internet only intermittently.

- Skill: Whoever will ultimately use the product must be able to understand how to use it. Are you getting a virus scanner for a group of tech-savvy engineers or a group of end users who are unlikely to be technically proficient?

- Technical: How does the virus scanner work? What methods does it use to scan? How often are the *.dat* files updated? How quickly does the vendor respond to new virus threats and release new *.dat* files?

All of these factors must be considered when selecting antivirus solutions. Too often security experts simply recommend a product they are familiar with without doing significant research. This section introduces a variety of antivirus solutions and the benefits of each.

McAfee VirusScan McAfee is a well-known antivirus vendor. This company offers solutions for the home user and large organizations. All of McAfee's products have some common features, including e-mail scanning and file scanning. They also scan instant messaging traffic.

McAfee scans e-mail, files, and instant messaging for known virus signatures, and uses heuristic methods to locate new worms. Given the growing use of worms (in contrast with traditional viruses), this is an important benefit. McAfee offers a relatively easy download and install, and you can get a trial version from the company's Web site. We will take a look at features of the home version, which functions similarly to the enterprise version.

Figure 9.2 shows the main screen of the McAfee antivirus software. You can see that McAfee has an integrated management screen for multiple security products, including its firewall and antivirus products. The main screen displays a security index for your computer, listed by category. You can get a detailed analysis for each security rating by clicking on the security index.

Select *virusscan>Options* to select what you wish to scan, how you wish to scan, and when you wish to scan. Figure 9.3 shows the *Options* dialog box. You can choose to scan inbound files, e-mail, instant messages, and so on. You can also choose to schedule scans to occur at set times, and then select whether you wish to scan the entire machine.

Of particular interest is the McAfee virus world map, shown in Figure 9.4. This is a map of virus activity currently going on in the world. This can be invaluable information for a security professional, particularly if your organization is geographically widespread.

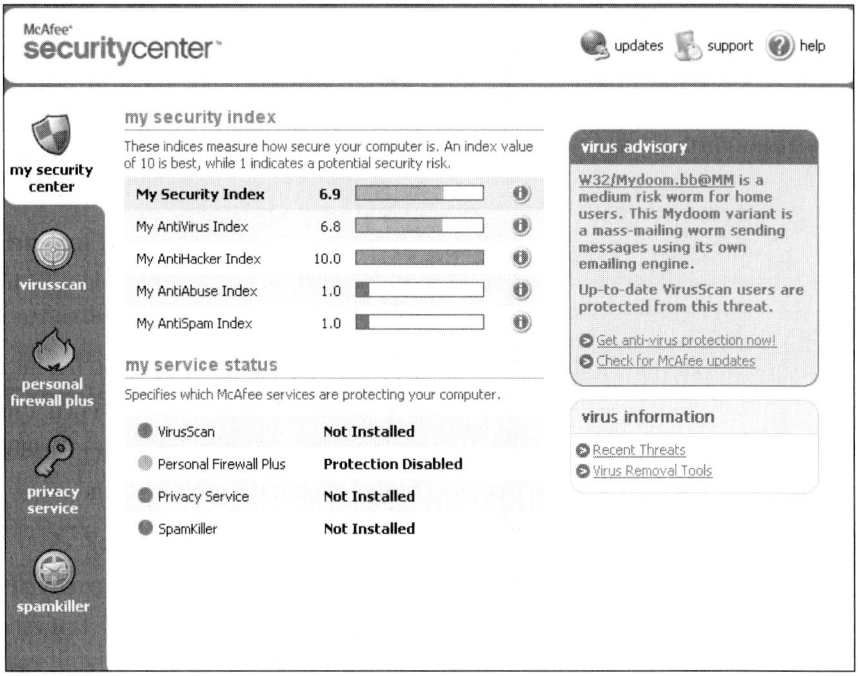

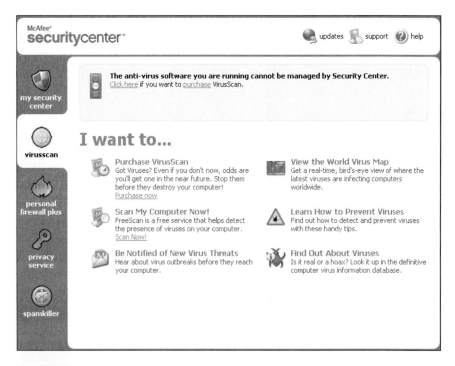

FIGURE 9.2 The McAfee antivirus main screen.

FIGURE 9.3 Scanning options.

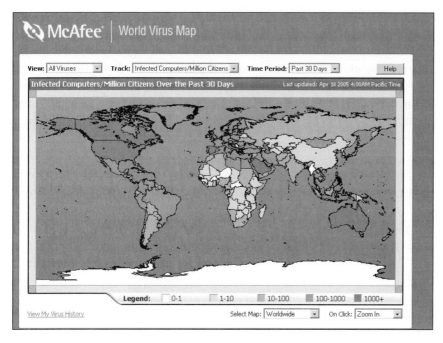

FIGURE 9.4 The McAfee virus world map.

This map is quite useful. You can select all viruses, or only the top 10. You can also choose to view by a specific geographical area any computers infected per million users, or how many files are infected per million users. If you click on any area of the map you will zoom down to that geographical area. You can continue to zoom until you are viewing individual cities, allowing you to find out a great deal about virus infections in any geographical region.

If you consider the four criteria we listed previously — budget, vulnerability, skill, and technical — McAfee rates quite well:

- It is very affordable.

- Different versions are available for different levels of vulnerability.

- It is relatively easy to use, requiring only limited skill to utilize.

- It is technically a very good scanner, using multiple modalities to scan for viruses. It also has interesting added features such as the virus infection map.

These features make McAfee a good choice for home users as well as corporate networks.

Norton AntiVirus Norton AntiVirus is also a widely known vendor of antivirus software. You can purchase Norton solutions for individual computers or for entire networks. Norton offers e-mail and file scanning, as well as instant messaging scanning. It also offers a heuristic approach to discovering worms and traditional signature scanning. Recent versions of Norton AntiVirus have also added anti-spyware and anti-adware scanning, both very useful features. An additional interesting feature of Norton AntiVirus is the pre-install scan. During the installation the install program scans the machine for any virus infections that might interfere with Norton. Because it is becoming more common to find virus attacks that actually seek to disable antivirus software, this feature is very helpful.

While Norton, like most antivirus vendors, offers versions for individual PCs and for entire networks, the individual version has a free trial version you can download and experiment with for 15 days without any charge. We will briefly examine this product to illustrate how Norton AntiVirus products function.

When you download the product, you get a self-extracting executable. Simply double-click on that in either Windows Explorer or My Computer, and it will install itself with very little interaction from you. When you launch Norton, the initial screen, shown in Figure 9.5, gives you valuable information. It lets you know what sorts of scans are turned on, when the last full system scan was done, and when the last update of virus definitions was accomplished. This is quite critical information. If your virus definitions have not been updated recently, then you simply are not protected

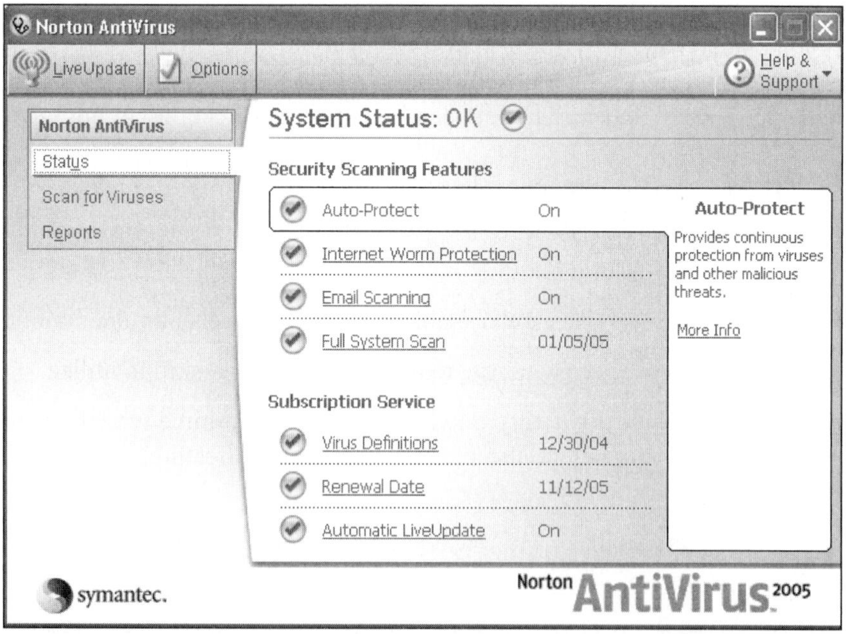

FIGURE 9.5 The main Norton screen.

against the newest viruses. Knowing when the last full system scan was done tells you how safe your computer currently is. Of course, you will also need to know what types of scans are turned on in order to know what threats Norton is protecting you against.

If you select *Scan for Viruses* on the left, you are given a number of options, shown in Figure 9.6. You can scan floppy disks, removable media, hard drives, or particular files and folders. The larger the area you select to scan, the longer the scan will take.

When a scan is done, Norton lists all suspect files and gives you the option of quarantining, deleting, or ignoring them, as shown in Figure 9.7. A fascinating aspect of Norton is that it also detects many common hacking tools. In Figure 9.7, you can see that Norton identified John the Ripper, a common password cracker, as a hacking tool. This can be quite useful because any hacking tools on your machine that you did not put there can be a sign that your machine has been hacked and that the hacker is continuing to use your machine. The intruder may even be using your machine to launch attacks on other machines.

On the main Norton screen there is also an important option labeled *Reports.* It gives you access to the virus encyclopedia maintained by Norton, as well as a report of all scans done. In an organizational setting you should probably periodically print and file this report. This provides valuable information for an audit. When you run any of these reports, it documents the

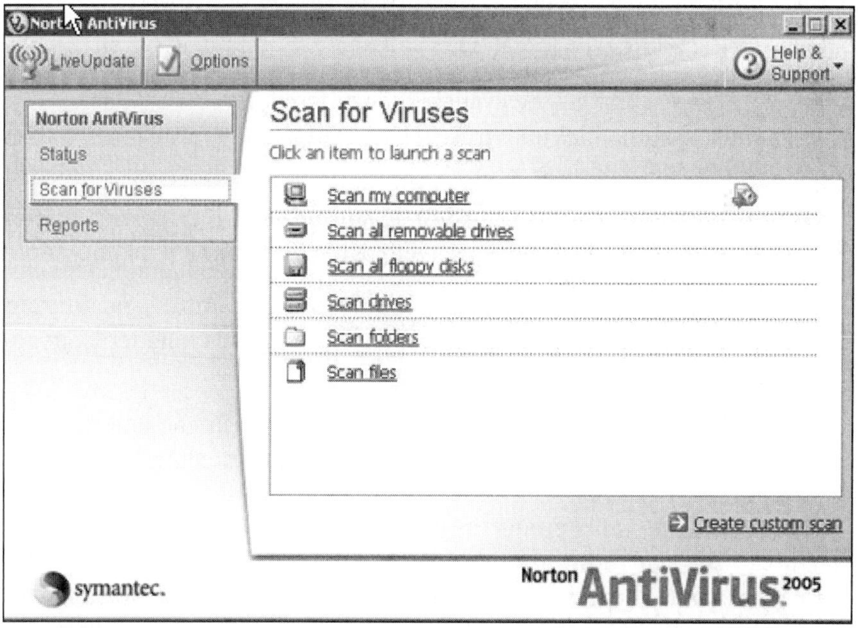

FIGURE 9.6 Scanning options with Norton AntiVirus.

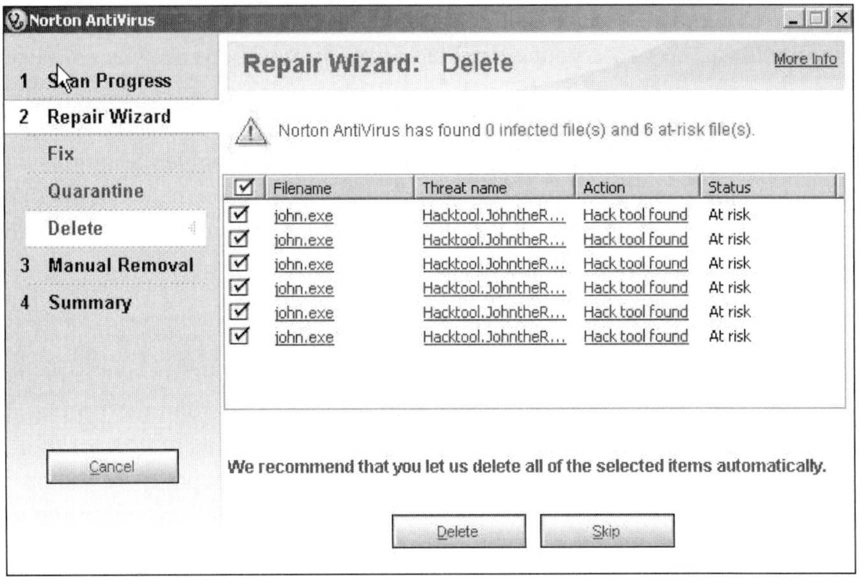

FIGURE 9.7 Norton scan results.

scans you did, for what viruses, and when you did them. These can be kept so that during any future audits you can easily verify the steps you have taken to prevent virus infections.

Again, if you consider the four criteria we listed previously — budget, vulnerability, skill, and technical — Norton also rates quite well:

- It is very affordable. McAfee and Norton are both similarly priced.

- Different versions are available for different levels of vulnerability. Most commercial antivirus vendors offer a range of products for different situations.

- Its graphical interface makes configuring and using Norton as easy as performing the same tasks with McAfee.

- It is technically a very good scanner, using multiple modalities to scan for viruses. The fact that it also picks up hacking tools, in addition to viruses, is an added benefit.

Like McAfee, Norton is a solid choice for both home and business users. It provides an easy to use tool that is also quite effective.

Avast! Antivirus This product is offered for free for home, noncommercial uses. You can download the product from the vendor's Web site: **www.avast.com/**. You can also find professional versions, versions for Unix or Linux, and versions specifically for servers. Of particular interest is that this product is available in multiple languages including English,

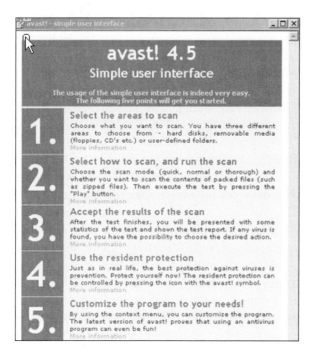

FIGURE 9.8 Avast! Antivirus main screen.

Dutch, Finnish, French, German, Spanish, Italian, and Hungarian. Figure 9.8 shows the main Avast! screen.

If you download it, you can see that Avast! opens up with a tutorial. This feature, combined with the fact that the home version is free, makes this a very attractive tool for the novice home user. The multilanguage and multioperating system supports make it attractive to many professionals. When it finds a virus, it sounds an alarm and then a voice states "Warning: There is a virus on your computer." However, when I scanned my PC with Avast!, it did not detect the older hacking tools as items of concern, unlike Norton.

Let's use our four criteria we listed previously — budget, vulnerability, skill, and technical — to evaluate Avast!:

- It is free, making it more affordable than either Norton or McAfee.

- There is a commercial version of Avast! for enterprise settings.

- It also has a graphical interface making it easy to use, and the fact that it initially launches with a tutorial makes it ideal for the novice.

- It is a reasonably good scanner. However, it lacks added features such as McAfee's virus map and Norton's ability to pick up hacking tools.

For a commercial setting you should probably use Norton or McAfee. However, Avast! is a good choice for the small office or home user. The fact that it is free means there is absolutely no reason why anyone should ever go without a virus scanner.

PC-cillin PC-cillin is a commercial product (**www.trendmicro.com**), with a free evaluation version available. The latest version of the product includes wireless antivirus scanning and anti-spyware/anti-phishing technology.

The main screen is very easy to use and allows you to immediately see the current status of your system (Figure 9.9). The event logs allow you to quickly see when the virus software was last updated, and the results of previous scans. This can be invaluable information for security audits.

The left-hand side includes buttons for e-mail scanning, system settings, updates, and other options. We won't examine all of these here, but you are encouraged to explore these options yourself. If you select *Network Control* on the left side of the screen, you will see a screen similar to Figure 9.10.

This is particularly interesting, as there are features here that are not found in more popular antivirus solutions. For example, you can block certain Web addresses. This can be important in both a home and a business environment.

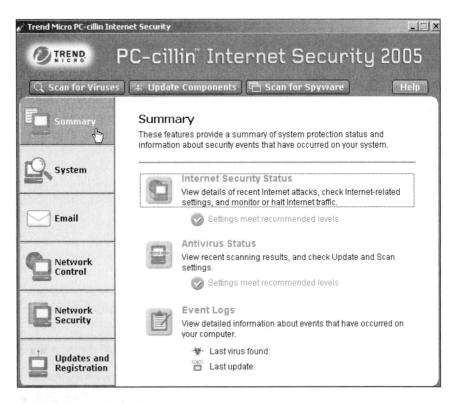

FIGURE 9.9 PC-cillin main screen.

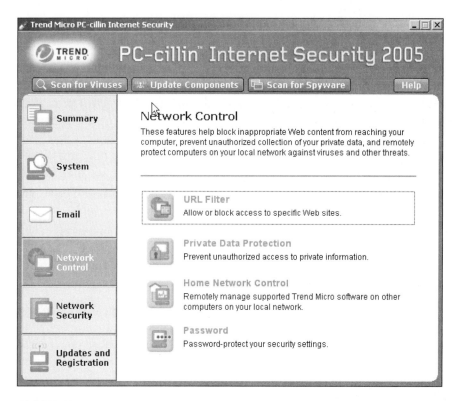

FIGURE 9.10 Network control settings.

The *Private Data Protection* option allows you to secure certain types of information on your PC. Finally, the *Home Network Control* allows you to remotely control the security settings of other computers on a home or small network.

Panda Panda (**www.pandasoftware.com**) is available in both commercial editions and free versions. The commercial version also comes with anti-spyware. Like Norton and McAfee, you can get a personal firewall bundled with the antivirus software. This product is available in English, French, and Spanish. This wide range of features makes this product a robust and effective solution.

Other Virus Scanners In addition to McAfee, Norton, Avast!, PC-cillin, and Panda there are a number of other antivirus packages available on the Internet. A simple Web search will reveal a plethora of antivirus products. As a security professional or a network administrator, it is critical that you be comfortable with multiple antivirus solutions and not simply rely on the most popular or widely known solution. It is important that you base decisions about what antivirus software to use on the facts regarding the product (how it works, ease of use, cost, etc.). The most popular product might not be the best product — or the ideal product — for your environment.

Antivirus Policies and Procedures

Examining how virus attacks spread and looking at specific attacks offers a clear picture of the dangers posed by viruses. We have also taken a look at how virus scanners work, including examining some commercial antivirus products. However, antivirus scanners are not the only facet of protecting yourself against viruses. In fact there are situations in which a virus scanner is simply not enough. You will need policies and procedures to complete your antivirus strategy. Policies and procedures are simply written rules that dictate certain actions that administrators and end users should take and other activities they should avoid. The following is a brief examination of appropriate antivirus polices. Policies will be discussed in greater detail in Chapter 11.

- Always use a virus scanner. McAfee and Norton are the two most widely known and used virus scanners. However, we have also examined other solutions. It costs only about $30 a year to keep your virus scanner updated. It can cost much more to not do it.

- If you are not sure about an attachment, do not open it. When you have specifically requested a file from someone, then opening an attachment from that person is probably safe. However, unexpected attachments are always cause for concern.

- Consider exchanging a code word with friends and colleagues. Tell them to put the code word in the title of the message if they wish to send you an attachment. Without the code word, do not open any attachment.

- Do not believe "security alerts" you are sent. Microsoft does not send out patches in this manner. Go check its Web site regularly, as well as one of the antivirus Web sites previously mentioned.

- Be skeptical of any e-mail you are sent. Keeping e-mail to official traffic will help reduce your danger. Jokes, flash movies, and so on simply should not be sent on a company e-mail system.

- Do not download files from the Internet. If you need a file downloaded, the IT department should do that, carefully scan the file, and then forward it to the user. Now clearly many people will choose to download files, so this admonition is an ideal that is unlikely to be realized. If you feel compelled to download files you should follow two simple rules:

  1. Only download from well-known, reputable sites.
  2. Download to a machine that is off the network first. Then you can scan that system for viruses. In fact, if you do request your IT department download something for you, this is likely to be the process they use.

These policies will not make a system 100 % virus proof, but they will go a long way in protecting it. Feel free to expand upon them any way you see fit.

Additional Methods for Defending Your System

Installing and running antivirus software and having solid antivirus policies are both very important steps in protecting your system. In fact, many organizations use only these two steps. However, there are other important steps you can take to secure your system against virus attacks:

- Set all browsers to block active code (ActiveX, scripts, etc.). Be aware that this will render some Web sites unviewable. A compromise between security and usability would be to set all browsers to warn the user before executing any active code.

- Set all user accounts so that they cannot install software or change browser security settings.

- Segregate subnetworks (especially high-risk subnets like college campus labs) and place a firewall that is tightly secured with its own virus scanning between that subnet and the rest of the network.

Clearly these items are extras. Many organizations do not segregate subnetworks nor do they block users from installing software or changing browser security settings. Many organizations are satisfied with simply installing antivirus scanners and setting up a few policies. However, if you want a truly complete antivirus strategy, these extra steps are part of that complete strategy.

What to Do If Your System Is Infected by a Virus

The unfortunate reality is that no matter what steps you take to prevent virus infections, there is still a chance your system will become infected with a virus. The next question is, what do you do? Some facets of your response will depend upon the severity of the virus and how far it has spread, but generally you need to focus on three things:

- Stopping the spread of the virus.

- Removing the virus.

- Finding out how the infection started.

The following sections examine each in detail and explain how to accomplish them.

Stopping the Spread of the Virus

In the event of a virus infection, the first priority is to stop the spread of the infection. How this is done will, of course, depend on how far the virus has spread. If the virus has only affected one machine, you can simply disconnect that machine from the network. However, it is unlikely that you will detect a virus before it has spread beyond a single machine. Given that fact, you will generally wish to follow these steps:

1. If the infection is on a segment of a WAN, then immediately disconnect from that WAN connection.
2. If the infection is on a subnetwork, immediately disconnect that subnetwork.
3. If there are servers with sensitive data that are connected (in any way) to the infected machine (or machines), disconnect those servers. This will prevent loss of sensitive data.
4. If there are backup devices connected to the infected machine or machines, disconnect them. This will prevent your backup media from becoming infected.

Obviously your goal is to avoid getting a virus on your system. However, should that unfortunate event occur, following these steps can minimize the damage and get your system back up and functioning in a shorter period of time.

Removing the Virus

Once you have isolated the infected machine or machines, the next step is to clean them. If you know the specific virus, then you should be able to remove it by either running an antivirus program, or you should be able to find virus removal instructions on the Internet. In the highly unlikely event that you cannot remove the virus, then you may have no other choice but to format the machine (or machines) and restore them from backups. However, it must be stressed that such a situation is very unlikely.

If you do successfully remove the virus, you will want to scan the machine thoroughly for any other virus infections before reconnecting it to your network. You want to make absolutely certain it is completely clean before putting it back online.

Finding Out How the Infection Started

Once you have contained and removed the virus, the next goal is to see that it does not recur. This is best done by finding out how the virus got onto your system in the first place. To do this, you need to investigate the situation in three ways:

- Talk to users of the infected machines and see if anyone opened any e-mail attachments, downloaded anything, or installed anything.

Since these are the three most likely avenues for virus infection, they should be checked first.

- Read any online documentation for that specific virus. It will tell you the normal method of propagation.

- If neither of those avenues tells you what occurred, check any activity logs that machine might have.

The key is to find out what went wrong in your current security strategy and correct it.

Summary

Virus attacks, and even virus hoaxes, are arguably the greatest threat to computer networks. The sophistication of virus delivery methods is increasing, with worms becoming more and more common. There are a number of steps you can take to mitigate the dangers posed by computer virus outbreaks.

Clearly the first step is to use a virus scanner. However, you absolutely must have a firm understanding of how virus scanners work in order to select the appropriate scanner for your situation. There are a variety of commercial and free antivirus solutions. Any security professional should be familiar with several of these. After installing and configuring an antivirus solution, the next step is establishing written policies and procedures. It is critical that you detail exactly how you want end users to use the system tools. Any situation you do not cover in your policies is an opportunity for a virus infection. Finally, you can take even more serious steps including blocking users from installing software, securely configuring the browser, and separating subnetworks in order to limit the spread of any virus that might infect your machines. Combining antivirus software with secure configuration of your systems, routine patching of software, firewalls, and sound security policies results in more complete protection. While the various topics in this book are segmented into chapters, it is critical that you remember that a complete security strategy must have all these elements working together.

Test Your Skills

MULTIPLE CHOICE QUESTIONS

1. In addition to any malicious payload, what is the most common way a virus or worm causes harm to a system?

   A. by increasing network traffic and overloading the system

   B. by overfilling your inbox

   C. by executing a DoS attack on a host

   D. by containing a Trojan horse

2. What differentiates a virus from a worm?

   A. Worms spread farther than viruses.

   B. Worms are more likely to harm the infected system.

   C. Worms propagate without human intervention.

   D. Worms delete system files more often than viruses do.

3. Which of the following is the primary reason that Microsoft Outlook is so often a target for virus attacks?

   A. Many hackers dislike Microsoft.

   B. Outlook copies virus files faster.

   C. It is easy to write programs that access Outlook's inner mechanisms.

   D. Outlook is more common than other e-mail systems.

4. What is the most common method of virus propagation?

   A. on infected floppy disks

   B. on infected CDs

   C. through instant messaging attachments

   D. through e-mail attachments

5. Which of the following did the most to contribute to the wide spread of the Zafi.d.worm?

   A. It claimed to be from the IRS.

   B. It claimed to be a holiday card and was released just prior to a major holiday.

   C. It used a script attachment rather than active code.

   D. It used active code rather than a script attachment.

6. What was the most dangerous aspect of Zafi.d?

    A. It deleted the registry.

    B. It tried to overwrite parts of virus scanners.

    C. It attempted to overwrite key system files.

    D. It sent out information about the infected computer.

7. What was the primary propagation method for the Mabutu virus?

    A. It used its own SMTP engine to e-mail itself.

    B. It "piggy backed" off of MS Outlook.

    C. It was on infected floppy disks.

    D. It was attached to Flash animations.

8. What additional malicious activity did the Mabutu virus attempt?

    A. It deleted the registry.

    B. It tried to overwrite parts of virus scanners.

    C. It attempted to overwrite key system files.

    D. It sent out information about the infected computer.

9. What was the taxpayer virus hoax?

    A. an e-mail that claimed that online tax submissions were infected and unsafe

    B. an e-mail that tried to get the victim to send tax checks to a phony address

    C. a virus that deleted all tax-related files from the target computer

    D. a virus that infected the U.S. Internal Revenue Service in 2003

10. In the context of viruses, what is a *.dat* file?

    A. a file containing system information

    B. a file that is infected

    C. a file with corrupt data

    D. a file with virus definitions

11. What is Heuristic scanning?

    A. scanning using a rules-based approach

    B. scanning based on a virus definition file

    C. scanning only system management areas (registry, boot sector, etc.)

    D. scheduled scanning

9

12. What is active code scanning?

    A. scanning that is occurring all the time, (i.e. actively)

    B. scanning for active Web elements (Scripts, ActiveX, etc.)

    C. actively scanning for malicious code

    D. actively scanning for worms

13. Which of the following should be the least important consideration when purchasing antivirus software?

    A. the type of scanning the software uses

    B. how quickly the software updates in response to new viruses

    C. how easy it is to configure and use

    D. cost of the software

14. Which of the following is a useful feature in McAfee not found in most other antivirus solutions?

    A. It does a pre-installation scan.

    B. It starts with a tutorial for new users.

    C. Its main screen has a security rating for your system.

    D. It uses heuristic scanning.

15. Which of the following is a useful feature in Norton AntiVirus not found in most other antivirus solutions?

    A. It does a pre-installation scan.

    B. It starts with a tutorial for new users.

    C. Its main screen has a security rating for your system.

    D. It uses heuristic scanning.

16. Which of the following is a useful feature in Avast! antivirus not found in most other antivirus solutions?

    A. It does a pre-installation scan.

    B. It starts with a tutorial for new users.

    C. Its main screen has a security rating for your system.

    D. It uses heuristic scanning.

EXERCISES

Note: These exercises will have you working with different antivirus products. It is critical that you uninstall one product before installing and using another.

Exercise 9.1: Using McAfee Antivirus

1. Download the trial edition of McAfee Antivirus.

2. Scan your machine.

3. Note what security rating the main McAfee screen gives your PC and the reasons why.

4. Note what the virus detector finds.

5. Experiment with settings and options, particularly scheduling.

Exercise 9.2: Using Norton AntiVirus

Note: If you did all of the projects in Chapter 2, then this first exercise will be familiar. However, here you will be asked to compare Norton with other antivirus solutions.

1. Download the trial edition of Norton AntiVirus.

2. Pay particular attention to the pre-install scan.

3. Scan your machine.

4. Note what the virus detector finds.

5. Experiment with settings and options, particularly scheduling.

Exercise 9.3: Using Avast! Antivirus

1. Download the trial edition of Avast! antivirus.

2. Scan your machine.

3. Examine the initial tutorial. Is it adequate for a novice user?

4. Note what the virus detector finds.

5. Experiment with settings and options, particularly scheduling.

9

Exercise 9.4: Using PC-cillin Antivirus

1. Download the trial edition of PC-cillin antivirus.

2. Scan your machine.

3. Note any features of PC-cillin that the other virus scanners do not have.

4. Note what the virus detector finds.

5. Experiment with settings and options, particularly scheduling.

Exercise 9.5: Using Panda Antivirus

1. Download the trial edition of Panda antivirus.

2. Scan your machine.

3. Note any features of Panda that the other virus scanners do not have.

4. Note what the virus detector finds.

5. Experiment with settings and options, particularly scheduling.

PROJECTS

Project 9.1: Comparing Antivirus Software

Compare the features of four antivirus packages, paying particular attention to:

1. Items that are unique to one solution.

2. What each scanner picks up (i.e., if they are all used to scan the same folder, do they all detect the same items?).

Project 9.2: Researching a Virus

1. Using various Web resources, find a new virus active in the last 90 days.

2. Describe how the virus propagates, what it does, and how widely it has spread (the McAfee virus map should help you with that).

3. Describe any known damage the virus has caused.

4. Describe measures being taken to combat the virus.

Project 9.3: Antivirus Policies

For this project you need to consult several antivirus policy documents (listed below). You will find some items in common, and some that exist in only some of them. Identify those items in common to all of these sources (thus indicating all the sources find them to be important) and explain why those are so critical.

- SANS Institute lab antivirus policies: **www.sans.org/resources/policies/ Lab_Antivirus_Policy.pdf#search='anti%20virus%20policy'**

- Dr. David Stang's antivirus policy: **vx.netlux.org/lib/static/vdat/ virpolic.htm**

- East Carolina University's antivirus policy: **www.ecu.edu/itcs/ policies/av.cfm**

Case Study

Denish is the network administrator for a small community college. He wishes to protect against virus outbreaks in student labs. He takes the following actions:

1. He installs Norton AntiVirus on all computers and schedules it to scan every Saturday at 2 A.M.

2. He publishes a policy in the school newspaper forbidding downloading.

What other steps might Denish take to secure the campus labs from virus attacks?

9

Chapter | **10**

Defending Against Trojan Horses, Spyware, and Adware

Chapter Objectives

After reading this chapter and completing the exercises, you will be able to do the following:

- Describe Trojan horses.
- Take steps to prevent Trojan horse attacks.
- Describe spyware.
- Use anti-spyware software.
- Create anti-spyware policies.

Introduction

Chapter 2 introduced Trojan horses and the threat they pose to a network. Trojan horse programs are a common threat for any system connected to the Internet. They are a particular problem if your users download software, screen savers, or documents from the Internet. Trojan horses are not quite as widespread as virus attacks or DoS attacks, but they are certainly a real threat to your systems. In order to have a secure network you must take steps to protect your network from Trojan horse attacks. In this chapter you will learn about some well known Trojan horse attacks and steps you can take to reduce the danger from these attacks.

In the past few years spyware has become an increasingly dangerous problem for computer users, both at home and in organizations. Many Web sites now drop spyware, or its close relative, adware, onto users' systems whenever the users open the Web site. Aside from the obvious threat to information security, these applications consume system resources. In this chapter we will examine the threats posed by spyware as well as methods you can use to combat them.

Trojan Horses

As Chapter 2 explained, a Trojan horse is an application that appears to have a benign purpose but actually performs some malicious function. This subterfuge is what makes these applications such a dangerous threat to your system. The Internet is full of useful utilities (including many security tools), screen savers, images, and documents. Most Internet users do download some of these things. Creating an attractive download that has a malicious payload is an effective way of gaining access to a person's computer.

One defense against Trojan horses is to prevent all downloading, but that is not particularly practical. The wonder and value of the Internet is the easy access it provides to such a wide variety of information — restricting that access in such a draconian manner subverts one of the most important reasons for giving employees Internet access. Instead of using such a heavy-handed tactic, you will learn other ways to protect your systems from Trojan horses.

Once you have a Trojan horse on your system, it may perform any number of unwanted activities. Some of the most common actions Trojan horses take include:

- Erasing files on a computer

- Spreading other malware, such as viruses. Another term for a Trojan horse that does this is a *dropper.*

- Using the host computer to launch Distributed Denial of Service (DDoS) attacks or send spam

- Searching for personal information such as bank account data

- Installing a back door on a computer system. This means providing the creator of the Trojan horse easy access to the system, such as creating a username and password she can use to access the system.

Of the items on the above list, installing back doors and executing distributed denial of service attacks are probably the most frequent results of a Trojan horse attack, though installing spyware and dropping viruses are becoming much more common as well.

Identifying Trojan Horses

In this section you will first learn about some well known Trojan horse attacks that have occurred in the past. This will give you an idea of how these applications actually work. You will then explore some of the methods and procedures you can implement to ameliorate the danger.

Back Orifice This rather crudely named Trojan horse is perhaps the most famous of the Trojan horses. Back Orifice is a remote administration system that allows a user to control a computer across a TCPIP connection using a simple console or GUI application. Some users download it thinking it is a benign administrative utility they can use. Others download it without even realizing they are downloading it. Back Orifice gives the remote user as much, if not more, control of the target machine than the person who downloaded it.

FYI: Is It a Trojan Horse?

Some experts argue that Back Orifice and a few other attacks such as NetBus are not actually Trojan horses because they do not appear to be legitimate applications. Other experts, including the author, feel this is incorrect for the following reasons:

- These programs can be attached to legitimate applications, creating a textbook example of a Trojan horse.
- Some users download the program thinking it is a legitimate administrative tool.
- Some users have the program downloaded without their knowledge while visiting some Web site. The Web site combined with the payload creates a Trojan horse.

10

Back Orifice is small and entirely self-installing. Simply executing the server on any Windows machine installs the server. Back Orifice can also be attached to any other Windows executable, which will run normally after installing the server. In other words it can be attached to a legitimate program the user downloads, thus installing Back Orifice in the background. Even more insidious is the fact that Back Orifice does not show up in the task list or close-program list. This program is also launched every time the computer is started. The remote administrative screen that Back Orifice provides the intruders is shown in Figure 10.1. This figure should give you some idea of just how much an intruder can do to your system with this utility.

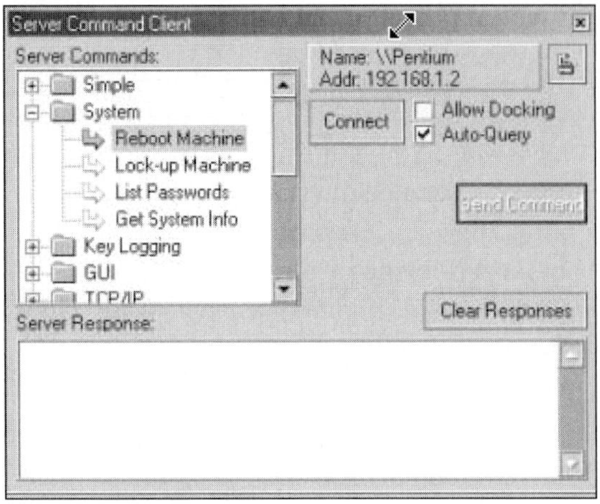

FIGURE 10.1 The Back Orifice Sscreen.

If you are already infected with Back Orifice (or wish to check to see if you are), going through the registry is the best way to remove it:

Caution

Registry Settings

Any change to the Windows Registry must be undertaken cautiously. Always be very careful, and if you are unsure of yourself, simply do not do it. You may wish to try this first on a lab machine rather than a live system.

1. Click *Start*.

2. Click *Run*, then type **Regedit**.

3. Using the + to expand the branches, locate the following key:

   HKEY_LOCAL_MACHINE\SOFTWARE\Microsoft\Windows\ CurrentVersion\RunServices

4. Double-click on the (default) "key." This opens a dialog box that shows the key and its current value (Value data), which is ".exe." Select this key and press *Delete* (not *Backspace*), and then click *OK*.

5. Close *Regedit* and reboot your machine.

6. Go to your command prompt and type

   del c:\windows\system\exe~1

Internet Explorer Trojan Horse In 2003 a Trojan horse that specifically targeted Microsoft's Internet Explorer began circulating the Internet. This Trojan program changes the DNS configuration on the Windows machine so that requests for popular Web search engines like Google and Alta Vista bring the Web surfer to a Web site maintained by the hackers, according to warnings from leading security companies (Roberts, 2003).

This attack relies on a vulnerability problem of Internet Explorer. This flaw allows Web sites, e-mails, or newsgroup messages to download and execute a file on your system without your knowledge. Microsoft released a patch for this vulnerability. The most difficult problem with this particular Trojan horse was that the patch released for it by Microsoft actually had additional security flaws. The following Web site will actually test

to see if your browser is vulnerable to either of these problems: Secunia:
http://secunia.com/MS03-032.

NetBus The NetBus Trojan is quite similar in effect to Back Orifice. A
NetBus worm tries to infect target machines with the NetBus Trojan. This
tool is a remote administration tool (often called a RAT), much like Back
Orifice. NetBus, however, operates only on port 20034. It gives the remote
user complete control of the infected machine, as if he were sitting at the
keyboard and had full administrative rights. The NetBus administration
screen is shown in Figure 10.2. You can see that the intruder can accomplish
a variety of high-level tasks on the infected machine.

It is a simple matter to check whether your computer is infected
with NetBus. Simply go to your command prompt and telnet with one
of the following commands. If you get a response, you are probably
infected.

    telnet 127.0.0.1 12345
    telnet 127.0.0.1 12346

If you are infected, then removal is best accomplished via the registry
by following these steps:

1. Using *regedit.exe* find the key *HKEY_LOCAL_MACHINE\Software\
   Microsoft\Windows\CurrentVersion\RunServices*.

2. Delete the key 666.

3. Reboot the computer.

4. Delete the file *SKA.EXE* in the Windows system directory.

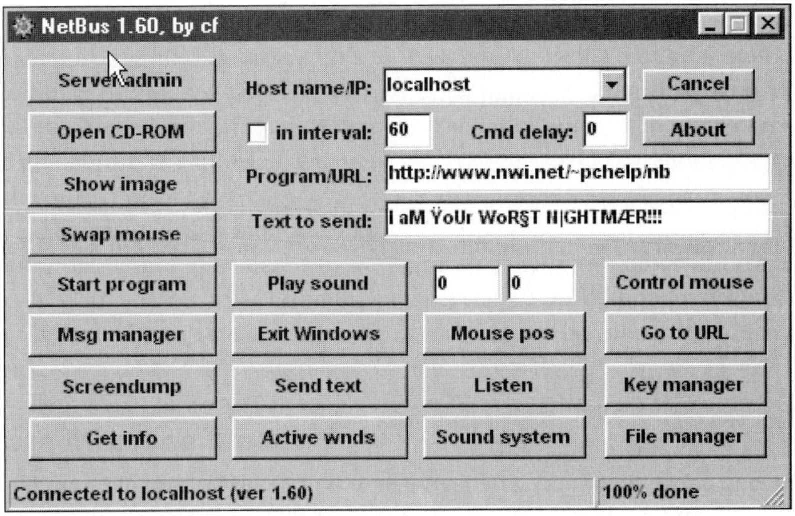

FIGURE 10.2 The NetBus administration screen.

Linux Trojan Horses It is common to find proponents of non-Microsoft operating systems touting the superior security of their systems. It is true that there are certain features in many Microsoft products that seem to favor usability over security. However, it has been the contention of some security experts that much of the apparently better security for non-Microsoft operating systems stems from the fact that they have a much smaller share of the PC market and are therefore less attractive targets to the creators of malware. As these operating systems become more popular, we will see more attacks focused on them. In fact there have already been Trojan horses aimed specifically at Linux.

There are a number of utilities available for Linux. Most ship with Linux distributions, but it is common for Linux users to download updates to these from the Internet. The *util-linux* file is one such download that includes several essential utilities for Linux systems. A Trojan horse was placed in the file *util-linux-2.9g.tar.gz* on at least one FTP server between January 22, 1999, and January 24, 1999. This Trojan horse could have been distributed to mirror FTP sites. It is impossible to tell how many mirror sites had this file or how many users downloaded it. The age of this Trojan horse should tell you that threats to Linux system are nothing new. With the growing popularity of Linux you should expect to see even more.

This particular Trojan horse was a classic back door Trojan. Within the Trojan horse *util-linux* distribution, the program */bin/login* was altered. The changes included code to send e-mail to the Trojan horse creator that contained the host name and log on information of users logging in. The distributors of the legitimate *util-linux* package updated their site with a new version; however, it is impossible to determine how many systems installed the Trojan version or how many systems were compromised as a result.

Portal of Doom This Trojan horse is also a back door administration tool. It gives the remote user a great deal of control over the infected system. The actions remote users can take, if they get control of your system via Portal of Doom, include but are not limited to:

- Opening and closing the CD Tray
- Shutting down the system
- Opening files or programs
- Accessing drives
- Changing the password
- Logging keystrokes
- Taking screen shots

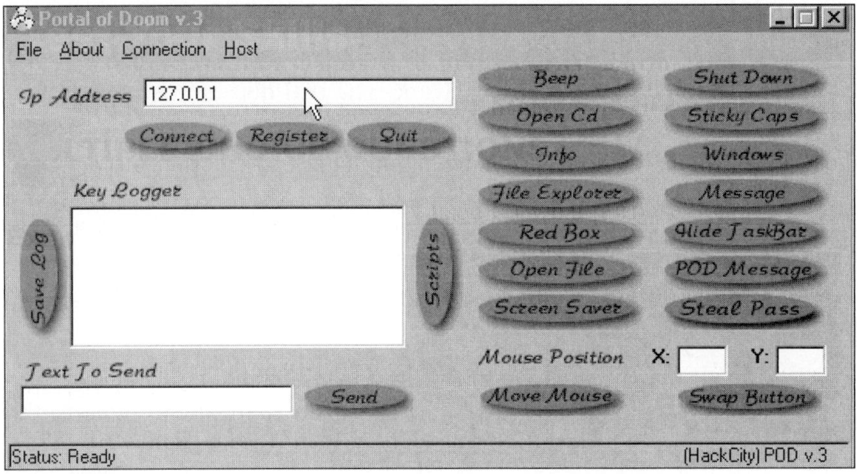

FIGURE 10.3 The Portal of Doom administrative screen.

Portal of Doom is quite similar to Back Orifice and NetBus. It is easy to use and has a graphical user interface, as you can see in Figure 10.3.

You can manually remove this Trojan horse with the following steps:

1. Remove the String key in the registry located at *HKEY_LOCAL_MACHINE\Software\Microsoft\Windows\CurrentVersion\RunServices*.

2. Use the task manager to shut down the process for *ljsgz.exe*. If you cannot shut it down, then reboot the machine. Now that you have altered the registry, the *ljsgz.exe* program will not start up again.

3. Delete the file *ljsgz.exe* from the Windows system directory.

Symptoms of a Trojan Horse

It is difficult to determine whether your system is the victim of a Trojan horse. There are a number of symptoms that might indicate that you have a Trojan horse. Assuming of course that you or another legitimate user are not making these changes, such symptoms include:

- Home page for your browser changing

- Any change to passwords, usernames, accounts, etc.

- Any changes to screen savers, mouse settings, backgrounds, etc.

- Any device (such as a CD door) seeming to work on its own

Any of these changes are symptoms of a Trojan horse and indicate your system is probably infected.

Preventing Trojan Horses

We have looked at several real world Trojan horses, which should give you a good understanding of how they work. The real question is how do you prevent your systems from being exploited by a Trojan horse? The answer is a hybrid approach using both technological measures and policy measures.

Technological Measures There are several technological measures that can protect your systems from the threat of Trojan horses. These measures are, of course, not a guarantee against Trojan horse attacks, but they can certainly provide a reasonable level of safety:

- Recall that NetBus worked using port 20034. This is yet another reason for blocking all unneeded ports on all machines, not just the servers or the firewall. A system that has port 20034 blocked on all servers, workstations, and routers is not susceptible to NetBus. If one of the network machines is infected with NetBus, it would be unusable by the attacker.

- Antivirus software is yet another way to reduce the dangers of Trojan horse attacks. Most antivirus software scans for known Trojan horses as well as viruses. Keeping antivirus software on all machines updated and properly configured can be a great help in preventing Trojan horse infections.

- Preventing active code in your browser can also help reduce the risk of Trojan horses. It will prevent users from viewing certain animations, but it can also stop several avenues for introducing a Trojan horse into your systems. At a minimum your browser should be set to warn users and get their approval prior to running any active code.

- You are probably already aware that, as a matter of general computer security policy, you should always give users the minimum privileges they need to perform their job tasks. This policy is particularly helpful with protecting against Trojan horses. If an end user cannot install software on her machine, it is more difficult for her to inadvertently install a Trojan horse.

Policy Measures Technology can go only so far in any facet of computer security, and protecting against Trojan horses is no different. End user policies are a critical part of protecting against Trojan horses. Fortunately, a few simple policies can greatly aid in protecting your system. You will probably note that many of these policies are the same ones used to protect your network from virus attacks.

- Never download any attachment unless you are completely certain it is safe. This means that unless you specifically requested an attachment, or at least expected one, and unless that attachment

TABLE 10.1 Ports used by well known Trojan horses.

Port(s) Used	Trojan Horse
57341	NetRaider
54320	Back Orifice 2000
37651	Yet Another Trojan (YAT)
33270	Trinity
31337 and 31338	Back Orifice
12624	Buttman
9872-9872, 3700	Portal of Doom (POD)
7300-7308	Net Monitor
2583	WinCrash

matches what you expected (i.e., is named appropriately, right format, etc.) do not download it.

- If a port is not needed, close it. Table 10.1 lists ports used by well known Trojan horses. This list is by no means exhaustive but should give you an idea of just how vulnerable your systems are if you are not shutting down unneeded ports.

- Do not download or install any software, browser skins, toolbars, screen savers, or animations on your machine. If you require one of these items, have the IT department scan it first to ensure safety.

- Be cautious of hidden file extensions. For example, a file you think is an image could be a malicious application. Instead of *mypic.jpg,* it may actually be *mypic.jpg.exe.*

Spyware and Adware

Spyware is a growing problem both for home computer users and for organizations. There is, of course, the risk that such applications might compromise some sensitive information. There is also the problem of these applications simply consuming too much of your system's resources. Spyware and adware both use memory. If your system has too many such applications, then they can consume so much of your system's resources that your legitimate software will have trouble running. I have personally seen computers that had so much spyware/adware running that the machine became unusable.

The primary difference between spyware and adware is what they do on your machine. They both infect your machine in the same manner. Spyware seeks to get information from your machine and make it available to some other person. This can be done in a number of ways. Adware seeks to create pop-up ads on your machine. Because these ads are not generated by the Web browser, many traditional pop-up blockers will not stop them.

Both spyware and adware are growing problems for network security and home PC security. This is an important element of computer security software that was at one time largely ignored. Even today, not enough people take spyware seriously enough to guard against it. Some of these applications simply change your home page to a different site (these are known as home page hijackers); others add items to your favorites (or read items from them). Other applications can be even more intrusive.

Identifying Spyware and Adware

Just as virus and Trojan horse threats eventually became well known to security professionals and hackers, there are certain adware and spyware products that are well known in the computer security community. Being aware of specific real world adware and spyware and how such applications function will help you to better understand the threats they pose.

Gator Gator is perhaps the most widely known adware product. This product is often distributed by being built into various free software packages you can download from the Internet. Once it is on your computer, you will be inundated with various pop-up ads. This company makes a significant profit from selling the ads they display. Because of this profit, they have recently begun suing anti-spyware companies that specifically target Gator. You can find more details on that development from the CNET news Web site: **news.com.com/2100-1032_3-5095051.html?tag=nefd_top**.

The manufacturer of Gator insists that its product is not spyware and will not send information from your computer. However, the number of pop-up ads you are subjected to can range from merely annoying to a significant productivity drain. For example, the Gator-related product Weather Scope uses 16 megabytes of memory itself. It is very easy for various adware products to use up more than 100 megabytes of your system's memory, which would produce a noticeable drain on your system's performance.

There are two ways to remove Gator (other than the use of anti-spyware, which may remove it for you automatically):

Method 1: Add/Remove Programs:

1. Right-click the Gator icon in the System Tray and click *Exit*.
2. Click the Windows *Start* button, select *Settings*, and then *Control Panel*.
3. Select the *Add/Remove Programs* icon.
4. Find the entry *Gator* or *Gator eWallet* in the list of installed programs. Select it and then click the Remove button.

Method 2: The Registry (useful if Method 1 does not work):

1. Right-click the Gator icon in the System Tray and click *Exit*.

2. Use *regedit* to open the registry and select the key *HKEY_LOCAL_ MACHINE \Software\Microsoft\Windows\CurrentVersion\Run*.

3. Find the entry *CMESys, GMT*, or *trickler*, and right-click it and click *Delete*.

4. Restart Windows.

5. Open *C:\Program Files\Common Files*. Delete the *CMEII* and *GMT* folders.

Either method should rid your computer of this piece of adware. In general manually removing spyware or adware will often require you to use the task manager to stop the running process. Then you will need to scan the hard drive to delete the application and use the *regedit* tool to remove it from the registry. You can see that this is a rather difficult process.

RedSheriff RedSheriff is spyware, not adware. This product is loaded as a Java applet embedded in a Web page you visit. Once you visit the Web site, this applet will collect information about your visit such as how long the page took to load, how long you stayed, and what links you visited. This information is sent to the parent company. A number of Internet Service Providers have begun including RedSheriff on their start pages, which are programmed to load every time the user logs on to the Internet. The problem with RedSheriff is twofold:

- No one (except the manufacturer) is really certain what data is collected or how it is used.

- Many people have a negative reaction to anyone monitoring their Web site usage habits.

The RedSheriff program is marketed as a reporting tool to measure how visitors use a Web site. You can view the vendor's own comments at its Web site **http://cexx.org/cache/redsheriff_products.htm**l.

Anti-Spyware

Anti-spyware is an excellent way to defend against spyware and adware, just as antivirus software defends against viruses and Trojan horses. Essentially, it is software that scans your computer to check for spyware running on your machine. Most anti-spyware works by checking your system for known spyware files. It is difficult to identify specific activities that identify spyware, as you can with viruses. Each application must simply be checked against a list of known spyware. This means that you must maintain some sort of subscription service so that you can obtain routine updates to your spyware definition list.

In today's Internet climate, running anti-spyware is as essential as running antivirus software. Failing to do so can lead to serious consequences. Personal data and perhaps sensitive business data can easily leak out of your organization without your knowledge due to spyware. You should also keep in mind that it is entirely possible for spyware to be the vehicle for purposeful industrial espionage. In this section we will examine a few popular anti-spyware utilities.

FYI: Anti-Adware

You are unlikely to find any software specifically designed to detect and remove adware. Most vendors group adware and spyware together, so most anti-spyware solutions also scan for adware.

Spy Sweeper   This product is available at **www.Webroot.com**. The vendor offers enterprise wide anti-spyware solutions as well as solutions for individual PCs. Most importantly you can download the software for free, but you will need to register it (and pay for it) in order to get updated spyware definitions. In addition to allowing scanning of your system, Spy Sweeper gives you real-time monitoring of your browser and downloads, and warns you of any changes. For example, if there is a change to your home page, Spy Sweeper asks you to confirm that change before it is committed.

This product's greatest advantage, however, is that it is simple and easy to use. If the person using the software is a novice, then Spy Sweeper is an excellent choice. Let's examine just a few features so you can see how it works. The initial screen, shown in Figure 10.4, makes it easy for the novice user to sweep, view quarantined items, update the software, and perform other tasks.

When you run the sweep, you see an ongoing, real time report of what is taking place. This is shown in Figure 10.5. This report tells you how many spyware definitions the application is testing for, how far along it is in the process, and what has been found so far.

Once the sweep is done, the suspect programs/files are identified, and you can elect to restore them, delete them, or quarantine them. Spy Sweeper does not automatically delete them. This is a beneficial feature, as it prevents the accidental deletion of items that might have been misidentified as spyware.

Another interesting feature of Spy Sweeper is the various shields it provides, shown in Figure 10.6. These shields can prevent changes to your Internet Explorer home page, favorites, Windows start up, programs in memory, and more. Most spyware and adware programs will attempt to alter one or more of these items. These shields require your direct approval before any such change can be made.

FIGURE 10.4 The Spy Sweeper opening screen.

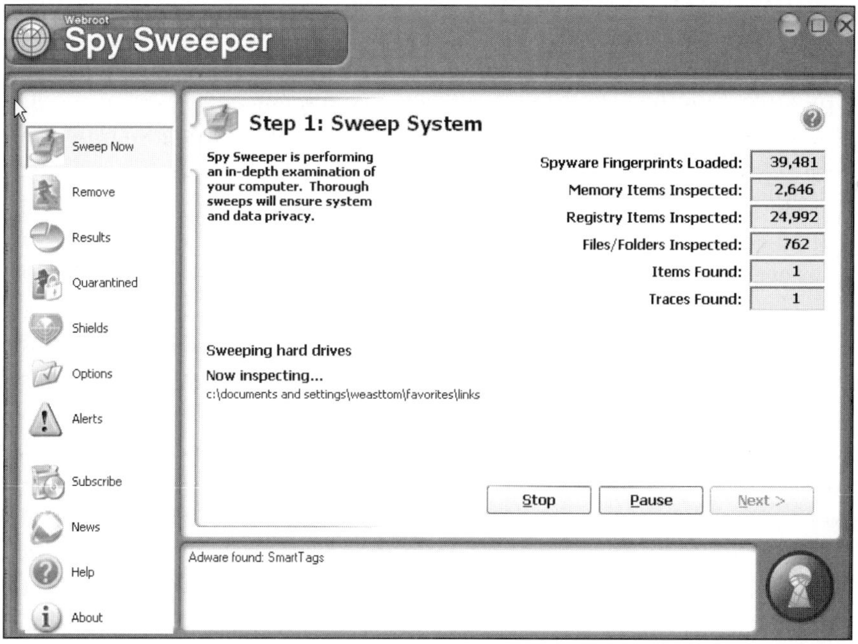

FIGURE 10.5 The Spy Sweeper sweeping process.

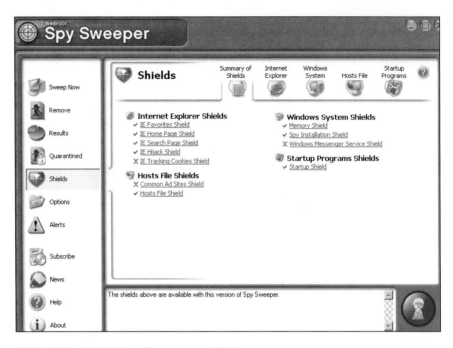

FIGURE 10.6 Spy Sweeper shields.

Spyware Doctor The Spyware Doctor is another anti-spyware product that offers a free trial version, which you can download from **www.pctools. com/spyware-doctor/**. Spyware Doctor is also easy to use and offers a number of options that can assist you in protecting your system. For example the Settings screen, shown in Figure 10.7, enables you to configure how Spyware Doctor handles suspected spyware, how it logs activities, how often it updates its spyware definitions, and whether to scan on start up.

Spyware Doctor offers an On Guard option that protects various aspects of your system. This is shown in Figure 10.8. Unlike Spy Sweeper, this option is available in only the registered version and has fewer options. However, Spyware Doctor can be purchased for only $19.95 online, whereas Spy Sweeper is $29.95.

Zero Spyware Zero Spyware is similar in function to Spy Sweeper and Spyware Doctor. Like the first two, it offers a free trial version that you can download from the company's Web site. Unlike the other anti-spyware options we have examined, this one has not received much press attention. Also, as you can see in Figure 10.9, its trial version is limited. It does not offer the home page shield or adware shield that the other options offer. It also has fewer scanning options.

One advantage of Zero Spyware is that it includes a system diagnostics utility not found in the other anti-spyware software packages we have

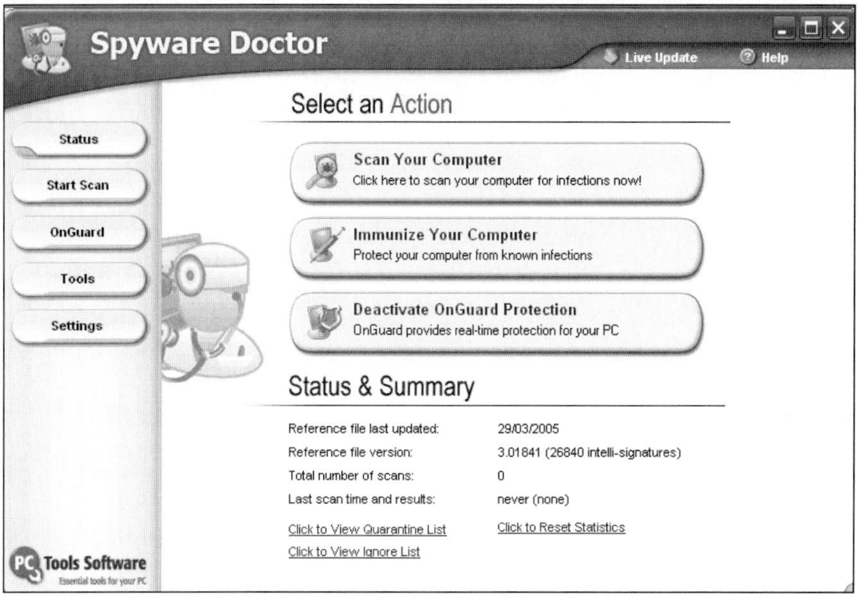

FIGURE 10.7 Spyware Doctor settings.

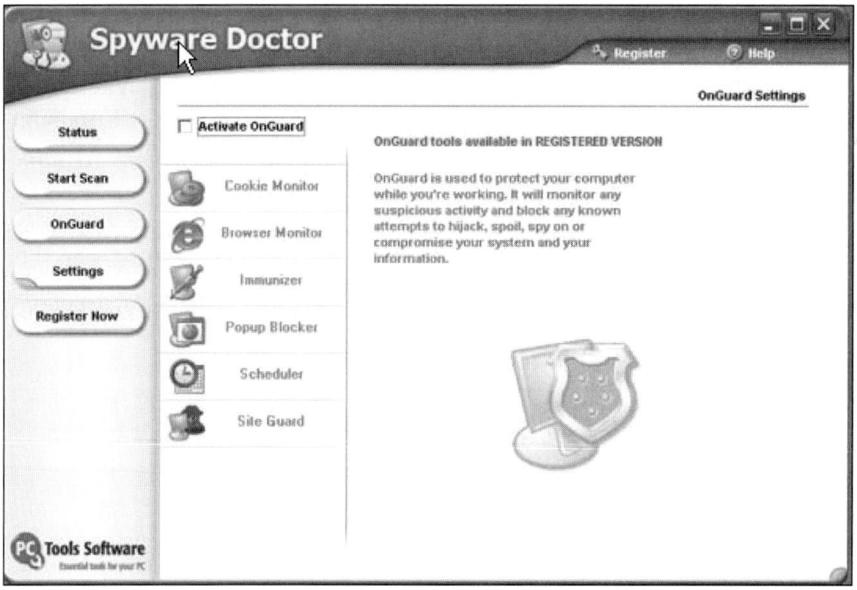

FIGURE 10.8 Spyware Doctor On Guard settings.

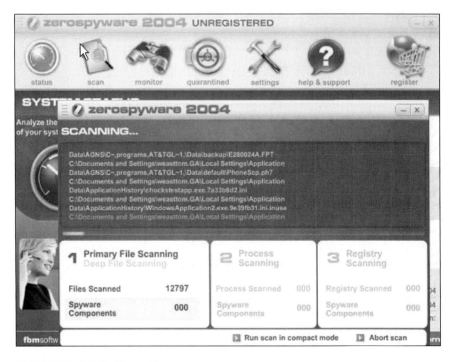

FIGURE 10.9 Zero Spyware screen.

examined. This utility places its results in a Web page, making them easy to view or display. Table 10.2 offers a brief comparison of the three top anti-spyware packages. Each feature is rated on a scale of one to five, with five being the best.

Creating a grid like this can be useful whenever you are evaluating any type of security product. Assigning values to various features and then

TABLE 10.2 Comparing Anti-spyware.

	Spy Sweeper	Spyware Doctor	Zero Spyware
Price	3	4	3
Shields	5	4	3
Spyware definitions	5	4	4
Trial version options	5	3	2
System diagnostics	2	2	5
Total	20	17	17

comparing the total score (as well as most important features) can help you decide which product is right for you.

Microsoft Anti-Spyware Microsoft has recently entered the anti-spyware market. Their Web site can be found at **www.microsoft.com/ athome/security/spyware/software/default.mspx**. Currently, the product is only in beta version and is available for free. It is unclear whether or not Microsoft will charge for the product in the future or bundle it as part of future Windows versions.

   As of this writing, there have been no conclusive independent reviews of this product. However, the fact that it is currently free and is made for Windows makes it worth mentioning.

Researching and Comparing Anti-Spyware Products As with antivirus, firewall, and other security products, there are many anti-spyware alternatives from which to choose. The following Web sites provide either anti-spyware or reviews of anti-spyware software you can use to help you evaluate the various products. Most products are priced from $19.95 to $39.95, and many have free trial editions you can download:

- Spyware Warrior vendor reviews: **http://spywarewarrior. com/asw-features.htm**

- Tech News World free anti-spyware utilities: **www.technewsworld.com/story/33188.html**

- Ars Technica anti-spyware reviews: **http://arstechnica.com/ reviews/apps/spyware-removal.ars**

- PC Magazine anti-spyware reviews: **www.pcmag.com/ article2/0,4149,1524223,00.asp**

- Spyware Avenger: **www.spywareavenger.com**

   This list is not comprehensive. A simple Web search will find a host of anti-spyware products. However, these are the more commonly used products and you should probably begin your exploration of anti-spyware with them.

Anti-Spyware Policies

As with all aspects of computer security, appropriate policies must be in place in order to protect your system against spyware and adware. Many of these policies are the same as the policies that protect your system from Trojan horses and virus infections.

- Never download any attachment unless you are completely certain it is safe. This means that unless you specifically requested an attachment, or at least expected one, and unless that attachment matches what you expected (i.e., is named appropriately, right format, etc.) do not download it.

■   Make sure your browser is configured to block cookies, or at most to allow cookies for only a very limited time. Cookies store information from a particular Web site, but any Web site you visit can read any cookie on your machine.

■   Your browser should be configured to block scripts that run without the user's awareness.

■   Some browsers (Netscape and Mozilla) also offer pop-up blocking. Pop-up ads are often a vehicle for adware. Blocking such ads is critical.

■   Never download any application, browser skin, screen saver, or utility from the Internet unless you are completely certain of its safety.

■   Block Java applets, or at least require that the user manually approve them before loading. This will stop RedSheriff and many other spyware utilities.

Summary

Both Trojan horses and spyware pose significant dangers to your network. Trojan horses and viruses frequently overlap (i.e., a virus may install a Trojan horse). Virus scanners and appropriate policies are your only protection against Trojan horses. For this reason it is particularly important that you carefully develop and implement your anti-Trojan horse policies.

Spyware and adware are growing problems for computer systems. Spyware can compromise security by revealing details of your system or confidential data on the system. Adware is mostly a nuisance rather than a direct security threat. However as your computer becomes infected with more adware, such programs can eventually drain your system's resources until your system becomes completely unusable.

You can protect yourself against adware and spyware with a combination of anti-spyware utilities and appropriate policies. There are several anti-spyware tools available, many of which were examined in this chapter.

Test Your Skills

MULTIPLE CHOICE QUESTIONS

1. Which of the following are the two most common things Trojan horse programs do?

   A. launche DDoS attacks and open back doors

   B. install spyware and launch Ping of Death attacks

   C. delete registry keys and alter system files

   D. hijack the home page and delete registry keys

2. What does Back Orifice do to a system?

   A. deletes or corrupts Microsoft Office applications

   B. installs a virus on the infected system

   C. provides a remote user complete administrative access to the machine

   D. launches a DDoS at Microsoft sites

3. Which of the following is the most insidious aspect of Back Orifice?

   A. It is small.

   B. It spreads via e-mail.

   C. It appears to be a legitimate program.

   D. It does not show up in the task list.

4. What was the worst aspect of the Internet Explorer Trojan horse of 2003?

   A. It corrupted the registry.

   B. It deleted system files.

   C. The patch for it had security flaws.

   D. There was no patch for it.

5. What effect did the *util-linux* Trojan horse of 1999 have?

   A. It sent out login information of users logging in.

   B. It deleted or corrupted the registry.

   C. It opened up port 1294 for a hacker to use.

   D. It used IRC to open a back door to the machine.

10

6. Which of the following most accurately explains why minimum necessary privileges for a user help protect against Trojan horses?

   A. If a user cannot remove programs, then he cannot remove anti-spyware and antivirus software accidentally.

   B. If the user cannot install programs, it is less likely that he will install a Trojan horse.

   C. If the user cannot install programs, it is completely impossible that he will install a Trojan horse.

   D. If the user cannot remove programs, he cannot alter the security settings you have put on his machine.

7. Why are hidden file extensions a security threat?

   A. Users might download an image that is really a malicious executable.

   B. Users cannot properly organize their systems without knowing accurate file extensions.

   C. Virus scanners have trouble with files whose extensions are hidden.

   D. Hidden extensions almost always indicate a worm.

8. What is Gator?

   A. adware that is downloaded automatically when you visit certain Web sites

   B. adware that is often attached to free programs found on the Internet

   C. spyware that gathers information about you when you visit a Web site

   D. spyware that gets banking information from your hard drive

9. What is RedSheriff?

   A. adware that is downloaded automatically when you visit certain Web sites

   B. adware that is often attached to free programs found on the Internet

   C. spyware that gathers information about you when you visit a Web site

   D. spyware that gets banking information from your hard drive

10. Which of the following is an advantage of Spy Sweeper over Spyware Doctor?

    A. Spy Sweeper is less expensive than Spyware Doctor.

    B. Spy Sweeper has more shield options than Spyware Doctor.

    C. Spy Sweeper is simply more effective than Spyware Doctor.

    D. Only Spy Sweeper catches adware as well as spyware.

11. Which of the following is an advantage of Spyware Doctor over Spy Sweeper?

    A. Spyware Doctor is less expensive than Spy Sweeper.

    B. Spyware Doctor has more shield options than Spy Sweeper.

    C. Spyware Doctor is simply more effective than Spy Sweeper.

    D. Only Spyware Doctor catches adware as well as spyware.

12. Manually removing spyware usually requires all but which of the following actions?

    A. formatting the hard drive

    B. removing keys from the registry

    C. reinstalling Windows

    D. reinstalling antivirus software

13. Why is blocking pop-up ads good for security?

    A. Pop-up ads reduce productivity.

    B. Pop-up ads can be a vehicle for hackers to get into your system.

    C. Pop-up ads can be a vehicle for spyware or adware to get into your system.

    D. Pop-up ads can corrupt memory on your system.

14. Which of the following is the most likely reason you might wish to restrict Java applets?

    A. Java applets can easily be modified to act as spyware.

    B. Java applets can delete files on your hard drive.

    C. Java applets usually contain viruses.

    D. Java applets serve no useful purpose other than virus delivery.

15. Why would you want to restrict cookies?

    A. Cookies consume system memory.

    B. Cookies take up hard drive space.

    C. Any Web site can read any cookie.

    D. Cookies are often infected with a virus.

10

EXERCISES

Exercise 10.1: Back Orifice

1. Obtain Back Orifice using one of the following Web sites:
   - **www.bo2k.com/**
   - **www.cultdeadcow.com/tools/bo.html**

2. Install it on a lab computer.

3. Use the remote administration features to alter the target system.

Exercise 10.2: NetBus

1. Obtain NetBus using one of the following Web sites:
   - **www.dark-e.com/archive/trojans/netbus/**
   - **www.windowsecurity.com/pages/article.asp?id=453**

2. Install it on a lab computer.

3. Use the remote administration features to alter the target system.

Exercise 10.3: Gator

1. Measure a lab computer's performance without Gator (processor usage, memory usage, etc.).

2. Download any application that has Gator attached. The following Web sites should help you:
   - **www.gator.com/**
   - **www.cexx.org/gator.htm**
   - **www.pcpitstop.com/gator/**

3. Monitor and graph usage changes by day and over a week's time with Gator installed.

Exercise 10.4: Spy Sweeper

1. Download Spy Sweeper onto a lab machine (preferably the one with Gator, Back Orifice, etc.).

2. Run the program and note what items it detects, but do not delete them.

Exercise 10.5: Spyware Doctor

1. Download Spyware Doctor to the same machine onto which Spy Sweeper was downloaded.

2. Run Spyware Doctor and note what items it picks up. Note any differences between the results from Spy Sweeper and Spyware Doctor.

PROJECTS

Project 10.1: Impact of Trojan Horses

Using the Web or other resources find out the following facts:

1. How common are Trojan horse attacks?

2. What effects do these have on businesses?

3. What steps do you recommend to help reduce the threat of Trojan horse attacks?

Project 10.2: Impact of Spyware and Adware

1. How common are spyware and adware?

2. What effects do these have on businesses?

3. What steps do you recommend to help reduce the threat of spyware and adware?

Project 10.3: Using Alternative Anti-spyware

1. Download one alternative anti-spyware product (i.e., one we have not examined thoroughly in this chapter).

2. Install it on a lab machine and run it.

3. Compare the results to what you got with Spy Sweeper and Spyware Doctor.

10

Case Study

Bob is the network administrator for a law firm. Due to issues like confidentiality and attorney-client privilege, spyware is a major concern for Bob. He takes the following steps:

1. Anti-spyware is installed and configured on all machines.

2. All browsers are set to allow only temporary session cookies.

3. All unnecessary ports are blocked.

Are these steps adequate? What else might Bob have done?

Chapter

Security Policies

Chapter Objectives

After reading this chapter and completing the exercises, you will be able to do the following:

- Create effective user policies.
- Outline effective system administration policies.
- Define effective access control.
- Generate effective developmental policies.

Introduction

Throughout this book we have occasionally mentioned the topic of policies; however, our primary focus has been on security technology. Unfortunately technology alone is not a panacea for network security problems. One reason is that technology cannot be effective if people do not follow appropriate procedures. Examples of this include:

- Virus software won't prevent a user from manually opening an attachment and releasing a virus.

- A technologically secured network is still very vulnerable if former employees (perhaps some unhappy with the company) still have working passwords or if passwords are simply put on Post-it notes on computer monitors.

- A server is not secure if it is in a room to which virtually everyone in the company has access.

Another reason that technology alone is not the answer is that technology must be appropriately applied. Policies can effectively guide you as you implement and manage security, including security technology. In this chapter we will examine computer security policies, including the elements for creating good security policies and examples of how to establish a network security policy.

Defining User Policies

In Chapter 1 we mentioned that misuse of systems is a major problem for many organizations. A large part of the problem comes from the difficulty in defining what exactly *misuse* is. Some things might be obvious misuse, such as using company time and computers to search for another job or to view illicit Web sites. However other areas are not so clear, such as an employee using her lunchtime to look up information about a car she is thinking of buying. Generally good user policies outline specifically how people may use systems and how they may not. For a policy to be effective it needs to be very clear and quite specific. Vague statements such as "computers and Internet access are only for business use" are simply inadequate.

Other areas for potential misuse are also covered by user policies, including password sharing, copying data, leaving accounts logged on while employees go to lunch, and so on. All of these issues ultimately have a significant impact on your network's security and must be clearly spelled out in your user policies. We will now examine several areas that effective user policies must cover:

- Passwords
- Internet use
- E-mail attachments
- Software installation and removal
- Instant messaging
- Desktop configuration

Passwords

Keeping passwords secure is critical. In Chapter 8 appropriate passwords were discussed as part of operating system hardening. You should recall that a good password is one that is six to eight characters long, uses numbers and special characters, and has no obvious relevance to the end user. For example a Dallas Cowboys fan would be ill-advised to use a password like "cowboys" or "godallas," but might be well advised to use a password like "%trEe987" or "123DoG$$" because those do not reflect the person's personal interests and therefore will not be easily guessed. Issues such as minimum password length, password history, and password complexity come under administrative policies, not user policies. User policies dictate how the end user should behave.

However, no password is secure, no matter how long or how complex, if it is listed on a Post-it note stuck to the user's computer monitor. This may seem obvious, but it is not at all uncommon to go into an office and find a password either on the monitor or in the top drawer of the desk. Every janitor or anyone who simply passes by the office can get that password.

It is also not uncommon to find employees sharing passwords. For example, Bob is going to be out of town next week, so he gives Juan his password so that Juan can get into his system, check e-mail, and so on. The problem is that now two people have that password. And what happens if, during the week Bob is gone, Juan gets ill and decides he will share the password with Shelly so she can keep checking that system while Juan is out sick? It does not take long for a password to get to so many people that it is no longer useful at all from a security perspective.

Issues like minimum length of passwords, password age, password history (all mentioned in Chapter 8 on operating system hardening) are issues of administrative policies. System administrators can force these requirements. However none of that will be particularly helpful if the users do not manage their passwords in a secure fashion.

All of this means you need explicit policies regarding how users secure their passwords. Those policies should specify:

- Passwords are never to be kept written down in any accessible place. The preference is that they not be written down at all, but if they are, they should be in a secure area such as a lock box at the user's home (i.e., not in the office right next to your computer).

- Passwords must never be shared with any person for any reason.

- If an employee believes his password has been compromised, he should immediately contact the IT department so that his password can be changed and so that log on attempts with the old password can be monitored and traced.

Internet Use

Most organizations provide users with some sort of Internet access. There are several reasons for this. The most obvious reason is e-mail. However, that is hardly the only reason to have Internet access in a business or academic setting. There is also the Web, and even chat rooms. All of these can be used for legitimate purposes within any organization but can also be serious security problems. Appropriate polices must be in place to govern the use of these technologies.

The Web is a wonderful resource for a tremendous wealth of data. Throughout this book we have frequently referenced Web sites where one can find valuable security data and useful utilities. The Internet is also replete with useful tutorials on various technologies. However, even nontechnology-related business interests can be served via the Web. Here are a few examples of legitimate business uses of the Web:

- Sales staff checking competitors' Web sites to see what products or services they offer in what areas, perhaps even getting prices

- Creditors checking a business's AM Best or Standard and Poor's rating to see how their business financial rating is doing

- Business travelers checking weather conditions and getting prices for travel

Of course there are other Web activities that are clearly not appropriate on a company's network:

- Using the Web to search for a new job

- Any pornographic use

- Any use which violates local, state, or federal laws

- Use of the Web to conduct employee's own business (i.e., an employee who is involved in another enterprise other than the company's business)

In addition, there are gray areas. Some activities might be acceptable to some organizations but not to others. Such activities might include:

- Online shopping during the employee's lunch or break time

- Reading news articles online during lunch or break time

- Viewing humorous Web sites

What one person might view as absurdly obvious might not be to another. It is critical that any organization have very clear policies detailing specifically what is and what is not acceptable use of the Web at work. Giving clear examples of what is acceptable use and what is not is also important. You should also remember that most proxy servers and many firewalls can block certain Web sites. This will help prevent employees from misusing the company's Web connection.

E-mail Attachments

Most business and even academic activity now occurs via e-mail. As we have discussed in several previous chapters, e-mail also happens to be the primary vehicle for virus distribution. This means that e-mail security is a significant issue for any network administrator.

FYI: E-mail Communications

Some people might still not fully grasp the extent and usefulness of e-mail communications. Many people today are working entirely or partially from home. Courses, and in fact entire degree programs, are offered on the Internet. Business associates in diverse geographical areas need to communicate. E-mail provides a way to send technical data, business documents, homework assignments, and more. More importantly, from a business/legal perspective, it provides a record of all communication. For many situations, e-mail is clearly far superior to phone communications.

As a case in point, the author of this book has never met anyone from the publishing company nor even his own agent in person. Except for a few brief phone calls, all communication pertaining to writing and producing this book has been done entirely via e-mail. Much of this involved e-mailing documents and images as attachments. This illustrates the growing importance of e-mail as an avenue for both academic and business communications.

It is difficult to find accurate statistics on office e-mail use. However if you enter any office in any type of organization and ask any employee about the amount of business e-mail traffic they receive, you will probably find the amount to be quite large. The proportion of e-mail communication to other communication such as phone and fax is likely to continue to increase.

Clearly you cannot simply ban all e-mail attachments. However you can establish some guidelines for how to handle e-mail attachments. Users should open an attachment only if it meets the following criteria:

- It was expected (i.e., the user requested documents from some colleague or client).

- If it was not expected, it comes from a known source. If so, first contact that person and ask whether they sent the attachment. If so, open it.

- It appears to be a legitimate business document (i.e., a spread sheet, a document, a presentation, etc.).

It should be noted that some people might find such criteria unrealistic. There is no question they are inconvenient. However, with the prevalence of viruses, often attached to e-mail, these measures are prudent. Many people choose not to go to this level to try to avoid viruses, and that may be your choice as well. Just bear in mind that millions of computers are infected with some sort of virus every single year.

11

No one should ever open an attachment that meets any of the following criteria:

- It comes from an unknown source.

- It is some active code or executable.

- It is an animation/movie.

- The e-mail itself does not appear legitimate. (It seems to entice you to open the attachment rather than simply being a legitimate business communication that happens to have an attachment.)

If the end user has any doubt whatsoever, then she should not open the e-mail. Rather, she should contact someone in the IT department who has been designated to handle security. That person can then either compare the e-mail subject line to known viruses or can simply come check out the e-mail personally. Then if it appears legitimate, the user can open the attachment.

FYI: About Attachments

The author of this book frequently follows the "better safe than sorry" axiom on this matter. This means that when forwarded some joke, image, Flash animation, and so on circulating the Internet, I simply delete it. That may mean that I miss many humorous images and stories, but it also means I miss many viruses. You would do well to consider emulating this practice.

Software Installation and Removal

This is one matter that does have an absolute answer. End users should not be allowed to install anything on their machine, including wall papers, screen savers, utilities — anything. The best approach is to limit their administrative privileges so they cannot install anything. However, this should be coupled with a strong policy statement prohibiting the installation of anything on users' PCs. If they wish to install something, it should first be scanned by the IT department and approved. This process might be cumbersome, but it is necessary. Some organizations go so far as to remove media drives (CD, floppy, etc.) from end users' PCs so installations can occur only from files that the IT department has put on a network drive. This is usually a more extreme measure than most organizations will require, but it is an option you should be aware of.

Instant Messaging

Instant messaging is also widely used and abused by employees in companies and organizations. In some cases instant messaging can be used for legitimate business purposes. However, it does pose a significant security risk. There have been viruses that propagated specifically via instant messaging. In one incident the virus would copy everyone on the users' buddy list with the contents of all conversations. Thus, a conversation the user thought was private was being broadcast to everyone with whom that user had messaged.

Instant messaging is also a threat from a purely informational security perspective. Without the traceability of an e-mail going through the corporate e-mail server, nothing stops an end user from instant messaging out trade secrets or other confidential information undetected. It is recommended that instant messaging simply be banned from all computers within an organization. If you find your organization absolutely must use it, then you must establish very strict guidelines for its use, including:

- Instant messaging may be used only for business communications, no personal conversations. Now this might be a bit difficult to enforce. Rules like this often are. More common rules, such as prohibiting personal Web browsing, are also quite difficult to enforce. However, it is still a good idea to have those rules in place. Then if you find an employee violating them, you can refer to a company policy that prohibits such actions. However, you should be aware that in all likelihood you will not catch most violations of this rule.

- No confidential or private business information should be sent via instant messaging.

Desktop Configuration

Many users like to reconfigure their desktop. This means changing the background, screen saver, font size, resolution, and so on. Theoretically speaking, this should not be a security hazard. Simply changing a computer's background image cannot compromise the computer's security. However there are other issues involved.

The first issue is where the background image comes from. Frequently end users download images from the Internet, creating an opportunity for getting a virus or Trojan horse, particularly one using a hidden extension (e.g., it appears to be a *mypic.jpg* but is really *mypic.jpg.exe*). There are also human resources/harassment issues if an employee uses a backdrop or screen saver that is offensive to other employees. Some organizations simply decide to prohibit any changes to the system configuration for this reason.

The second problem is technical. In order to give a user access to change screen savers, background images, and resolution, you must give her rights that also allow her to change other system settings you might not want changed. The graphical display options are not separated from all other configuration options. This means that allowing the user to change her screen saver might open the door for her to alter other settings that would compromise security (such as the network card configuration or the Windows Internet connection firewall).

Final Thoughts on User Policies

This section has provided an overview of appropriate and effective user policies. It is critical that any organization implement solid user policies. However these policies will not be effective unless you have clearly defined consequences for violating them. Many organizations find it helpful to spell out specific consequences that escalate with each incident such as:

- The first incident of violating any of these policies will result in a verbal warning.

- A second incident will result in a written warning.

- The third incident will result in suspension or termination (in academic settings this would be suspension or expulsion).

You must clearly list the consequences, and all users should sign a copy of the user policies upon joining the organization. This prevents anyone claiming they were not aware of the policies.

It is also important to realize that there is another cost to misuse of corporate Internet access. That cost is lost productivity. How much time does the average employee spend reading personal e-mail, doing nonbusiness Web activities, or instant messaging? It is hard to say. However for an informal view, go to **www.yahoo.com** on any given business day during business hours, and click on one of the news stories. At the bottom of the story you will see a message board for this story. It lists the dates and times of posts. See how many posts are done during business hours. It is unlikely that all of the people posting these messages are out of work, retired, or at home sick.

Defining System Administration Policies

In addition to determining policies for users, you must have some clearly defined policies for system administrators. There must be a procedure for adding users, removing users, dealing with security issues, changing any system, and so on. There must also be procedures for handling any deviation.

New Employees

When a new employee is hired, the system administration policy must define specific steps to safeguard company security. New employees must be given access to the resources and applications their job functions require. The granting of that access must be documented (possibly in a log). It is also critical that each new employee receive a copy of the company's computer security/acceptable use policies and sign a document acknowledging receipt of such.

Before a new employee starts to work, the IT department (specifically network administration) should receive a written request from the business unit for which that person will be working. That request should specify exactly what resources this user will need and when she will start. It should also have the signature of someone in the business unit with authority to approve such a request. Then, the person who is managing network administration or network security should approve and sign the request. After you have implemented the new user on the system with the appropriate rights, you can file a copy of the request.

Leaving Employees

When an employee leaves, it is critical to make sure all of his logins are terminated and all access to all systems is discontinued immediately. Unfortunately, this is an area of security that all too many organizations do not give enough attention to. When an employee leaves, you cannot be certain which employee will bear the company ill will and which will not. It is imperative to have all of the former employee's access shut down on his last day of work. This includes physical access to the building. If a former employee has keys and is disgruntled, nothing can stop him from returning to steal or vandalize computer equipment. When an employee leaves the company, you should ensure that on his last day the following actions take place:

- All logon accounts to any server, VPN, network, or other resource are disabled.

- All keys to the facility are returned.

- All accounts for e-mail, Internet access, wireless Internet, cell phones, etc., are shut off.

- Any accounts for mainframe resources are cancelled.

- The employee's workstation hard drive is searched.

The last item might seem odd. But if an employee was gathering data to take with him (proprietary company data) or conducting any other improper activities, you need to find out right away. If you do see any evidence of any such activity, you need to secure that workstation and keep it for evidence in any civil or criminal proceedings.

All of this might seem a bit extreme to some readers. It is true that with the vast majority of exiting employees, you will have no issues of concern. However, if you do not make it a habit of securing an employee's access

11

when he departs, you will eventually have an unfortunate situation that could have been easily avoided.

Change Requests

The nature of IT is change. Not only do end users come and go, but requirements change frequently. Business units request access to different resources, server administrators upgrade software and hardware, application developers install new software, Web developers change the Web site, and so on. Change is occurring all of the time. Therefore, it is important to have a change control process. This process not only makes the change run smoothly but allows the IT security personnel to examine the change for any potential security problems before it is implemented. A change control request should go through the following steps:

- An appropriate manager within the business unit signs the request, signifying approval.

- The appropriate IT unit (database administration, network administrator, e-mail administrator, and so on) verifies that the request is one they can fulfill (from both a technological and a budgetary/business perspective).

- The IT security unit verifies that this change will not cause any security problems.

- The appropriate IT unit formulates a plan to implement the change and a plan to roll back the change in the event of some failure.

- The date and time for the change is scheduled, and all relevant parties are notified.

Your change control process might not be identical to this one; in fact, yours might be much more specific. However, the key to remember is that in order for your network to be secure, you simply cannot have changes happening without some process for examining their impact prior to implementing them.

IN PRACTICE: Extremes of Change Control

Anyone with even a few years of experience in the IT profession can tell you that when it comes to change control there are all sorts of different approaches. The real problem is those IT groups that implement unreasonable extremes. This author has personally seen both. Without using the real names of the companies involved, let's examine a real case of each extreme:

Software consultant's company X was a small company that did custom financial applications for various companies. They had a staff of fewer than twenty developers, who frequently traveled to client locations around the country. They literally had

- No documentation for any of their applications, not even a few notes.
- No change control process at all. When someone did not like a setting on a server or some part of the network configuration, they simply changed it.
- No process for handling former employee access. In one case a person had been gone for six months and still had a valid logon account.

Now clearly this is alarming from several perspectives, not just from a security viewpoint. However, that is one extreme, one that makes for a very chaotic environment that is very insecure. Security-minded network administrators tend to move towards the opposite extreme, one which can have a negative impact on productivity.

Company B had more than 2,000 employees and an IT staff of about 100 people. In this company, however, the bureaucracy had overwhelmed the IT department to the point that their productivity was severely impacted. In one case, the decision was made that a Web server administrator also needed database administration rights on a single database server. The process, however, took three months with one face-to-face meeting between his manager and the CIO, as well as two phone conferences and a dozen e-mails between his manager and the manager of the database group.

The company's convoluted change control process had a severely negative impact on productivity. Some employees informally estimated that even the low level IT supervisors spent 40 percent of their time in meetings/conferences, reporting on meetings/conferences, or preparing for meetings/conferences. And the further one went up the IT ladder, the more of one's time became consumed by bureaucratic activities.

Both of these examples are meant to illustrate two extremes in change control management that you should try to avoid. Your goal in implementing change control management is simply to have an orderly and safe way of managing change, not to be an impediment to productivity.

11

Security Breaches

Unfortunately, the reality is that your network will probably, at some point, have a security breach of some kind. This could mean that you are the target of a DoS attack, your system is infected with a virus, or a hacker gains entrance and destroys or copies sensitive data. You must have some sort of plan for how to respond should any such event occur. This book cannot tell you specifically how to deal with each and every event that might occur, but we can discuss some general guidelines for what to do in certain, general situations. We will look at each of the main types of security breaches and what actions you should take for each.

Virus Infection When a virus strikes your system, immediately quarantine the infected machine or machines. This means literally unplugging the machine(s) from the network. If it is a subnet, then unplug its switch. Isolate the infected machines (unless your entire network is infected, in which case simply shut down your router/ISP connection to close you off from the outside world and prevent spread beyond your network). After implementing the quarantine, you can safely take the following steps:

- Scan and clean each and every infected machine. Because they are now off the network, this will be a manual scan.

- Log the incident, the hours/resources taken to clean the systems, and the systems that were affected.

- When you are certain the systems are clean, bring them online in stages (a few at a time). With each stage check all machines to see that they are patched, updated, and have properly configured/running antivirus.

- Notify the appropriate organization leaders of the event and the actions you have taken.

- After you have dealt with the virus and notified the appropriate people, you should then have a meeting with appropriate IT staff to discuss what can be learned from this breach and how you might prevent it from occurring in the future.

Denial of Service Attacks If you have taken the steps outlined earlier in this book (such are properly configuring your router and your firewall to reduce the impact of any attempted DoS), then you will already be alleviating some of the damage from this type of attack. Use your firewall logs or IDS to find out which IP address (or addresses) originated the attacks. Note the IP address(es), and then (if your firewall supports this feature, and most do) deny that IP address access to your network.

- Use online resources (interNIC, etc.) to find out who the address belongs to. Contact that organization and inform them of what is occurring.

- Log all of these activities and inform the appropriate organizational leaders.

- After you have dealt with the DoS and notified the appropriate people, you should then have a meeting with appropriate IT staff to discuss what can be learned from this attack and how you might prevent it from occurring in the future.

Intrusion by a Hacker

- Immediately copy the logs of all affected systems (firewall, targeted servers, etc.) for use as evidence.

- Immediately scan all systems for Trojan horses, changes to firewall settings, changes to port filtering, new services running, and so on. In essence you are performing an emergency audit (described in greater detail in Chapter 12) to determine what damage has been done.

- Document everything. Of all of your documentation, this must be the most thorough. You must specify which IT personnel took what actions at what times. Some of this data may later be part of court proceedings, so absolute accuracy is necessary. It is probably a good idea to log all activities taken during this time and to have at least two people verify and sign the log.

- Change all affected passwords. Repair any damage done.

- Inform the appropriate business leaders of what has happened.

- After you have dealt with the breach and notified the appropriate people, you should then have a meeting with appropriate IT staff to discuss what can be learned from this breach and how you might prevent it from occurring in the future.

These are just general guidelines, and some organizations may have much more specific actions they want taken in the event of some security breach. You should also bear in mind that throughout this book when we have discussed various sorts of threats to network security, we have mentioned particular steps and policies that should be taken. The policies in this chapter are meant to complement any already outlined. It is an unfortunate fact that some organizations have no plan for what to do in case of an emergency. It is important that you do have at least some generalized procedures you can implement.

Defining Access Control

An important area of security policies that usually generates some controversy in any organization is access control. There is always a conflict between users' desire for unfettered access to any data or resources on the

> ### FYI: The "CIA" Triad
>
> No, this is not a nefarious plot, nor does CIA stand for Central Intelligence Agency in this instance. CIA is an acronym for confidentiality, integrity, and availability. This has direct bearing on access to resources. The concept is that data must be kept confidential. That means that only those personnel with a need to know will have access to the data. Secondly, the data integrity must be maintained. This means that the data must be reliable. That involves limiting who can alter the data and under what conditions they can alter it. Finally, all data must be available to be accessed.
>
> It is worth keeping this acronym in mind when thinking about access control. You goal is to make sure the data is accurate, confidential, and available only to authorized parties.

network and the security administrator's desire to protect that data and resources. This means that extremes in policies are not practical. You cannot simply lock down every resource as completely as possible because that would impede the user's access to those resources. Conversely, you cannot simply allow anyone and everyone complete access to everything.

This is where the least privileges concept comes into play. The idea is simple. Each user, including IT personnel, gets the least access they can have to effectively do his job. Rather than asking the question "Why not give this person access to X," you should ask "Why give this person access to X?" If you do not have a very good reason, then do not provide the access. This is one of the fundamentals of computer security. The more people who have access to any resource, the more likely some breach of security is to occur.

Clearly tradeoffs between access and security must be made. Examples abound. One common example involves sales contact information. Clearly a company's marketing department needs access to this data. However what happens if competitors get all of your company's contact information? That information could allow them to begin targeting your current client list. This requires a tradeoff between security and access. In this case you would probably give sales people access only to the contacts that are within their territory. No one other than the sales manager should have complete access to all contacts.

Defining Developmental Policies

Many IT departments include programmers and/or Web developers. Unfortunately many security policies do not address secure programming. No matter how good your firewalls, proxy server, virus scanning, and policies, if your developers create code that is flawed, you will have security breaches. Clearly the topic of secure programming requires a separate volume to explore thoroughly. Nonetheless, we can consider a brief checklist for defining secure development policies. If your company currently has no secure programming initiatives, this checklist is certainly better than developing in a vacuum. It can also serve as a starting point to get you thinking, and talking, about secure programming.

- All code, especially code done by outside parties (contractors, consultants, etc.) must be checked for back doors/ Trojan horses.

- All buffers must have error handling which prevents buffer overruns.

- All communication (such as using TCP sockets to send messages) must adhere to your organization's secure communications guidelines.

- Any code that opens any port or performs any sort of communication is thoroughly documented and the IT security unit is apprised of the code, what it will do, and how it will be used.

- All vendors should supply you with a signed document verifying that there are no security flaws in their code.

Following these steps will not guarantee that no flawed code is introduced into your system, but it will certainly lower the odds significantly. The unfortunate fact is that these simple steps alone are more than most organizations are taking.

Summary

In this chapter we learned that technology is not enough to ensure a secure network. You must have clear and specific policies detailing procedures on your network. These policies must cover employee computer resource use, new employees, outgoing employees, access rights, emergency response procedures, and the security of code in applications and Web sites.

User policies must cover all aspects of how the user is expected to use company technology. In some cases, such as instant messaging and Web use, policies may be difficult to enforce, but that does not change the fact that they must still be in place. If your user policies fail to cover a particular area of technology use, then you will have difficulty taking any action against any employee who performs that particular misuse.

We also learned that it is not just the end user who needs policies. The IT staff needs clearly delineated policies covering how to handle various situations. Of particular concern will be policies dictating how to handle new and exiting users. You also need a carefully considered change management policy.

11

Test Your Skills

MULTIPLE CHOICE QUESTIONS

1. Which of the following does not demonstrate the need for policies?

   A. Antivirus software cannot prevent a user from downloading infected files.

   B. The most secure password is not at all secure if posted on a note by the computer.

   C. End users are generally not particularly bright and must be told everything.

   D. Technological security measures are dependent upon the employees' implementation.

2. Which of the following is not an area user policies need to cover?

   A. minimum length of passwords

   B. a description of Web sites users may or may not visit

   C. if and when to share passwords

   D. what to do when the user believes your password has been compromised

3. Which of the following is not an example of a user password policy?

   A. Users may not keep copies of passwords in their office.

   B. Passwords must be eight characters long.

   C. Users may share passwords only with their assistants.

   D. Passwords may not be shared with any employee.

4. What should an employee do if she believes her password has been revealed to another party?

   A. If it is a trusted employee or friend, just ignore it.

   B. Change her password immediately.

   C. Notify the IT department.

   D. Ignore it.

5. Which of the following should not be recommended as acceptable e-mail attachments?

   A. Flash animations

   B. Excel spreadsheets from a colleague

   C. attachments the user expected

   D. plain text attachments from known sources

6. Which of the following is the best reason users should be prohibited from installing software?

   A. They may not install it correctly, which could cause security problems for the workstation.

   B. They may install software that disables existing security programs on your machine.

   C. Software installation is often complex and should be done by professionals.

   D. If a user's account does not have privileges to install, then it is likely that a Trojan horse will not be inadvertently installed under their account.

7. Which of the following is not a significant security risk posed by instant messaging?

   A. Employees may send harassing messages.

   B. Employees might send out confidential information.

   C. A virus or worm might infect the workstation via instant messaging.

   D. An instant messaging program could actually be a Trojan horse.

8. What is the most important characteristic all user policies must have in order to be effective?

   A. They must be reviewed by an attorney.

   B. They must have consequences.

   C. They must be notarized.

   D. They must be properly filed and maintained.

11

9. Which of the following is the appropriate sequence of events for a new employee?

   A. IT is notified of the new employee and the requested resources. > Employee is granted access to these resources. > Employee is briefed on security/acceptable use policies. > Employee signs acknowledgement of receipt of company security rules.

   B. IT is notified of the new employee and the requested rights. > Employee is given access to these resources. > Employee signs acknowledgement of receipt of company security rules.

   C. IT is notified of the new employee and assigns default rights. > Employee is briefed on security/acceptable use. > Employee signs acknowledgement of receipt of company security rules.

   D. IT is notified of the new employee and assigns default rights. > Employee signs acknowledgement of receipt of company security rules.

10. Which of the following is the appropriate sequence of events for a departing employee?

    A. IT is notified of the departure. > All logon accounts are shut down. > All access (physical and electronic) is disabled.

    B. IT is notified of the departure. > All logon accounts are shut down. > All access (physical and electronic) is disabled. > The employee's workstation is searched/scanned.

    C. IT is notified of the departure. > All physical access is shut down. > All electronic access is shut down.

    D. IT is notified of the departure > All electronic access is shut down. > All physical access is shut down.

11. Which of the following is the appropriate sequence for a change request?

    A. Business unit manager requests change. > IT unit verifies request. > Request is implemented.

    B. Business unit manager requests change. > IT unit verifies request. > Security unit verifies request. > Request is scheduled with rollback plan. > Request is implemented.

    C. Business unit manager requests change. > IT unit verifies request. > Request is scheduled with rollback plan. > Request is implemented.

    D. Business unit manager requests change. > IT unit verifies request. > Security unit verifies request. > Request is implemented.

12. What is the first step after discovering a machine or machines has been infected with a virus?

    A. Log the incident.

    B. Scan and clean infected machines.

    C. Notify appropriate management.

    D. Quarantine infected machines.

13. What is the best rule of thumb in access control?

    A. Allow the most access you can securely give.

    B. Allow the least access job requirements allow.

    C. Standardize access for all users.

    D. Strictly limit access for most users.

14. After dealing on a technical level with any security breach, what is the last thing to be done for any security breach?

    A. Quarantine infected machines.

    B. Study the breach to learn how to prevent a re-occurrence.

    C. Notify management.

    D. Log the incident.

15. Which of the following is a list of items that should be implemented in all secure code?

    A. all code checked for back doors or Trojans, all buffers have error handling to prevent buffer over runs, and all communication activity thoroughly documented

    B. all code checked for back doors or Trojans, all buffers have error handling to prevent buffer over runs, all communications adheres to organizational guidelines, and all communication activity thoroughly documented

    C. all code checked for back doors or Trojans, all buffers have error handling to prevent buffer over runs, and all communications adheres to organizational guidelines

    D. all code checked for back doors or Trojans, all communications adheres to organizational guidelines, and all communication activity thoroughly documented

11

EXERCISES

Each of these exercises is intended to give you experience writing limited portions of a policy. Taken together, the exercises represent a complete policy for a college campus computer network.

Exercise 11.1: User Policies

1. Using the guidelines provided in this chapter (and other resources as needed), create a document that defines end user policies in an academic setting.

2. The policies should clearly define acceptable and unacceptable use for all personnel.

3. You may require some separate policies for administration, faculty, and students.

Exercise 11.2: New Student Policy

1. Using the guidelines provided in this chapter (and other resources as needed), create a step-by-step IT security policy for implementing a new user account for a student.

2. The policy should define which resources the student will have access to, what she will not have access to, and the duration of her access.

Exercise 11.3: Departing Student Policy

1. Using the guidelines provided in this chapter (and other resources as needed), create a step-by-step IT security policy for handling user accounts/rights for a student that is leaving prematurely (drops, is expelled, etc.).

2. You will need to consider specialized student scenarios, such as a student who works as an assistant to a faculty member or as a lab assistant in a computer lab who may have access to resources most students do not.

Exercise 11.4: New Faculty/Staff Policy

1. Using the guidelines provided in this chapter (and other resources as needed), create a step-by-step IT security policy for implementing a new user account for a faculty or staff member.

2. The policy should define what resources the employee will have access to, what she will not have access to, and any restrictions. (*Hint:* Unlike student policies, you will not need to define time length since it should be indefinite).

Exercise 11.5: Leaving Faculty/Staff Policy

1. Write a policy for how to handle a faculty or staff member's departure (e.g., quit, fired, retired, etc.). Use the guidelines in this chapter and any other resources you like to get you started.

2. Make certain you consider not only shutting down access but the possibility of proprietary research material existing on the faculty or staff member's workstation.

Exercise 11.6: Student Lab Use Policy

1. Considering the material in this chapter, create a set of policies for acceptable use of computer lab computers.

2. Make sure to specify Web use, e-mail use, and any other acceptable uses.

3. Carefully spell out unacceptable usage (e.g., Is game playing acceptable?).

PROJECTS

Project 11.1: Examining Policies

1. Examine the following Web resources that discuss security policies:
   - Level 3 acceptable use policy: **www.level3.com/764.html**
   - Earthlink acceptable use policy: **www.earthlink.net/about/ policies/use/**
   - Sans institute policies: **www.sans.org/resources/policies/**
   - Information Security Policy World: **www.information-security-policies-and-standards.com/**

2. Summarize the main theme of these policy recommendations. Pay particular attention to any area in which these recommendations differ from or exceed the recommendations of this chapter.

3. Choose the policy recommendation you believe is the most secure, and state the reasons for your choice.

11

Project 11.2

1. Ask a local business or your college for a copy of its security policies. Study the policies carefully.

2. Summarize the main theme of these policy recommendations. Pay particular attention to any area in which these recommendations differ from or exceed the recommendations of this chapter.

3. Choose the policy recommendation you believe is the most secure, and state the reasons for your choice.

Project 11.3

Note: This project works well as a group project.

1. At this point in the book you have studied security, including policies. After this chapter and the proceeding exercises and projects, you have examined several polices from various Web resources, as well as the policies of some actual organizations.

2. Take the brief policies you created for the Exercises in this chapter and expand them to create an entire working security policy for your academic institution. You will need to add administrative policies, developmental policies, and more.

▶▶ Case Study

Hector is a security administrator for a defense contractor. This business frequently works with highly sensitive, classified material. Hector has developed a policy for departing employees. This policy handles everything mentioned in this chapter:

- All logon accounts to any server, VPN, network, or other resource are disabled.

- All keys to the facility are returned.

- All accounts for e-mail, Internet access, wireless Internet, cell phones, and so on are shut off.

- Any accounts for mainframe resources are cancelled.

- The employee's workstation hard drive is searched.

Given the highly sensitive nature of the work at this company, what other actions might you add to this policy?

Chapter 12

Assessing a System

Chapter Objectives

After reading this chapter and completing the exercises, you will be able to do the following:

- Evaluate a system's security.
- Scan a system for vulnerabilities.
- Evaluate the overall security of a network.
- Use the "Six Ps" of security.
- Apply a patch to your system.
- Document your security.

Introduction

As you learn more about computer security, you will learn new techniques for securing a particular system. However, the ability to assess a system's security is critical. Before you can begin administering system security, you must have a realistic assessment of the system's current state of security. This chapter discusses the essential steps that you should follow in assessing a system's security level. It is very important to assess a system's security level prior to implementing any security measures. You must be cognizant of the current state of affairs in order to appropriately address vulnerabilities. You should also conduct periodic security audits to ensure that the appropriate level of security is being maintained.

It is also commonplace for security professionals and firms to be contracted to audit a system's security. Whatever your purpose for assessing a system's security, you will need to have some framework within which to conduct your review. This chapter gives you an understanding of how to approach such a review, and what to look for.

Evaluating the Security Risk

In Chapter 1 we provided a method for assigning a numeric value to your system's security risk based on several factors. In this section we will expand upon that system. Recall that we evaluated three aspects of your system:

- Attractiveness to attackers

- Nature of information

- Level of security

The system being evaluated was given a numeric designation between 1 and 10 for each of these factors. The first two are added together, and then the third number (level of security) is subtracted. The lower the number, the more secure your system; the higher the number the greater your risk. The best rating is for a system that:

- Receives a 1 in attractiveness to hackers (i.e., a system that is virtually unknown, has no political or ideological significance, etc.)

- Receives a 1 in informational content (i.e., a system that has no confidential or sensitive data on it)

- Receives a 10 in security (i.e., a system with an extensive layered, proactive security system complete with firewalls, ports blocked, antivirus software, IDS, anti-spyware, appropriate policies, all workstations and servers hardened, etc.)

This hypothetical system would get a score of $1 + 1 - 10$, or -8. That is the lowest threat score possible. Conversely, the worst rating is for a system that:

- Receives a 10 in attractiveness (i.e., a well-known system that has a very controversial ideological or political significance)

- Receives a 10 in informational content (i.e., a system that contains highly sensitive financial records or classified military data)

- Receives a 1 in security (no firewall, no antivirus, no system hardening, etc.)

This system would get a $10 + 10 - 1$, or a 19. Such a hypothetical system is, in effect, a disaster waiting to happen. As a systems administrator, you are unlikely to encounter either extreme. Evaluating system attractiveness to hackers is certainly quite subjective. However, evaluating the value of informational content or the level of security can be done with simple metrics.

To evaluate the value of the informational content on your systems, you have to consider the impact of such data being made public. What would be the worst-case scenario of that data being made public? Table 12.1 divides data into categories, based on worst-case impact, and gives examples of types of data that fit that specification.

You can use similar metrics to evaluate the security level of any network. Table 12.2 shows an example.

A few observations about Table 12.2 should be made here. The first is that Level 3 is actually the bare minimum any person should be using. Because both Windows XP and Linux have built-in firewalls, there is no reason that even a home user would not achieve Level 3. Most organizational networks should be able to get a minimum standard of Level 5 or 6. It should also be noted that you probably will not find networks that fit exactly into

TABLE 12.1 Value of data.

1	Negligible, at most some personal embarrassment	Non-sensitive data: video rental records, book sales records
2-3	Slight loss of competitive advantage	Low-level business data: basic process and procedure documents, customer contact lists, employee lists
4-5	Significant loss of competitive advantage (business or military)	More sensitive business data: business strategies, business research data, basic military logistical data
6-7	Significant financial loss, significant loss of reputation, possible negative impact on operations	Financial/personal data: Social Security numbers, credit card numbers, bank account numbers, detailed military logistical data, military personnel records, confidential health records
8-9	Significant business profit loss, significant negative military/operational impact	Sensitive research data/patent product data, classified military information
10	Serious loss of life, danger to national security	Top secret data, weapons specifications, troop locations, lists of agent identities

12

TABLE 12.2 Security level assessment.*

1	No security at all	Many home users
2	Basic antivirus software	Many home users
3	Antivirus, some security browser settings, basic filtering firewall	Small office/home office users (SOHO)
4	Level 3 plus routine patches and perhaps some additional security measures such as stronger browser security and anti-spyware	Small business/schools
5	Level 4 plus router hardening, strong password requirements, perhaps an IDS, basic policies about downloading, acceptable usage policies, sensitive servers hardened	Networks with a full-time network administrator
6-7	Level 5 with both IDS and anti-spyware, all unnecessary ports closed, subnets filtered, strong password policies, good physical security, encryption used for sensitive data, all servers hardened, back-up media destroyed appropriately, stateful packet inspection firewall on perimeter, Web servers located in a DMZ, packet filtering on all subnet routers, very extensive policies on all aspects of computer security	Networks with a larger IT staff, possibly a full-time security professional
8-9	Level 6-7 with regular internal and external security audits, hard drive encryption (such as Windows EFS), possible use of biometrics in physical security (finger print scan), extensive logging, background checks on all IT personnel, all workstations/servers completely hardened, all personnel wear security ID badges, all data transmissions encrypted	Networks with a full-time security professional
10	Level 8-9 plus security clearance for all IT personnel, monthly updates/patching/auditing, routine penetration testing, Internet usage extremely restricted or blocked altogether, no portable media (CD, floppy, etc.) on workstations, strong physical security including armed guards	Military/research installations

*This does not mean that this level should be found at these types of organizations; this is just where it is likely to be found.

one of these levels. However, this chart should give you some guidelines for how to evaluate the security level of these systems.

This system is somewhat simplistic, and parts of it are clearly subjective. It is hoped that this will form a basis for you as you begin working on security for your network. Having numerical values to evaluate your threat level can be a great assistance when assessing your security level. The real issue is that you have some quantifiable method for evaluating the security of a given system. This system is presented to you simply because there are very few similar systems in existence today. Most security evaluations are somewhat subjective. This numerical grading system (which is the invention of this author) is offered as a starting point. You should feel encouraged to expand upon it.

Making the Initial Assessment

Disaster recovery, access rights, and appropriate policies are topics that are often overlooked by those new to security. To keep it simple and easy to remember, the stages of assessing a system's security can be separated into the "Six Ps":

- Patch

- Ports

- Protect

- Policies

- Probe

- Physical

The first three are discussed in this section. The fifth — probe — is discussed in the next section, and policies are covered in Chapter 11. You should note that these Six Ps are the invention of this book's author (just as the numerical grading system was), and are not yet standards in the security industry. They are provided here as a framework for approaching system security.

12

Patches

Patching a system is perhaps the most fundamental part of security. Therefore, when assessing any system's security, you should check to see whether a procedure is in place to govern the routine updating of all patches. And you should also, of course, check to see that the machines actually have current patches and updates. A written policy is essential, but when performing a security audit, you need to ensure that those policies are actually being followed.

As you are aware, operating system and application vendors occasionally discover security flaws in their products and release patches to correct these flaws. Unfortunately, it is not uncommon to find organizations in which patches have not been applied as late as 30 days or more after their release.

Applying Patches Applying patches means that the operating system, database management systems, development tools, Internet browsers, and so on are all checked for patches. In a Microsoft environment this should be easy because the Microsoft Web site has a utility that scans your system for any required patches to the browser, operating system, or office products. It is a very basic tenet of security to ensure that all patches are up-to-date. This should be one of your first tasks when assessing a system. Regardless of the operating system or application vendor, you should be able to go to its Web site and find information regarding how to download and install the latest patches.

Once you have ensured that all patches are up-to-date, the next step is to set up a system to ensure that they are kept up-to-date. One simple method is to initiate a periodic patch review where, at a scheduled time, all machines are checked for patches. There are also automated solutions that will patch all systems in your organization. It is imperative that all machines be patched, not just the servers.

Automated Patch Systems Manually patching machines can be quite cumbersome, and in larger networks, simply impractical. However, there are automated solutions that will patch all systems on your network. These solutions scan your systems at preset times and update any required patches. A few are listed here:

- **Windows Update:** For systems running Microsoft Windows, you can set up Windows to automatically patch your system. Recent versions of Windows have this turned on automatically. If your system is older, simply go to **www.microsoft.com** and click on the link on the left-hand side that says "Update Windows." This will give that individual machine routing updates for the Windows operating system. This approach does have a few shortcomings, the first being that it will only update Windows and not any other applications on your machine. The second drawback is that it does not provide any way to check patches on a test machine before deploying them to the entire network. Its main advantages are that it is free, and integrated with the Windows operating system.

- **HFNetChkPro:** This product is available from **www.deerfield.com/products/hfnetchkpro/**. It automatically administers and manages patches, including rebooting the patched machines. It is sold on a per seat license, with five seats going for about $200 and 100 seats selling for about $2,100.

- **Zen Works Patch Management:** This product is available from Novell at **www.novell.com/news/press/archive/2004/03/pr04020. HTML**. If you are currently using a Novell network, then it might make sense for you to also use their patch management software. There is a licensing fee of about $18 per each device to be patched.

- **PatchLink:** Available from **www.patchlink.com/**, this product also manages and automates the patching process. PatchLink uses an agent-based system. This means an intelligent agent is installed on each workstation to manage patching.

- **McAfee ePolicy Orchestrator:** This product (**www.mcafeesecurity. com/us/products/mcafee/mgmt_solutions/epo.htm**) is both interesting and popular. It handles the automated patching of your system, and it includes a number of other features. One interesting feature is that it monitors the network for any devices that are connected to the network that are not set up via ePolicy Orchestrator. This prevents "rogue" machines. In larger organizations people setting up their own machines and servers can be a significant security risk. ePolicy Orchestrator also monitors other aspects of your network defense, including antivirus and firewall software.

Other patch management software solutions are available. These four are provided to give you an example of the solutions available and the price range you can expect to pay for them. A simple Internet search using any major search engine should give you several more options you may want to consider.

The choice of patch management system is often affected by other considerations, such as what other software the company uses. For example if you already use McAfee Firewall and antivirus software, then using their patch management system is definitely an option you should seriously consider.

If no automated patch management system is used, then the next best option is scheduled, periodic manual patching. This means that the IT department in that organization has a schedule wherein they routinely scan each machine and update its patches. How frequently this is done is dependent upon the security needs of the organization. Patching quarterly should be considered the absolute minimum for any organization. Monthly is probably appropriate for most businesses. If a higher level of security is desired, then manual patching is probably not the appropriate choice.

Ports

As we have discussed in previous chapters, all communication takes place via some port. This is also true for many virus attacks. Frequently virus attacks will utilize some uncommon port to gain access to your system. Recall that ports 1 through 1024 are assigned and used for well-known protocols.

12

We have examined viruses, Trojan horses, and other dangers that operate on specific port numbers. If those ports are closed, then your vulnerability to these specific attacks is significantly reduced.

Unfortunately some system administrators do not make a policy of closing unused ports. This is probably due to the fact that many administrators think that if the firewall is blocking certain traffic, then there is no need to block that port on individual machines. However, this approach provides you with only perimeter security, not layered security. By closing ports on individual machines, you provide a backup in case the firewall is breached. As a rule, any port you do not explicitly need for operations should be closed, and communication should be disallowed on this port. A port is usually associated with a service. For example an FTP service is often associated with ports 21 and 20. In order to close a port on an individual machine, you would need to shut down the service that uses that port. This means those unused services on servers and individual workstations should be shut down.

Both Windows XP and Linux have built-in port-filtering capability. Windows 2000 Professional also has port-filtering capability whereas Windows XP has a complete firewall solution built into the operating system. This means in addition to shutting down the particular unneeded services on all client machines, you should also shut down the ports. The end of this chapter has exercises that specifically walk you through closing down services on a Windows 2000 or Windows XP machine.

You should also shut down any unused router ports in your network. If your network is part of a larger wide area network (WAN), then it is likely you have a router connecting you to that WAN. Every open port is a possible avenue of entry for a virus or intruder. Therefore, every port you can close is one less opportunity for such attacks to affect your system. The specifics of how to close a port on a router are particular to the individual router. The documentation that came with your router or the vendor should be able to provide you with specific instructions for how to accomplish this. If you have a vendor servicing your router, then you should make a list of all required ports and request that the vendor close all other ports on the router.

Protect

The next phase is to ensure that all reasonable protective software and devices are employed. This means at a minimum having a firewall between your network and the outside world. Firewalls were discussed in Chapters 3 and 4. Clearly more advanced firewalls such as stateful packet inspection firewalls are preferred. When auditing a system, you must note not only whether the system has a firewall, but what type of firewall it has.

You should also consider using an intrusion detection system (IDS) on that firewall and any Web servers. An IDS is considered nonessential by some security experts; you can certainly have a secure network without one.

IN PRACTICE: Closing Ports

Many companies tend to concentrate on port filtering at the firewall. However, there is always a chance that an intruder or a virus could get inside your network. It is therefore prudent to block ports and services on each machine. When doing so, you must make sure you do not block ports that you need. The following process is recommended for blocking ports on workstations:

1. Using a port scanner, make a list of all open ports for that machine.

2. Try to find out what each port is used for, then note on your list which ports are actually needed.

3. On a single test machine, block the ports you believe are not needed. In fact block all ports except the ones you listed as being necessary.

4. Try to use all of your standard applications and see if they still work.

Assuming step 4 works, then apply the same blocking to 1 or 2 beta testers' machines and let them use it for several days.

Now you are ready to begin blocking ports on all workstations. It is critical that you make sure your blocking won't disable or impede legitimate applications and network processes.

However, they are the only way to know of impending attacks, and there are free, open source IDS available. For that reason, most experts highly recommend them. The firewall and IDS will provide basic security to your network's perimeter, but you also need virus scanning. Each and every machine, including servers, must have a virus scanner that is updated regularly. The point has already been made that a virus infection is the greatest threat to most networks. As also previously discussed, it is probably prudent to consider anti-spyware software on all of your systems. This will prevent users of your network from inadvertently running spyware on the network.

Finally, a proxy server, also discussed in Chapter 2, is a very good idea. It not only masks your internal IP addresses, but most proxy servers allow you to discover what Web sites users visit and put on filters for certain sites. Many security experts consider a proxy server to be as essential as a firewall.

In addition to protecting your network, you must also protect data that is transmitted, particularly outside your network. All external connections should be made via a VPN. Having data encrypted prevents hackers from intercepting the data via a packet sniffer. For more secure locations you might even look for all internal transmissions to be encrypted as well.

In short, when assessing the protection of the network, check to see whether the following items are present, properly configured, and functioning:

- Firewall

- Antivirus protection

- Anti-spyware protection

- IDS

- Proxy Server or NAT

- Data transmissions encryption

Be aware that the first two items are met in most networks. Any network that does not have a firewall or antivirus software is so substandard that the audit should probably stop at that point. In fact, it is unlikely that such an organization would even bother to have a security audit. The IDS and data encryption options are probably less common; however, they should be considered for all systems.

Physical

In addition to securing your network from unwanted digital access, you must also ensure that it has adequate physical security. The most robustly secure computer that is left sitting unattended in an unlocked room is not at all secure. You must have some policy or procedure governing the locking of rooms with computers as well as the handling of laptops, PDAs, and other mobile computer devices. Servers must be in a locked and secure room with as few people as is reasonably possible having access to them. Backup tapes should be stored in a fireproof safe. Documents and old backup tapes should be destroyed before disposal (e.g., by melting tapes, magnetizing hard disks, breaking CDs).

Physical access to routers and hubs should also be tightly controlled. Having the most hi-tech, professional information security on the planet but leaving your server in an unlocked room to which everyone has access is a recipe for disaster. One of the most common mistakes in the arena of physical security is co-locating a router or switch in a janitorial closet. This means that, in addition to your own security personnel and network administrators, the entire cleaning staff has access to your router or switch, and any one of them could leave the door unlocked for an extended period of time.

There are some basic rules you should follow regarding physical security:

- **Server Rooms:** The room where servers are kept should be the most fire-resistant room in your building. It should have a strong door with a strong lock, such as a deadbolt. Only those personnel who actually have a need to go in the room should have a key. You might also consider a server room log wherein each person logs in when they enter or exit the room. There are actually electronic locks that record who enters a room, when they enter, and when they leave. Consult local security vendors in your area for more details on price and availability.

- **Workstations:** All workstations should have an engraved identifying mark. You should also routinely inventory them. It is usually physically impossible to secure them as well as you secure servers, but you can take a few steps to improve their security.

- **Miscellaneous Equipment:** Projectors, CD burners, laptops, and so forth should be kept under lock and key. Any employee that wishes to use one should be required to sign it out, and it should be checked to see that it is in proper working condition and that all parts are present when it is returned.

IN PRACTICE: Physical Security

How much physical security is enough? Well, that depends entirely on your situation. The very first step, one that many companies use, is to simply not let nonemployees roam around the building. All employees are given ID badges that they wear. Anyone without such a badge should be stopped and asked to return to the reception area (unless accompanied by an employee). That alone is a step forward for security.

Another step is to make sure all sensitive equipment is locked. Many companies do this, but then allow a large number of people to have copies of the keys. That degrades the level of security provided by locks. The fewest number of people possible should have keys. If someone does not have a clear need for access, then they should not have a key.

Biometrics are becoming more common as they become cheaper. Such systems control access to equipment by a fingerprint. This has the advantage of not being easily copied or lost, as a key might be. This also allows you to easily verify who accesses what equipment and when it is accessed.

12

These measures should be considered by all organizations. Some organizations go much further in ensuring physical security, and we will list some of the more extreme measures here. Most are probably more extreme

than businesses require. However if you deal with highly sensitive or classified data, then you might want to consider some or all of these measures.

- Biometric locks to all server rooms, or equipment storage rooms.
  Such locks are triggered by a fingerprint scan, and the identity of
  the person as well as the time they entered the room are recorded.

- All visitors to the building are logged in (both their entry and exit
  time) and are escorted by an employee at all times.

- All bags are inspected when personnel leave, or at least some bags
  are inspected at random.

- No portable devices that might record data are allowed on the
  premises. This includes USB drives, camera phones, or any device
  that might copy data or record screen images.

- All printing is logged. Who printed, the time the printing occurred,
  the document name, and the document size.

- All copying is logged, similarly to printing.

If you are in a situation that demands a greater than normal security
level, these measures may be considered.

Probing the Network

Perhaps the most critical step in assessing any network is to probe the network for vulnerabilities. This means using various utilities to scan your network for vulnerabilities. Some network administrators skip this step. They
audit policies, check the firewall logs, check patches, and so on. However,
the probing tools discussed in this section are the same ones that most hackers use. If you want to know how vulnerable your network is, it is prudent to
try the same tools that an intruder would use. In this section we will review
the more common scanning/probing tools.

NetCop

The first scanner we will examine is NetCop. This particular scanner is not
necessarily the most widely used in the security or hacking communities,
but it is easy to use and therefore makes a very good place for us to start.
This utility can be obtained from many sites, including **www.cotse.com/
pscan.htm**. When you download NetCop, you get a simple self-extracting
executable that will install the program on your machine and will even
place a shortcut in your program menu. Launching NetCop brings up the
screen shown in Figure 12.1. As you can see from this image, this scanner is
relatively simple and intuitive to use.

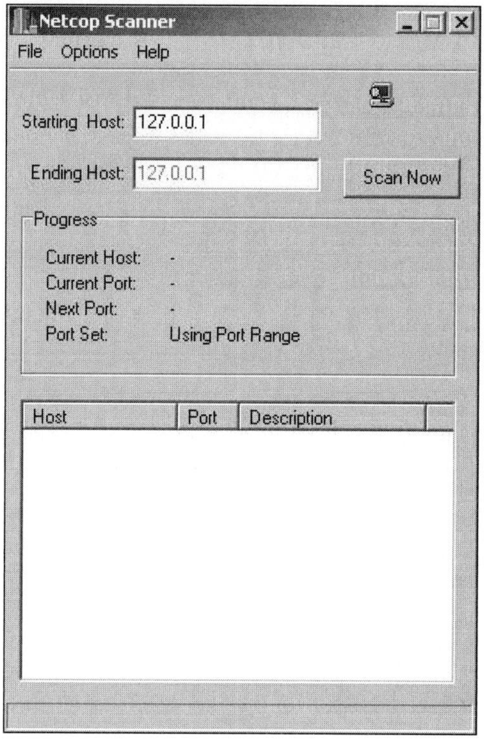

FIGURE 12.1 NetCop port scanner.

The first selection you make is how to scan the IP address. You can either choose to scan a single IP address or a range of IP addresses. The latter option makes this tool particularly useful for network administrators who want to check for open ports on their entire network. For our purposes we will begin by scanning a single IP address, our own machine. To follow along on your own computer, you will need to type in your machine's IP address. You can either type your machine's actual IP address or simply the loop back address (127.0.0.1). When you type in a single IP address and click on *Scan Now,* you can watch the display showing that it is checking each and every port, as shown in Figure 12.2. This is very methodical but also a bit slow.

You can stop the scan if you wish to do so; however, if you let the scan run through all of the ports, you will then see something similar to what is shown in Figure 12.3. Of course, different machines you examine will have different ports open. That is the entire point of scanning, to find out which ports are open.

Finding out which ports are open on a given machine is only half the battle. It is important that you know what each port is used for, and which ones you can shut down without negatively impacting the machine's purpose.

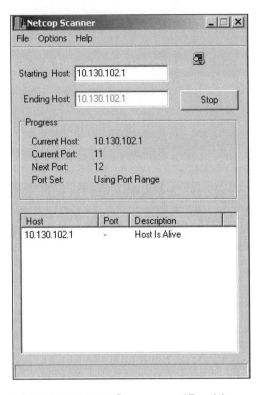

FIGURE 12.2 Screen an IP address
with NetCop.

Over time you will probably memorize several commonly used ports. For a
complete list of all ports, you can check any of these Web sites:

- **www.networksorcery.com/enp/protocol/ip/ports00000.htm**

- **www.iana.org/assignments/port-numbers**

- **www.techadvice.com/tech/T/TCP_well_known_ports.htm**

Consider what sort of information these ports tell you. Machines running
port 80 are probably Web servers. But other ports can give a hacker even more
useful information. For example, ports 137, 138, and 139 are used by NetBios,
which is most often associated with older versions of Windows. If an intruder
realizes that the target machine is using an older version of Windows, she
knows she can exploit flaws that have been corrected in newer versions. Other
ports can indicate if the target machine is running a database server, e-mail
server, or other vital services. This information not only helps hackers to compromise systems, but also helps them identify information-rich targets.

If you are working within an organizational structure, the best course
of action is to make a list of all open ports and identify which ones you

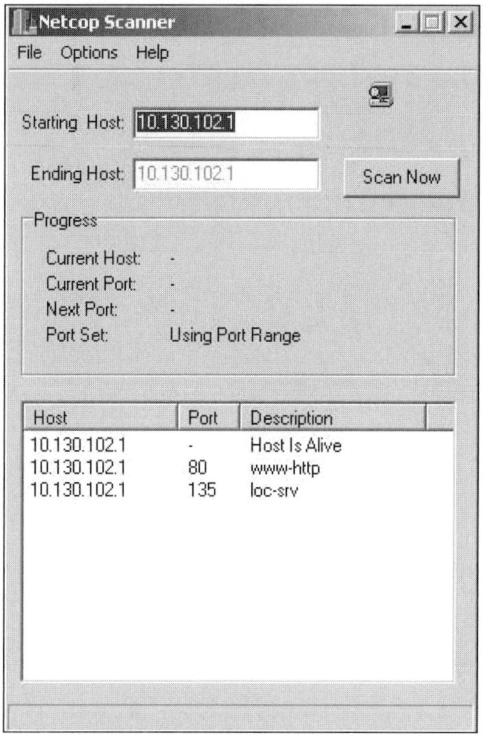

FIGURE 12.3 IP Scan results.

believe are required for operations and which ones are not. You should then forward that list to relevant parties such as other network administrators, the IT manager, and the security manager. Give them a chance to identify any additional ports that may be needed. Then you can proceed to close all the ports not needed.

NetBrute

Some port scanners do more than simply scan for open ports. Some also give you additional information. One such product is NetBrute from RawLogic, located at **www.rawlogic.com/netbrute/**. This one is quite popular with both the security and hacker community. No computer security professionals should be without this item in their tool chests. This utility will give you open ports, as well as other vital information. Once you install and launch NetBrute, you will see a screen such as the one depicted in Figure 12.4.

As you can see in Figure 12.4, there are three tabs. We will concentrate on the NetBrute tab first. You can elect to scan a range of IP addresses (perfect for network administrators assessing the vulnerability of their own systems),

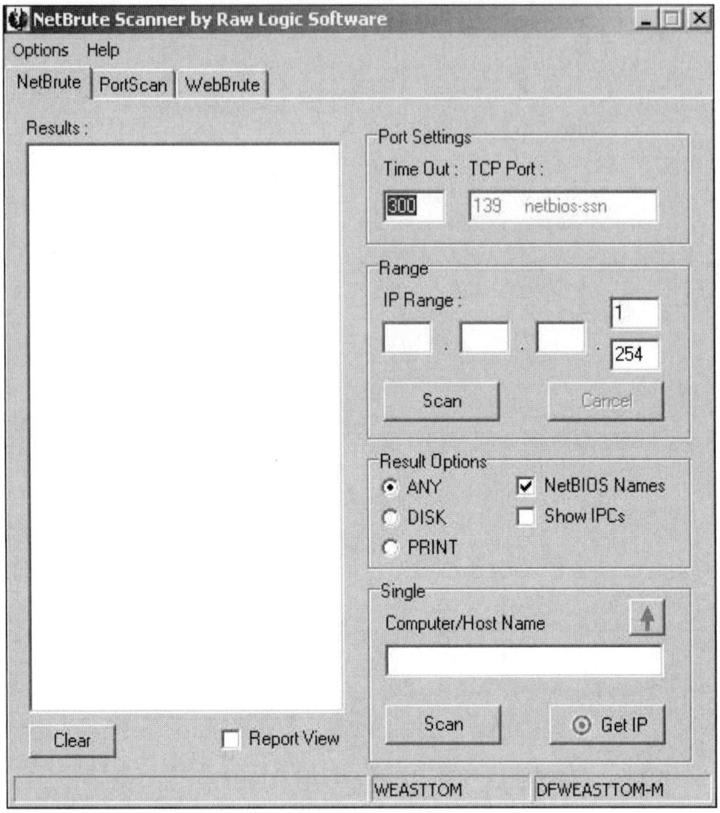

FIGURE 12.4 NetBrute main screen.

or you can choose to target an individual IP. When you are done, it will show you all the shared drives on that computer, as you see in Figure 12.5.

Shared folders and drives are important to security because they provide one possible way for a hacker to get into a system. If the hacker can gain access to that shared folder, she can use that area to upload a Trojan horse, virus, key logger, or other device. The rule on shared drives is simple: If you don't absolutely need them, then don't have them. Any drive or folder can be shared or not shared. Unless you have a compelling reason to share a drive, you should not. And if you do decide to share it, then the details of that shared drive — including content and reason for sharing it — should be in your security documentation.

With the PortScan tab, you can find ports. It works exactly like the first tab except that instead of giving you a list of shared folders/drives, it gives you a list of open ports. Thus, with NetBrute, you get a port scanner *and* a shared folder scanner. In essence the second tab contains the most pertinent information you might obtain from other products such as NetCop.

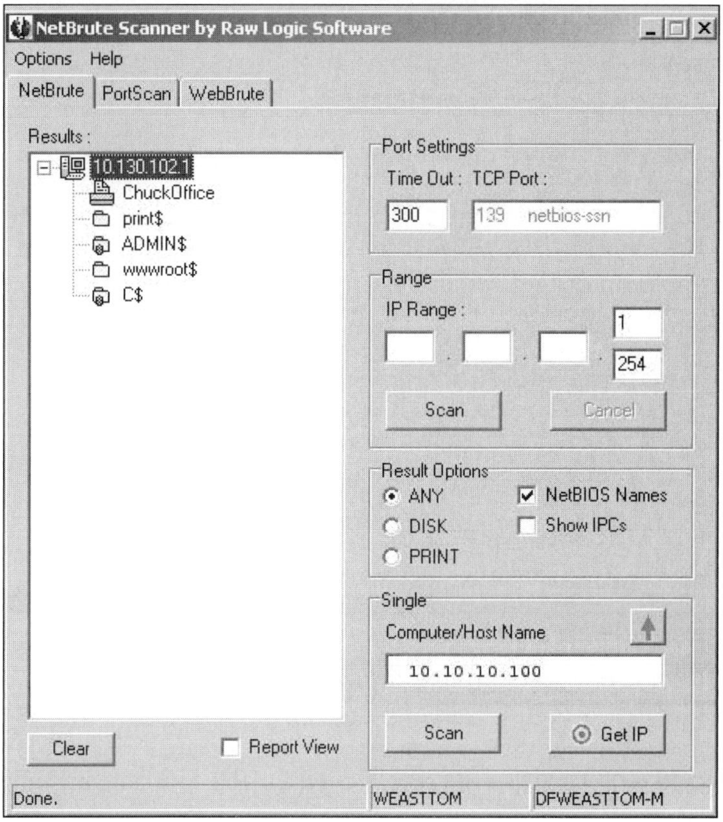

FIGURE 12.5 Shared drives.

When scanning your own network, these first two tabs will be the most important. However if you wish to check the security of your Web server you would want to use the WebBrute tab. The WebBrute tab allows you to scan a target Web site and obtain information similar to what you would get from Netcraft. This scan gives you information such as the target system's operating system and Web server software.

NetBrute is easy to use and provides most of the basic information you might need. The ability to track shared folders and drives in addition to open ports is of particular use. This tool is widely used by hackers as well as security professionals.

Cerberus

One of the most widely used scanning utilities, and a personal favorite of this author, is the Cerberus Internet Scanner, available as a free download from **www.cerberus-infosec.co.uk/cis.sHTML** (alternative download locations are listed in the Appendices at the back of this book, or you can simply do a

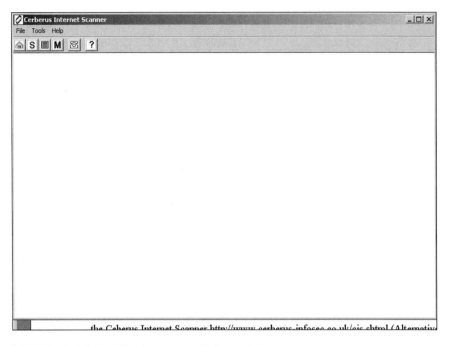

FIGURE 12.6 The Cerberus Internet Scanner.

Web search with your favorite search engine). This tool is remarkably simple to use and very informative. When you launch this tool, you will see a screen like the one shown in Figure 12.6.

From this screen you can click on the button on the far left that has an icon of a house. Or you can go to *File* and select *Host*. You then simply key in either the URL or the IP address of the machine that you wish to scan. Click either the button with the "S" on it or go to *File* and select *Start Scan*. Cerberus will then scan that machine and give you a wealth of information. You can see in Figure 12.7 all the various categories of information that you get from this scan.

Click on the third button to review the report. The report will launch a Hypertext Markup Language (HTML) document (thus the document is easy to save for future reference) with links to each category. Click on the category you wish to view. As a rule you should save all such security reports for future audits. In the event of litigation it may be necessary for you to verify that you were practicing due diligence in implementing and auditing security. It is also important to document these activities as a part of the record of security precautions you take. This documentation could be crucial in the case of any external audit or even in helping a new IT security professional get up to speed on what actions have already been taken. This information should be stored in a secure location, as it is of great value to someone wishing to compromise your system security. An example of the report is shown in Figure 12.8.

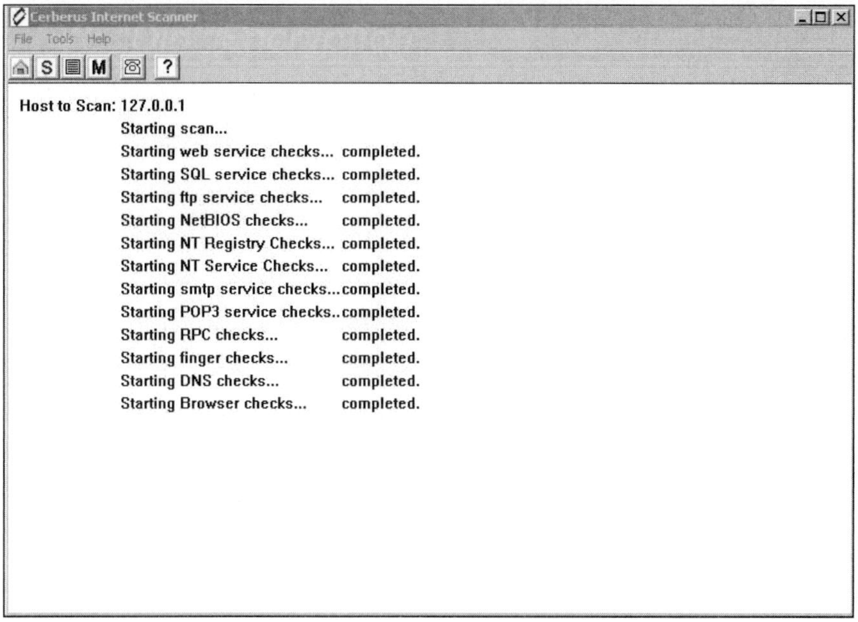

FIGURE 12.7 Cerberus scan results.

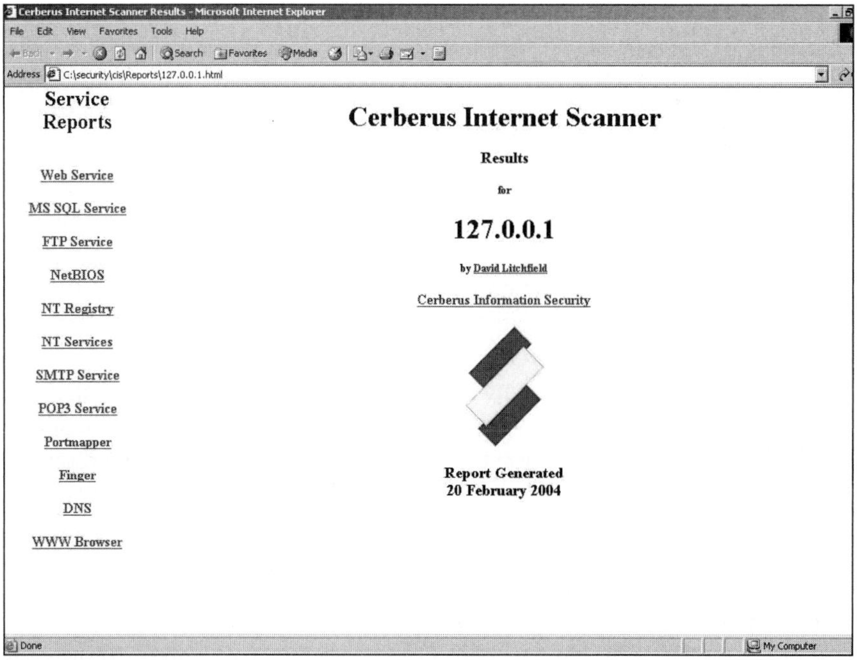

FIGURE 12.8 The Cerberus Report.

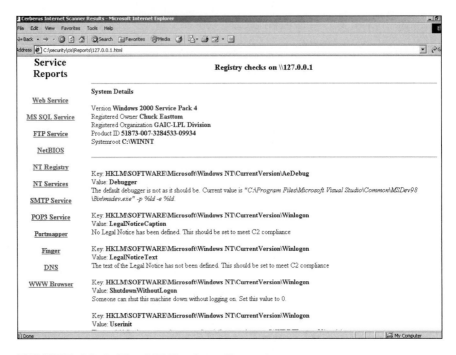

FIGURE 12.9 The NT Registry Report.

One of the most interesting sections to review, particularly for a security administrator, is the NT Registry report. This report will examine the Windows Registry and inform you of any security flaws found there and how to correct them. This report is shown in Figure 12.9.

This list shows specific Windows Registry settings, why those settings are not particularly secure, and what you can do to secure them. For obvious reasons, this tool is very popular with hackers. Cerberus can provide a great map of all of a system's potential vulnerabilities including, but not limited to, shared drives, insecure registry settings, services running, and known flaws in the operating system.

You may have noted that more detail was given on Cerberus than some of the other scanners. This is for two reasons. The first is that this particular scanner gives more information than most port scanners. The second reason is that this scanner is a particular favorite of the author. My recommendation to you is that if you have to go with just one scanner, this is the one.

Port Scanner for Unix: SATAN

One tool that has been quite popular for years with Unix administrators (as well as hackers) is SATAN. This tool is not some diabolical supernatural entity, but rather an acronym for Security Administrator Tool for Analyzing Networks. It can be downloaded for free from any number of Web sites.

Many of these sites are listed at **www.fish.com/satan/mirrors.HTML**. This tool is strictly for Unix and does not work in Windows.

SATAN was created by Dan Farmer, author of COPS (Computer Oracle and Password System) and Wietse Venema and from the Eindhoven University of Technology in the Netherlands. It was originally released on April 5, 1995. It should be noted that SATAN, as well as many other probing tools, was originally used by hackers to find out about a target system. Over time, the more creative network administrators began to use these tools for their own purposes. Clearly if you wish to protect your system against intruders, it can be quite helpful to try the same tools that intruders use.

The user can enter either a single machine or an entire domain of machines to attack. There are three classes of attacks:

- **Light:** A light attack simply reports what hosts are available and what Remote Procedure Call services those hosts are running.

- **Normal:** A normal attack probes the targets by establishing various connections including telnet, FTP, WWW, gopher, and SMTP. These are used to discover what operating system the host is running and what vulnerabilities may be available.

- **Heavy:** A heavy attack includes everything that a normal attack does with the addition of a search for several other known vulnerabilities, such as writable anonymous FTP directories or trusted hosts.

The history of this particular product is quite illuminating. It began with the work of two computer scientists, Dan Farmer of Sun Microsystems and Wietse Venema of Eindhoven University of Technology. Together they published a paper entitled "Improving the Security of Your Site by Breaking Into It" (**www.alw.nih.gov/Security/Docs/admin-guide-to-cracking.101.HTML**). In it, they discussed using hacking techniques to attempt to break into your own system and thereby discover its security flaws. In the process of writing this paper, they developed the SATAN tool in order to aid network administrators in carrying out the recommendations of their paper. This means SATAN is the product of computer scientists working to improve computer security. It is not a commercial product and can be freely downloaded from numerous Web sites.

SAINT®

SAINT (Security Administrator's Integrated Network Tool is a network vulnerability assessment scanner (**www.saintcorporation.com/products/saint_engine.HTML**) that scans a system and finds security weaknesses. It prioritizes critical vulnerabilities in the network and recommends safeguards for your data. SAINT can benefit you in several ways:

- Prioritized vulnerabilities let you focus your resources on the most critical security issues. This is probably the most distinctive feature of SAINT.

12

- Fast assessment results help you identify problems quickly.

- Highly configurable scans increase the efficiency of your network security program.

- It allows network administrators to design and generate vulnerability assessment reports quickly and easily. Such reports are particularly useful when conducting audits.

- The product is automatically updated whenever a scan is run.

This product is newer than Cerberus and SATAN, and is gaining widespread acceptance in both the hacking and security communities.

Nessus

Nessus, or the "Nessus Project," is another extremely powerful network scanner. It is open source and can be downloaded from **www.nessus.org**. Nessus is fast and reliable, with a modular architecture that allows you to configure it to your needs. Nessus works on Unix-like systems (MacOS X, FreeBSD, Linux, Solaris, and more) and also has a Windows version (called NeWT).

Nessus includes a variety of plug-ins that can be enabled, depending on the type of security checks you want to perform. These plug-ins work cooperatively with each test specifying what is needed to proceed with the test. For example, if a certain test requires a remote FTP server and a previous test showed that none exists, that test will not be performed. Not performing futile tests speeds up the scanning process. These plug-ins are updated daily and are available from the Nessus Web site.

The output from a Nessus scan of a system is incredibly detailed, and there are multiple formats available for the reports. These reports give information about security holes, warnings, and notes. Nessus does not attempt to fix any security holes that it finds. It simply reports them and gives suggestions for how to make the vulnerable system more secure.

Some security professionals complain that Nessus can give false positives. This means it can report a problem where there is none. This product is also not as widely used as Cerberus, SATAN, or some of the other scanners we have examined.

NetStat Live

One of the most popular protocol monitors is NetStat, which ships free with Microsoft Windows. A version of this, NetStat Live (NSL), is freely available on the Internet from a variety of sites, such as **www.analogx.com/contents/download/network/nsl.htm**. This product is an easy-to-use TCP/IP protocol monitor that can be used to see the exact throughput on both incoming and outgoing data whether you are using a modem, cable modem, DSL, or a local network. It allows you to see the speed at which your data goes from your computer to another computer on the Internet. It even tells you how many other computers your data must go through to get to its destination. NSL also graphs the CPU usage of a system. This can be especially useful if, for example, you are experiencing slowed connection speeds. It can identify whether your computer or your Internet connection is the reason for the slowdown.

The NetStat Live screen is shown in Figure 12.10. This display shows the last 60 seconds of data throughput. It displays the average datarate, the total amount of data sent since last reboot, and the maximum datarate. It tracks these for all incoming and outgoing messages.

To enable or disable a pane, simply right-click on the window, choose *Statistics,* and then place a check next to any statistics that you would like to see. Your choices are:

- **Local Machine.** The current machine name, IP address, and network interface being monitored

- **Remote Machine.** The remote machine, including average ping time and number of hops

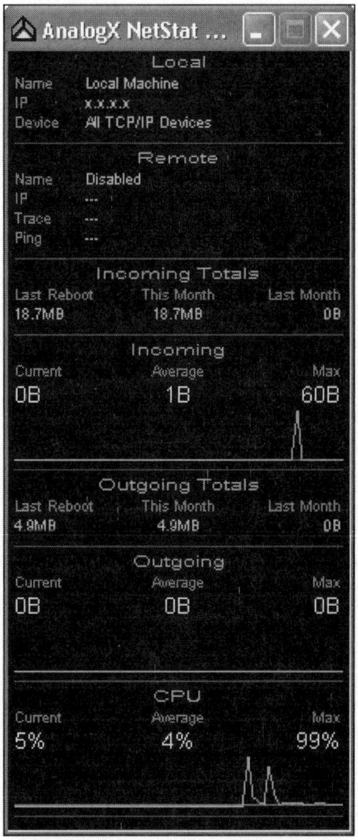

FIGURE 12.10 NetStat Live.

- **Incoming Data.** Data on the incoming (download) channel

- **Incoming Totals.** Totals for the incoming data

- **Outgoing Data.** Data on the outgoing (upload) channel

- **Outgoing Totals.** Totals for the outgoing data

- **System Threads.** Total number of threads currently running in the system

- **CPU Usage.** Graphs the CPU load

Notice that the Remote section has a machine listed and some information pertaining to it. You can easily change the server for which you are gathering information. Simply open your Web browser, go to a Web page, and copy the URL (including "http://") into the clipboard (by using Ctrl+C). When you return to viewing NSL, you will see that the server has been replaced with information on the site to which you browsed. One of the most important reasons to use NetStat or NetStat Live is to find out what the normal traffic flow is to a given server (or your entire network). It is difficult to determine whether abnormal activity is taking place if you do not know the characteristics of normal activity.

IN PRACTICE: When Doing an Audit

As we previously discussed, a very early step in assessing a network is checking its documentation. This step can give you invaluable information about the organization's security approach. Whether you are doing an internal audit or are an outside party auditing another organization, there are some telltale signs in documentation that can tell you how thorough the organization's approach to security is.

For example, an organization that has documented the normal traffic flow to its servers is probably paying close attention to the details of its security architecture. There are some other items that will indicate good security practices:

- A documented patch maintenance program

- A documented change control process

- A diagram of the entire network, complete with details of what is on each machine. This documentation must be secured and not generally available to unauthorized people.

- Documentation of the security training/certifications of the network staff

- Ongoing in-house security training
- Routine review of security literature, journals, and Web sites

All of these items can indicate to you that this organization takes security seriously. On the other hand, there may also be items in the documentation that would indicate the opposite. Some of these include:

- Very limited or outdated documentation
- Unsecured network documentation that is easy for unauthorized personnel to get to
- Overly vague security policies
- Security policies that do not mention any negative outcome for violations
- Lack of logs (Most changes—database, server, security, etc.—should be logged.)

These are just a few items to look for when you are reviewing documentation for any organization.

Active Ports

Active Ports is another easy-to-use scanning tool for Windows. You can download it for free from **www.protect-me.com/freeware.HTM**L. This program enables you to monitor all open TCP and UDP ports on the local computer. Figure 12.11 shows the main screen of Active Ports. Active Ports maps ports to the owning application so you can watch which process has opened which port. It also displays a local and remote IP address for each connection and allows you to terminate the process that is using that port.

Active Ports lacks some of the features you would find in more advanced tools such as Cerberus or SATAN. It is a good place to start, though, especially if you have no experience port scanning at all.

Other Port Scanners

There are many more port scanners and security tools available on the Internet, a few of which are listed here:

- Like Active Ports, Fport reports all open TCP/IP and UDP ports and maps them to the owning application. Additionally, it maps those ports to running processes. Fport can be used to quickly identify unknown open ports and their associated applications. This product is available at **www.ibiblio.org/security/articles/fport.HTM**L.

12

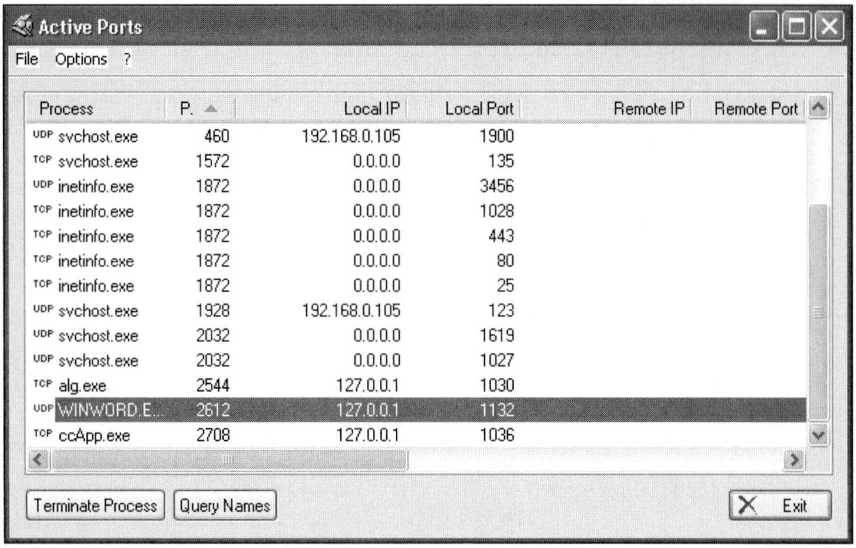

FIGURE 12.11 Active Ports user interface.

■ TCPView is a Windows program that will show you detailed listings of all TCP and UDP endpoints on your system, including the remote address and the state of TCP connections. TCPView provides a conveniently presented subset of the NetStat program. You can find this product at **www.sysinternals.com/ntw2k/source/tcpview.shtml**.

■ SuperScan is a port scanner from Foundstone Inc. It is available as a free download at **www.foundstone.com/**. This particular scanner gives its report in HTML format. What is most interesting about SuperScan is the wide variety of tools also available at that same Web site, including tools that scan for any number of very specific vulnerabilities. Exploring this Web site is well worth your time.

The specific port scanner you use is often more a matter of personal preference than anything else. The best approach is to use three or four separate scanners to ensure that you are checking all the possible vulnerabilities. Using more than three or four scanners provides limited incremental benefits and can be very time consuming. I would definitely recommend that Cerberus be one of the scanners you use. You may also wish to fully test your password with some of the password crackers we mentioned in Chapter 6 to ensure that your passwords cannot be easily cracked.

More security savvy network administrators will use these tools on their servers, just to check security. Full-time security professionals should try to stay abreast of trends in the hacking community, and may even use the same tools as hackers. This is a proactive and important step for a network administrator to take.

Security Documentation

Throughout this chapter, and this book, we have frequently mentioned security documentation. By this point you are undoubtedly aware that you need to document your security. However you may not be clear as to exactly what documents you should have. Unfortunately this is an area of network securities for which there are not firm industry standards. There is no manual on documentation.

In this section we will explore some essential documents you should have, and what they should contain. To make this simpler, many of these documents relate directly to the aforementioned Six Ps of security.

Physical Security Documentation

You should have a document that lists physical security that is in place. Where are the machines located? This means documenting the location of every single server, workstation, router, hub, or other device. The documentation should contain serial numbers as well as what personnel have access to them. If a device is in a locked room, then the documentation should also have a list of who has keys to that room.

If you log entry to secured rooms, then copies of those logs should be filed with your other physical documentation. In even a medium-sized network this would quickly become a rather hefty file rather than a single document. You may consider implementing some method whereby after a certain period of time (1 year, for example) the access logs are archived, then after a longer period of time (such as 3 years) they are destroyed.

Policy and Personnel Documentation

All policies *must* be on file. Any revisions should be filed along with the originals. Assuming you have employees sign an agreement stating they are aware of the policies (and you absolutely should), then copies of that should also be on file.

Along with policy documentation, you should keep a list of personnel along with what items they have access to. This includes physical access as well as any machines (servers, workstations, or routers) that they have login rights to. You should also note what level of access they have (standard user, power user, administrator, and so on).

Probe Documents

Any time you conduct any security audit, a report of that audit should be filed. Even audits done by outside consultants should be kept on file. The audit report should include any flaws found, and have a follow-up report of what steps were taken to correct them.

Should you have a security incident (such as a virus infection or intruder), there should be at least a brief memo summarizing what occurred. That document should state what the security incident was, when it occurred, what machines were affected, and how it was corrected.

Network Protection Documents

The most obvious item to document is exactly what network protections you have in place. This documentation should detail the following:

- What firewall are you using and how is it configured?

- What IDS are you using and how is it configured?

- What antivirus and/or anti-spyware are you using?

- Have you configured any honey pots?

- What individual machine security measures (such as workstation firewalls) have you taken?

One note of caution: These documents should be kept under lock and key, with only limited access. If an intruder were to get access to these documents, they would have a detailed analysis of your network's weaknesses.

Summary

Periodic security audits must be a part of any proper security plan. The audit must include the following steps, at a minimum:

- Check for appropriate security policies.

- Check to see that all systems have updated patches for the operating system and applications. Also check to see whether a patch management plan is in place and documented.

- Check physical security.

- Probe the system using port scanners and other software to detect and correct any flaws.

- Document the specific steps taken in the security audit, any flaws found, and any corrective actions that were taken or are recommended.

Test Your Skills

MULTIPLE CHOICE QUESTIONS

1. Which of the following scanners provides information regarding the target system's registry?

   A. Cerberus

   B. NetCop

   C. NetBrute

   D. Active Ports

2. What is the minimum level of security (using the chapter's 1–10 scale) that any organizational network should have?

   A. 1

   B. 3

   C. 5

   D. 7

3. Which of the following is the most fundamental aspect of security?

   A. shutting down unused services

   B. implementing an IDS

   C. patching the operating system

   D. conducting periodic security audits

4. What is the best device, method, or technique to help you be aware of attacks in progress?

   A. server logs

   B. firewall logs

   C. IDS

   D. NAT

5. VPNs should be used for what type of communications?

   A. all external connections to your network

   B. all external connections that might transmit sensitive data

   C. all internal communications

   D. all internal communications that might transmit sensitive data

12

6. What is not a primary reason for documenting your security activities and audits?

   A. to prove due diligence in case of litigation

   B. to provide information in case of any external or internal audit

   C. to get new personnel up to speed on the current state of security

   D. to demonstrate how much work the network administrators actually do

7. Which of the following is the least necessary security device/software?

   A. firewall at the perimeter

   B. anti-spyware on all machines

   C. antivirus on all machines

   D. encryption for all internal transmission

8. How should used media be disposed of?

   A. It should not be. It should be archived.

   B. It should be disposed of normally after 5 years.

   C. It should be destroyed thoroughly prior to disposal.

   D. It should be archived and never destroyed if it contains sensitive data.

9. Which of the following utilities can reveal shared drives on a system?

   A. NetCop

   B. NetBrute

   C. NetGuard

   D. NetMaster

10. Which of the following scanners provides information about the Windows Registry?

   A. NetCop

   B. SATAN

   C. Cerberus

   D. SAINT

11. Which of the following scanners is a Unix-only tool popular with hackers?

    A. NetCop

    B. SATAN

    C. Cerberus

    D. SAINT

12. What is the most distinctive feature of SAINT?

    A. its registry report

    B. its prioritization of vulnerabilities

    C. its scans for shared drives

    D. its capability to map network traffic

13. What is the most important reason to use NetStat or NetStat Live?

    A. to detect DoS attempts

    B. to find registry vulnerabilities

    C. to check passwords

    D. to determine normal network traffic

14. What is the best approach when using scanners?

    A. Pick any single scanner and use it.

    B. Use three or four different scanners.

    C. Find the most thorough scanner and use it.

    D. Use every scanner type you can find.

15. What tools, besides port and security scanners, might you wish to use to assess security?

    A. an IDS

    B. a firewall

    C. a virus

    D. a password cracker

12

EXERCISES

Exercise 12.1: Using NetBrute

1. Download NetBrute and install it according to the instructions found in the product.

2. Scan either a laboratory computer or your own PC for open ports.

3. Document what you find. Also note anything that NetBrute provides that NetCop did not.

Exercise 12.2: Using Cerberus

1. Download Cerberus and install it according to the instructions found in the product.

2. Scan either a laboratory computer or your own PC for open ports.

3. Note what you found that neither NetCop nor NetBrute detected.

Exercise 12.3: Using SATAN

Note: This exercise requires a Unix-based operating system

1. Download SATAN and install it according to the instructions found in the product.

2. Scan either a laboratory computer or your own PC for open ports.

3. Document what you find. Particularly note any differences between the results from SATAN and the Windows-based software.

Exercise 12.4: Using Other Port Scanners

1. Download any other port scanner and install according to the instructions found.

2. Scan either a laboratory computer or your own PC for open ports.

3. Document differences between the results from that port scanner and NetCop, NetBrute, and Cerberus.

Exercise 12.5: Patching a System

1. Take a lab machine, preferably one that has not been checked for patches in some time.

2. Go to **www.microsoft.com** and run the Windows Update you will find on the left-hand side of the screen.

3. Note how many critical and recommended patches the machine has.

Exercise 12.6: Physical Security

Note: This is ideal for a group exercise.

1. Consider your educational institution. Examine (as much as possible) the physical security for servers and technology.

2. Devise your own plan for improving security.

3. Your plan might include additions such as
   - Biometrics
   - Alarms
   - Restricting access to keys
   - Putting routers under lock and key

PROJECTS

Project 12.1: Using the Security Rating Scale

Using the Security Rating Scale outlined at the beginning of this chapter, rate the security of your campus computer systems and network. Provide clear reasons for each of your ratings on the scale and recommendations for ways to improve the system's security.

12

Project 12.2: Assessing Security Policies

Find an organization that will allow you to review their security policies. You can try inquiring at any place you work, asking friends and relatives if you might check with their company's IT department, or checking with your college/university IT department. Make sure the organization has no objection to your review before you proceed.

The organization you review should have written security policies. Summarize the organization's policies and make recommendations for changes you feel are needed to improve security there. You can also use resources that define appropriate security policies to compare against the policies of your chosen organization. Some sources for this information include:

- Information Security Policy World, 2004: **www.information-security-policies-and-standards.com/**
- Sans Institute, 2003: **www.sans.org/resources/policies/**
- *Writing Information Security Policies* by Scott Barn, 2001

Project 12.3: Performing a Full Audit

Note: This exercise requires a fully equipped lab (at least 10 machines) and is probably best done in groups.

You and your team should conduct a complete audit of the chosen lab and write a detailed account of what you find. The audit must include a review of lab policies, probing the machines, checking for patches, and all other items mentioned in this chapter.

Case Study

Tom works for a security consulting firm. He has been asked to audit a small business network (40 workstations, 5 servers). He takes the following steps:

1. Checks all machines to see whether they have updated patches.
2. Checks physical security.
3. Checks to see that there is a properly configured and operating firewall, IDS, and proxy server (or NAT device).
4. Checks to see that all machines have properly configured antivirus software.
5. Probes the perimeter and all servers with NetCop.

Was this adequate? What other steps should Tom have taken?

Chapter | **13**

Security Standards

Chapter Objectives

After reading this chapter and completing the exercises, you will be able to do the following:

- Apply the U.S. Department of Defense's *Orange Book* computer security criteria.
- Utilize the U.S. Department of Defense's entire Rainbow Series computer security criteria.
- Use the Common Criteria computer security criteria.
- Employ other security models, including the Bell-LaPadula, Clark-Wilson, Biba Integrity, Chinese Wall, and State Machine models.

Introduction

Network security, as a field of study, has matured greatly in the past few decades. This means that there are a number of well-studied and widely accepted security standards already in place. There are also a variety of security models in place that you can use to assist in your approach to security. Understanding these standards and models is essential to developing a complete security strategy for your network. Through the preceding twelve chapters you have studied firewalls, proxy servers, antivirus software, defenses against DoS attacks, security policies, and more. Adding to that knowledge an understanding of security standards and models will give you a very solid understanding of network security.

Using the *Orange Book*

The *Orange Book* is the common name of one of several books published by the United States Department of Defense (DoD). Because each book is color-coded, the entire series is referred to as The Rainbow Series. (We will look at the series as a whole in the next section of this chapter.) The full name of the *Orange Book* is *The Department of Defense Trusted Computer System Evaluation Criteria, (DOD-5200.28-STD)*. It is a cornerstone for computer security standards, and one cannot be a security professional without a good understanding of this book.

This book outlines the criteria for rating various operating systems. In the chapters you have already read, we have primarily focused on Windows with some attention to Linux. For most settings these operating systems provide enough security. However, you need to be aware of the various security levels of secure operating systems available. If you are considering operating systems for key servers, you should consider the underlying security rating for that operating system. If your organization intends to do any work with any military, defense, or intelligence agencies, you may be required to have operating systems that reach a specified level of security.

Actual copies of the *Orange Book* are notoriously difficult to obtain for anyone not working for the U.S. government, which makes understanding the security ratings difficult. The book is not classified; it simply is not widely published. However, you can find excerpts, chapters, and standards from it at the following Web addresses:

- The Orange Book Site: **www.dynamoo.com/orange/**

- Department of Defense *Orange Book*: **http://nsi.org/Library/Compsec/orangebo.txt**

- The Department of Defense Standard: **http://csrc.nist.gov/publications/history/dod85.pdf#search='the%20orange%20book%20computer%20security**

The DoD security categories are designated by a letter ranging from D (minimal protection) to A (verified protection). The *Orange Book* designations are generally used to evaluate the security level of operating systems rather than entire networks. However, your network will not be particularly secure if the operating systems running on your servers and workstations are not secure. We will take a moment to examine each of these categories.

D - Minimal Protection

This category is for any system that does meet the specifications of any other category. Any system that fails to receive a higher classification gets a D classification. In short, this is a classification that is so low that they simply did not bother to rate it. In other words, a D rating means an operating system that has not been rated. By default any operating system that is not given any other rating is given a D rating. It is very rare to find any widely used operating system that has a D rating.

C - Discretionary Protection

Discretionary protection applies to Trusted Computing Bases (TCBs) with optional object (e.g., file, directory, devices, etc.) protection. This simply means that there is some protection for the file structure and devices. This is a rather low level of protection. C is a general class where all of its members (C1, C2, etc.) have basic auditing capability. That means that security events are logged. If you have ever looked at the event viewer in Windows 2000 or Windows XP, then you have seen an example of security audit logs. Operating systems will actually fall into a subcategory such as C2, rather than the general class C.

FYI: What Is a Trusted Computing Base?

A ***trusted computing base,*** or ***TCB,*** is a term referring to the totality of protection mechanisms within a computer system, including hardware, firmware, and software, the combination of which is responsible for enforcing a security policy. The ability of a trusted computing base to enforce correctly a unified security policy depends on the correctness of the mechanisms within the trusted computing base and the correct input of parameters related to the security policy.

C1 - Discretionary Security Protection C1 – discretionary security protection is the C protection with a bit more added to it. The following list defines a number of additional features required to achieve C1-level protection. This level of security was found frequently in the past, but for the past decade, most operating system vendors have aimed for C2.

- Discretionary access control, for example access control lists (ACLs), user/group/world protection

- Usually for users who are all on the same security level.

- Periodic checking of the trusted computing base (TCB). The trusted computing base is the *Orange Book's* general term for any computing system.

- Username and password protection and secure authorizations database

- Protected operating system and system operations mode

13

- Tested security mechanisms with no obvious bypasses

- Documentation for user security

- Documentation for systems administration security

- Documentation for security testing

This list may not be particularly clear to some readers. In order to clarify exactly what C1 security is, let's look at a few actual excerpts from the *Orange Book* about C-level and then explain what these excerpts mean:

- "The TCB shall require users to identify themselves to it before beginning to perform any other actions that the TCB is expected to mediate. Furthermore, the TCB shall use a protected mechanism (e.g., passwords) to authenticate the user's identity. The TCB shall protect authentication data so that it cannot be accessed by any unauthorized user."

This simply means that users must log in before they can do anything. That may sound obvious, but earlier versions of Windows (3.1 and before) did not require users to log in. This was true of many older desktop operating systems.

- "The security mechanisms of the ADP system shall be tested and found to work as claimed in the system documentation. Testing shall be done to assure that there are no obvious ways for an unauthorized user to bypass or otherwise defeat the security protection mechanisms of the TCB."

That sounds pretty vague. It simply means that the operating system has been tested to ensure that it does what its own documentation claims it will do. It says nothing about what level of security the documentation should claim, merely that there must have been testing to ensure the operating system meets the claims made in the documentation. The reader may also wish to note that ADP stands for *automatic data processing.* It refers to any system that processes data without direct step-by-step human intervention. This may sound like a description of most computer systems, and it is. Remember that the *Orange Book* was first conceived many years ago.

C2 - Controlled Access Protection C2, as the name suggests, is C1 with additional restrictions.

- Object protection can be on a single-user basis, e.g., through an ACL or Trustee database.

- Authorization for access may be assigned only by authorized users.

- Mandatory identification and authorization procedures for users, e.g., username/password

- Full auditing of security events (the event, date, time, user, success/failure, terminal ID)

- Protected system mode of operation

- Documentation as C1 plus information on examining audit information

You will find this level of certification in IBM OS/400, Windows NT/2000/XP, and Novell Netware. Again it might be helpful to explain this level of security by examining what the *Orange Book* actually says and elaborating on that a bit.

- "The TCB shall define and control access between named users and named objects (e.g., files and programs) in the ADP system. The enforcement mechanism (e.g., self/group/public controls, access control lists) shall allow users to specify and control sharing of those objects by named individuals, or defined groups of individuals, or by both, and shall provide controls to limit propagation of access rights. The discretionary access control mechanism shall, either by explicit user action or by default, provide that objects are protected from unauthorized access. These access controls shall be capable of including or excluding access to the granularity of a single user. Access permission to an object by users not already possessing access permission shall only be assigned by authorized users."

What this means in plain English is that once a user has logged on and has access to specific objects, that user cannot easily "promote" himself to a higher level of access. It also means that for an operating system to be rated C2, you must be able to assign security permissions to individual users rather than simply to entire groups.

- "All authorizations to the information contained within a storage object shall be revoked prior to initial assignment, allocation or reallocation to a subject from the TCB's pool of unused storage objects. No information, including encrypted representations of information, produced by a prior subject's actions is to be available to any subject that obtains access to an object that has been released back to the system."

This paragraph means that if one user logs on and uses some system object, all of its permissions are revoked before that object can be reused by another user. This prevents a user with lower security access from logging on immediately after a user with higher security access and perhaps reusing

13

some system object the previous user left in memory. It is yet another way to prevent a user from accessing items that he may not be authorized to access.

- "The TCB shall require users to identify themselves to it before beginning to perform any other actions that the TCB is expected to mediate. Furthermore, the TCB shall use a protected mechanism (e.g., passwords) to authenticate the user's identity. The TCB shall protect authentication data so that it cannot be accessed by any unauthorized user. The TCB shall be able to enforce individual accountability by providing the capability to uniquely identify each individual ADP system user. The TCB shall also provide the capability of associating this identity with all auditable actions taken by that individual."

In short this paragraph means that not only should security activities be able to be logged, but they should also be associated with a specific user. That way an administrator can tell which user did what activity. Again, if you have ever looked at a Windows Security log, you will see this. Figure 13.1 shows an event from a Windows 2000 event log. Note that the individual username is shown.

B - Mandatory Protection

Category B is a rather important category because it provides a higher level of security. It does this by specifying that the TCB protection systems should be mandatory, not discretionary. Like the C category this is a broad

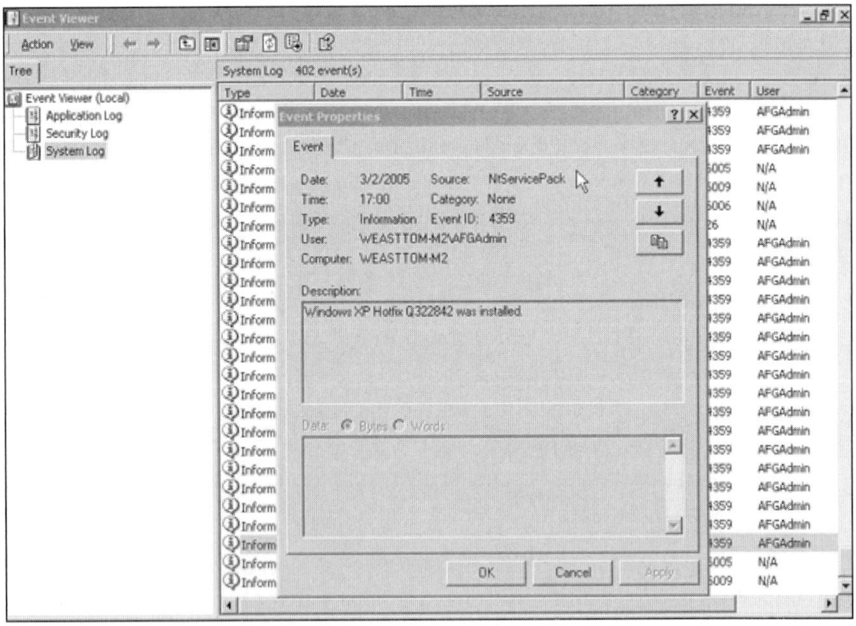

FIGURE 13.1 Windows 2000 event log.

category containing several subcategories. You will not encounter an operating system that is simply rated B; it would be B1, B2, and so on.

B1 - Labeled Security Protection This is just like B, only with a few added security features.

- Mandatory security and access labeling of all objects. The term *objects,* in this context, encompasses files, processes, devices, and so on.

- Auditing of labeled objects

- Mandatory access control for all operations

- Ability to specify security level printed on human-readable output (e.g., printers)

- Ability to specify security level on any machine-readable output

- Enhanced auditing

- Enhanced protection of operating system

- Improved documentation

Let us again turn to what the *Orange Book* actually states about this security level and use that as a guide to better understanding this particular security rating.

- "Sensitivity labels associated with each subject and storage object under its control (e.g., process, file, segment, device) shall be maintained by the TCB. These labels shall be used as the basis for mandatory access control decisions. In order to import non-labeled data, the TCB shall request and receive from an authorized user the security level of the data, and all such actions shall be auditable by the TCB."

This paragraph tells us that in a B1-rated system there are security levels (label) assigned to every single object (that would include any file and any device) and for every subject (user). No new subject or object can be added to the system without a security level. This means that unlike C1 and C2 systems where such access control is discretionary (i.e., optional), it is impossible to have any subject or object in a B1 system that does not have access control defined. Consider again the Windows 2000 operating system. Many items in that system have restricted access (often restricted only to administrators). This includes the control panel and various administrative utilities. However, some items (such as the accessories) have no access control. In a B1- (or higher) rated system, everything in that system has access control.

13

These security labels are the real key to B1 security ratings. Much of the *Orange Book* documentation regarding the B1 rating surrounds how such labels are imported or exported.

- "The TCB shall require users to identify themselves to it before beginning to perform any other actions that the TCB is expected to mediate. Furthermore, the TCB shall maintain authentication data that includes information for verifying the identity of individual users (e.g., passwords) as well as information for determining the clearance and authorizations or individual users. This data shall be used by the TCB to authenticate the user's identity and to ensure that the security level and authorizations of subjects external to the TCB that may be created to act on behalf of the individual user are dominated by the clearance and authorization of that user. The TCB shall protect authentication data so that it cannot be accessed by any unauthorized user. The TCB shall be able to enforce individual accountability by providing the capability to uniquely identify each individual ADP system user. The TCB shall also provide the capability of associating this identity with all auditable actions taken by that individual."

Now this paragraph may sound like the same paragraph from the C category indicating that security activities should be audited. However, this goes a bit further. Every action is not only audited along with the user that performed that action, but the users' access rights/security level are also noted. This provides a clear indication of any user attempting to perform some action that is beyond his security rights.

This level of operating system security can be found on several very high-end systems such as:

- HP-UX BLS (a highly secure version of Unix)

- Cray Research Trusted Unicos 8.0 (an operating system for the famous Cray research computers)

- Digital SEVMS (a highly secure VAX operating system)

B2 - Structured Protection   As the name suggests this is an enhancement to the B category. It includes everything B does, plus a few added features.

- Notification of security level changes affecting interactive users

- Hierarchical device labels

- Mandatory access over all objects and devices

- Trusted path communications between user and system

- Tracking down of covert storage channels

- Tighter system operations mode into multilevel independent units

- Improved security testing

- Version, update, and patch analysis and auditing

This level of security is actually found in a few operating systems:

- Honeywell Multics: This is a highly secure mainframe operating system

- Cryptek VSLAN: This is a very secure component to network operating systems. The Verdix Secure Local Area Network (VSLAN) is a network component that is capable of interconnecting host systems operating at different ranges of security levels allowing a multi-level secure (MLS) LAN operation.

- Trusted XENIX: This is a very secure Unix variant.

Examining the *Orange Book* will give us a better view of the differences between B2 and B1 levels of security. A few paragraphs seem to really illustrate the primary differences:

- "The TCB shall support a trusted communication path between itself and user for initial login and authentication. Communications via this path shall be initiated exclusively by a user."

This paragraph tells us that not only must the user be authenticated before accessing any of the system's resources, but that the communication used to authenticate must be secure. This is particularly important in client server situations. A B2-rated server allows clients to log on only if their log-on process is secure. This means the log-on communication should be encrypted via a VPN or some other method that keeps the username and password secure. Notice that the first two B2-rated operating systems are for distributed environments.

- "The TCB shall immediately notify a terminal user of each change in the security level associated with that user during an interactive session. A terminal user shall be able to query the TCB as desired for a display of the subject's complete sensitivity label."

In this excerpt we see that if a user is logged on to the system and something should change in either his security level or in the security level of some object he is accessing, that the user will immediately be notified and, if necessary, his access will be changed. In many systems you are probably most familiar with (Windows, Unix, Linux), if a user's permissions are changed, the changes do not take effect until the next time the user logs on. With a B2-rated system the changes take effect immediately.

13

B3 - Security Domains Yes, this category is yet another enhancement to the B category.

- ACLs additionally based on groups and identifiers
- Trusted path access and authentication
- Automatic security analysis
- Auditing of security auditing events
- Trusted recovery after system down and relevant documentation
- Zero design flaws in the TCB and a minimum of implementation flaws

To the best of this author's knowledge, there is only one B3-certified operating system, Getronics/Wang Federal XTS-300. This is a highly secure Unix-like operating system, complete with a graphical user interface. There are a couple of fascinating segments of the *Orange Book's* description of the B3 security rating that help illustrate the differences between B2 and B3.

- "The TCB shall define and control access between named users and named objects (e.g., files and programs) in the ADP system. The enforcement mechanism (e.g., access control lists) shall allow users to specify and control sharing of those objects, and shall provide controls to limit propagation of access rights. The discretionary access control mechanism shall, either by explicit user action or by default, provide that objects are protected from unauthorized access. These access controls shall be capable of **specifying, for each named object, a list of named individuals and a list of groups of named individuals with their respective modes of access to that object. Furthermore, for each such named object, it shall be possible to specify a list of named individuals and a list of groups of named individuals for which no access to the object is to be given.** Access permission to an object by users not already possessing access permission shall only be assigned by authorized users."

This paragraph (note the portion in bold) says that access control is taken to a higher level with B3 systems. In such a system every single object must have a specific list of authorized users and may have a specific list of prohibited users. This goes beyond the C level, where an object may have a list of authorized users. It also goes beyond the lower B ratings with its list of specifically disallowed users.

- "The TCB shall be able to create, maintain, and protect from modification or unauthorized access or destruction an audit trail of accesses to the objects it protects. The audit data shall be protected by the TCB so that read access to it is limited to those who are authorized for audit data. The TCB shall be able to record the following types of events: use of identification and authentication mechanisms, introduction of objects into a user's address space (e.g., file open, program initiation), deletion of objects, and actions taken by computer operators and system administrators and/or system security officers and other security relevant events. The TCB shall also be able to audit any override of human-readable output markings. For each recorded event, the audit record shall identify: date and time of the event, user, type of event, and success or failure of the event. For identification/authentication events the origin of request (e.g., terminal ID) shall be included in the audit record. For events that introduce an object into a user's address space and for object deletion events the audit record shall include the name of the object and the object's security level. The ADP system administrator shall be able to selectively audit the actions of any one or more users based on individual identity and/or object security level. The TCB shall be able to audit the identified events that may be used in the exploitation of covert storage channels. **The TCB shall contain a mechanism that is able to monitor the occurrence or accumulation of security auditable events that may indicate an imminent violation of security policy. This mechanism shall be able to immediately notify the security administrator when thresholds are exceeded, and if the occurrence or accumulation of these security relevant events continues, the system shall take the least disruptive action to terminate the event."**

Again, pay particular attention to the bold section. This paragraph tells us that auditing in a B3 system is taken to a higher level. In such a system not only are all security related events audited, but any occurrence or accumulation of occurrences that might indicate a potential violation of a security policy will trigger an alert to the administrator. This is conceptually similar to an intrusion detection system. However, in this incident it is not simply signs of intrusions that are being monitored but any event or series of events that might lead to any compromise of any part of the operating system's security.

13

A - Verified Protection

Division A is the highest security division. It is divided into A1 and A2 and beyond. A2 and above are simply theoretical categories for operating systems that might someday be developed. There are currently no such operating systems in existence.

A1 - Verified Protection This level includes everything found in B3 with the addition of formal methods and proof of integrity of TCB. The biggest difference between A-rated and B-rated operating systems lies in the development process. For A-rated systems the *Orange Book* carefully delineates specific controls that must be in place during the development of the system and testing standards that must be adhered to. This basically means that an A-rated system has had every aspect of its security carefully verified during its development. Doing this requires a great deal of effort and expense. You will note that the only two A1 systems we list are for military use.

You can actually find a few A1-certified systems:

- Boeing MLS LAN: This is a highly secure and specialized network operating system.

- Honeywell SCOMP (Secure Communications Processor): This is a highly secure and specialized network operating system.

IN PRACTICE: The *Orange Book* in Your Organization

Many IT professionals select operating systems based on one of three factors:

- Cost
- What they are most familiar with
- What has the most software available for it

This means that in many businesses you will see Windows on the desktop and Windows, Linux, or Unix servers. However, as security becomes a greater concern, perhaps other criteria should be considered, at least for servers. Note that Windows 2000 and XP are C2-rated systems. That means that a Windows 2000 or Windows 2003 server is also rated C2. For many businesses this is enough.

However, you may wish to consider a more secure solution, at least for your most critical servers. Even a C3- or B1-rated system generally suffices. This would probably mean some version of Unix (though it is hoped that Microsoft will eventually release a more secure server version, perhaps one with a B1 or better rating). You could still have Windows workstations, and even use Windows for less critical servers such as Web servers. But use the more secure Unix version for your major database servers that contain critical data such as credit card data.

There even has been a great deal of talk in the Linux community about someone making a much more secure version of this open source operating system specifically for use in highly secure settings. So far, to the best of this author's knowledge, that product has not been released. However, given the history of the open source software community, it seems only a matter of time.

Using the Rainbow Series

As we mentioned, the *Orange Book* is only one part of the Rainbow series. You will see the *Orange Book* mentioned most often, but there are other books you should be aware of. Each of these books is part of the United States Department of Defense guide to information security. You can view the series at the following Web sites:

- FAS Rainbow Series page: **www.fas.org/irp/nsa/rainbow.htm**

- Computer Security Resource Center: **http://csrc.nist.gov/secpubs/ rainbow/**

- Introduction to the Rainbow Series: **www.palowireless.com/wireless/ security_rainbow.asp**

Below is a list of the books in the series, along with a brief description of each. Some books are more applicable to your study of network defense than others. For those books that are less relevant to our study, the description is briefer. You may think that if you are not directly involved in systems related to defense or intelligence, you do not need to be familiar with these standards. However, consider that when you are trying to secure any network, would it not be useful to consider the security standards and requirements of the most secure systems? Many private companies have done just that and have adopted one or more of these standards for their own use.

- *Tan Book - A Guide to Understanding Audit in Trusted Systems* [Version 2 6/01/88]. This book describes recommended processes for auditing trusted systems. Recall that event auditing is a significant feature of several security classifications in the *Orange Book*. The *Tan Book* describes exactly how auditing should be done. This book is a worthwhile read for any security professional.

- *Bright Blue Book - Trusted Product Evaluation - A Guide for Vendors* [Version 1 3/1/88]. As the name indicates, this is a guide for vendors. This will be of use to you only if your company is attempting to market secure systems to the United States Department of Defense.

13

- *Orange Book - A Guide to Understanding Discretionary Access Control in Trusted Systems.* This section has been examined in great detail in the first portion of this chapter.

- *Aqua Book - Glossary of Computer Security Terms.* Bookstores and the Internet are replete with computer security glossaries. Appendix B of the textbook you are reading right now is such a glossary. The *Aqua Book* is the Department of Defense computer security glossary. It is worth at least a cursory examination.

- *Burgundy Book - A Guide to Understanding Design Documentation in Trusted Systems.* As the name suggests, this book examines what is required for documentation. As with most government agencies, the standard here is for a lengthy amount of documentation probably much more detailed than most organizations will require.

- *Lavender Book - A Guide to Understanding Trusted Distribution in Trusted Systems.* This book discusses standards for security in distributed systems. In this day of e-commerce it would be quite useful for any security professional to spend some time studying these standards.

- *Venice Blue Book - Computer Security Subsystem Interpretation of the Trusted Computer System Evaluation Criteria.* This book describes criteria for evaluating any hardware or software that is to be added to an existing secure system. While the specifics of this particular document are not critical to your study of network defense, the concept is. Recall in Chapter 12 we discussed change control processes. One reason this is so important is that even a very secure system can have its security compromised by the addition of a device or software that is not secure.

- *Red Book - Trusted Network Interpretation Environments Guideline - Guidance for Applying the Trusted Network Interpretation.* In this book you will find criteria for evaluating network security technologies. This is closely related to the material in the *Lavender Book.*

- *Pink Book - Rating Maintenance Phase Program Document.* In this document you will see the criteria for rating maintenance programs. This again relates back to change control processes discussed in Chapter 12 and is related to the *Venice Blue Book.* Routine maintenance of a secure system can either enhance or compromise system security, depending on how it is executed.

- *Purple Book - Guidelines for Formal Verification Systems.* For a vendor developing a system it wishes to be rated according to Department of Defense guidelines, this book outlines the process of verifying the security of that system.

- *Brown Book - A Guide to Understanding Trusted Facility Management* [6/89]. Because secure systems must reside in some building/facility, then the management of that facility is of concern to a security professional. This book details guidelines for the management of a trusted facility.

- *Yellow-Green Book - Writing Trusted Facility Manuals.* Anyone familiar with government documents of any type is accustomed to a great deal of paperwork and an excessive amount of manuals. This particular book is a guide to writing manuals.

- *Light Blue Book - A Guide to Understanding Identification and Authentication in Trusted Systems.* In this manual the process of authentication is explored in great detail. This information is critical to you only if you are attempting to create your own authentication process rather than using one of the many existing authentication protocols.

- *Blue Book - Trusted Product Evaluation Questionnaire* [Version-2 - 2 May 1992]. This document is closely related to the *Orange Book,* as it contains questions that must be answered in order to get an operating system rated according to *Orange Book* standards.

- *Grey/Silver Book - Trusted UNIX Working Group (TRUSIX) Rationale for Selecting Access Control List Features for the UNIX System.* For readers using Unix this book is of particular value. It examines the standards for choosing specific access control list options in a Unix operating system.

- *Lavender/Purple Book - Trusted Database Management System Interpretation.* As the name suggests, this book details the requirements for a secure database management system. Given that databases are at the heart of all business programming, the security of such database systems is an important issue.

- *Yellow Book - A Guide to Understanding Trusted Recovery.* Should any failure occur (hard drive crash, flood, fire, etc.), you must restore your systems. For secure systems, even such recovery must be done in accordance with security guidelines, which this book outlines.

- *Forest Green Book - A Guide to Understanding Data Remanence in Automated Information Systems.* This particular book covers requirements for the secure storage of data.

13

■ *Hot Peach Book - A Guide to Writing the Security Features User's Guide for Trusted Systems.* This book is yet another manual on how to write manuals.

■ *Turquoise Book - A Guide to Understanding Information System Security Officer Responsibilities for Automated Information Systems.* In many government agencies or in defense contractor companies, there is a designated security officer with overall responsibilities for security. This book outlines the responsibilities of such an officer. It is not directly relevant to network defense but can provide background information when formulating organizational security policies.

■ *Violet Book - Assessing Controlled Access Protection.* In this particular book the reader will find standards related to how to assess access control procedures. Most operating systems (at least C-rated or better) have some sort of access control (discretionary in C-rated systems, mandatory in B-rated systems).

■ *Blue Book - Introduction to Certification and Accreditation.* This manual explains the process of achieving Department of Defense certification for a product.

■ *Light Pink Book - A Guide to Understanding Covert Channel Analysis of Trusted Systems* [11/93]. One feature of some higher rated systems (B2 and above) is the handling of communication channels. This document discusses analyzing such channels in great detail.

Clearly no one can be expected to study, much less memorize, all of these books. The *Orange Book* is commonly used, so you should certainly have a basic familiarity with it. Beyond that, simply select the one or two books that are most pertinent to your job role or to your personal research interests, and familiarize yourself with those. The most important thing to gather from this section is what the various books are responsible for. You should know which book to consult for a given purpose.

Using the Common Criteria

The *Orange Book* and the entire Rainbow series are excellent guidelines for security. Several other organizations and other nations have also established their own security guidelines. Each of these separate security criteria overlap on some issues. Eventually, the organizations responsible for the existing security criteria in the United States, Canada, and Europe began a project to fuse their separate criteria into a single set of IT security criteria that became known as the Common Criteria. The first version of it was completed in January 1996.

The Common Criteria originated out of three standards:

- ***ITSEC (Information Technology Security Evaluation Criteria),*** a European standard used by UK, France, the Netherlands, Germany, and Australia. You can learn more about ITSEC at **www.iwar.org.uk/ comsec/resources/standards/itsec.htm**. However, remember that in most cases this has been supplanted by the Common Criteria.

- The United States Department of Defense *Orange Book.*

- ***CTCPEC (Canadian Trusted Computer Product Evaluation Criteria),*** the Canadian standard. This standard is roughly equivalent in purpose to the *Orange Book.*

The Common Criteria is essentially a fusion of these three standards. While they can now be applied to any product, the original intent was to outline standards for companies selling computer products for use in defense or intelligence organizations.

As with most things in information technology, the Common Criteria was eventually revised. Version 2.0 of the Common Criteria was released in April 1998. This version of the Common Criteria was adopted as ISO (International Standards Organization) International Standard 15408 in 1999. Subsequent minor revisions of the Common Criteria were also adopted by ISO. The Common Criteria was originally developed to supercede parts of the Rainbow Series and similar standards used in Europe and Canada. However, its use has gone well beyond defense-related applications. The Common Criteria are now often used in private organizational security settings. In fact, a basic knowledge of this standard is part of the CISSP (Certified Information Systems Security Professional) certification test. This certification and others are discussed in detail in Appendix B.

Clearly the Common Criteria is important and widely used, but what exactly does it cover? The Common Criteria (often abbreviated as just CC) defines a common set of security requirements. These requirements are divided into functional requirements and assurance requirements. The CC further defines two kinds of documents that can be built using this common set:

- Protection Profiles: This is a document created by a user that identifies user security requirements.

- Security Targets: This is a document created by the developer of a particular system that identifies the security capabilities of a particular product.

Frequently, organizations ask for an independent evaluation of a product to show that the product does in fact meet the claims in a particular security target. This evaluation is referred to as the *Target of Evaluation,* or *TOE.* The Common Criteria has built-in mechanisms to support these independent evaluations.

13

The Common Criteria outlines some requirements/levels of security assurance. These levels are usually called ***Evaluation Assurance Levels*** (EALs). These EALs are numbered 1 to 7, with higher numbers representing more thoroughly evaluated security. The idea is to rate security products, operating systems, and security on a numeric scale. The criteria for each level are well established and are the same for all parties using the Common Criteria.

Using Security Models

The *Orange Book* and the Common Criteria are designed to evaluate the security levels of operating systems, applications, and other products. Ensuring that the products your organization uses meet a certain security standard is certainly a key part of securing your network. This process of evaluating systems, as well as everything else we have discussed in this book, has been very direct and very practical. However, now it is time to delve into the theoretical aspects of computer security. In this section we will discuss various widely used models that are used to form the underlying basis for an organization's security strategy. Let me reiterate that a person can certainly secure a network using only the practical guidelines found in the preceding 12 chapters of this book. However, in some organizations, particularly larger organizations, you will find that a particular security model is first chosen and then the security strategy is built. In small to midsize organizations, a security model is generally not selected.

It must be stressed that these models are theoretical frameworks that can assist you in guiding your network defense strategy. You can certainly be successful at defending networks without them, but in this book our goal is to give you a well-rounded understanding of network defense.

FYI: Security Models and the CISSP

The CISSP exam covers several of these models, so familiarizing yourself with them now can be advantageous to you should you later take that exam.

Bell-LaPadula Model

The ***Bell-LaPadula model*** is a formal security model that describes various access control rules. This was one of the earliest computer security models. It was developed by two researchers named Bell and LaPadula in 1973. It was designed enforcing access control in government and military applications. The entire model is based on a principle it refers to as the *basic security theorem*. That theorem states that:

A system is secure if and only if the initial state is a secure state and all state transitions are secure, then every subsequent state will also be secure, no matter what inputs occur.

In other words if you start out with a secure system, and then every single transaction that occurs that might change the state of the system in any way is also secure, then the system will remain secure. Therefore the Bell-LaPadula model focuses on any transaction that changes the system's state.

The model divides a system into a serious of subjects and objects. A *subject* is any entity that is attempting to access a system or data. That usually refers to an application or system that is accessing another system or data within that system. For example, if a program is designed to perform data-mining operations, requiring it to access data, then that program is the subject, and the data it is trying to access is the *object*. An object, in this context, is literally any resource the user may be trying to access.

The model defines the access control for these subjects and objects. All interactions between any subjects and objects are based on their individual security levels. There are usually four security levels:

- Unclassified

- Confidential

- Secret

- Top secret

It is no coincidence that these are the same four classifications the United States military uses. This particular model was originally designed with military applications in mind.

There are two properties that describe the mandatory access in this model. These are the simple-security property and the * property:

- **Simple-security property** (also referred to as **ss-property**): This means that a subject can read an object only if the security level of the subject is higher than or equal to the security of the object. This is often referred to as read-down. What this means is that if the subject has a secret level of security it can read only secret, confidential, and un-classified materials. That subject cannot read top secret material.

- ***. Property** (also referred to as the **star property**): A subject can write on an object only if the security level of the object is higher than or equal to the security level of the subject. This is often referred to as write up. It may seem odd to allow a system to write to a higher security level than itself; however, the key is to use a broad definition for the word *write*. What this means is that a system that is classified secret cannot output less than secret. This prevents a secret system from classifying its output as confidential or unclassified.

13

The Bell-LaPadula model also has a third rule that is applied to *discretionary access control (DAC)*, called the *Discretionary Security Property*. Discretionary access is defined as the policies that control access based on named users and named objects.

- Discretionary security property (also called *ds-property*): Each element of the set of current accesses, as well as the specific access mode (for example, read, write, or append) is included in the access matrix entry for the corresponding subject-object pair.

Biba Integrity Model

The ***Biba Integrity Model*** is also an older model, having been first published in 1977. This model is similar to the Bell-LaPadula model in that it also uses subjects and objects; in addition, it controls object modification in the same way that Bell-LaPadula controls data disclosure, what the Bell-LaPadula model referred to as write up.

The Biba Integrity model consists of three parts. The first two are very similar in wording and concept to the Bell-LaPadula model but with wider applications.

- A subject cannot execute objects that have a lower level of integrity than the subject.

- A subject cannot modify objects that have a higher level of integrity.

- A subject may not request service from objects that have a higher integrity level.

Essentially this last item means that a subject that has a confidential clearance cannot even request a service from any object with a secret or top secret clearance. The idea is to prevent subjects from even requesting data from objects with higher security levels.

Clark-Wilson Model

The ***Clark-Wilson Model*** was first published in 1987. Like the Bell-LaPadula model it is a subject-object model. However, it introduces a new element, programs. In addition to considering subjects (systems accessing data) and objects (the data), it also considers subjects accessing programs. With the Clark-Wilson model there are two primary elements for achieving data integrity:

- Well-formed transaction
- Separation of duties

Well-formed transaction simply means users cannot manipulate or change the data without careful restrictions. This prevents transactions from inadvertently altering secure data. *Separation of duties* prevents authorized users from making improper modifications, thus preserving the external consistency of data.

The Clark-Wilson model uses integrity verification and transformation procedures to maintain internal and external consistency of data. The verification procedures confirm that the data conforms to the integrity specifications at the time the verification is performed. What this means in simple terms is that this model explicitly calls for outside auditing to ensure that the security procedures are in place and effective. The model essentially encompasses three separate but related goals:

- Prevent unauthorized users from making modifications

- Prevent authorized users from making improper modifications

- Maintain internal and external consistency

Chinese Wall Model

In business, the term *Chinese wall* is used to denote a complete separation between parts of a firm. It literally means to establish some mechanism to make sure that different parts of the firm are kept separate so that information does not circulate between the two segments. It is often used to prevent conflicts of interest.

The **Chinese Wall Model** was proposed by Brewer and Nash. This model seeks to prevent information flow that can cause a conflict of interest. For example, write access is granted only if no other object containing unsanitized information can be read. Unlike Bell-LaPadula, access to data is not constrained by attributes of the data in question but by what data the subject already holds access rights to. Also unlike Bell-LaPadula and Biba, this model originates with business concepts rather than military concepts. With this model sets of data are grouped into "conflict of interest classes" and all subjects are allowed access to at most one dataset belonging to each such conflict of interest class.

The basis of this model is that users are allowed access only to information that is not considered to be in conflict with any other information that they already possess. From the perspective of the computer system, the only information already possessed by a user must be information that the user has previously accessed.

State Machine Model

The **State Machine Model** looks at a system's transition from one state to another. It starts by capturing the current state of a system. Later the system's state at that point in time is compared to the previous state of the system to determine whether there has been a security violation in the interim. It looks at several things to evaluate this:

- Users

- States

- Commands

- Output

A state machine model considers a system to be in a secure state when there is no instance of security breach at the time of state transition. In other words, a state transition should occur only by intent; otherwise, it is a security breach. Any state transition that is not intentional is considered a security breach.

Summary

Computer security has a theoretical foundation that should be studied in addition to the hands-on practical techniques and procedures. The United States Department of Defense has the Rainbow series, a series of color-coded manuals that dictate every aspect of security. The most widely known of these manuals is the *Orange Book,* which is used to evaluate the security of systems, particularly operating systems.

The Common Criteria is another series of criteria formed by a merger of the criteria used by several different nations. This Common Criteria is also used to evaluate the security of systems, particularly systems that are intended for use by defense or intelligence related organizations.

Security can also be viewed from the perspective of different models. The Bell-LaPadula model, the Clark-Wilson model, and the Biba Integrity model all view data access as a relationship between subjects and objects. These models originated in the defense industry. The Chinese Wall model, on the other hand, originated in private business and views information security from a conflict of interest perspective. Finally we examined the state machine model, which concerns itself with system transitions from one state to another.

Test Your Skills

MULTIPLE CHOICE QUESTIONS

1. The *Orange Book* is primarily used for what purpose?
   A. evaluating programs for security levels
   B. evaluating overall security of networks
   C. evaluating security of operating systems
   D. assessing the security of firewalls

2. To which of the following does the C2 rating apply?
   A. most firewalls
   B. Windows 2000
   C. Honeywell Multics
   D. networks with appropriate security

3. Mandatory access over all objects and devices is required at what level of security rating?
   A. C2
   B. B1
   C. B2
   D. A2

4. Which operating systems qualify for an A2 rating?
   A. Honeywell SCOMP
   B. Trusted XENIX
   C. Windows 2000
   D. none

5. Which book in the Rainbow series would you consult to look up a particular security term?
   A. *Orange Book*
   B. *Aqua Book*
   C. *Pink Book*
   D. *Red Book*

13

6. If you wanted to study methods for verification of trusted systems, which book in the Rainbow series should you consult?

   A. *Purple Book*

   B. *Orange Book*

   C. *Red Book*

   D. *Blue Book*

7. What Canadian standard was used as one basis for the Common Criteria?

   A. ITSEC

   B. *Orange Book*

   C. CTCPEC

   D. CanSec

8. The Common Criteria applies mostly to what types of system?

   A. home user systems

   B. military/intelligence systems

   C. business systems

   D. commercial systems

9. What is an EAL?

   A. evaluation authority level

   B. execution assurance load

   C. execution authority level

   D. evaluation assurance level

10. Which of the following models focuses on any transaction that changes the system's state?

    A. Biba Integrity

    B. ITSEC

    C. Clark-Wilson

    D. Bell-LaPadula

11. What does the concept of "write up" mean?

    A. writing files to a secure location

    B. sending data to an object at a higher security level

    C. documenting security flaws

    D. logging transactions

12. Which of the following subject-object models introduced the element of programs?

A. Bell-LaPadula

B. Chinese Wall

C. Clark-Wilson

D. Biba Integrity

13. What is a Chinese wall, in the context of business practices?

A. a barrier to information flow within an organization

B. a highly secure network perimeter

C. a barrier to information flow between organizations

D. an A2-rated network perimeter

14. Which of the following models is based on the concept of conflict of interest?

A. Biba Integrity

B. State Machine

C. Chinese Wall

D. Bell-LaPadula

15. Which of the following models considers a system to be in a secure state when there is no instance of security breach at the time of state transition?

A. Clark-Wilson

B. State Machine

C. Bell-LaPadula

D. Chinese Wall

EXERCISES

Exercise 13.1: Applying the *Orange Book*

1. Pick an *Orange Book* level C2 or better.

2. Select an operating system that matches this particular level.

3. Using the *Orange Book* guidelines and the documentation for that operating system (you may even find this online), identify specific features of that operating system that satisfy the *Orange Book* level.

13

Exercise 13.2: Using the *Aqua Book*

1. Using the *Aqua Book,* find the definitions for the following terms.

   DAC

   entrapment

   environment

   hand shaking

   You can find the *Aqua Book* online at: **www.fas.org/irp/nsa/rainbow/ tg004.htm**.

Exercise 13.3: Using the *Blue Book*

1. Using the *Blue Book,* found at **www.fas.org/irp/nsa/rainbow/ tg019-2.htm,** define the following:

   subject

   object

Exercise 13.4: Applying the Common Criteria

1. Using the Web or other resources, find out what the Common Criteria version 2.1's guiding philosophy is. (*Hint:* It is clearly stated as such in the CC documentation.)

2. Find some examples of organizations that use the Common Criteria.

3. What are some advantages and disadvantages of the Common Criteria?

4. What situations are most appropriate for the Common Criteria?

Exercise 13.5: The Biba Integrity Model

1. Using the Web or other resources, identify the company that created the Biba Integrity model. (*Hint:* Web Searches on Biba Integrity model will reveal Web sites that include this detail.)

2. What was the original purpose of the development of this model?

3. Identify companies or organizations that use this model today.

4. What are some advantages and disadvantages of this model?

5. What situations are most appropriate for this model?

PROJECTS

Note: These projects are meant to guide the student into exploring other security models and standards.

Project 13.1: Applying ITSEC

1. Using various resources including Web sites listed below, find the following information about ITSEC.

   ■ Is the system still being used?

   ■ If so, where?

   ■ On what areas of security does the system focus?

   ■ What are some advantages and disadvantages of this system?

   The following Web sites may help:

   ■ IT Security Dictionary: **www.itsecurity.com/dictionary/itsec.htm**

   ■ The Information Warfare Site: **www.iwar.org.uk/comsec/resources/ standards/itsec.htm**

   ■ ITSEC Criteria: **www.boran.com/security/itsec.htm**

Project 13.2: CTCPEC

1. Using various resources including Web sites listed below, look up information on CTCPEC, and find answers to the following questions.

   ■ Is the system still being used?

   ■ If so, where?

   ■ On what areas of security does the system focus?

   ■ What are some advantages and disadvantages of this system?

   The following Web sites may help:

   ■ Nation Master.Com: **www.nationmaster.com/encyclopedia/ CTCPEC**

   ■ Computer Security Evaluation FAQ: **www.opennet.ru/docs/FAQ/ security/evaluations.html**

   ■ Canadian Communications Security: **www.cse-cst.gc.ca/en/home/ home.html**

13

Project 13.3: The Common Criteria

1. Using the Web and other resources, write a brief essay on the Common Criteria. Feel free to elaborate on areas that interest you, but your paper must address the following questions:

    ■ What is the current version being used?

    ■ When was it released?

    ■ How does this version define the scope of security?

    ■ What industry certifications use the common criteria?

Case Study

Jennifer is the security administrator for a small company. Previously this company has developed accounting software for private companies, but now it wishes to market accounting software to the Department of Defense. Jennifer takes the following actions:

- She chooses Windows XP as the platform to develop on because it has a C2 rating.

- She uses SQL Server 2000 because it is so well integrated with other Microsoft development tools.

Has she taken the proper steps? Are there additional steps you would recommend? Additional standards she should consider or guidelines she should consult?

Chapter | **14**

Computer-Based Espionage and Terrorism

Chapter Objectives

After reading this chapter and completing the exercises, you will be able to do the following:

- Defend against computer-based espionage.
- Employ defenses against computer-based terrorism.
- Choose appropriate defense strategies for your network.
- Employ defenses against information warfare.

Introduction

To this point, we have covered a wide variety of threats to computer networks, but these threats have primarily been carried out by lone perpetrators, including virus infections that spread randomly via e-mail and the Internet. Because computer systems and networks are such an integral part of all types of organizations, it is only natural that they have become a primary target for espionage and terrorism. Computer-based espionage, which is the use of computer systems to obtain confidential information, can be directed at all types of organizations, including businesses, governments, and political organizations. Because most sensitive data is stored on computer systems, it is only reasonable to assume that most illegal efforts to acquire that data will be a remote attack via the computer network.

The threat of computer-based terrorist acts, or cyber terrorism, is also growing. People around the world are aware of the threat of terrorist attacks in the form of bombs, hijackings, releasing a biological agent, or other means. Unfortunately, many people have not considered the possibility of cyber terrorism. Cyber terrorism is the use of computers and the Internet connectivity between them to launch a terrorist attack. It is a strong possibility that, in time, someone or some group will use computer methods to launch a military or terrorist attack against our nation. Some experts make the case that the MyDoom virus was an example of domestic economic terrorism.

Defending Against Computer-Based Espionage

Espionage is not necessarily making daring midnight raids into the files of some foreign government. Though that scenario makes the best plots for movies, espionage is simply any attempt to acquire information to which you do not have legitimate access. Whether by law or by some company policy, the person perpetrating espionage is not supposed to be accessing this information but is trying to do so anyway. Generally speaking, a spy wishes to get unauthorized information without anyone realizing he has acquired the data, so espionage is best conducted without any of the drama typically shown in novels or movies.

A variety of motives can lead a person or organization to engage in espionage. Most people think of political/military motivations for espionage, and those often are the motivation for spying. However, there are also economic motivations that might lead one to commit acts of espionage. It is a widely known fact that some businesses will purchase information from less-than-reputable sources. This information might well be sensitive data from a competitor.

Consider that most business data, scientific research data, and even military data is stored on computer systems and transmitted over telecommunications lines. As a result, any person or group interested in retrieving that data illicitly can attempt to compromise the security of those systems to get the data rather than attempt to physically infiltrate the target organization. This means that the tactics we have discussed for hackers can also be used for illicitly gathering information from a target. Of course, spyware can also play a role in computer-based espionage. Having spyware on a target computer can allow an intruder access to sensitive data directly from the machine that is producing the data.

Even if a person is physically located within the organization and wishes to steal information, computer technology can be used to facilitate this process. Employees from within an organization are frequently the source for leaks of sensitive or confidential data. This can be for a variety of reasons, including any of the following:

- For money: The person will be compensated by some other party who is interested in the data.

- Due to a grudge: The person believes he has been wronged in some way and wishes to exact retribution.

- Due to ideology: The person feels ideologically opposed to some course of action the organization is taking and chooses to divulge some information in order to disrupt the organization's activities.

Whatever the motivation, you must be aware that it is entirely possible for a member of your organization to divulge data to an outside party. Technology makes this easier to do. A person carrying out boxes of documents is likely to arouse suspicion, but a USB flash drive or CD fits in a pocket or briefcase. Camera-enabled cell phones can be used to photograph diagrams, screens, and so on and to send them to some other party. Some companies ban the use of camera cell phones as well as removing portable media (floppy drives, CD drives, etc.) from workstations. These measures may be more extreme than most organizations require. Even so, you must take some steps to decrease the danger posed by members of your own organization disclosing data. The following list includes 11 steps you might take. You must make the decision of which steps to include based on a complete assessment of the organization's security needs:

1. Always use all reasonable network security: firewalls, intrusion-detection software, anti-spyware, patching and updating the operating system, and proper usage policies.

2. Give the personnel of the company access to only the data that they absolutely need to perform their jobs. Use a "need-to-know" approach. One does not want to stifle discussion or exchange of ideas, but sensitive data must be treated with great care.

3. If possible, set up a system for those employees with access to the most sensitive data in which there is a rotation and/or a separation of duties. In this way, no one employee has access and control over all critical data at one time.

4. Limit the number of portable storage media in the organization (such as CD burners, zip disks, and flash drives) and control access to these media. Log every use of such media and what was stored. Some organizations have even prohibited cell phones because many phones allow the user to photograph items and send the pictures electronically.

5. Do not allow employees to take documents/media home. Bringing materials home may indicate a very dedicated employee working on her own time or a corporate spy copying important documents and information.

6. Shred documents and melt old disks/tape backups/CDs. A resourceful spy can often find a great deal of information in the garbage.

7. Do employee background checks. You must be able to trust your employees, and you can only do this with a thorough background check.

14

Do not rely on "gut feelings." Give particular attention to information technology (IT) personnel who will, by the nature of their jobs, have a greater access to a wider variety of data. This scrutiny is most important with positions such as database administrators, network administrators, and network security specialists.

8. When any employee leaves the company, scan his or her PC carefully. Look for signs that inappropriate data was kept on that machine. If you have any reason to suspect any inappropriate usage, then store the machine for evidence in any subsequent legal proceedings.

9. Keep all tape backups, sensitive documents, and other media under lock and key, with limited access to them.

10. If portable computers are used, then encrypt the hard drives. Encryption prevents a thief from extracting useable data from a stolen laptop. There are a number of products on the market that accomplish this encryption, including the following:

   ■ CryptoEx Navastream from (**www.navastream.com**). The CryptoEx family of products has different components to suit different needs. CryptoEx Pocket enables you to protect a personal digital assistant (PDA) and CryptoEx Volume enables you to encrypt hard drives.

   ■ CryptoGram Folder from Imecom Group (**www.securemessaging. com/products/cgfolder/index.htm**). CryptoGram Folder provides features that enable you to protect your files, hard drive, and e-mail.

   ■ SafeHouse from Envoy Data Corporation (**www.smartcardsys. com/security/**). SafeHouse also enables you to encrypt data on either a notebook or desktop personal computer. This list is not exhaustive; therefore, it is highly recommended that you carefully review a variety of encryption products before making a selection.

11. Have all employees with access to any sensitive information sign nondisclosure agreements. Such agreements give you, the employer, a recourse should an ex-employee divulge sensitive data. It is amazing how many employers do not bother with this rather simple protection.

Unfortunately, following these simple rules will not make you totally immune to corporate espionage. However, using these strategies will make any such attempts much more difficult for any perpetrator and, thus, you will improve your organization's data security.

Packet Sniffers

Clearly, spyware is an important method of espionage attack. A key logger can record passwords and usernames, a screen capture utility can create images of confidential documents, and even cookies can reveal sensitive information. However, all of these items require software to be physically installed on the target system. A ***packet sniffer,*** however, need not be on the target system in order to gather information. A packet sniffer is an application that intercepts packets traveling on a network or the Internet and copies their contents. Some packet sniffers simply give a raw dump of the contents in hexadecimal format. Other sniffers are more sophisticated. We will look at a few of the most widely used packet sniffers here.

CommView CommView is available for purchase from **www.tamos.com/ download/main/**, but there is also a free trial version you can download at the same URL. In addition to basic packet sniffing, it also gives you statistics regarding any packets it captures. There is also a version of CommView for wireless packet sniffing as well. There is even a 64-bit version of this product. This particular product was originally developed specifically for use by security professionals. The vendor, TamoSoft, produces security products for a number of major companies like Cisco and Lucent. As we explore other packet sniffers you will see that some of them were originally designed as tools for hackers. Recall in Chapter 11 we used hackers' tools to analyze security vulnerabilities on your network.

When you first launch this product you will see a screen like the one shown in Figure 14.1. From the tool bar or the various drop-down menus you can select a number of options including:

- Start Capture

- Stop Capture

- View Statistics

- Change Settings/Rules

If you choose View Statistics, you see a screen like the one shown in Figure 14.2. From this dialog box, you can elect to view protocol type, source/destination IP or MAC address, packets per second, and more. This sort of information is more useful for network analysis than for packet interception.

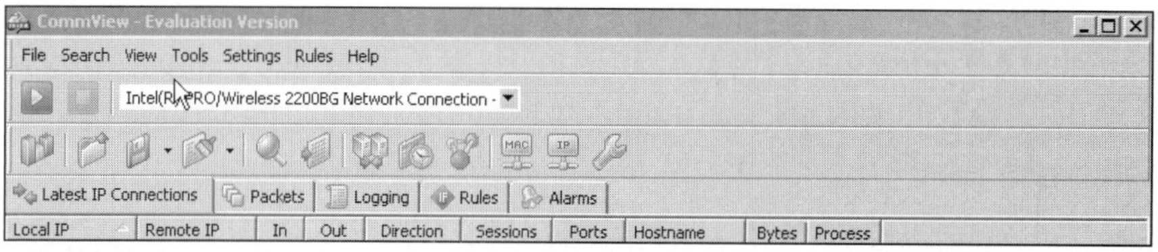

FIGURE 14.1 CommView main screen.

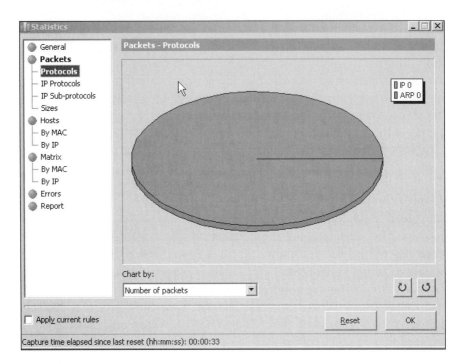

FIGURE 14.2 The CommView Statistics.

Once you have initiated packet capture, you can view packets on the main screen, including the raw hexadecimal contents, as shown in Figure 14.3. Once you have the hexadecimal contents of the packet, you can convert the hexadecimal data into actual readable text. The hexadecimal data is in ASCII Format and can be converted to ASCII Code, thus yielding the actual data contained in the packet.

EtherDetect EtherDetect is a widely known and used Windows-based packet sniffer available at **www.etherdetect.com/**. It is unclear whether EtherDetect was originally developed for security professionals or for hackers. However, some of its features, such as the ability to focus on specific packets, seem more appropriate for hackers. This, however, makes it an excellent tool for a security professional to study. This packet sniffer is much simpler than CommView; however, it also is not as feature-rich. For example, it does not offer the statistical analysis or graphs of CommView, but for basic packet sniffing, it does just fine. In Figure 14.4 you can see the output from EtherDetect, including the raw packet information.

Ethereal The primary strength of Ethereal (**www.ethereal.com/**) is the fact that it works on multiple platforms. It is available for Windows, Linux, Solaris, and even Macintosh. It is also open source. That means that you can actually see the source code, and if you have the skills, modify it to suit your needs.

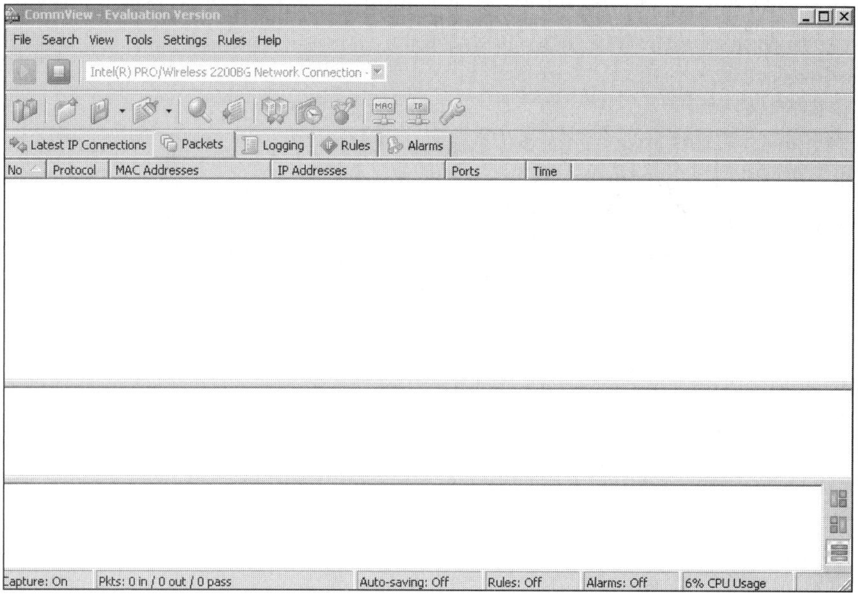

FIGURE 14.3 CommView packet data.

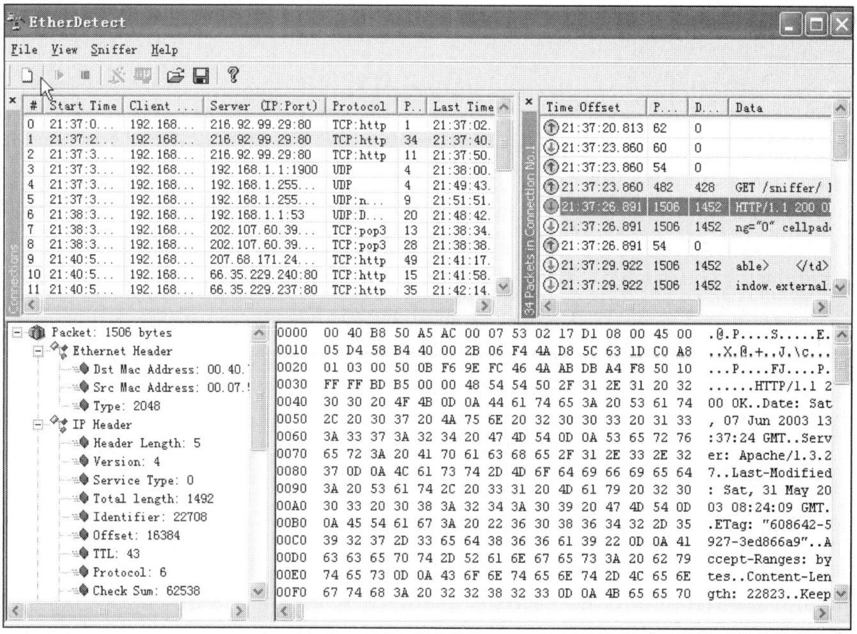

FIGURE 14.4 EtherDetect.

You can find many other packet sniffers on the Internet. The fact that these products are so widely available should make you realize that anyone can intercept and copy data from packets being sent. That is why you should, at a minimum, encrypt all data that leaves your network. You should also consider encrypting data that is going from PC to PC within your network. Many home wireless network kits offer the option of encrypting all wireless transmissions.

What to Look for with a Packet Sniffer A packet sniffer can be of use to either a hacker or a security professional. The hacker is, obviously, hoping first and foremost to get data from the packets. If your data is unencrypted, then it can be read right out of the packet. Secondly she may be hoping to find out information about your network such as the IP address of servers, routers, or workstations. This information can be useful if she wishes to execute a Denial of Service attack, IP spoofing, or many other forms of attacks.

For the security professional, there are many things you might use a packet sniffer for:

- Checking to see if your packets are encrypted.
- Checking to see if the encryption is strong enough.
- Establishing a baseline of normal activity on your network.
- Monitoring traffic when it exceeds the level of normal activity.
- Looking for malformed packets. These may signal a buffer overflow attempt.
- Monitoring a suspected attempted DoS in progress.

The specifics of configuring a packet sniffer are unique to each product. However most offer very simple instructions that any competent network administrator can follow. Virtually all packet sniffers display the following data:

- Source IP address of the packet
- Destination IP address of the packet
- Protocol of the packet
- Contents of the packet, usually in hexadecimal form

For some readers, getting information from hexadecimal form may be difficult. Remember that hexadecimal numbers can be easily converted to decimal with the free Windows calculator. Also many ASCII tables give hexadecimal and decimal. This is useful because this data you are viewing in a packet sniffer is, in most cases, simply ASCII codes. So once you convert the hexadecimal to its ASCII code you can put together the data.

Defending Against Computer-Based Terrorism

When discussing computer-based terrorism, or ***cyber terrorism,*** the first question might be "What is terrorism?" According to the FBI, "cyber terrorism is the premeditated, politically motivated attack against information, computer systems, computer programs, and data that results in violence against noncombatant targets by sub-national groups or clandestine agents" (Savino, 2000). In short, cyber terrorism is just like other forms of terrorism. It is only the means of the attack that has changed. Clearly the loss of life due to a cyber attack would be much less than that of a bombing. In fact it is highly likely that there would be no loss of life at all. However significant economic damage, disruptions in communications, disruptions in supply lines, and general degradation of the national infrastructure are all quite possible via the Internet.

FYI: The U.S. Government Takes Cyber Terrorism Seriously

Throughout 2003 and 2004, there have been a number of reports in reliable news sources, such as Cable News Network (CNN), of the U.S. government hiring hackers to test the security of various systems. The job of these hackers is to attempt to breach security of a sensitive system in order to find security flaws so they can be corrected before a more maliciously motivated hacker exploits them. Clearly, the U.S. government considers the concept of cyber terrorism to be a real threat and is taking steps to secure information.

There are several ways that a computer- or Internet-based terrorist attack could cause significant harm to a nation. These include:

- Direct economic damage
- Economic disruption
- Compromising sensitive/military data
- Disrupting mass communications

Economic Attack

There are a variety of ways that a cyber attack can cause economic damage. Lost files and lost records are one way. In addition to stealing that data, it could simply be destroyed, in which case the data is gone and the resources used to accumulate and analyze the data are wasted. To use an analogy, consider that a malicious person could choose to simply destroy your car rather than steal it. In either case, you are without the car and will have to spend additional resources acquiring transportation.

In addition to simply destroying economically valuable data (remember that there is very little data that does not have some intrinsic value), there are other ways to cause economic disruption. Some of those ways include stealing credit cards, transferring money from accounts, and fraud. But it is a fact that anytime IT staff is involved with cleaning up a virus rather than developing applications or administering networks and databases, there is economic loss. The mere fact that companies now need to purchase antivirus software, intrusion-detection software, and hire computer security professionals means that computer crime has already caused economic damage to companies and governments around the world. However, the general damage caused by random virus outbreaks, lone hacking attacks, and online fraud is not the type of economic damage that is the focus of this chapter. This chapter is concerned with a concerted and deliberate attack against a particular target or targets for the exclusive purpose of causing direct damage.

A good way to get a firm grasp on the impact of this type of attack is to walk through a scenario. Group X (which could be an aggressive nation, terrorist group, activist group, or literally any group with the motivation to damage a particular nation) decides to make a concerted attack on our country. They find a small group of individuals (in this case, six) that are well versed in computer security, networking, and programming. These individuals, motivated either by ideology or monetary needs, are organized to create a coordinated attack. There are many possible scenarios under which they could execute such an attack and cause significant economic harm. The example outlined below is just one of those possible attack modalities. In this case, each individual has an assignment, and all assignments are designed to be activated on the same specific date.

- Team member one sets up several fake e-commerce sites. Each of these sites is only up for 72 hours and portends to be a major stock brokerage site. During the brief time they are up, the site's real purpose is only to collect credit card numbers/bank account numbers and so forth. On the predetermined date, all of those credit card and bank numbers will be automatically, anonymously, and simultaneously posted to various bulletin boards/Web sites and newsgroups, making them available for any unscrupulous individual that wishes to use them.

- Team member two creates a virus. This virus is contained in a Trojan horse. Its function is to delete key system files on the predetermined date. In the meantime, it shows a series of business tips or motivational slogans, making it a popular download with people in business.

- Team member three creates another virus. It is designed to create distributed Denial of Service attacks on key economic sites, such as those for stock exchanges or brokerage houses. The virus spreads harmlessly and is set to begin its distributed Denial of Service attack on the predetermined date.

- Team members four and five begin the process of footprinting major banking systems, preparing to crack them on the predetermined date.

- Team member six prepares a series of false stock tips to flood the Internet on the predetermined date.

If each of these individuals is successful in his or her mission, on the predetermined date, several major brokerages and perhaps government economic sites are taken down, viruses flood networks, and files are deleted from the machines of thousands of businesspeople, economists, and stock brokers. Thousands of credit cards and bank numbers are released on the Internet, guaranteeing that many will be misused. It is also highly likely that the cracking team members four and five will have some success—meaning that possibly one or more banking systems are compromised. It does not take an economist to realize that this would easily cost hundreds of millions of dollars, perhaps even billions of dollars. A concerted attack of this nature could easily cause more economic damage to our country than most traditional terrorists attacks (i.e., bombings) have ever done.

You could extrapolate on this scenario and imagine not just one group of six cyber terrorists, but five groups of six — each group with a different mission and each mission designed to be committed approximately two weeks apart. In this scenario, the nation's economy would literally be under siege for two and one-half months.

This scenario is not particularly far-fetched when you consider that, in past decades, nuclear scientists were sought after by various nations and terrorist groups. More recently, experts in biological weapons have been sought by these same groups. It seems extremely likely that these groups will see the possibilities of this form of terrorism and seek out computer security/hacking experts. Given that there are literally thousands of people with the requisite skills, it seems likely that a motivated organization could find a few dozen people willing to commit these acts.

Compromising Defense

Economic attacks seem the most likely form of attack because the process is relatively easy (for someone with appropriate technical skills) and it carries low risk for the attacker. However, more direct assaults on a nation's national defense, via computer, are certainly possible. When computer security and national defense are mentioned together, the obvious thought that comes to

14

mind is the possibility of some hacker breaking into highly secure systems at the Department of Defense, Central Intelligence Agency (CIA), or National Security Agency (NSA). However, such an intrusion into one of the most secure systems in the world is very unlikely — not impossible, but very unlikely. The most likely outcome of such an attack would be that the attacker is promptly captured. Such systems are hyper-secure, and intruding upon them is not as easy as some movies might suggest. By "hyper-secure," think back to the numeric security ratings we gave in Chapter 12 and think about systems with a rating of 9 or 10. This means systems with intrusion detection, multiple firewalls, anti-spyware, honey pots, hardened operating systems, dedicated IT staff, and more. However, there are a number of scenarios in which breaking into less secure systems could jeopardize our national defense or put military plans at risk. Two such scenarios are outlined here.

Consider less sensitive military systems for a moment, for example, systems that are responsible for basic logistical operations (e.g., food, mail, fuel). If someone cracks one or more of these systems, he could perhaps obtain information that several C-141s (an aircraft often used for troop transports and parachute operations) are being routed to a base that is within flight distance of some city — a city that has been the focal point of political tensions. This same cracker (or team of crackers), also finds that a large amount of ammunition and food supplies, enough for, perhaps, 5,000 troops for two weeks, is simultaneously being routed to that base. Then on yet another low-security system the cracker (or team of crackers) notes that a given unit, for example, two brigades of the 82nd airborne division, have had all military leaves cancelled. It does not take a military expert to conclude that these two brigades are preparing to drop in on the target city and secure that target. Therefore, the fact that a deployment is going to occur, the size of the deployment, and the approximate time of that deployment have all been deduced without ever attempting to break into a high-security system.

Taking the previous scenario to the next level, assume the hacker gets deep into the low-security logistical systems. Then assume that he does nothing to change the routing of the members of the brigades or the transport planes — actions that might draw attention. However, he does alter the records for the shipment of supplies so that the supplies are delivered two days late and to the wrong base. So there would be two brigades potentially in harm's way, without a re-supply of ammunition or food en route. Of course, the situation could be rectified, but the units in question may go for some time without re-supply — enough time, perhaps, to prevent them from successfully completing their mission.

These are just two scenarios in which compromising low-security/ low-priority systems can lead to very significant military problems. This further illustrates the serious need for high security on all systems. Given the interconnectivity of so many components of both business and military computer systems, there clearly are no truly "low-priority" security systems.

> ## FYI: Why Include Such Scenarios in This Book?
>
> Some people may suggest that including such scenarios in this book might give a terrorist an idea he did not previously have. However, experience has shown that criminals and terrorists tend to be quite creative in their illicit endeavors. It seems highly unlikely that none of them have envisioned a scenario like this. Including such things in this book, or any other, ensures that the "good guys" are also thinking about these possible dangers. It also helps to imbue the reader with a certain healthy level of paranoia. In this author's opinion, a network administrator who is not a little bit paranoid is in the wrong job.

General Attacks

The previously outlined scenarios involve specific targets with specific strategies. However, once a specific target is attacked, defenses can be readied for it. There are many security professionals that work constantly to thwart these specific attacks. What may be more threatening is a general and unfocused attack with no specific target. Consider the various virus attacks of late 2003 and early 2004. With the exception of MyDoom, which was clearly aimed at the Santa Cruz Organization, these attacks were not aimed at a specific target. However, the sheer volume of virus attacks and network traffic did cause significant economic damage. IT personnel across the globe dropped their normal projects to work to clean infected systems and to shore up the defenses of systems.

This leads to another possible scenario in which various cyber terrorists continuously release new and varied viruses, perform DoS attacks, and work to make the Internet in general, and e-commerce in particular, virtually unusable for a period of time. Such a scenario would actually be more difficult to combat, as there would not be a specific target to defend or a clear ideological motive to use as a clue to the identity of the perpetrators.

Certainly no incidents of the magnitude I have described in these scenarios have yet occurred. However, several smaller, less destructive incidents lend credence to the fear that cyber terrorism is a growing threat. These incidents were reported in testimony before the U.S. House of Representatives Special Oversight Panel on Terrorism Committee on Armed Services (Denning, 2000):

- In 1996, a computer hacker allegedly associated with the White Supremacist movement temporarily disabled a Massachusetts ISP and damaged part of the ISP's record-keeping system. The ISP had

14

attempted to stop the hacker from sending out worldwide racist messages under the ISP's name. The hacker signed off with the threat, "You have yet to see true electronic terrorism. This is a promise."

- In 1998, ethnic Tamil guerrillas swamped Sri Lankan embassies with 800 e-mails a day over a two-week period. The messages read, "We are the Internet Black Tigers and we're doing this to disrupt your communications." Intelligence authorities characterized it as the first known attack by terrorists against a country's computer systems.

- During the Kosovo conflict in 1999, NATO computers were blasted with e-mail bombs and hit with DoS attacks by hacktivists protesting the NATO bombings. In addition, businesses, public organizations, and academic institutes received highly politicized virus-laden e-mails from a range of Eastern European countries, according to reports. Web defacements were also common. After the Chinese Embassy was accidentally bombed in Belgrade, Chinese hacktivists posted messages such as, "We won't stop attacking until the war stops!" on U.S. government Web sites.

- In Australia in 2000, a disgruntled former consultant hacked into a waste management control system and released millions of gallons of raw sewage on the nearby town.

- In 2001, two hackers cracked a bank system used by banks and credit card companies to secure the personal identification numbers of their customers' accounts. Of even more concern is the fact that the same system is used by the U.S. Treasury Department to sell bonds and treasury bills to the public over the Internet.

- Most readers who even occasionally read or watch the news are aware of the conflict between India and Pakistan regarding control of the Kashmir province. Fewer people are aware that hackers have gotten involved in this conflict as well. According to the *Hindustan Times News*, in April of 2003 Pakistani hackers defaced 270 Indian Web sites. Indian hackers calling themselves "Indian Snakes" spread the Yaha worm as "cyber-revenge." The worm aimed at performing DDoS attacks on some Pakistani sources, including ISPs, the Web site of Karachi Stock Exchange, and governmental sites.

- Also in 2003 a group calling itself the Arabian Electronic Jihad Team (AEJT) announced its existence and stated that its goal was to destroy all Israeli and American Web sites as well as any other "improper" sites.

Clearly cyber terrorism is a growing problem. In this author's opinion (as well as the opinions of many other security experts), the only reason we have not seen more damaging and more frequent attacks is that many terrorist groups do not have the computer skills required. It can therefore only be a matter of time before such groups either acquire those skills or recruit those who do.

FYI: What Is Hacktivism?

Hacktivism is a term for hacking activities that are motivated by purposes the perpetrator feels are ethically valid. For example, if a particular government is guilty of significant human rights violations, a hacktivist might attempt to compromise its systems. In many cases they will try to crack the target group's Web site and post embarrassing information on that Web site. It is important to keep in mind that, whatever your motives, any unauthorized access of any system is a crime.

The good news is that these particular attacks caused little damage and were clearly the product of amateurs. However, it is my contention that it may only be a matter of time before more damaging attacks are perpetrated by far more skilled cyber terrorists. Yet, it is clear that cyber terrorism, at least on a low intensity scale, has already actually happened. As a network administrator or security professional you have the choice either to heed these warnings and begin to take these issues seriously or simply wait until disaster strikes.

Choosing Defense Strategies

At this point, you have gained an awareness of the dangers of cyber terrorism and computer-based espionage. Now the question is what can be done to prepare an adequate defense. For businesses and individual organizations, the following steps can be taken:

- Ensure that you have as tight a security as is practical for your organization. Realize that failure to secure your network is not simply a danger to your organization but might be a threat to national security.

- Make certain you do adequate background checks for all network administrators and security personnel. You do not wish to hire someone who is likely to participate in cyber terrorism or espionage.

- If a computer breach occurs or is even attempted, report the incident to the appropriate law enforcement agency. This may not lead to the capture of the perpetrator, and your organization may not even consider the incident worthy of prosecution. However, if law enforcement agencies are not aware of such incidents, they cannot investigate and prosecute them.

14

What can be done on a state and national level to defend against this sort of attack?

- Greater law enforcement attention to computer crimes: Computer crimes often do not get the attention that other crimes do and, therefore, might not be as thoroughly investigated.

- Better training for law enforcement: Simply put, most law enforcement agencies are well-equipped to track down thieves, murderers, and even con men but not to track down hackers and virus writers.

- Industry involvement: More involvement from industry is critical, such as Microsoft's offering of cash bounties for information leading to the capture of virus writers.

- Federal government involvement: Also critical is more involvement by the FBI, Defense Department, and other agencies in defense against computer-based crime and terrorism. A coordinated planned response should be formulated.

Nothing can make one completely safe from any attack. However these steps can be taken to decrease the dangers.

Of even more immediate interest to companies is protecting against industrial espionage. As we have pointed out, this is a real phenomenon and one which you must guard against. If the espionage is conducted by a hacker breaking into your system to steal information, then the various security techniques we have discussed throughout this book are the appropriate defense. However, what can you do to stop an employee who has access to sensitive data and decides to participate in such espionage? Remember that this can occur for many reasons. Perhaps that employee is angry over being passed over for promotion, perhaps he feels the company is doing something unethical and wants to damage the company, or it could be as simple as that person committing espionage for monetary gain.

Whatever the reason, protecting yourself against authorized users divulging data is much harder. Remember the seven steps we mentioned in the section on industrial espionage (removing floppy drives, prohibiting camera phones, etc.). These can also be helpful. Also recall our discussion in Chapter 11 on least privileges. Even if a person requires access to sensitive data, she should have access only to the data she absolutely needs. For example, a manager of your eastern region marketing division would clearly need access to sales data for that region, but she would not need access to the sales data for the entire nation.

Defending Against Information Warfare

We have examined the use of computers and the Internet for espionage and for terrorism. Now let's look at a third type of attack. *Information warfare* certainly predates the advent of the modern computer and, in fact, may be as old as conventional warfare. In essence, information warfare is any attempt to manipulate information in pursuit of a military or political goal. When you attempt to use any process to gather information on an opponent or when you use propaganda to influence opinions in a conflict, these are both examples of information warfare. Previously we discussed the role of the computer in corporate espionage. The same techniques can be applied to a military conflict in which the computer can be used as a tool in espionage. Although information gathering will not be re-examined in this chapter, information gathering is only one part of information warfare. Propaganda is another aspect of information warfare. The flow of information impacts troop morale, citizens' outlooks on a conflict, the political support for a conflict, and the involvement of peripheral nations and international organizations.

Propaganda

Computers and the Internet are very effective tools that can be used in the dissemination of propaganda. Many people now use the Internet as a secondary news source, and some even use it as their primary news source. This means that a government, terrorist group, political party, or any activist group could use what appears to be an Internet news Web site as a front to put their own political spin on any conflict. Such a Web site does not need to be directly connected to the political organization whose views are being disseminated; in fact, it is better if it is not directly connected. The Irish Republican Army (IRA), for example, has always operated with two distinct and separate divisions: one that takes paramilitary/terrorist action and another that is purely political. This allows the political/information wing, called Sinn Fein, to operate independently of any military or terrorist activities. In fact, Sinn Fein now has their own Web site where they disseminate news with their own perspective (**www.sinnfein.org**). In this situation, however, it is fairly clear to whoever is reading the information that it is biased toward the perspective of the party sponsoring the site. A better scenario (for the party concerned) occurs when there is an Internet news source that is favorably disposed to a political group's position without having any actual connection at all. This makes it easier for the group to spread information without being accused of any obvious bias. The political group (be it a nation, rebel group, or terrorist organization) can then "leak" stories to this news agency.

Information Control

Since World War II, control of information has been an important part of political and military conflicts. Below are just a few examples.

- Throughout the Cold War, Western democracies invested time and money for radio broadcasts into communist nations. This well-known campaign was referred to as Radio Free Europe. The goal

14

was to create dissatisfaction among citizens of those nations, hopefully encouraging defection, dissent, and general discontent. Most historians and political analysts agree that this was a success.

- The Vietnam War was the first modern war in which there was strong and widespread domestic opposition. Many analysts believe that opposition was due to the graphic images being brought home via television.

- Today, the government and military of every nation are aware of how the phrases they use to describe activities can affect public perception. They do not say that innocent civilians were killed in a bombing raid. Rather, they state that there was "some collateral damage." Governments do not speak of being the aggressor or starting a conflict. They speak of "preemptive action." Dissenters in any nation are almost always painted as treasonous or cowards.

Public perception is a very important part of any conflict. Each nation wants its own citizens to be totally in support of what it does and to maintain a very high morale. High morale and strong support lead to volunteers for military service, public support for funding the conflict, and political success for the nation's leader. At the same time, you want the enemy to have low morale—to doubt not only their ability to be successful in the conflict, but also their moral position relative to the conflict. You want them to doubt their leadership and to be as opposed to the conflict as possible. The Internet provides a very inexpensive vehicle for swaying public opinion.

Web pages are just one facet of disseminating information. Having people post to various discussion groups can also be effective. One full-time propaganda agent could easily manage 25 or more distinct online personalities, each spending time in different bulletin boards and discussion groups, espousing the views that his political entity wants to espouse. These can reinforce what certain Internet news outlets are posting or they could undermine those postings. They can also start rumors. Rumors can be very effective even when probably false. People often recall hearing something with only a vague recollection of where they heard it and whether it was supported by any data.

Such an agent could have one personality that purports to be a military member (it would take very little research to make this credible) and could post information "not seen in newscasts" that would cast the conflict in either a positive or negative light. She could then have other online personas that entered the discussion who would agree with and support the original position. This would give the initial rumor more credibility. Some people suspect this is already occurring in Usenet newsgroups and Yahoo discussion boards.

Closely related to propaganda, disinformation is yet another type of information warfare. It is a given that one's opponent is attempting to gather

FYI: Is Cyber Information Warfare Happening Now?

Anyone familiar with Yahoo news boards has probably noticed an odd phenomenon. At certain times, there will be a flood of posts from anonymous users, all saying essentially the exact same things—even using the exact same grammar, punctuation, and phrasing—and all in support of some ideological perspective. These flurries often happen in times when influence of public opinion is important, such as when an election is nearing. Whether or not these postings are coordinated by any well-known or official organization is debatable. However, they are an example of information warfare. One person or group of people attempt to sway opinion by flooding one particular media (Internet groups) with various items advocating one view. If they are lucky, some individuals will copy the text and e-mail it to friends who do not participate in the newsgroups, thus crossing over to another medium and spreading opinions (in some cases entirely unfounded) far and wide.

Of particular interest were posts made immediately prior to the 2004 United States presidential election. As the election drew closer, there were literally thousands of posts, in many cases repeating outright lies about one candidate or the other. Whether or not this was an organized effort, or if it even swayed the election, is certainly debatable. However, it does seem that as more and more people use the Internet as a vehicle for news and discussions, it will also become a vehicle for swaying opinions.

Some marketing firms already use the Internet for what is termed stealth marketing. For example if a new video game is released, the marketing firm might hire someone to begin frequenting relevant chat rooms and discussion boards, use numerous different identities, and begin discussions that cast the new product in a favorable light. So it is a fact that this technique has been applied in the realm of product marketing. If it has not yet been applied to political issues, then it would seem to be only a matter of time before it is.

information about one's troop movements, military strength, supplies, and so on. A prudent move would be to set up systems that had incorrect information and were just secure enough to be credible but not secure enough to be unbreakable. For example, a user may send an encrypted coded message that seems to say one thing when intercepted and decrypted but actually has a different message to a recipient who can complete the code. There are encryption

14

schemes that do just this. The actual message is "padded" with "noise." That noise is a weakly encrypted false message, and the real message is more strongly encrypted. This way if the message is decrypted, there exists a high likelihood that the fake message will be decrypted, not the real one. Marine General Gray put it best when he said "Communications without intelligence is noise; intelligence without communications is irrelevant" (Gray, 2004).

Actual Cases

In addition to some of the cases already listed, there have been other credible threats or actual incidents of cyber attacks in the past several years. Let's briefly examine some of these cases.

- In 2002, Counterpane Internet Security reported a credible threat of a Chinese-backed, all-out cyber attack planned on the United States and Taiwan (2002). A private group of Chinese hackers, called the China Eagle Union, planned to attack routers and Web servers across the United States and Taiwan. The attack never materialized, but unconfirmed reports suggested that the CIA took the threat seriously.

- In June of 2000, Russian authorities arrested a man they accused of being a CIA-backed hacker. This man allegedly hacked into systems of the Russian Domestic Security Service (FSB) and gathered secrets that he then passed on to the CIA (BBC Report, 2000). This example illustrates the potential for a skilled hacker using his knowledge to conduct espionage operations. This espionage is likely occurring much more often than is reported in the media, and many such incidents may never come to light.

Alternative media sources have been reporting that both the CIA and NSA have employed hackers for some time. This might be easily dismissed as false were it not for the fact that such hackers have actually been caught, as in the Russian story. One might even go so far as to say that, in our modern age, for intelligence gathering agencies not to employ cyber intelligence-gathering techniques would be a dereliction of their duty.

One problem with attempting to collect data on cyber espionage or cyber terror is the fact that many stories may never be made public, and of those that are, it is likely that not all the facts are made public. In fact if one is truly successful in any espionage act, it never becomes public.

Summary

Computer-based espionage is the use of computers, networks, and telecommunications lines to attempt to illicitly acquire information. It is also possible for employees to use portable media to smuggle data out of an organization in order to give it to a third party. There are a variety of motivations for either activity, but regardless of the motivation, you must be aware of the threat to your system's data. Remember that the hardware is simply there to house the data; ultimately the data itself is the commodity.

There have been some low-level incidents of cyber terrorism. It also seems likely that there will be more such incidents in the future. Clearly the potential for such threats exists, and in this chapter we have examined some possible scenarios. We have also examined the role computers and the Internet can play in information warfare. It seems likely, from anecdotal evidence, that such activities are already taking place.

Test Your Skills

MULTIPLE CHOICE QUESTIONS

1. Which of the following best defines espionage?
   A. the use of spies to acquire military information
   B. the use of any technique to acquire military information
   C. any acquisition of any data via illicit means
   D. the use of any technique to acquire any data of military or political value

2. Which of the following is not one of the recommended measures to prevent employee-based industrial espionage?
   A. Remove all floppy drives.
   B. Monitor all copying from servers.
   C. Have all employees sign confidentiality agreements.
   D. Perform random polygraph tests.

3. Which of the following best defines cyber terrorism?
   A. computer crime that is directed at military installations
   B. computer crime conducted solely for political motivation
   C. computer crime that is directed at any government entity
   D. computer crime conducted for political or ideological motivation

14

4. Which of the following best defines a packet sniffer?

   A. a product that scans the Internet seeking out packets

   B. a utility that finds packets of a specific protocol

   C. a program that intercepts packets and copies their contents

   D. a program that provides statistical analysis of packet traffic

5. Excessive network traffic between a server and a single workstation would most likely indicate what?

   A. The workstation has spyware on it.

   B. A large amount of file copying to the workstation is occurring.

   C. The workstation is sending a lot of e-mails.

   D. The server is not working correctly.

6. What is the most likely damage from an act of cyber terrorism?

   A. loss of life

   B. compromised military strategy

   C. economic loss

   D. disrupted communications

7. Which of the following is the most likely way in which cyber terrorism could lead to loss of life?

   A. by causing a missile launch

   B. by causing a plane to crash

   C. by disrupting safeguards at a power or chemical plant

   D. by electrical discharge through a computer keyboard

8. Without compromising highly secure systems, which of the following is not a likely way for a terrorist to disrupt military operations using hacking?

   A. hacking logistical systems and disrupting supplies

   B. monitoring information to derive information about troop and supply movement and locations

   C. causing (or stopping) the launch of a missile

   D. gleaning information about troop morale from unsecured communications

9. Which of the following attacks may have been an example of domestic cyber terrorism?

   A. the Sasser virus

   B. the Mimail virus

   C. the Sobig virus

   D. the MyDoom virus

10. What differentiates cyber terrorism from other computer crimes?

   A. It is organized.

   B. It is politically or ideologically motivated.

   C. It is conducted by experts.

   D. It is often more successful.

11. Which of the following is the least likely reason the United States has not yet been the victim of a significant, large scale cyber terrorist attack.

   A. Terrorist groups underestimate the impact of such attacks.

   B. There are simply no people around with the requisite skills.

   C. The number of people with sufficient skills is small.

   D. Because such an attack would be ineffectual and not cause much damage.

12. What is information warfare?

   A. only spreading disinformation

   B. spreading disinformation or gathering information

   C. only gathering of information

   D. any use of information to manipulate any political/military situation

13. Which of the following would not be considered information warfare?

   A. spreading lies about a political opponent via the Internet

   B. broadcasting messages into a hostile area that cast your viewpoint in a positive light

   C. a factual political documentary

   D. sending false information in order to deceive a hostile group

14

14. If a group were using the Internet in information warfare, which of the following would be the least likely use?

    A. to spread propaganda

    B. to spread disinformation about opponents

    C. to plant slanted news stories

    D. to directly recruit new members

15. Sending a false message with weak encryption, intending it to be intercepted and deciphered, is an example of what?

    A. poor communications

    B. disinformation

    C. a need for better encryption

    D. propaganda

EXERCISES

Exercise 14.1 Analyzing Incidents

1. Using the Web or other resources, find any example of computer-based espionage or terrorism not already mentioned in this book.

2. Describe how the attack took place — what methods were used by the attackers?

3. Describe the effects of the attack. Were they economic, political, or social? Did they affect you personally in any way?

4. What steps might have been taken to prevent the attack?

Exercise 14.2: The Kosovo Crisis

1. Using the Web or other resources, research the use of cyber warfare as part of the Kosovo crisis.

2. Describe the various cyber attacks you can find. What methods were used by the attackers?

3. Describe the effects of the attack. Were they economic, political, or social? What effect might these attacks have had on you if you were living in Kosovo?

4. What steps might have been taken to prevent the attack?

Exercise 14.3: Key Loggers and Espionage

1. Recall from earlier chapters we discussed spyware and how it works. Specifically think about key loggers.

2. Describe how key loggers might be used in spying and how serious you feel the danger is.

3. How might you combat this threat?

Exercise 14.4: CommView

In earlier chapters we discussed encrypting transmissions to prevent packet sniffers from picking them up. Also in this chapter we discussed packet sniffers in some detail. In a lab setting:

1. Download and install CommView on a lab computer.

2. Use it to intercept data sent between other lab computers.

3. Observe the data you pick up going across the network. Note how a packet sniffer can be used for espionage, especially if the data is not encrypted.

Exercise 14.5: Other Packet Sniffers

In earlier chapters we discussed encrypting transmissions to prevent packet sniffers from picking them up. Also in this chapter we discussed packet sniffers in some detail. In a lab setting:

1. Download and install EtherDetect or another packet sniffer on a lab computer.

2. Use it to intercept data sent between other lab computers.

3. Describe how a packet sniffer can be used for espionage, especially if the data is not encrypted.

4. Describe the data you intercepted. Could any of the contents be considered sensitive or confidential?

5. How could you safeguard the lab's computers from this type of attack?

14

PROJECTS

Project 14.1: Hackers and Espionage

Clearly, hacking techniques can be used in espionage (whether the espionage is political or economic in nature). Find a case of espionage in which hacking was used and carefully examine the techniques used. Describe the results of the case and preventative measures that should have been used. The following Web sites might be useful to you in this search:

- Hacking and Industrial Espionage:
  www.fidex.com/hackinglaws.htm

- American Management Corporation Corporate Espionage:
  www.amopi.com/corporate_espionage.htm

Project 14.2: Information Warfare

Using the Internet, locate communications (Web sites, chat rooms, newsgroups, etc.) that you consider to be examples of information warfare. Explain what type of information warfare they are (disinformation, propaganda, etc.) and why you consider these to be examples of information warfare.

Project 14.3: Cyber Terrorism Scenario

1. Select one of the theoretical cyber terrorism scenarios presented in this chapter.

2. Study it carefully, and then write a security and response plan that addresses the scenario and protects against that specific threat, the key being a plan against a specific threat. Whatever threat you select, you should provide details regarding what technologies should be used and what policies should be implemented to defend against that specific threat.

▶▶ Case Study

Harrold handles security for a database server at a company that ships supplies to military units. Supplies include food, equipment, and sometimes ammunition. The information is not highly classified, but it is sensitive. He has taken the following steps:

1. He installed a firewall with all unneeded ports closed.

2. Anti-spyware is installed on all machines.

3. All outside transmissions are done securely over a VPN.

Is this adequate? If you believe it is, explain why. If not, what other recommendations would you make to Harrold? Explain your reasons for each of your recommendations.

14

Appendix A

Resources

This appendix is divided into three segments. The first is a list of security-related Web sites broken down by category. The second is a list of recommended security books. The third lists security organizations that may be of interest.

Web Sites

General Network Security

The Network Security Library: **secinf.net/**

The SANS Institute: **www.sans.org/**

Insecure's top 75 security tools: **www.insecure.org/tools.html**

CERT Coordination Center: **www.cert.org/**

Firewall Sites

Symantec Firewall: **www.symantec.com/sabu/nis/npf/**

McAfee Firewall: **us.mcafee.com/root/package.asp?pkgid=101&WWW_URL=www.mcafee.com/myapps/firewall/ov_firewall.asp**

Zone Alarms Firewall: **www.zonelabs.com/store/content/home.jsp**

Cisco Firewall: **www.cisco.com/warp/public/cc/pd/fw/sqfw500/**

D-Link Firewall: **www.dlink.com/products/category.asp?cid=9&sec=0**

Check Point Firewall: **www.checkpoint.com/products/firewall-1/**

Antivirus Sites

Symantec's antivirus site: **www.symantec.com/avcenter/**

Computer Associates' virus information center: **www3.ca.com/virusinfo/**

F-Secure: **www.f-secure.com**

About.Com antivirus: **antivirus.about.com/**

General Computer Security and Computer Crime Resources

Cyber Crime: **www.cybercrime.gov/**

Computer Security: **www.cert.org**

Computer Crime Research resources: **mailer.fsu.edu/~btf1553/ccrr/ welcome.htm**

Department of Justice Computer Crime: **www.usdoj.gov/criminal/ cybercrime/compcrime.html**

Department of Defense Cyber Crime: **www.dcfl.gov/home.asp**

Encryption

Cryptography World: **www.cryptographyworld.com/**

Ohio State Cryptography FAQ: **www.faqs.org/faqs/cryptography-faq/**

International Association for Cryptologic Research: **www.iacr.org/**

Cryptographic Algorithms: **www.cryptographyworld.com/ algo.htm**

General Hacking

IRC Hacking: **users.techline.com/sheldon/hack/irc.htm**

IRC Security: **www.irchelp.org/irchelp/security/**

Hacking Link: **www.hideaway.net/home/public_html/index.php**

Hacking Link: **www.xs4all.nl/~l0rd/**

Hacking Link: **www.hackinthebox.org/**

Hacker History: **www.tranquileye.com/hackerculture/ home.html**

Hacker History: **www.sptimes.com/Hackers/ history.hacking.html**

Port Scanners and Sniffers

www.hackfix.org/software/port.html

www.rawlogic.com/netbrute/

www.all-internet-security.com/security_scanners.html

www.mycert.org.my/resource/scanner.htm

is-it-true.org/pt/ptips13.shtml

www.prosolve.com/software/winscan.php

Password Crackers

www.password-crackers.com/

www.pcmag.com/article2/0,4149,696,00.asp

Countermeasures

Preventing port scanning: **www.nwfusion.com/links/Encyclopedia/P/792.html**

Detecting port scanning: **cs.baylor.edu/~donahoo/NIUNet/portscan.html**

Various security and hacking tools: **www.insecure.org**

Snort, an open source IDS system: **www.snort.org/**

The SANS Institute IDS FAQ: **www.sans.org/resources/idfaq/**

The Association of Computing Machinery IDS page: **www.acm.org/crossroads/xrds2-4/intrus.html**

Spyware

www.youarethespy.com/spy-software.htm

www.keystrokekeyloggers.com/spy_anywhere.asp

www.keyloggers.com/

www.bestspyware.com/

www.spectorsoft.com/

www.spywareguide.com/

www.spywareinfo.com/

www.softactivity.com/

Anti-Spyware Sites

theplanet.tucows.com/preview/305123.html

www.webroot.com/wb/products/spysweeper/index.php

www.spywarenuker.com/overture.php

www.webroot.com

www.enigmasoftwaregroup.com/jump8.shtml

Books

Hacking Exposed: Network Security Secrets & Solutions, 4th ed., by Stuart McClure, Joel Scambray, George Kurtz. McGraw-Hill, 2003.

Maximum Security, 4th ed., by Anonymous. Sams Publishing, 2002.

Windows 2000 Security by Roberta Bragg. Sams Publishing, 2000.

Writing Information Security Policies by Scott Barman. Sams Publishing, 2001.

Cryptography and Network Security: Principles and Practice, 3rd ed., by William Stallings. Prentice Hall, 2003.

Organizations

International Information Systems Security Certification Consortium: **www.isc2.org/cgi-bin/index.cgi**

Computer Security Institute: **www.gocsi.com/**

Information Systems Security Association: **www.issa.org/**

Appendix | B

Computer Security Education and Certifications

After studying this book and completing the exercises, you should now have a strong basic understanding of network defense. For those readers intending to pursue a career in programming, Web design, network administration, or a non-IT field, then this is clearly enough. In fact at this point you probably have more knowledge about computer security than many of your colleagues in those fields. However, for those readers who wish to have a career in computer/network security, then this book has simply laid a solid foundation. You will require more training.

The problem is that security has become one of the hottest topics in IT. It seems that every technical college, trade school, and community college wants to offer a computer security degree. And quite a few vendors offer security-oriented certifications or training. How do you choose which one is truly going to prepare you for a career? Unfortunately not all of them are of equal validity and quality. In fact, a few are simply not worth your time or money. In this appendix we will discuss some things to look for in any program. This should help you decide which one to choose.

Academic Training and Programs

First and foremost, you must realize that a bachelor's degree is necessary to pursue a career in computer security. Quite a few community and technical colleges now offer associate's degrees in security. I personally have never seen a computer security job ad that did not require a bachelor's degree. It is possible that there are a few out there, but they will be very few. That does not mean that pursuing an associate's degree in computer security is a bad idea. Many people find that taking their first two years of college at a community or technical college is very cost effective and convenient. Just be aware that the associate's degree will simply be laying the foundation for the bachelor's degree and is not an end in itself.

Next you have to decide what to actually major in. Obviously a computer security degree would be nice, but there are many other majors that will help prepare you for this field as well. Most professionals in the field now began long before there were computer security majors. There are a variety of computer science, engineering, computer information systems, as well as computer security programs from which one can choose. It is likely that you are currently enrolled in some college program. The real question is not what the major is called but what courses you take within the program.

In any degree program you generally have flexibility in choosing both electives and a minor. This flexibility should allow you to formulate an appropriate program. The following list details what training you will need for computer security:

- **Network:** First and foremost you should take as many network courses as possible. Expertise in computer networks is a cornerstone of computer security. This cannot be over emphasized.

- **Programming and Database:** You will need at least introductory courses in these fields. Security extends well beyond simple firewalls. It extends into software development, database management, and all other aspects of IT. It is therefore critical that you have at least a cursory understanding of these topics. A few introductory programming courses and an introductory database course should be sufficient.

- **Telecommunications:** If at all possible an introductory course in basic telecommunications should be taken. If you can take additional courses, do so. You will often find these offered through electrical engineering or electronics departments. Recall that many aspects of security depend on telecommunications. There is even an entire branch of hackers that specialize in hacking phone lines.

- **Security:** Obviously if your college offers any specific courses in computer security take them.

- **Math:** If you intend to get a better understanding of encryption you will need mathematics up to and including number theory. Number theory is generally a post-calculus course. Of course it is entirely possible to be a security professional with only a cursory knowledge of the math behind encryption algorithms. You simply have to be able to recommend and implement encryption, not design your own algorithms. Of course this author has the biased opinion that there is no such thing as too much math!

- **Law/Criminology:** Because computer security often involves data forensics, it can be useful to have a basic understanding of the law and basic criminology.

You can see that network security is a very broad field and touches on a number of other fields. This means a broad educational background is necessary to truly be effective in this endeavor. The real key to any training program in any field is an appropriate mix of solid grounding in theory with hands-on practice. As in this book you have had numerous hands-on exercises as well as reading/research projects. Any good program will combine theory and research with hands-on practice. Studying how firewalls work is not much use unless you have actual experience installing a firewall.

It is also important to know something about the instructors of security courses. Security is becoming the hottest buzzword in IT, and unfortunately some academic institutions are so eager to provide security courses that they might be tempted to use instructors who may not have adequate backgrounds. A few questions about the instructor should help you determine whether he or she has the appropriate background. Has the instructor/professor had professional hands-on security experience? What is her background related to security? Usually faculty members are eager to announce their credentials on their faculty Web site. If you do not see any security-related experience or credentials, this might be a matter of concern to you.

Industry Certifications

Industry certifications are a significant part of the computer industry. It is unlikely that you have progressed very far in any IT-related program without being aware of these certifications. Microsoft Certified Software Engineers, Red Hat Certified Engineers, and Certified Java Programmers are all part of the IT profession. Certifications can be a very controversial issue because people's attitudes towards certifications vary a great deal. Some professionals will tell you that they would never hire a person who is not certified. Some job ads either require or prefer one certification or another. Other professionals will tell you certifications are worthless. Both extremes come from two factors:

- **Misunderstanding what certification means.** Some people think certification is meant to show complete mastery of a topic. So if such a person hires a CompTIA A+ certified technician who has not completely mastered PC hardware, then the employer might decide certifications are not worthwhile. The problem is that one or both parties in this case misunderstood what a certification means. A particular certification means a person has demonstrated a minimum level of competency with that product or technology. Certifications indicate that the person holding them has achieved a certain level of competency; they do not indicate that the person in question has completely mastered the topic at hand.

- **Use of "cheat sheets."** The Internet is replete with "study guides" that are in fact cheat sheets for certification exams. These study guides often have the real questions and answers from a particular certification exam. A person could quite easily memorize such a cheat sheet, pass a test, and not truly understand the material. Such study guides are very good resources for helping a person identify areas in which they may need more study. If used in conjunction with hands-on experience and thorough study of reference material, they are then useful study aids. However, they are often used simply as cheat sheets, thus demeaning the value of certifications.

Once you have a realistic idea of what certifications mean, the next question that arises is: What certifications are truly meaningful in security? The short answer is that there are certainly some certifications that are essential to a career in computer security. Unfortunately, computer certifications are not regulated as medical licenses, real estate licenses, and so on. Anyone can publish a certification and make bold claims about it. Let's examine the well-known certifications, what they actually measure, and how much credibility they have in the industry.

Security+

This certification is administered by the Computer Technology Industry Association (CompTIA) famous for A+, Network+, and Linux+ certifications (as well as others). The test itself covers general security concepts rather than specific implementations. It is not a hands-on test, but rather a test of one's general security knowledge. The questions will ask you about firewalls, honey pots, and other issues but will not ask you how to configure a router, how to perform stack tweaking, or any of the actual hands-on security practices. This certification is a good gateway to other certifications. For a network administrator or programmer who simply wants a broad understanding of security, this certification is perfect. For a security professional, it will need to be combined with experience, formal education, and possibly other certifications (Microsoft Certified Systems Engineer, Certified Novel Engineer, etc.). For the novice trying to enter the security profession, this test is an excellent place to start. Details are available at **www.comptia.org/certification/security/.**

CIW Security Analyst

This exam is quite similar in content to the Security+ exam. It asks general security knowledge questions. Its content is a bit more broad and inclusive than that of Security+, but like the Security+, it does not delve into hands-on security knowledge. However, it has one very significant advantage over Security+: Before you can take this exam, you must first pass the

CIW Security professional exam and the CIW Foundations exam, as well as one of the following:

- Microsoft Certified Systems Administrator (MCSA)
- Microsoft Certified Systems Engineer (MCSE)
- Certified Novell Engineer (CNE)
- Cisco Certified Network Professional (CCNP)
- Cisco Certified Network Associate (CCNA)
- Cisco Certified Internetwork Expert (CCIE)
- Linux Professional Institute (LPI) Level 2

This means that in addition to basic security knowledge, the holder of this certification has had at least two other CIW certifications, as well as at least one major network certification. This combination of certifications is a likely indicator of competence in network security. You can find out more about this exam at **www.ciwcertified.com/**.

MCSE Security Specialization

Microsoft offers a very widely used operating system, and Microsoft-based networks can be found in most businesses. For that reason, many companies prefer to hire Microsoft Certified Systems Engineers for administering such networks. Microsoft has added a specialized track within the MCSE specifically for those people interested in security. In addition to the basic fundamentals of the MCSE, the security specialization requires three security-specific certification tests:

- Designing Security for a Microsoft Windows 2000 Network
- Implementing and Administering Security in a Microsoft Windows 2000 Network
- Installing, Configuring, and Administering Microsoft Internet Security and Acceleration (ISA) Server 2000, Enterprise Edition

If your goal is to secure Microsoft networks, then this particular certification is very important. You can find out more about it at **www.microsoft.com/learning/mcp/mcse/security/windows2000.asp**.

CISSP

The Certified Information Systems Security Professional designation is the gold standard in security certifications. This designation is simply the most sought-after security certification. You cannot take this certification until you have a few years of practical experience, but once you do, you are strongly advised to get this certification. The reason is simply the rigorous standards required to get the exam. The requirements are as follows:

- Pass a grueling exam that takes several hours.

- Have at least four years of security experience, or three years and a bachelor's degree. This experience must be certified by either another CISSP or by an officer in your corporation.

- Meet certain continuing education requirements every 36 months in order to retain your certification. In other words even after you have achieved the CISSP, you will need to keep your training and skills current in order to retain the certification.

- A certain percentage of those who pass the exam are randomly selected for an audit and investigation of their background.

With the CISSP the test itself is not what makes the certification meaningful. It is the requirement for verifiable work experience as well as ongoing continuing education. For someone looking to excel in the computer security profession, this certification is certainly desirable.

You can find out more about this test at **www.isc2.org**.

SANS Institute Certifications

The Sans Institute (**www.sans.org**) is a very well-respected source for security information. You have probably noticed that its site and its documents have been referenced many times in this book. You would probably find the same in other computer security books. However, their computer security certifications have not been widely used within the security industry. This is most likely due to the fact that they are relatively new and not widely marketed. However it seems likely that in the coming years their certifications will gain wide acceptance. You can find out more details at **www.giac.org/ subject_certs.php**.

What Is the Ideal Security Professional?

This is clearly a matter that is quite controversial, and anything you see in this section is the author's opinion. You would easily find other authors, instructors, professors, and professionals that strongly disagree with these positions. However, I believe I can make a strong case for my claims. At a minimum, by reading this you will have some idea of what goals you need to achieve to be a security professional or what to look for when hiring a consultant.

The first point to make, and perhaps the most controversial, is that a security professional should have a perfectly clean criminal history. Hiring convicted hackers is simply a bad idea. Now you will find many people who disagree with this opinion. I take this position for two reasons:

- Would you hire a convicted burglar as a security guard? Or perhaps a convicted car thief to work at an auto dealership? The answer is, of course not. Why then do you think a convicted hacker is going to be an ideal security consultant? This person has already proven that they are not trustworthy. Do you really wish to give him access to your systems?

- Some people assume that convicted hackers have some esoteric knowledge that other security professionals do not have. I have simply not found this to be the case. First of all, one can now study hacking techniques in legitimate laboratory settings and have all the experience and skill of an actual hacker without violating any laws. The second issue is that the convicted hacker clearly is not the best hacker around; he or she was caught. What you have is the hacker that knew enough to perpetrate the crime but not enough to get away with it. Perhaps their knowledge is not as deep as you may have thought.

After you have established that an applicant has a clean criminal history, next look at his or her education and training. You will have different requirements for an entry-level security position than you might for a seasoned professional or consultant. Here are what I consider to be ideal backgrounds for each.

Entry-Level

- At a minimum an associate's degree in computer security or a closely related field with security courses. Preferably a bachelor's degree with the same major/concentrations.

- One of the major certifications (Security+, MCSA, Network+)

- A minimum of one year of network administration, programming, or technical support experience.

Recall that this is for an entry-level security position. You might certainly find companies that require more or less than this, but this is my recommendation. If you want a computer security job, you should consider achieving these three things before seeking an entry-level position in computer security.

Experienced/Consultant

For a more experienced position, such as a security administrator or a consultant, the following is recommended:

- A minimum of a bachelor's degree in computer security or a closely related field with security courses. A master's degree is always a nice thing to have on a résumé, but it is not critical for this sort of job.

- At least one of the major networking certifications (MSCA, MCSE, CNE, CCIE, CCNA, etc.) and at least one major security certification (Security+, CIW Security Analyst, etc.) OR simply the CISSP. In essence, if you do not have the CISSP, you need to have a major networking designation and a major security designation. Of course, having more is desirable. A CISSP who also has the MCSE and CCNA is certainly going to attract some attention from employers.

- At least five years of experience in IT (programming, networking, etc.) with at least two of those years directly related to security.

These are some guidelines that might help you plan your career path. If you are currently in college and wish to become a security professional, a good career path might include:

- Complete your degree with as many networking and security courses as you can.

- While in school try to achieve some certification (Security+, MCSA, etc.).

- When you graduate, look for a job in network administration or something related. You may find entry-level security positions that will hire you with no experience, especially if you worked part-time during college doing technical support or something similar.

- In your first two years of post-college employment try to achieve at least one or two other certifications (CIW security analyst, CCNA, etc.).

- After three to four years, start seeking the CISSP.

This may seem like a long and arduous journey. However, most professions require extensive training. Attorneys get a bachelor's degree and then attend three years of law school. Doctors have college, then four years of medical school, then residency.

Glossary

Some terms in this glossary come from the hacker community and others from the security professionals' community. To truly understand computer security one must be familiar with both worlds. General networking terms are also included in this glossary.

A

access control   The process of limiting access to some resource only to authorized users, programs, or systems.

access control authentication   The process of authenticating users, in order to control access.

access control list   A list of entities, together with their access rights, that are authorized to have access to a resource.

access lockout policies   Policies regarding how many login attempts should be allowed before the account is locked.

account policies   Policies regarding account settings.

admin   Short for system administrator.

AES   Advanced Encryption Standard, a modern encryption method that is widely used, including in some high-end firewalls.

anomaly detection   An intrusion-detection strategy that depends on detecting anomalous activities.

application gateway firewall   A firewall type that verifies specific applications.

ASCII code   Numeric codes used to represent all standard alphanumeric symbols. There are 255 different ASCII codes.

auditing   A check of a system's security usually including a review of documents, procedures, and system configurations.

authenticate   The process of verifying that a user is authorized to access some resource.

Authentication Header (AH)   A field that immediately follows the IP header in an IP datagram and provides authentication and integrity checking for the datagram.

B

back door   A hole in the security system deliberately left by the creator of the system.

bagbiter   Something, such as a program or a computer, that fails to work or works in a remarkably clumsy manner.

banishment vigilance   Blocking all traffic from a suspect IP address (i.e., banishing that address).

basic security theorem   A theorem that states that a system is secure if and only if the initial state is a secure state and all state transitions are secure, then every subsequent state will also be secure, no matter what inputs occur.

bastion host   A single point of contact between the Internet and a private network.

Bell-LaPadula Model   One of the oldest security models, based on the basic security theorem.

Biba Integrity Model   An older security model with similarities to Bell-LaPadula.

binary numbers   Numbers that use the base 2 number system.

binary operations   Operations on base 2 (i.e., binary) numbers. The operations include XOR, OR, and AND.

black hat hacker   A hacker with a malicious purpose, synonymous with cracker.

blocking   The act of preventing transmissions of some type.

Blowfish   A well-known encryption algorithm.

braindump   The act of telling someone everything one knows.

breach   To successfully break into a system (e.g., "to breach the security").

brute force   To try to crack a password by simply trying every possible combination.

buffer overflow   An attack that seeks to overwrite a memory buffer with more data than it is designed to hold.

bug   A flaw in a system.

C

Caesar cipher   One of the oldest encryption algorithms. It uses a basic mono-alphabetic cipher.

call back   A procedure for identifying a remote connection. In a call back, the host discon-nects the caller and then dials the authorized telephone number of the remote client to re-establish the connection.

certificate authority   An agency authorized to issue digital certificates.

CHAP   Challenge Handshake Authentication Protocol, a commonly used authentication protocol.

Chernobyl packet   Also called Kamikaze Packet. A network packet that induces a broadcast storm and network meltdown.

Chinese Wall Model   An informational barrier preventing information flow between different groups within the same organization.

cipher   Synonym for cryptographic algorithm.

cipher text   Encrypted text.

circuit level gateway firewall   A firewall that authenticates each user before granting ac-cess.

Clark-Wilson Model   A subject-object model first published in 1987 that attempts to achieve data security via well-formed transactions and a separation of duties.

code   The source code for a program, or the act of programming, as in "to code an algorithm."

codegrinder   An unflattering reference to one who works in an uncreative corporate pro-gramming environment.

Common Criteria   A set of standards for com-puter security. This is a fusion of United States Department of Defense standards with European and Canadian standards.

compulsory tunneling   Tunneling that is mandatory, not optional. This is in reference to VPN technologies. Some protocols allow the user to choose whether to use tunneling.

confidentiality of data   Ensuring that the con-tents of messages will be kept secret.

cookie A small file containing data that is put on your machine by a Web site you visit.

cracker One who breaks into a system in order to do something malicious, illegal, or harmful. Synonymous with black hat hacker.

cracking Hacking with malicious intent.

crash A sudden and unintended failure, as in "my computer crashed."

CTCPEC Canadian Trusted Computer Product Evaluation Criteria.

Cyber terrorism Terrorism using computers, computer networks, telecommunications, or the Internet.

D

daemon A program that runs in the background. Often used to perform various system services. *See also* service.

DDoS Distributed Denial of Service, a DoS attack launched from multiple sources.

decryption The process of un-encrypting an encrypted message.

demigod A hacker with years of experience, a national or international reputation.

DES Data Encryption Standard, a widely used encryption standard that is considered quite secure.

digital signature A file that digitally verifies the identity of the sender.

discretionary access control An administrator's option either to control access to a given resource or simply allow unrestricted access.

discretionary security property The policies that control access based on named users and named objects.

Distributed Reflection Denial of Service A specialized type of DDoS that uses Internet routers to perform the attack.

DMZ Demilitarized zone. A firewall type consisting of two firewalls with an intermediate zone between them

DoS Denial of Service, an attack that prevents legitimate users from accessing a resource.

dropper A type of Trojan horse that drops another program onto the target machine.

dual-homed host A type of firewall that literally has two NICs.

dynamic security approach An approach to security that is proactive rather than reactive.

E

EAP Extensible Authentication Protocol.

encapsulated Wrapped up.

Encrypting File System Also known as EFS, this is Microsoft's file system that allows users to encrypt individual files. It was first introduced in Windows 2000.

encryption The act of encrypting a message, usually by altering a message so that it cannot be read without the key and the decryption algorithm.

ESP Encapsulated Security Payload, one of the two protocols (ESP and AH) that make up IPSec.

ethical hacker One who hacks into systems in order to accomplish some goal that he or she feels is ethically valid.

Evaluation Assurance Levels Numeric levels (1 through 7) that define security assurance as defined in the Common Criteria.

executable profiling   A type of intrusion detection strategy that seeks to profile the behavior of legitimate executables and compare that against the activity of any running program.

F

false positive   An erroneous flagging of legitimate activity as an attempted intrusion by an intrusion detection device.

firewall   A barrier between the network and the outside world.

G

gray hat hacker   A hacker whose activities are normally legal but occasionally delves into activities that may not be legal or ethical.

Group Policy Objects   Objects in Microsoft Windows that allow you to assign access rights to entire groups of users or computers.

H

hacker   One who tries to learn about a system by examining it in detail and reverse engineering it.

handshaking   The process of verifying a connection request. It involves several packets going from client to server and back.

honey pot   A system or server designed to be very appealing to hackers, when in fact it is a trap to catch them.

I

ICMP packets   Network packets often used in utilities such as Ping and Tracert.

Internet Key Exchange (IKE)   A method for managing the exchange of encryption keys.

infiltration   The act of gaining access to secure portions of a network. *See also* intrusion.

Information Technology Security Evaluation   Security guidelines created by the Commission of the European Communities, analogous to the Common Criteria.

information warfare   Attempts to influence political or military outcomes via information manipulation.

integrity of data   Ensuring that data has not been modified or altered and that the data received is identical to the data that was sent.

international data encryption algorithm (IDEA)   A block cipher designed as a replacement for DES.

intrusion   The act of gaining access to secure portions of a network. *See also* infiltration.

intrusion deflection   An IDS strategy that is dependent upon making the system seem less attractive to intruders. It seeks to deflect attention away from the system.

Intrusion-Detection System (IDS)   A system for detecting attempted intrusions.

intrusion deterrence   An IDS strategy that attempts to deter intruders by making the system seem formidable, perhaps more formidable than it is.

IP   Internet Protocol, one of the primary protocols used in networking.

IPComp   IP compression protocol. A protocol designed to reduce the size of IP packets sent over the Internet.

IPSec   Internet Protocol Security, a method used to secure VPNs.

IP spoofing   Making packets seem to come from a different IP address than they really originated from.

K

key logger   Software that logs key strokes on a computer.

L

L2TP   Layer 2 tunneling protocol, a VPN protocol.

layered security approach   A security approach that also secures the internal components of the network, not just the perimeter.

M

malware   Any software that has a malicious purpose such as a virus or Trojan horse.

Microsoft Point-to-Point Encryption   An encryption technology designed by Microsoft for use with virtual private networks.

mono-alphabet cipher   An encryption cipher using only one substitution alphabet.

MS-CHAP   A Microsoft Extension to CHAP.

multi-alphabet substitutions   Encryption methods that use more than one substitution alphabet.

N

network address translation   A replacement technology for proxy servers.

network host-based   A firewall solution that runs on an existing server.

network intrusion-detection   Detecting any attempted intrusion throughout the network, as opposed to intrusion-detection that only works on a single machine or server.

NIC   Network interface card.

Non-repudiation   The process of verifying a connection so that neither party can later deny, or repudiate the transaction.

null sessions   How Windows represents an anonymous user.

O

object   In reference to computer security models, an object is any file, device, or part of the system a user wishes to access.

open source   Software where the source code itself is freely available to the public.

operating system hardening   The process of securing an individual operating system. This includes proper configuration and applying patches.

P

packet filter firewall   A firewall that scans incoming packets and either allows them to pass or rejects them.

packet sniffer   Software that intercepts packets and copies their contents.

PAP   Password Authentication Protocol, the most basic form of authentication in which a user's name and password are transmitted over a network and compared to a table of name-password pairs.

passive security approach   An approach to security that awaits some incident to react to, rather than being proactive.

password policies   Policies that determine the parameters of a valid password including minimum length, age, and complexity.

penetration testing   Assessing the security of a system by attempting to break into the system. This is the activity most sneakers engage in.

perimeter security approach   A security approach that is concerned only with securing the perimeter of a network.

PGP   Pretty good privacy, a widely used public key encryption algorithm.

phreaker   Someone who hacks into phone systems.

phreaking   The process of hacking into a phone system.

Ping of Death   A DoS attack that sends a malformed Ping packet hoping to cause the target machine to error out.

playback attacks   This attack involves recording the authentication session of a legitimate user, and then simply playing that back in order to gain access.

port scan   Sequentially pinging ports to see which ones are active.

PPP   Point-to-point protocol, a somewhat older connection protocol.

PPTP   Point-to-point tunneling protocol, an extension to PPP for VPNs.

proxy server   A device that hides your internal network from the outside world.

public key system   An encryption method where the key used to encrypt messages is made public and anyone can use it. A separate, private key, is required to decrypt the message.

Q

quantum encryption   A process that uses quantum physics to encrypt data.

quantum entanglement   A phenomena from quantum physics where two subatomic particles are related in such a way that a change to the state of one instantaneously causes a change to the state of the other.

R

resource profiling   A monitoring approach that measures system-wide use of resources and develops a historic usage profile.

Rijndael algorithm   The algorithm used by AES.

RSA   A public key encryption method developed in 1977 by three mathematicians, Ron Rivest, Adi Shamir, and Len Adleman. The name RSA is derived from the first letter of each mathematician's last name.

RST cookie   A simple method for alleviating the danger of certain types of DoS attacks.

S

screened host   A combination of firewalls; in this configuration you use a combination of a bastion host and a screening router.

script kiddy   A slang term for an unskilled person who purports to be a skilled hacker.

security template   Preset security settings that can be applied to a system.

service   A program that runs in the bacground, often performing some system service. *See also* daemon.

session hacking   The process of taking over the session between a client and a server in order to gain access to the server.

simple-security property   This means that a subject can read an object only if the security level of the subject is higher or equal to the security of the object.

single-machine firewall   A firewall that resides on a single PC or server.

Slammer   A famous Internet worm.

Smurf attack   A specific type of DDoS attack.

sneaker   Someone who is attempting to compromise a system in order to assess its vulnerability.

sniffer   A program that captures data as it travels across a network. Also called a packet sniffer.

Snort   A widely used, open source, Intrusion-Detection System.

social engineering   The use of persuasion on human users in order to gain information required to access a system.

SPAP   Shiva Password Authentication Protocol. SPAP is a proprietary version of PAP.

spoofing   Pretending to be something else, as when a packet might spoof another return IP address (as in the Smurf attack) or when a Web site is spoofing a well known e-commerce site.

spyware   Software that monitors computer use.

stack tweaking   A complex method for protecting a system against DoS attacks. This method involves reconfiguring the operating system to handle connections differently.

Stateful packet inspection   A type of firewall that not only examines packets but knows the context within which the packet was sent.

State Machine Model   The state machine model looks at a system's transition from one state to another. It starts by capturing the current state of a system. Later the system's state at that point in time is compared to the previous state of the system to determine whether there has been a security violation in the interim.

subject   In computer security models the sub-

ject is any entity that is attempting to access a system or data.

symmetric key system   An encryption method where the same key is used to encrypt and decrypt the message.

SYN cookie   A method for ameliorating the dangers of SYN floods.

SYN flood   Sending a stream of SYN packets (requests for connection) then never responding, thus leaving the connection half open.

T

transport mode   One of two IPSec modes, the transport mode works by encrypting the data in each packet but leaves the header unencrypted.

target of evaluation   Also TOE, an independent evaluation of a product to show that the product does, in fact, meet the claims in a particular security target.

threshold monitoring   Monitoring a network or system looking for any activity that exceeds some predefined limit or threshold.

Tribal Flood Network   A tool used to execute DDoS attacks.

Trin00   A tool used to execute DDoS attacks.

Trojan horse   Software that appears to have a valid and benign purpose but really has another, nefarious purpose.

trusted computing base   The trusted computing base (TCB) is everything in a computing system that provides a secure environment.

tunnel mode   One of two IPSec modes. The tunnel mode encrypts both the header and the data and is thus more secure than the transport mode but can work a bit slower.

V

virus   Software that is self-replicating and spreads like a biological virus.

virus hoax   A notification of a virus that is not true. Often the notification attempts to convince the user to delete some critical file, claiming that file is a virus.

voluntary tunneling   Tunneling that allows the user to either use tunneling or to simply use a standard (i.e., nontunneled) connection.

W

War-dialing   Dialing phones waiting for a computer to pick up, usually done via some automated system.

war-driving   Driving and scanning for wireless networks that can be compromised.

well-formed transactions   Transaction in which users cannot manipulate or change the data without careful restrictions.

white hat hacker   A hacker who does not break the law, often synonymous with ethical hacker.

worm   A virus that can spread without human intervention.

X

X.509   A widely-used standard for digital certficates.

References

Chapter 1

100th Congress. Computer Security Act of 1987. Public Law 100-235. **www.epic.org/crypto/csa/csa.html** (accessed June 2004).

CERT. Denial of Service Attacks. **www.cert.org/tech_tips/denial_of_service.html** (accessed August 2003).

CNN/Technology. Hacker Accesses 5.6 Million Credit Cards. February 18, 2003. **www.cnn.com/2003/TECH/02/17/creditcard.hack/index.html** (accessed 15 December 2004).

Computer Security Institute. Cyber Crime Bleeds U.S. Corporations, Survey Shows; Financial Losses from Attacks Climb for Third Year in a Row. April 7, 2002. **www.gocsi.com/press/20020407.jhtml; jsessionid=J5CTJV4ZKSD3MQSNDBGCKHSCJUMEKJVN?_requestid=219439** (accessed 15 December 2004).

DefCon II. Wardriving Statistics. Las Vegas, NV. August 2003. **www.defcon.org/html/defcon-11/defcon-11-postcon.html** (accessed 15 December 2004).

F-Secure. F-Secure Virus Descriptions. 2003. **www.f-secure.com/v-descs/_new.shtml** (accessed 15 December 2004).

Glossary of Hacker Terminology. June 2004. **www.cs.usask.ca/undergrads/kwm519/490/project/details/glossary.htm** (accessed 15 December 2004).

Hacker Dictionary. April 2003. **www.hacker-dictionary.com/**.

Landesman, Mary. What Is a Virus? **http://antivirus.about.com/cs/tutorials/a/whatisavirus.htm** (accessed November 2004).

Lemos, Robert. Mitnick Teaches Social Engineering. *ZDNet* News. July 16, 2000. **http://zdnet.com.com/2100-11-522261.html?legacy=zdnn** (accessed 15 December 2004).

Poulsen, Kevin. War Driving by the Bay. *SecurityFocus*. April 12, 2001. **www.securityfocus.com/news/192** (accessed 15 December 2004).

Raymond, Eric S. 2003. *The New Hacker's Dictionary*. 3rd ed. Cambridge, MA: The MIT Press.

Chapter 2

Delio, Michelle. My Doom Targets Linux Antagonist. *Wired News*. January 27, 2004. **www.wired.com/news/linux/0,1411,62058,00.html** (accessed 15 December 2004).

F-Secure. F-Secure Virus Descriptions: Sobig. April 23, 2003. **www.f-secure.com/v-descs/sobig.shtml** (accessed 15 December 2004).

Gibson, Steve. Description and Analysis of a Potent, Increasingly Prevalent, and Worrisome Internet Attack. *Distributed Reflection Denial of Service*. **http://grc.com/dos/drdos.htm** (accessed 15 December 2004).

Gudmundsson, Atli, and Scott Gettis. W32.Mimail.A@mm.*Symantec*. July 28, 2003. **http://securityresponse.symantec.com/avcenter/ venc/data/w32.mimail.a@mm.html** (accessed 15 December 2004).

Huegen, Craig. The Latest in Denial of Service Attacks: Smurfing. **www.governmentsecurity.org/articles/THELATESTINDENIALOF-SERVICEATTACKSSMURFING.php** (accessed November 2004).

Hypponen, Mikko; Tocheva, Katrin; Rautiainen Sami. My Doom Virus Description. **www.f-secure.com/v-descs/novarg.shtml** (accessed November 2004).

Kapersky Lab. The Virus List Web Site, Zafi Worm. **www.viruslist.com/ en/viruslist.html?id=1666973** (accessed December 2004).

Moore, David; Paxson, Vern; Savage, Stefan; Shannon, Colleen; Staniford, Weaver; Stuart, Nicholas. Inside the Slammer Worm. **http:// csdl.computer.org/comp/mags/sp/2003/04/j4033abs.htm** (accessed August 2004).

Rooney, Paul. Gates Says SCO's Case Against IBM Will Harm Linux's Commercial Prospects. **www.crn.com/sections/ breakingnews/dailyarchives.jhtml;jsessionid= NHYCTYPFXMPGGQSNDBCSKHSCJUMEKJVN? articleId=18839636&_requestid=1042690** (accessed 25 July 2003).

SCO/Linux. 2003. **swpat.ffii.org/patente/wirkungen/sco/index.en.html** (accessed 15 December 2004).

Tanasc, Matthew. IP Spoofing: An Introduction. March 11, 2003. **www.securityfocus.com/infocus/1674** (accessed 1 November 2004).

Vmyths.com jdbgmgr.exe Virus. July 7, 2002. **www.vmyths.com/ hoax.cfm?id=275&page=3** (accessed 16 December 2004).

Webopedia. Buffer Overflow Attack. 2004. **www.webopedia.com/ TERM/b/buffer_overflow.html** (accessed 14 November 2004).

Webopedia. Denial of Service Attack. 2004. **www.webopedia.com/ TERM/D/DoS_attack.html** (accessed 15 December 2004).

Chapter 4

Canavan, John, and Rodney Andres. MyDoom Virus Alert. July 20, 2004. **http://securityresponse.symantec.com/avcenter/venc/data/w32. mydoom.m@mm.html** (accessed 20 July 2004).

Check Point Firewall-1 Data Sheet. **www.checkpoint.com/products/ downloads/firewall-1_datasheet.pdf** (accessed October 2004).

D-Link. Product Data Sheet. **ftp://ftp10.dlink.com/pdfs/products/ DFL-300/DFL-300_ds.pdf** (accessed October 2004).

SonicWALL Data Sheet. **www.firewalls.com/sonicwall-tz-170-10.asp** (accessed October 2004).

Chapter 6

Burnett, Steve and Stephen Paine. 2001. *RSA Security's Official Guide to Cryptography.* New York, NY: McGraw-Hill.

Curtin, Matt. Snake Oil Warning Signs: Encryption Software to Avoid. April 10, 1998. **www.interhack.net/people/cmcurtin/snake-oil-faq.html** (accessed 16 December 2004).

Federal Information Processing Standards. Data Encryption Standards (DES). Publication 46-2. December 30, 1993. **www.itl.nist.gov/ fipspubs/fip46-2.htm** (accessed 16 December 2004).

Hershey, J. E. 2003. *Cryptography Demystified.* New York, NY: McGraw-Hill.

International PGP. Home Page. **www.pgpi.org/** (accessed March 2004).

McCune, Tom. Tom McCune's Page for Pretty Good Privacy. **www.mccune.cc/PGP.htm** (accessed March 2004).

MyCrypto.Net. Encryption Algorithms. **www.mycrypto.net/encryption/ crypto_algorithms.html** (accessed April 2004).

Security in Computing. Letter Frequency Distributions in the English Alphabet. 1988. **arapaho.nsuok.edu/~rosener/mis4313/freq- distribution.html** (accessed 16 December 2004).

Zimmerman, Philip. Philip Zimmerman: Creator of PGP. **www.philzimmermann.com/EN/background/index.html** (accessed March 2004).

Chapter 7

Salamone, Salvatore. Does Everybody Really Know What a VPN Is? *Internet Week.* December 14, 1998. **www.internetweek.com/ VPN/paper-2.htm** (accessed 19 August 2004).

Chapter 9

F-Secure. F-Secure Virus Descriptions: Sobig. April 23, 2003. **www.f- secure.com/v-descs/sobig.shtml** (accessed 15 December 2004).

F-Secure. F-Secure Virus Descriptions: Mabutu. July 29, 2004. **www.f-secure.com/v-descs/mabutu.shtml** (accessed 15 December 2004).

Kaspersky Labs. Zafi Worm. July 2004. **www.kaspersky.com/ removaltools** (accessed 13 October 2004).

McAfee Virus Hoax Listings. **us.mcafee.com/virusInfo/ default.asp?id=description&virus_k=100151** (accessed December 2004).

Vmyths.com. jdbgmgr.exe Virus. July 7, 2002. **www.vmyths.com/ hoax.cfm?id=275&page=3** (accessed 16 December 2004).

Chapter 10

Roberts, Paul. Trojan Horse Hijacks IE: Attack Sends Browsers Aiming for Search Engines to Hackers' Site Instead. *PC World.* October 2, 3003. **www.pcworld.com/news/article/0,aid,112732,tfg,tfg,00.asp** (accessed 05 July 2004).

Chapter 14

BBC News. Russians Arrest "CIA Hacker." June 26, 2000. **http://news.bbc.co.uk/1/hi/world/europe/806984.stm** (accessed 17 December 2004).

Denning, Dorothy E. Cyberterrorism. May 23, 2000. **www. cosc. georgetown. edu/~denning/infosec/cyberterror.html** (accessed 17 December 2004).

Gray, Alfred. **www.securityfocus.com/archive/12/75718** (accessed 03 June 2004).

Savino, Adam. Cyber-Terrorism. **www.cybercrimes.net/Terrorism/ct.html** (accessed 01 November 2004).

Index